Guarding Greensboro

# Guarding Greensboro

A Confederate Company in the Making of a
Southern Community ★ G. WARD HUBBS

THE UNIVERSITY OF GEORGIA PRESS ★ ATHENS & LONDON

© 2003 by the University of Georgia Press
Athens, Georgia 30602
All rights reserved
Designed by Louise OFarrell
Set in 10/13 Minion by Graphic Composition, Inc.,
Athens, Georgia
Printed and bound by Maple-Vail
The paper in this book meets the guidelines for permanence
and durability of the Committee on Production Guidelines
for Book Longevity of the Council on Library Resources.

Printed in the United States of America
07   06   05   04   03   C   5   4   3   2   1

Library of Congress Cataloging-in-Publication Data

Hubbs, G. Ward, 1952–
Guarding Greensboro : a Confederate company in the making
of a Southern community / G. Ward Hubbs.
          p. cm.
Includes bibliographical references and index.
ISBN 0-8203-2505-8 (hardcover : alk. paper)
1. Greensboro (Ala.)—History—19th century. 2. Greensboro
(Ala.)—History, Military—19th century. 3. Greensboro
(Ala.)—Social conditions—19th century. 4. Confederate States
of America. Army. Alabama Infantry Regiment, 5th. 5. Civil-
military relations—Alabama—Greensboro—History—19th
century. 6. Alabama—History—Civil War, 1861–1865—Social
aspects. 7. Alabama—History—Civil War, 1861–1865—Regimental histories. 8. United States—History—Civil War, 1861–
1865—Social aspects. 9. United States—History—Civil War,
1861–1865—Regimental histories. I. Title.
F334.G7 H83 2003
976.1'43—dc21          2002154239

British Library Cataloging-in-Publication Data available

*For Jess* ★ *For Molly* ★ *For Claire*

# Contents

# Illustrations

# Preface

Too many years ago, Ron Cartee walked into my office, politely introduced himself as head of the University of Alabama's Air Force ROTC, and asked what to do with a diary that had passed down to his wife. The thin little journal covered only a single month (January 1863) in the life of John H. Cowin, an Alabama soldier in Robert E. Lee's Army of Northern Virginia. I suggested that Ron try to find out if Cowin had written more. A week later, Ron came back with a substantial hardbound manuscript that opened with the words, "After the election of Abraham Lincoln to the presidency of the United States by the abolitionists of the North, . . ." This turned out to be a great find.

Cowin entitled his diary "A record of events transpiring in the Campaign of the Greensboro Guards, 5th Regt Ala Vols," an appropriate title, for he was recording as much his company's story as his own. Like most Civil War soldiers, Cowin fought alongside friends and relatives. Among well-constructed depictions of battles and camp life, I was surprised to come across a few names that seemed familiar. Sure enough, two fellow members of the Greensboro Guards had also written diaries that I had once read. Over the next few years, I found a total of eight diaries written by various Greensboro Guards (collected in a companion volume, *Voices from Company D,* also published by the University of Georgia Press) along with hundreds of wartime letters. I decided to tell what appeared to be an engaging and, as far as I knew, untold tale: the career of a single Confederate company from Manassas to Appomattox.

Then I discovered that the Guards had not been born from the political turmoil of 1860–1861. They had first mustered as a militia company in the 1820s. Not for four years but for four decades the Guards had belonged to the small cotton town of Greensboro, Alabama. Limiting my study to the time they spent fighting Yankees in Virginia ignored a major part of the real story, the Guards' long-standing relationship to their town.

Greensboro turned out to be something quite different from what its elegant old homes and endless fields suggested. Instead of a stable community of close-knit citizens, rowdy and rootless itinerants once filled Greensboro's streets. Thousands came, stayed a few days or a few years, and then continued further westward when new opportunities beckoned. These individualists, intent on making their fortunes from cotton and slaves, were poor material for uniting into a single community. But they did cooperate to create multiple, temporary, and overlapping communities—associations such as churches, committees to promote railroads or schools, fraternal lodges, and the like—that advanced personal self-interests.

Among these associations was the Greensboro Guards, a typical militia company of its day. The Guards drilled and met irregularly, dressed in their finest regalia to march in patriotic parades, and took off after Creek Indians when the state went to war against them in 1836. Such public fuss hid the Guards' quiet role in community-building. Membership in the company united those who otherwise had nothing in common. Even more important, by joining the Guards, men assumed responsibility for the safety of their fellow citizens. The militiamen were gradually and unknowingly moving Greensborians beyond self-interest.

Upon receiving news of Fort Sumter's bombardment, a hundred Guards marched off to fight as part of the Fifth Alabama Infantry Regiment, strongly supported by the efforts of those citizens who remained behind. At Seven Pines and Malvern Hill, many Guards were permanently disabled, and several were killed. The company was captured first at South Mountain and then again at Chancellorsville after leading Stonewall Jackson's corps on its famous flanking movement. The Guards helped drive the bluecoats back through Gettysburg on the first day of the battle and less than a year later repulsed the Yankee attack at Spotsylvania's Bloody Angle. When Jubal Early looked down on Washington from the Maryland hills, so did the Guards. The war ended for them in the trenches of Petersburg—except for a lone Greensboro Guard who made it to Appomattox.

Veterans returned to their homes defeated but with memories and convictions they would forge into a new kind of community. Marching together in sweltering summers and sharing quarters in the cold winters had certainly drawn these men closer. But they became irrevocably tied to each other and their town when injury, death, and the overwhelming sense of loss at the war's end were added. Instead of the antebellum relationships of self-interest, Greensborians now formed a closed community based on the exclusive bonds that the war had forged. The town had never been more unified or more Southern.

*Guarding Greensboro* is about people in a particular place—but not all the people. Women, I found, left a great deal of material, particularly letters to distant family members. They were less directly involved in building a civic community, however, for they neither voted, held office, nor joined fraternal societies. During the Civil War, women did not don uniforms to fight with the Guards, of course, but women waged war in their own ways. Their main influence remained in the home, where they sought to shield their families from an acquisitive and often dangerous world. I also wanted to write more about Greensboro's slave and free black communities, particularly because they would furnish distinct contrasts to the exclusive white community that emerged after the war. Unfortunately, the scant records these groups left made doing so virtually impossible. Knowing these limitations, I was even more determined to read every surviving scrap written by Greensborians between 1823 and 1873, as well as local newspapers and other selected materials well into the twentieth century.

Other challenges emerged as I proceeded. For starters, Greensboro was somewhat isolated: the railroad and telegraph did not arrive until after the Civil War; steamboats could come only to within about ten miles; and roads south were impassable during and after rains, while the road north to Tuscaloosa crossed hills. An 1868 courthouse fire destroyed legal records. Perhaps most daunting, Greensboro never contained more than a thousand white inhabitants at any one time during its first half century, and many—probably most—stayed only briefly before departing and taking their experiences with them. During the Civil War, this small town seemed to grow even smaller. With the bulk of its men gone and its economy on hold, Greensborians turned their focus away from civic life and toward their soldiers in Virginia. These men left an extraordinary cache of diaries and letters, but I would surely have had access to even more material had I been writing on a corps, for example, or a major city. I continued despite these hurdles because certain primary social relationships can be revealed only at local levels.

Many historians write as if communities spontaneously appear when people live together in hamlets, villages, or towns. If just left alone, the argument goes, such islands of social warmth and mutual reliance would persist indefinitely. But communities seem to be constantly in decline, so these scholars have assumed the task of seeking out and identifying the sources of division that have turned people from their natural relationships. Economic differences in particular are thought to create disharmony as the richer band together to exploit the poorer, often through politics.[1]

This book starts from very different premises indeed. Unlike those who assert that communities are natural and inevitable, I believe that establishing enduring commitments requires great efforts. Thus, I am less interested in what divides people than in what unites them, less interested in identifying and blaming those who destroy communities than in discovering circumstances that allow communities to be created. A mere assemblage of like-minded people does not make a community. The autonomous frontiersmen who flocked to the region in its early decades found no community to greet them. Greensborians, like other Americans, generally lived at a distance from each other—not physically, of course, but psychically—as all pursued their own paths. Yet in time and in crisis, the inhabitants of this Alabama town drew themselves together into something resembling the tight-knit Southern community of myth and legend.

To understand these people and the relationships they built required an imaginative leap into the world as they saw it, suppressing my urge to write from the vantage of historical omniscience. On a trivial level, this involved keeping their nonstandard spellings and relying on the reader's good sense to catch writers' meaning, rather than repeatedly inserting *sic*. Similarly, I referred to battles by their Southern names, often used *ladies* where the modern preference is for *women,* and kept many of the familiar names that Greensborians called each other. On a deeper level, this account of the Guards' experiences in combat, for example, is written largely from their perspective—not from Lee's, Grant's, or even God's. Such an approach to the Civil War years may trouble a few, and my portrayal of the violence that continued after the war, when black and white Greensborians pursued different directions, may strike more than a few as insensitive. Be assured, however, that my hesitation to render moral judgments—to depict Reconstruction Greensboro simply as a morality play of good people versus bad—arose neither from ethical dullness nor, worse, from a covert agenda to defend Southern racism or romanticism. Rather, I became convinced that self-righteous indignation toward those long dead would only hinder my efforts. That white citizens created a loyal community was a notable achievement of surmounting the anomic self-interest that had characterized their lives. But one cannot deny the fact that their unity came by actively (and sometimes violently) ostracizing the Yankees, former slaves, and Unionists whom the former Confederates dismissed as enemies or betrayers.

Every place has its own unique story, and the South was much more diverse than is often presumed. Nonetheless, I believe that Greensboro may well have been typical of the hundreds of small towns spread out across the Southern landscape. Here a recurring theme played itself out yet again: a social good accomplished by accepting a social evil, the benefits to some gained by sacrificing the rights of others. Building a community in Greensboro was a drama of emerging loyalties, but it was also a tragedy of continuing exclusion.

And finally, for those who find my portrait of antebellum Greensborians too individualistic—or my portrait of postbellum Greensborians not enough so—I say, fine. Drawing lines will be a source of endless quibbling. But I remain convinced that the conflict changed these people profoundly and that painting with a broad brush is quite in order if this shift is to be grasped.

★ ★ ★

Ron Cartee's entrance into my office was also the beginning of many acts of generosity and goodwill by a host of individuals. Private documents were offered for my use by many individuals, including John McCall, who generously gave me free rein to read his extensive collection of papers from the Pickens family, and David Nelson. The staff members at various archives located numerous obscure things for me: I am especially grateful to those at the Alabama Department of Archives and History (Director Ed Bridges, who shared James Williams' account, and Bob Bradley, Rickie Brunner, Bob Cason, Norwood Kerr, Victor Nielsen, Mark Palmer, Debbie Pendleton, and Ken Tiley) and at the W. S. Hoole Special Collections Library at the University of Alabama (particularly Clark Center, who discovered the constitutions of the Greensboro Guards). Alan Pitts sent me his research on the Fifth Alabama. Norvin W. Richards of the University of Alabama Department of Philosophy discussed the concept of loyalty with me. Craig Remington at the University of Alabama Cartographic Laboratory drew the maps. Jessica Hubbs helped enter into the computer economic and demographic data that my colleague Kathleen Greer Rossmann, despite her particularly hectic schedule, then turned into the graphs comparing precincts. At the recommendation of Ronald Rogers, dean of the graduate school, the University of Alabama National Alumni Association appointed me Graduate Fellow in 1996–1997, a generous award that allowed me time to complete my research.

I cannot begin to list every Greensborian who offered me help, but any list would have to include Willie Jean Arrington, Mary Esther Coleman, Carolyn Hemstreet, Ann Langford, Ed Lowry, Kitty Rugg, Minnie Brown Sledge, and Sara Bayol Taylor. In particular, the Nicholas and Winifred Cobbs family willingly shared their resources and straightened out some of my mistakes; I still immensely enjoy arguing with Nick over scalawags and such.

Those who read the manuscript at various stages—Paula Barnes, David Beito, Nick Cobbs, Peter Donahue, Mike Fitzgerald, Gary W. Gallagher, John McCall, Jennifer McClure, Fred L. Ray, and Adam Tate—all pointed out specific passages for improvement. Rich Megraw and Johanna Shields (who read the manuscript thrice) made especially penetrating criticisms for which I am the richer and this book the better.

The Wednesday breakfast bunch contributed significantly to this book. John Hall read the manuscript and offered his usual curmudgeonly comments. Jim Stovall, who has heard my account of the Guards for more years than he would wish, spent a couple of Saturdays on his computer drawing several of the charts. And George C. Rable offered strong criticisms, actively pushed this book's publication, and continues to send me tidbits that fall his way. I have come to depend on their personal support and Christian goodwill.

Over countless cups of brewed caffeine (a cheap vice), Lawrence Frederick Kohl and I struggled with organization, wording, and argument. His insistence that I never leave the big questions unanswered both frustrated and saved me. All professional debts I owe Larry, however, pale beside my personal debts—debts that I cannot hope to repay and that he would never seek to collect.

Finally, three generations of the Hubbs family made the mistake of encouraging me to write this book. For that they put up with poor salaries and vaporized weekends. My parents, LaMar and Louise, took up much of the slack on a daily basis. My wife, Pat, remained unfailingly supportive—even enthusiastic. We told our three daughters—Jess, Molly, and Claire—that their interruptions prolonged this project, but this was a lie. Their interruptions gave me a reason to continue. Thanks.

# PART I

# Autonomy

# CHAPTER 1

# The Stone Soldier

Ages are made up of moments, fountains
of drops, and human character of little
words and actions. ✶ John G. Harvey, 1871

Greensboro, Alabama, like other Southern towns, has its memorial to the Confederate soldier. He stands before the courthouse, his uniform looking nearly new, his slouch hat shielding his eyes from the glaring sun. This marble man faces north, holding his musket vertically, guarding the town's citizens from attack. Below him a particularly large base bears the names of some five hundred local men who fought in the Civil War. Many of them were members of the Greensboro Guards, Fifth Alabama Infantry Regiment.

John H. Cowin's name is there. He left Greensboro first to study at the University of Virginia, then transferred to Philadelphia's Thomas Jefferson University, where he earned his medical doctorate. The following year, 1861, Dr. Cowin joined the Guards as a private, fought in the Army of Northern Virginia, and died at the battle of Chancellorsville.

The names of Francis Edward Bayol and Jules Honoré Bayol are also inscribed on the base. The brothers' grandfather came to Greensboro after fleeing a bloody slave rebellion in Santo Domingo. The brothers enlisted together in August 1861. Jules was killed a year later, assaulting Malvern Hill; Ned, as he was known, was discharged for wounds to his hip and leg received at the battles of South Mountain and Chancellorsville.

Charles von Badenhausen, a German lieutenant in the Austrian army, was teaching school on a plantation when the war broke out. He joined the Guards and was quickly appointed chief regimental musician. At Malvern Hill he lost his left arm and a finger of his right hand, but he survived the war and moved to North Carolina.

George Nutting fell mortally wounded while bearing the Fifth Alabama's flag at Gettysburg. His last words to his fellow Guards, "Come on boys," were the same last words shouted by numerous other color-bearers, Confederate and Union alike, as they led assaults on each other's lines.

The Confederate Memorial in Greensboro, Alabama.

The Pickens brothers, Samuel and James, probably could have avoided service altogether. Their mother, who in 1860 reported assets approaching a half million dollars from land, slaves, and cotton, would have shielded them. But they both joined the Guards and survived the war to resume their lives as cotton planters.

William Lyles, a farmer, signed his name with an X on the oath of allegiance he took when the war ended.

More than one hundred Guards marched off from Greensboro in 1861. Others joined later to fill vacancies. Only one—Edward T. Hutchinson, son of a local Methodist minister—is reported to have witnessed General Robert E. Lee's surrender at Appomattox Court House. Hutchinson's grandson chuckles when recalling that he never heard Edward use the word *Yankee* without inserting *damn* before it.

Greensboro's stone soldier stands alone. The town has no statue to James Williams, for example, a slave who escaped from a nearby plantation in 1837 and spent months wandering northward to freedom. Nor does Greensboro honor Dr. William T. Blackford, who, after serving the Guards as a surgeon, made the mistake of joining the Republican Party after the war. No monuments honor women, celebrated as they may be in other ways. Greensboro does have a small black slab inscribed with the names of locals who died in twentieth-century wars, but there are no statues of national figures—no presidents, no artists, not even a general—because national issues were understood only in local contexts.[1]

Greensboro's stone soldier stares out at a town that seems not to have changed for at least a century. The antebellum homes built with cotton money—including the mellifluously named Magnolia Hall, Greenwood, Multi Flora, Japonica Path, Seven Pines, Tunstall House, and Glencairn—are easily among the finest in the state, if not the South. St. Paul's, the third-oldest Episcopal church in Alabama, was consecrated in 1843 by the Right Reverend Leonidas Polk, the future Confederate general. Main Street has its own charm. Folks amble along, shaded by rusting storefront awnings. Greensboro could never be mistaken for anything but a venerable old Southern town.

Outmoded buildings, the slow pace and personal scale of a small place, perhaps even our nostalgia for simpler times—whatever the cause—we tend to believe that communities such as Greensboro have stood for a long time, islands of calm in the torrent of modernity. But Greensboro was once young. During its rowdy first decades, the town was besieged by thousands of young men—both independent bachelors and fathers with families in tow—who left the confines of their parents' homes in search of fortune. These people shared only a willingness to become rich by exploiting land and slaves. Some made money; many did not. Some stayed for a few weeks, some a few years, but most resumed their march westward, eyeing the main chance. When the Civil War broke out, Greensboro was hardly four decades old, and many of its columned homes were barely finished. Those who joined the Greensboro Guards included some who had arrived in town only a few months earlier.

The first white Greensborians were once modern. They lived in a lonely, rootless anonymity where all were equal in their solitude, where the pursuit of lucre overwhelmed mutual dependence. On the Alabama frontier they were forced to face head-on the great American problem: How do individualists form communities?

They answered through voluntary efforts to build churches, reform committees, fraternal associations, and the like. These were typically American solutions, but the peculiar institution would make their society peculiar. The ever-increasing reliance on slaves to grow cotton made Greensborians wealthier even as they felt less secure. By 1830 the county's black slaves equaled the number of white citizens, but on the eve of secession, slaves outnumbered the free population by three to one. The rise in the slave population made the problem of community-building all the more crucial, as Greensborians began to fear that their slaves would rise up against them. Thus, one voluntary association, the Greensboro Guards, assumed prominence above the others. Over a half century, this militia company came to embody the ideals of brotherhood and sacrifice that the citizens cherished but were otherwise unable to effect.

Greensboro's network of overlapping voluntary communities could not withstand the challenge posed by the Civil War. The Guards marched off to protect their town from the Yankees, who were believed to be planning to end slavery and foment a race war. The Guards failed to stop the Yankee threat but succeeded at something else. Greensboro's soldiers forged another type of community based not on self-interest and contract but on loyalty.

Greensboro's stone soldier stands on the courthouse square—the center of civic life—because those soldiers were largely responsible for creating the town's civic life. The story of the Greensboro Guards is thus Greensboro's story. What appears first as a heroic melodrama of courage and commitment to a lost cause—and it was that—became a defining moment, the crisis that turned this frontier town into a Southern community.

CHAPTER 2

# A Land of Strangers

There is little or no society, the people
are from all quarters & care no more for
each other than dogs do, except . . . to
cheat you.  ★  William B. Beverley, 1831

Some came by wagon, others by steamboat. Some hailed from Virginia and the Carolinas, others from Connecticut, Nova Scotia, Ireland, and Germany. Some arrived
alone, others with wives and children. Some were greeted by sisters and brothers
who had gone before; others knew not a soul. Some brought only their own clothes
wadded in a carpetbag; others brought wagons and dozens of slaves. All came to
make their fortunes. The fertile soil of west Alabama promised great riches but
could not promise that a community would emerge among the grasping individualists who settled there. These frontiersmen would found their town, Greensboro,
and they would have their community—or, rather, communities—but the path
would be neither easy nor direct.

The land that attracted them was known as the Canebrake, in Alabama's Black
Belt and bordered roughly on the east and west by the Cahaba and Black Warrior
Rivers. The name was taken from the extensive stands of large cane (native bam-
boo) that flourished in marshes and along river and creek banks. Some canebrakes
grew so dense that wandering cattle never found their way out. In one spectacular
example, a continuous band of cane thirty feet high once stretched 170 miles up the
winding Black Warrior from Demopolis to the fall line at Tuscaloosa. The Canebrake included about seven hundred square miles of prairie land plus the adjacent
river bottoms east of the Warrior. Another region, known as the Fork, began on the
other side of the Warrior, stretched westward to the Tombigbee, and was considerably smaller but geologically identical to the Canebrake.[1]

Describing the prairie land beyond the lush cane taxed the early visitors' vocab-
ularies. "Fancy yourself for a moment in such a situation," wrote one observer in
1821. "Before you a wide and extended meadow, to the right and left intervening
strips of oaks and pines; proceeding onwards, the prospect seems terminated by the
surrounding woods; anon you catch a glimpse of the opening vista; and now again

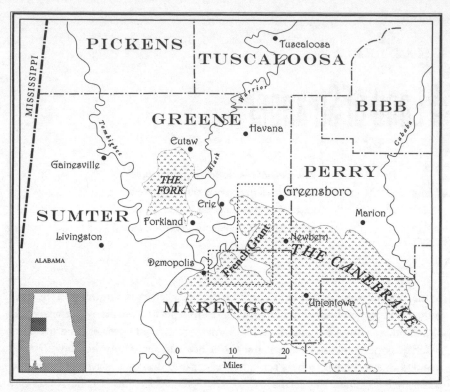

The Canebrake. Prairies are shaded, but the Canebrake and the Fork are considered to extend to the rivers. (Map by Craig Remington, University of Alabama Cartographic Laboratory, Tuscaloosa)

the prospect expands into the wide spread horizon of an extensive prairie." Others noted that the prairies varied according to elevation: the higher regions were bare, the lower ones wet, and between them lay islands of trees bedecked in Spanish moss. These prairies appeared to be "rolling in long waves," broken up by "mounds, or gentle swells, with circular bases." Some observers distinguished between the desirable "bald prairies," covered with grasses that would yield easily to the plow, and the "timbered prairie," where grew white and red oak, sweet gum trees, poplar, and towering cedars sometimes three feet in diameter—but no pine trees. The prairies, then, were not continuous but rather were large meadows ending at woodland hummocks, the whole appearing as an uneven checkerboard.[2]

The Canebrake's distinctive topography resulted from its distinctive soil. Unlike the red clay found in much of Alabama, the Canebrake's soil was a dingy bluish to yellowish white when dry but black when wet. The soil of the Canebrake and the Fork formed the richest part of the Black Belt, a stratum of what was called limestone or chalk (actually marl, a combination of lime and clay) cutting across the center of the state. Settlers found that this ancient sea floor was not of uniform thickness. At its northern edge, the limestone was but a few feet thick, but thirty miles south, where the Canebrake ended, the limestone was nearly a thousand feet thick. Over the eons, decaying plant material mixed with air and water to produce a soft and exceedingly rich two-foot layer of soil known as "rotten limestone." Many thought this to be the best soil in the South, ideally suited for growing cotton.[3] Here fortunes could indeed be made.

But before that could occur, the problem of water had to be solved. Rainfall was plentiful—an average of an inch a week—but the limestone subsoil could not absorb it. A thunderstorm on the relatively flat land instantly turned the surface of the Canebrake into a proverbial sea of mud. And it was a particularly sticky mud. Pigs' tails had to be cut off to prevent their turning into mud anchors. Roads routinely became impassable. Ironically, an even greater problem was the scarcity of drinking water. Because the impermeable limestone had no aquifer to flow into ordinary cistern wells, rainfall had to be collected and stored, a problem that apparently had kept even the Indians from settling there. The Canebrake might make a good place to grow crops, but more than one labeled it "the worst place in the world to live in."[4] Towns would have to be located just outside the Canebrake, where wells could be dug and mud was not a problem.

Statehood in 1819 ignited an Alabama land fever. Most immigrants were poor farmers who could pack their families and possessions into a wagon or two. They had little to lose and much to gain by leaving their worn-out farms on the eastern seaboard. Often a few families migrated together. Word of the rich black soil of the Canebrake, however, attracted men of a different sort. They planned to assault the new land and squeeze great profits from it.

Among the first to arrive was Israel Pickens, a North Carolina congressman of considerable means. During one of their regular meals together in Washington, General Andrew Jackson had told Pickens that the land between the Alabama and Tombigbee Rivers looked promising. By the first day of 1815, Pickens was already planning a tour through the Southwest, since he would shortly be assuming the enviable position of land registrar at St. Stephens, the future territorial capital of Alabama located 120 river miles up the Tombigbee from Mobile. As registrar, Pickens would be perfectly placed to select and purchase the best lands for himself and his family. Within two years of his arrival, Pickens had established his brother, James, as a storekeeper in St. Stephens and was planning to purchase sizable tracts of land for his relatives. Israel Pickens had already sold his old plantation and sent his slaves to a farm below St. Stephens.[5]

Pickens acquired land fearlessly. One tract he purchased with only forty acres cleared, and much of that was choked with fallen timber; he immediately cleaned off the rest of the land, hired an additional dozen slaves to supplement his own, and within six months had a hundred acres planted with corn and fifty with cotton. When he combined this tract with others, Pickens held about a thousand acres of good land. At an April 1819 land sale he purchased another fifteen hundred acres, and six months later, just after Alabama's admission to the Union, Pickens was eyeing some rich prairie land, "the most valuable & inexhaustible of any other in this country." There, "fevers, agues &c. are perfect strangers," he claimed, and both cotton and wheat would do well. Pickens paid only seventeen dollars per acre for eight hundred acres of timbered prairie in the Canebrake, about ten miles from another tract of bottomland he had purchased the previous April. (Those without Pickens' well-placed position as land registrar had to pay as high as thirty to fifty dollars per acre from those who beat them there.)[6]

Such purchases forestalled competitors and gave Pickens a valuable investment. He displayed no particular interest in his newly acquired holdings other than as a means for acquiring wealth—subsistence farming this was not. He also founded the Tombeckbe Bank in 1818 and followed carefully the prospects of a proposed canal to open south Alabama by connecting the Coosa River to the Tennessee. Similarly, he purchased slaves by weighing price, risk, and yield. His letters betrayed not an ounce of sentiment.[7]

"I consider my settlement now *permanent,*" Pickens wrote of his Canebrake home in 1822. By that time he had been elected governor of Alabama after a campaign that called for common men to throw off the oppressive yoke of their "royal" opponents, as he disingenuously labeled them. "Numerous emigrants have come in this winter, & we have already a very dense neighbourhood of respectable settlers." Yet just a year later, the governor was pondering whether to leave his "permanent" home and move to Tennessee, ever in search of personal advantage.[8]

Israel Pickens had little attachment to the land, but he was attached to his family. He helped set up his brothers and sisters near him on plantations that generated enormous profits. And despite dragging his wife and family around the Old Southwest, probably against their will, Israel left them a significant inheritance when he died in 1827.[9] Pickens' drive, timing, and success certainly set him apart, but his character was not fundamentally distinct from that of those who followed in his footsteps. They all sought money.

Frontier life on the northern edge of the Canebrake was unrefined. Pickens had established his family near the short-lived Russell's Settlement, named for three brothers from Georgia who arrived in 1816 but soon abandoned their home after several Indian attacks. The village of Troy appeared a few miles west, still some ten miles from the Black Warrior River. Troy consisted of a couple of dry goods stores—hastily erected of round pine logs and measuring twelve by fifteen feet—that catered to nearby farmers, herdsmen, and the occasional Indian. A dwelling house and cotton gin completed the commercial establishments. The homes were mud-chinked log huts, and their furnishings were equally rough: three-legged stools, a high bench for a table, and beds made by laying boards across rails bored into the cabin walls.[10]

Alabama's admission into the Union in 1819 imposed political order on the region. Troy was included in the new county of Greene, whose western border was the Tombigbee River and whose eastern border with Perry County was along a township line splitting the Canebrake. The Black Warrior River ran right through the middle of Greene County, dividing it informally into east and west Greene, with the Canebrake in the east and the Fork in the west. The legislature located the county seat at Erie, a small port along the Black Warrior, an obvious attempt to unite east and west. (The county government would be relocated to Eutaw in 1838.)

Because the law mandated that the sixteenth section of every township be reserved for education and because Troy was in the sixteenth section, the town had to be moved less than a mile westward to "new" Troy. In December 1823, at the request of a few residents, the General Assembly of Alabama incorporated Troy, renaming it Greensborough. (The common practice of dropping the final letters soon rendered it Greensboro.) The new name, like the county's, honored Revolutionary War hero Nathanael Greene. The incorporation established councillors and an intendant with powers to appoint and tax. This did not mean that only those living along the town's streets identified themselves as Greensborians. Many people living six, eight, or even ten miles away looked to the town as the locus of their activities. Membership lists for Greensboro's churches, lodges, and other organizations always included those who lived well into the Canebrake. The town lay just north of the prairie, where the soil did not turn to mud and where natural springs ensured drinkable water. The flat land left surveyors free to orient the town along Main Street, which formed a strong east-west axis, and its intersection with the Tuscaloosa Road, which ran north-south. The few secondary streets, which were not even named until the 1880s, were laid out in a grid oriented along Main and Tuscaloosa.[11]

The rude log homes did not last, and by the late 1820s the first of Greensboro's fine homes were starting to appear. The spacious brick residence of John Gayle (governor 1831–1835), for example, was built on a large parcel on the west end of town. The Peck place boasted vine-covered pillars and sat on a lot with circular paths, a paling fence, and a two- or three-acre vineyard.[12] Houses were set back from the streets, with enough room for vegetable gardens and outbuildings.

By contrast, the businesses erected along Main Street lined the boardwalks. Transients arriving in the early 1830s could stay in one of three shabby hotels made of logs, but a "first-rate" brick hotel was soon built. "There is not, so far as I can learn, a vacant room in the place," wrote one newcomer forced to eat in a tavern and sleep in a loft; single young men commonly sought out families with whom to board. The town also boasted a tinner, printing office, and carriage maker; one female and two male academies; a couple of cabinetmakers, blacksmiths, tailors, and saddlers; three physicians, "tippling shops," and churches (Presbyterian, Baptist, and Methodist); and eight stores selling either dry goods or groceries.[13]

Henry Watson's routine typified Greensboro's success-hungry bachelors. A Connecticut émigré, he and another young lawyer boarded together at the hotel, sharing a snug, small room sparsely furnished with a table, chairs, and books;

Watson hung old prints on the walls. In the mornings a boy made the fire before the two got up, washed, and then read until breakfast. They then departed for work, Watson to a law office he shared with the successful and prominent John Erwin, at that time president of the state senate. Theirs was a single building faced with unplaned and unpainted clapboards and squeezed between two stores. The office, raised on four wooden posts, was set only a few feet back from the walk. Inside was a single room about twenty feet square, without a ceiling below the joists. The window had a shutter but no sash; the door was kept wide open to let in light and because no one would enter if it were closed. "It is finished off about as nicely as our long barn," Watson wrote to his father back in New England.[14]

An unattached young man out to make his fortune, Watson could have settled anywhere. He had considered the Fork across the Black Warrior in west Greene. It too was filling up—and lacked a lawyer. Lands that had sold there for $1.25 an acre in 1832 were going for $5 to $10 only two years later. In the end, however, Watson decided that the "active and busy population" in Greensboro held more promise. The choice was a good one. Within a year of setting up his law practice with John Erwin, Watson could boast that land prices had doubled generally and in Greensboro were rising at an incredible 20 percent monthly. The population soared as well. "New settlers are continually pouring in," wrote one new resident of Greensboro. The county's population, both black and white, had jumped from a mere forty-five hundred in 1820 to fifteen thousand ten years later, when it ranked as Alabama's second most populous county.[15]

Soaring land prices and booming populations were hardly unusual in the Old Southwest of the early 1830s. Because of a recent technological breakthrough, however, Greensboro's future seemed brighter and on a firmer economic base than that of other frontier towns. The fertile prairie lands were exceptionally well suited for growing America's greatest cash crop, cotton. But the lack of drinking water had held up exploitation of both the Canebrake and the Fork by restricting the size of the workforce. Drinking water had to be carried eight miles or more during times of drought. This critical problem was overcome in 1830 when John M. Cooper, a determined and inventive Vermont-born well borer, arrived in the Canebrake to apply his innovative techniques. Wells soon were routinely reaching hundreds of feet in depth in order to break through the limestone stratum and allow water to gush upward to the surface.[16] Artesian wells had finally opened the Canebrake to commercial exploitation.

Planters wasted no time in amassing gangs of slaves to exploit the Canebrake. In 1820 a bit more than one-third of Greene County's population were slaves; the figure had risen to half ten years later; and by 1840 more than two-thirds of the population held this status. On the eve of the Civil War, slaves would comprise more than three-quarters of Greene County's population. They were concentrated in the Canebrake, the Fork, and the river bottoms. (In an extreme example, one precinct reported 2,479 black residents and only 81 white, or 3 percent of the total, in 1870.)

Slave prices, too, reflected demand. In 1830 field hands who sold for three hundred dollars in the Carolinas commanded seven or eight hundred dollars in Greensboro.[17] Despite the development of artesian wells, few white families lived on the prairies; most preferred such villages and towns as Marion, Greensboro, and Eutaw, where people could avoid the insurmountable problem of mud and have access to schools and other services. House servants lived with their owners' families in Greensboro, while the majority of the slaves remained on the plantations. The Canebrake's thousands of black slaves and few white overseers—encircled by white settlements standing like bastions—added significantly to white jitters that those slaves would revolt.

These slaves began to transform the Canebrake for their masters. The bald prairies could be plowed and planted immediately, but the timbered prairies first had to be cleared by felling the smaller trees and girdling the largest. Many of the smaller trees were used in fences that surrounded the crops, since livestock at that time grazed on the open range. Fields were then ready to be plowed and planted. Much of the land was devoted to corn (520,000 bushels in 1840), but such grains as wheat, oats, and rye were also planted. Sweet potatoes were abundant, and even peaches were being cultivated in the 1830s.[18] Planters, however, were not enthused about growing food crops.

"*Cotton, Cotton* is all they talk about," wrote Martha Hatch when she first arrived in Greensboro in late 1832. "They dont appear to care for any thing else." And the whole country was "*mud* and *mire*." Her husband had rented a place six miles from Greensboro where he planned to keep his most valuable slaves; he was renting them presently at fifty cents per day. She had seen a good many acquaintances, but all they ever talked or cared about was cotton and money, both "very abundant," it seemed. "Every acre possible bearing the semblance of profit has been put in cotton, & we could plant more had we the ground," reported another farmer in the mid-1830s. Even Indians were hired to pick cotton in the fall. Within four years of the first locomotive in America, planters were subscribing a railroad to run from Greensboro through the Canebrake to the Alabama River, where their cotton could be loaded on steamboats and shipped to Mobile and foreign markets.[19]

Production statistics bear out these reports. By 1840 Greene County produced nearly eight thousand bales (at four hundred pounds per bale), by 1850 that figure had risen to more than twenty-five thousand bales, and by 1860 it had reached nearly fifty-eight thousand bales. Greene County's cotton production during these years remained third or fourth in the state. Perhaps more telling of the settlers' drive was that Greene led all other Alabama counties in the amount of land in production. In fact, Greene had nearly as much improved land as unimproved, a percentage exceeded by only two other Alabama counties during the antebellum era.[20]

The Canebrake was no place for subsistence farmers or the faint of heart. Agriculture there was a calculated business venture, and planters filled their journals and letters home with precise lists of expenditures and profits combined with detailed proposals of future prospects. When in late 1832 Thomas Johnston arrived with his family in Greensboro, he quickly purchased a Canebrake plantation of 320 acres and a good well lying ten miles south of Greensboro. "I never have seen any lands to excel it," he boasted to his brother, George. "I think the minimum calculation & a safe one on the average would be one thousand lbs of cotton & fifty bushels of corn to the acre when well tended." He paid forty-four hundred dollars, just over thirteen dollars per acre, and prices were rising again. Thomas intended to travel to New York to stock a store he was about to start and wanted George to join him as a business partner. In July 1833, Thomas was still trying to persuade his brother by explicitly detailing the legal and financial obligations that the arrangement would involve. More opportunities had developed when he wrote to his brother again the next month. The federal government was opening up lands purchased from the Choctaw in Mississippi, and the chances for "profitable speculation" were ripe. Many of the settlers there had improved land they did not own and would now be unable to pay for it. "There is no risque at all in this business," for none had lost money and some were quickly becoming wealthy through speculation alone. Thomas regretted not purchasing more land when he first arrived. "I would have made a fortune," he lamented, "but I was afraid."[21]

Greensborians easily balanced cotton planting with other professions. "I find here is a fine field for action in business," wrote Benjamin King back home to North Carolina in 1832. A friend or relative had just been hired in a mercantile store in Greensboro and was working continuously. "It runs them to death to keep up with it. The Clerks are up untill 12 Oclk every night." King had been offered two positions in business. Despite the offers, however, he was purchasing land. The practice of law was especially lucrative where so much land was changing hands. Henry Watson first came as a teacher, left, and then returned as a lawyer. C. C. Scott wrote in August 1832 from his home near Springfield, Virginia, that he intended to leave shortly with his wife for Greensboro or perhaps for nearby Linden. He planned to board at a respectable public or private house while establishing his law practice. Once the new counties in the Choctaw nation farther west were organized and laid off, Scott, like Johnston, planned to move there and start again.[22]

William B. Beverley arrived expecting to rent plantation land but instead purchased 450 acres for forty-three hundred dollars. The price would have been far higher in the Canebrake, but Beverley purchased ridge land some five miles from Greensboro. He was assured that within two years his cotton crop would pay for the land and all expenses and "with good luck & good management, make a good deal more." The price nonetheless staggered him. "My mind dwells with horror on my debt."[23]

Indeed, Greensboro's economy during the 1830s operated almost entirely on credit. Because banks and specie were scarce, individuals seldom paid in cash. A creditor could wait a year to settle up with a debtor, who manufactured excuses not to pay (but was more likely waiting for the price of cotton to rise or, worse, had already borrowed elsewhere to make other investments). When payment was demanded, the answer always came back, "you must wait. I *can't* pay you, I *must* buy a negro, it is out of the question, I have the money but I *must* buy a *negro*." Because profits exceeded the 8 percent in interest due, the debtor would hold out as long as possible, asking his creditor to wait. Finally, the debtor would be brought into court. He would offer no defense, and the judge would order that the debt be paid in full, with all the costs.[24]

"It is all business and bustle, and men and 'niggars,'" a young Connecticut-born girl discovered when she first reached Greensboro. The economy was heating up all over the country but even more so on the cotton frontier. Greensboro's isolation contributed to the high prices charged for everything not made locally. But the pace of the economy had an even larger effect. Provisions, labor, and goods were all expensive. Cotton was "high, very high" and getting higher. Lands were selling at unprecedented rates. Everyone was going into debt. These were the Flush Times.[25]

The varied enterprises of Robert W. Withers revealed much about the entrepreneurs who came to the Canebrake. A Virginian who graduated from Yale before studying medicine at the University of Pennsylvania, Dr. Withers had made his way into the Canebrake by the age of twenty-five (about 1823), twenty-four hundred dollars in debt and owning merely a horse. Then he married a young woman with forty slaves and a plantation. She promptly died, and Withers was on his way. By 1831 he owned eighty slaves and cultivated seven hundred acres on two plantations. At his home along the Black Warrior, he established a cotton warehouse and a hotel. There travelers could cross the river on his ferry or take his four-horse stage to Greensboro, ten miles to the east. To power his grist- and sawmills, Withers first used steam but later introduced turbines powered by artesian wells. He also turned the power of the turbines, which yielded eight horsepower, to hauling goods from the river up an inclined plane to the top of the fifty-foot bluff. Marrying well and harnessing the artesian wells were not the only ways in which Dr. Withers exploited his opportunities. In addition to growing cotton, he experimented with grapes and, after visiting Louisiana, introduced sugarcane. He manured his land by driving his two hundred head of cattle into a particular enclosure, where they would stay for eight or nine nights before moving to another spot, and he experimented with such crops as beans and peas to replenish nutrients in the soil.[26]

"Goes all for making money," sniffed Watson on first meeting Dr. Withers. But before long the Connecticut-born Watson would also get caught up in the contagion, using his position as a lawyer to found Greensboro's first bank and to invest heavily in slaves and land himself. None were immune. An early settler admitted that he and everyone else "thought of little else but making money [and] came to this new country for that particular purpose." Such acquisitiveness was encouraged by the frontier's unsettled population and lack of institutions, by the immigrants' young age, and certainly by the examples of those who succeeded. While most, of course, did not succeed, seemingly all—successful or otherwise—could agree with

Greene County planter Henry Tayloe when he admitted, "I came here to make money."[27]

* * *

Perceptive contemporary observers were struck by Americans' cupidity. Americans were clever but not profound, boastful yet egalitarian, unrefined, and certainly acquisitive. Alexis de Tocqueville accused Americans of an "excessive care for worldly welfare" and noted their calculating opportunism. With an extreme single-mindedness, Americans moved about their country in search of their main chance. Traditions were dismissed as restraints on personal success, and shrewd business dealings were applauded.[28]

Such unfettered and successful would-be entrepreneurs welcomed the opportunities and personal freedom that they found on the frontier. Israel Pickens, for example, had used an 1820 oration celebrating the nation's independence as an opportunity to proclaim the individual's independence: "Man is known here by his proper test, of talents and virtue; instead of the capricious distinctions of birth and fortune, and is left to pursue his happiness, according to the dictates of his own inclination." Another observer described this new country as a place where a man "is thrown upon his own resources; where his only friends are his talents; where he sees energy leap at once into prominence; where those only are above him whose talents are above his; where there is no *prestige* of rank, or ancestry, or wealth, or past reputation—and no family influence." The frontier was an open field of rivalry, with every man pursuing the glittering prize. To enter the lists was a manly deed. "You have done a solemn act," a friend wrote to Watson when he came to live in Greensboro. Such a decision "requires an uncommon and perhaps, uninviable hardihood to leave, home, country, friends, early recollections and associations, all the endearments of life: and seek in a land of strangers, a resting place for the hopes of our young ambition. . . . You may and doub[t]less will receive all the civilities, which you can reasonably expect—but they come from Strangers."[29]

Alongside cupidity, observers of the American character were struck by the glorification of the individual. No self-respecting young man, for example, would have admitted a debt to his family for his economic and social status. To be manly was to stand apart, as demonstrated by a willingness to set out alone into the frontier. And yet migrants' repeated references to other family members, both with them and back home, give pause. Young men regularly seemed to look to their fathers for financial backing, for example. And as extended families settled together, they built kinship groups, or "cousinries," especially in the Canebrake. (Truly unattached young men did seem to cluster in towns, such as Greensboro.) Thus, letters and diaries celebrating personal independence were probably exaggerated.[30] Such documents should not be dismissed lightly, however, for they convey more than self-deception; indeed, the perception of frontiersmen as being self-made probably holds more significance than their actual status. The celebration of personal independence suggests just how demanding the cult of individualism was. The challenge to these young men was not so much to acknowledge family ties as to transcend those ties and begin to establish a civic culture, a community, among themselves. It would be a formidable task, especially when confronted with the sins that the frontier encouraged: lawlessness, pretense, and anomie.

Unscrupulous men on the make seemed to overrun this unsettled region. Local legend has it that Andrew Russell, one of the three brothers who arrived in 1816, was victimized by a "land shark" when he tried to purchase the land he had settled at an 1820 public sale at Cahawba. A local man approached Russell and demanded $3.50 for each of the 160 acres that he had considered his own; otherwise, the shark and his confederates would enter the auction and force the bidding higher. Russell got his land for $4.75 an acre, but only $1.25 went to the government.[31]

A more serious affront to order occurred during an 1833 election in Greensboro for justice of the peace. The two candidates were a lawyer named John Street and a member of the Stollenwerck family. Dr. J. S. W. Hellen, a young physician, spoke out strongly against Street, sarcastically ridiculing his abilities and talents and even calling him a drunken vagabond. Hellen apparently also had been indulging freely: swearing that he would whip Street, Hellen rushed into the building where the candidate was staying and collared and then struck at him, although the blow missed. At this point, someone fatally stabbed the doctor through the heart. John Street and his brother, William, who was also present, were both arrested. At the trial, held in Marengo County because of local prejudice against the Streets, many witnesses came forward, but both men were acquitted because no one could be sure which one had held the knife. Twenty years later, a North Carolina businessman who witnessed the crime finally returned to Greensboro and identified the murderer as John Street, the candidate himself.[32]

Another legend recounted the story of a young Greensboro merchant named Brown returning from an 1833 business trip to Mobile carrying a large sum of money. Brown met several professional gamblers on board the steamboat and foolishly agreed to play cards. Although no novice, Brown lost enormous sums. When he discovered that the dice were loaded, he grabbed a carving fork, stuck it through the gambler's wrist into the table, and pointed a cocked pistol at the man's head. The gambler was stripped of his weapons and left on a low sandbank in the middle of the river. The night was black, the current strong, and as the steamboat continued upstream toward Greene County, the gambler's cries could be heard growing more distant.[33]

These unbridled Alabamians particularly fascinated novelists and literati. When Joseph Glover Baldwin heard of the "exhilarating prospects of fussing, quarrelling, murdering, violation of contracts, and the whole catalogue of *crimen falsi*," he left his native Virginia for Sumter County, immediately west of Greene and experiencing the same chaos. He found that the reality exceeded the wildest rumors. Society was "wholly unorganized" in this new country, and the law "powerless." A charlatan without cash could buy land and slaves simply by proclaiming that he was good for the money; if anyone dared refuse him credit, a quick hand on the bowie knife would redress that insult. "What country could boast more largely of its crime?" asked Baldwin rhetorically. "What more splendid role of felonies! What more terrific murders! What more gorgeous bank robberies!"[34]

The lawlessness of murderers, cheating gamblers, and bank robbers were but the overt manifestation of a deeper problem. Far from a network of friends and relatives to vouch for one's character, in a land devoid of enduring institutions, a man's reputation could be whatever he said it was. The parson's face sometimes hid an evil soul. The well-dressed young man might have a warrant on his head back east. An ignorant horse doctor could set up a sign reading "Physician and Surgeon," or a constable could call himself a lawyer. "A Dandy Absconded" read the headlines in one typical newspaper account; a confidence man, it seems, had set up a school in the county seat and then bolted without paying his numerous creditors. "Nobody knew who or what they were," wrote Baldwin of these virtuosi of duplicity, "except as they claimed, or as a surface view of their characters indicated."[35] Among strangers, who could deny anyone's reputation?

In such circumstances, legends were made. Newspaperman Johnson Jones Hooper published his sketches of a fictitious confidence man in the national best-seller, *Adventures of Captain Simon Suggs*. The stories recount Suggs' travels through frontier Alabama, gaining lucre by deceiving everyone he meets. His first real success comes when he becomes a land shark and, like those who cheated the Russell brothers, convinces a man to give him $170 and a horse in return for *not* buying a piece of land. Suggs himself, of course, had no money to buy any land. Any fool could speculate with money, ruminates Hooper, with tongue in cheek. "But to buy, to sell, to make profits, without a cent in one's pocket—this required judgment, discretion, ingenuity—in short, genius!" Suggs' next adventure finds him in a stagecoach heading for the state capital, Tuscaloosa. Allowing himself to be mistaken for a legislator, Suggs accepts a bribe from a fellow traveler. "You'll use your influence with your senator and other friends?" the traveler asks. "Look me in the eye!" demands Suggs. "You see *honesty* thar—don't you?" And with that solemn assurance, Suggs pockets the money. Suggs' victims should themselves have heeded the motto that Suggs adopted, "It is good to be shifty in a new country."[36]

Future novelist W. Gilmore Simms of South Carolina made his first journey through Alabama in 1822 at the age of sixteen. After several more trips west, he merged his experiences into the adventure story *Richard Hurdis: A Tale of Alabama*, published in 1838. Simms' novel drew on the career of John A. Murrell, whose notorious gang of conspirators terrorized the Natchez Trace region and threatened to launch slave rebellions.[37] *Richard Hurdis* begins with the hero proudly and stoically leaving his mother, father, and sweetheart in the Canebrake in order to make his way to the Choctaw lands opening in Mississippi. Hurdis is ambushed en route, his friend killed, and his money taken. Resolving to avenge his friend's death, Hurdis changes his name and disguises himself as a riverboat gambler. On a steamboat along the Tombigbee, he meets Clement Foster, a Methodist preacher from the Alabama Conference who warns him of a secret society of fifteen hundred men, the Mystic Brotherhood. Outwardly professing religion, law, medicine, planting, shop keeping, and all manner of legitimate practices, the Brotherhood members are actually murdering rogues who have sworn allegiance to the bidding of their leader. Members of the Brotherhood had robbed Hurdis and murdered his friend. Hurdis sees through Foster's disguise; the preacher is in fact their leader. Hurdis is asked to join the Brotherhood, and when the steamboat docks, he rides with the members to a meeting in the Sipsey River swamp west of Tuscaloosa. But before they can commit another great robbery, Hurdis escapes to Tuscaloosa, gives warning, and together with a posse ambushes the Brotherhood. All the miscreants are killed or captured, with one exception, Foster, who escapes, vowing to meet Hurdis again in Arkansas.

The novel's two main antagonists, Foster and Hurdis, are both seeking to make their own way on the frontier, this tabula rasa of possibilities. In one revealing passage, Foster relates the circumstances of his youth. He was born poor and worked hard trying to get ahead until one day he asked himself how many years he was willing to spend futilely trying to make an honest living. And then it occurred to him that there were thousands of others like him. "We all have a family likeness in our hearts, however disguised by habits, manners, education." The usual external clues were unreliable. The dandies appear to be the most upright of gentlemen, and the most evil—the leader of the Mystic Brotherhood—is dressed as a Methodist minister. Shorn of institutions and webs of enduring relationships, each is on his own. This is the "true picture of our social condition. Man is the prey of man—the weak of the strong—the unwary of the cunning."[38] The impostors succeeded because the frontier freed men to pursue selfish impulses.

This new country was unlike the older communities of these men's youth, where a network of restraints confined a man, observed Baldwin. Chains of habit, fashion, prejudice, custom, and opinion held him back. He was trampled under the feet of "wealth, family, influence, class, caste, fashion, coterie and adventitious circumstances of all sorts, . . . he acts not so much from his own will and in his own way, as from the force of these arbitrary influences." His character becomes "artificial and conventional; less bold, simple, direct, earnest and natural"—in short, less effective. Once on the frontier and adrift from his moorings, a man could act decisively. But he could also act recklessly. "Vulgarity—ignorance—fussy and arrogant pretension—unmitigated rowdyism—bullying insolence," wrote Baldwin, "*seemed* to wield unchecked dominion." Swindling did not merely become respectable but "was raised to the dignity of the fine arts." Fortunes multiplied as houses and lands changed hands, "real estate see-sawed up as morals went down on the other end of the plank." The resulting profits were spent appropriately. The groceries, as saloons were known, did a roaring business. Horse races came before all else: one judge twice adjourned his court to officiate at races. And gambling at the table was but an extension of gambling on land and slaves. Religion was scarcely mentioned, except when some swearing was needed.[39]

Simms was even more damning. Cheap Western lands and promises of quick riches, he charged, had seduced individuals into renouncing their moral obligations. (As a two-year-old, Simms had been left behind with his grandmother when his father abandoned the family to pursue planting in Mississippi.) Frontiersmen might gain great wealth, Simms admitted, but "the nicer harmonies of the moral world become impaired; the sweeter cores of affection are undone or rudely snapped asunder, and a rude indifference to the claims of one's fellow, must follow every breaking up of the old and stationary abodes."[40]

★ ★ ★

Greensborians, too, were troubled by the problems created by avarice and unrestrained individuals. Henry Watson—perhaps because he was so far removed from his family, perhaps because his native Connecticut was so established, perhaps simply because he was unusually sensitive—wrote plaintive letters back home. He asked his father, "Do you forget that I am in a wilderness, cut off from all mankind," only tenuously connected with "all those I hold most dear?" And a few months later, Watson wrote to his mother, "Here have I been now for three years and all the time most pleasantly situated, and so constantly & so pleasantly employed, . . . and yet I never for a moment have felt my self *at home*."[41] He would not call Greensboro his home for some time.

Surely it was distressing for Watson and other Greensborians to be isolated, far from their roots. But the problems ran deeper: "To be in a strange land," as the *Green[e] County Sentinel* put it, "surrounded by those who feel no particular interest in your situation" was the ruinous result of their own rapacious selfishness. They had "little or no society," as William Beverley complained to his father back in Virginia; "the people are from all quarters & care no more for each other than dogs do, except [if] it is to cheat you." No Greensborian took notice of a stranger, because everyone was a stranger. But as if to overcome their separateness, they saluted each other with the moniker *friend*. One's "friend," however, might turn out to be another disguised criminal. "Beset with scoundrels," concluded Beverley, with "no confidence in one another, all is suspicion & distrust."[42]

Greensborians certainly socialized with each other but did so in ways unfamiliar to settled easterners. The men generally neglected the women, preferring to congregate in saloons. Because each man considered himself as good as any other, parties were given without invitations, and each individual put himself forward rather than rely on another's introductions. Wedding invitations were sent indiscriminately to everyone, "whether known or not and without regard to character." This was a radical sort of egalitarianism where, unable to discriminate genuine character from fake, grasping individuals masked their deep-seated suspicions with a good-natured slap on the back. "A heterogenious mass of people," decided Beverley, "they dont know, nor do they care for each other."[43]

How credible was it to call someone a friend when the two might easily never see each other again? "A friendship," Watson objected, "is by no means the result of an hour." Although the overall number of Greene County's white residents leveled off during the 1830s, restless individuals constantly moved in and out at least until 1860. As one person arrived in Greensboro from the East, another left for the West. An analysis of Masonic membership, for example, shows a persistence rate during the 1830s of only between 3 and 14 percent, and by 1850, less than half the Masons were likely to stay more than five years.[44]

"The great objection to this country," wrote Watson, "is that the population is so changeable, nobody seems to consider himself settled, they remain one, two, three or four years & must move to some other spot. Since I came here [two years earlier], the entire population of this Town, with a dozen or two exceptions, has changed. . . . if a man is away six months & returns, he must expect to find himself among strangers. . . . no man knows when he gets acquainted with another whether he will ever know him long enough to make it worth his while to cultivate his friendship." A fair problem indeed. "Of course," concluded Watson, that such ephemeral relationships were so common "has its effect upon the feelings of the community."[45]

As if real friendships were not difficult enough to establish among transients, a downturn in the economy drove these already disparate individuals even further apart. "The cry is money! money!! money!!! and nobody has any money!" complained Watson a full year before the Panic of 1837 officially struck. Bankruptcies were soaring, unlike anything he had ever experienced. "Since I have been here I have not seen a time like the present—The rich and the poor alike are pinched, perhaps the rich the most so, as they have had the least prudence. . . . It seems to me now as if [we are] on the brink of destruction." Debts were called in, and citizens tried to sell their assets. Land was offered for sale at low prices. Slaves were said to be more common than five-dollar bills, and none sold in Greensboro during the summer of 1837. Cotton prices dropped to less than nine cents per pound. Merchants stopped traveling to New York to replenish their stock of goods because New Yorkers would require the payment of debts. Banks ceased to pay in specie.[46]

Greensborians believed that they suffered disproportionately because land and slave speculation was at the heart of their economy, and they petitioned the governor for relief. He called into session the General Assembly, which passed acts extending debts owed to banks and issued state bonds raising the assets of the state bank. The problem was made worse because Alabama's state banking system had been capitalized with money generated from land sales that Congress had earmarked for internal improvements. The Bank of Alabama had been so successful that the General Assembly had improvidently abolished direct taxation in 1836 in expectation of relying on state bank profits to run the government. But without taxes to raise revenue, the bank was forced to float a $7.5 million bond issue. The strategy failed and with it the bank. Direct taxation was reinstituted, a move that covered only the interest on the debt, and liquidation of the bank's assets followed.[47]

Some Greensborians blamed the crisis on the Jackson administration's Specie Circular—a requirement that all public lands be purchased with hard money, an especially scarce commodity on the frontier. Others singled out the paper notes that banks had been allowed to issue far in excess of their assets, comparing the bloated currency's effect on the populace to that of "Liquor on the toper."[48] Whatever the cause, Greensborians were worried and responded variously: the local Masonic lodge received an unprecedented number of new members; some citizens left for the Republic of Texas; others demanded legal redress.

Lawyers had more business than they could possibly handle trying to sort out the tangle of debts that had been at the root of the local economy. When prices for cotton and slaves were growing faster than inflation, speculators had purchased wildly, delaying repayment as long as possible. "Every man says he will pay when he can collect and in this way every one is dependant upon another," observed Watson. But this was hardly the sort of mutual dependency on which to build a community. When the economic bubble burst, banks began calling in promissory notes. Merchants in turn called in their debts, and when they could not collect, businesses failed. The mercantile store Harrison and Haywood, for example, sold out for a dollar, although more than two hundred individuals owed the firm a total of nearly fifty thousand dollars (of which thirty thousand dollars was owed by one person), this in a town of only a few hundred.[49]

Waggish lawyer and author Baldwin estimated, with some exaggeration, that the panic had produced four or five thousand lawsuits in adjacent Sumter County. "It was a pleasant sight to professional eyes," he wrote, "to see a whole people let go all holds and . . . move off to court" in this one-against-all contest for survival. Watson, also a lawyer, did not once go to bed before midnight for the first few months of the panic. Two years later, he was still working long hours "without change and incident. . . . talking & writing, receiving and paying money, bringing suits & settling them, keeping people out of scrapes when out, and getting them out when in." From supper until midnight he stayed in his room at a private boardinghouse, researching obscure legal points and writing letters and legal documents. It was numbingly routine. "The dirty streets & confined prospects of a small village afford nothing romantic," he sighed.[50]

Greensboro would one day have its community. But the way was not plain, and the materials—transient and autonomous self-seekers—unpromising.

PART II

# Cooperation

# CHAPTER 3

# Voluntary Communities

Individuals, as well as communities, look very much
to their own interest.  ✷  John G. Harvey, 1852

"The frequent interchange of those social feelings, which bind us to each other, and render life pleasant, though highly prized by me, is denied," wrote Methodist minister Eugene LeVert to his brother. His yearning was accentuated by the Panic of 1837 but had deeper roots in the separation from his family. LeVert's plight was common enough. He, like other young men, saw a move to the Southwest as an opportunity to escape from the confines of long-standing family influence and to achieve economic success. But independence had a price that became clear only with time and distance.[1]

Unattached young men were not the only people to make their way to Greensboro, of course. Many men brought wives and children. Some migrants left their old residences to join kinfolk who had settled previously. By entering an existing family network, these people were getting a head start, and by building their homes near each other, neighborhoods became identified with families. But even those newcomers with relatives already in Greensboro found relationships inconstant and tentative. Letters back home testified to the regret women in particular faced at having to leave their relatives and friends to confront a frontier lacking in the community feelings they so cherished.

Familial society—whether realized in kinship neighborhoods or coveted by single young men and uprooted wives—represented, settlers believed, the most basic social unit. The relationships and responsibilities among husband, wife, and children were deemed natural and were never openly challenged. Beyond this bedrock lay great uncertainty. Some saw no need to extend or expand familial society. Such impulses meshed easily with other notions of negative liberty, small government, and attempts to avoid entanglements in the market economy. Most Greensborians, however, were heavily engaged in commerce and seemed to recognize the limitations that dissociative individuals faced. Residents also came to recognize that while Greensborians shared aspirations of success, they lacked a common past that would foster moral—not simply legal or contractual—obligations beyond their families.

Southern University, designed by Adolphus Heinman. (From Southern University catalog, 1870–1871, Birmingham-Southern College Archives, Birmingham)

How could a civil society be established among self-serving strangers? New, more flexible solutions would be required to bind such dynamic individualists together—they were not about to change what they were. Yet within a few decades, improvising Greensborians would do something extraordinary. As town leaders persuaded residents to enter into joint projects—to promote commerce, establish fraternal organizations and churches, and push for moral and educational reforms—the germ of community feelings began to appear. The more successful of these efforts enlisted the greater number of citizens, but these people were not building a single community as much as cobbling together a nexus of overlapping communities. More than merely enlisting citizens and successfully completing a project, these endeavors necessarily brought with them certain latent visions of how society should ultimately be organized.

Leadership roles in these projects were generally—but not necessarily—assumed by long-standing and generally prosperous residents. Membership was fluid, based on an individual's particular interest or the prospects for personal advantage, and most people did not limit themselves to just one organization but joined a second or a third.[2] The newspaper editor's public profile suggests that he, more than any other single individual, had the pivotal role. In Greensboro's case it was "Colonel" John G. Harvey, who, after retiring from the army as a captain, purchased the *Alabama Beacon* in 1843 and remained its editor and Greensboro's most fervent town booster for all but a few months until his death in 1890. His advocacy or rejection of a particular program carried great weight. But more than the editor's backing, the single most significant factor in the success of a project was whether participation was likely to incur personal benefits.

Rigid autonomy yielded to cooperation. This was not a difficult transition, for cooperation implied an equality of interchange that easily complemented self-interest and reliance on contract. Cooperating Greensborians were thus not that far removed from autonomous Greensborians, for in both cases they acted to advance their own interests. In this respect, Greensboro, with its wealth of voluntary communities, resembled countless other small towns across the American frontier.[3]

★ ★ ★

Self-interested cooperation was first and most clearly seen in railroad building. The advantages were clear to Greensborians: A railroad through the Canebrake would facilitate getting their cotton to large markets, where early arrival secured a better price. A railroad would also go far in overcoming the Canebrake mud that stopped wagons and horses from traveling after a rain. Further, trains could bring in the manufactured goods that commanded such high prices in the hinterlands. In short, a rail line would help to end the town's isolation, promote wealth, and open the town to the world of progress. By calling public meetings, setting up committees, and sending out volunteers to solicit support, railroad building promoted community-building as it promised prosperity.[4]

Plans were drawn in 1833 to connect Greensboro by rail south to Prairie Bluff (Daletown) along the Alabama River between Cahaba and St. Stephens. By the end of the year, the company's stock was subscribed as individuals rushed to purchase Canebrake land along the proposed road before prices soared. At the same time, other railroad companies were planning to run lines through the Canebrake east of Demopolis, and one was being subscribed to connect Greensboro and the county seat at Erie, along the Black Warrior River. Estimated costs ran at sixty-five hundred dollars per mile. "All these will operate to the benefit of this part of the county," wrote Henry Watson.[5]

Greensborians enthusiastically embraced new technologies and commercial opportunities. Alabama's first railway, around the Shoals on the Tennessee River, had been in operation only a year (and the first steam locomotive in America only three) when Greensborians were agitating for a railroad. At nearly the same time that the new railroads were being subscribed, artesian wells were starting to become commonplace in the Canebrake, and Dr. Robert W. Withers was about to introduce turbines. His complex at Millwood, west of Greensboro along the river, was described in leading journals as a "wonder of the earth" and attracted such renowned scientists as Sir Charles Lyell, who wanted to see it for themselves.[6]

This was the Age of Progress, and the industrious Canebrakers were marching in the parade. Dr. Withers pondered in his private journal whether humankind had been improved by the progress of arts and civilization in society. He had no real doubts. His description of the prior "Savage State"—perpetual wars, vengeance, ignorance, a precarious subsistence, limited intellectual powers, and a hard insensibility—seemed to have been lifted straight out of Thomas Hobbes' *Leviathan*. In full agreement, Withers' neighbor, Jacob Cribbs, the editor of the *Erie Gazette*, could scarcely control his exuberance for the times. "It is with much pleasure," the editor wrote in one of his columns, "that we see the exertions of enterprise, intelligence and improvement so cheerfully manifested, and so fully and effectually completed." The woodsman's axe and the unwearied labor of the farmer had tamed these wild wastelands and densely woven forests. Twenty years earlier, the Indian had roamed free. Now, the land was filled with happy cottages and farmhouses, fertile fields and bulging barnyards, growing villages and towns. Twenty years earlier, Indians had floated leisurely down the Black Warrior in ill-constructed canoes. Now, weekly steamboats speedily and conveniently turned distant places into virtual neighbors. Now, "praise and thanksgiving, peace and liberty, have led the way; edifices of learning, and temples of piety have been erected . . . monuments of good for the rising greatness of this FAR, FAR, SOUTH-WEST."[7]

The Panic of 1837 squelched much of Greensboro's optimism, and the railroad projects quickly ended. With no funds to assist companies directly, the Alabama General Assembly tried a new course. Liberal charters were granted that allowed new companies to barter stock for land, supplies, and labor; the right of eminent domain was extended to the railroad companies; and restrictions on voting shares were dropped in order to entice wealthy Alabamians to invest. The new policies ultimately succeeded, but not until meetings to promote railroads finally started appearing again in the late 1840s. Greensborians then joined others to promote a railroad link between the Alabama and Tennessee Rivers. Its advantages would include speed, safety, economy, and—significantly—a vast increase in property values. Such an endeavor would be in keeping with "the progressive and improving spirit of the age," touted the *Alabama Beacon,* and the line's completion would not only add immensely to the state's wealth but also unite closely and fraternally different sections of the state.[8]

"You will find a considerable change here for the better," wrote Israel Pickens' brother, Samuel, in the mid-1850s. "We too are beginning to turn our attention to the 'progress of the age.'" In addition to the Mobile and Ohio and the Alabama and Tennessee Rivers, several other railroads were either under construction or being planned to run from Jackson, Mississippi, to Selma; from Montgomery to Pensacola, Florida; and from Alabama's northeast corner through Tuscaloosa and Eutaw to Meridian, Mississippi. The railroad-building boom of the 1850s resulted from the convergence of several economic developments: the reestablishment of sound banks, the beginnings of Alabama's exploitation of its mineral district, and a high demand for cotton. At the beginning of the 1850s, only three railroads were operating or under construction, but by the end of the decade, Alabama boasted 610 miles of rail.[9]

Greensborians pushed to have their town connected to this emerging system. In 1852 the chance came for a line to come directly into town. The Greensboro, Newbern, and Woodville Rail Road had, of course, the solid backing of the *Beacon*. Correspondents touted the advantages of cooperation, with editor Harvey warning that "unless each one acts his part, the object cannot be effected": the opposition of only a few people would be enough to kill the venture. In conjunction with barbecues held to attract subscribers, the *Beacon* published a series of articles relentlessly supporting the proposal. The problem, according to Harvey, was that in most enterprises of this sort, "individuals, as well as communities, *look very much to their own interest*"; the solution, therefore, lay in identifying the different interests and explaining how each would benefit. He then proceeded to list the usual advantages, including ease in getting goods to market and increased property values. But more than that, Harvey continued, a railroad was a means for bringing individuals together, making them better informed, and cultivating their social and better feelings—technology building community.[10]

Despite high hopes, the project failed, as another would in late 1858 when a Planters' Rail Road was proposed to run from Uniontown, through Newbern and Greensboro, across the Black Warrior to the Tombigbee River. Correspondents again wrote letters to the newspapers appealing to self-interest and the prospects of increasing prosperity. "Cotton is King," one proclaimed, "let Steam be his Chariot Steed." When other proposed railroads—from Cahaba to Marion to Greensboro, from Gainesville to Greensboro—competed for subscriptions, complaints surfaced of too many meetings, too many speeches, too many barbecues, and too little effect. The complaints were all too accurate. By 1861 a line snaked northward from Uniontown to Newbern, nine miles from Greensboro, and ended. Greensboro had little to show for nearly three decades of efforts to bring a railroad. Railroads were simply beyond the town's means if funds came voluntarily only from those whose land would be directly improved.[11]

"Whilst we are prosecuting plans for the construction of railroads and manufactories," an article reprinted in the *Beacon* reminded readers, "let us not neglect farming," humanity's most independent and honorable occupation. As the editor saw it, the two were completely compatible, for farmers had to keep pace in this age of improvement. Beginning in 1849, Harvey declared the *Beacon* an agricultural paper and politically neutral. (The policy would not last.) He encouraged farmers to adopt modern agricultural techniques and printed reports of the latest developments and theories. Some articles counseled moving away from cotton by diversifying into naval stores, lumber, sugarcane, and such. When Greensboro's John DuBois received a patent on improvements to the cotton gin, the newspaper prominently displayed the illustration. Harvey touted a public meeting in Forkland to address the practicability of establishing a local cotton factory. And when Canebrakers advanced a plan to build drainage systems and plank roads to overcome the prairie mud, that effort too received prominent billing; again, despite printed endorsements in the *Beacon* and lists of financial advantages, the enterprise came to nothing.[12]

Planters, farmers, and experimenters willingly shared their ideas for agricultural reform. Dr. Withers, despite charges of being "all for money," openly called for agriculturalists to improve their land, not only for their own sake but also to improve the public good. Withers published scientific analyses of the Canebrake soil and delivered the first anniversary address to the Agricultural Society at Greensboro in 1830. The society was active in promoting new plants and breeds and in applying scientific principles to rescue nature from the tyranny of ignorance and old habits. The agriculturalists hoped to accomplish collectively what individual action could not: stop the wasting of the soil that threatened to turn to Canebrake into the latest worn-out region. Planter Isaac Croom even pushed for the University of Alabama to hire a professor of scientific agriculture and, joining other planters, physicians, and entrepreneurs, petitioned the governor to look into setting up a display at London's Crystal Palace Exhibition of 1851. Croom became one of the delegates to an 1852 industrial convention in New Orleans. He returned to champion the benefits of industrial conventions "in multiplying population, diversifying labour, bringing to light dormant resources, advancing agricultural and mechanical improvement." Industry, he asserted, would enrich, ennoble, and adorn the state and thereby discourage individuals from leaving their fragile society.[13]

Personal profit and public good—did one preclude the other? Planters would cooperate in sharing ideas about agricultural reforms, but self-interest always seemed to intrude. When the Agricultural Society failed to meet, editor Harvey knew the problem. "So long as the acquisition of negroes and lands constitutes the all-engrossing subject of interest with us, neither Agricultural Societies, nor Societies of any other sort, are likely to effect much good."[14] The planters and businessmen who comprised the commercial community—if indeed it was a community—exacted few obligations from each other. Individuals were linked by bonds no thicker than a bank note.

✯ ✯ ✯

While rampant individualism worked its effects, certain voluntary associations—including the Freemasons, the churches, and reform movements—offered alternative models of moral behavior to counter Greensboro's market-inspired anomie. On the American frontier, Freemasonry emerged as a means of adjusting to the destabilizing effects of commerce and the Age of Progress. Masons proclaimed older, seemingly outdated Enlightenment ideals of fraternity and disinterested virtue for which individualistic entrepreneurs and town boosters seemed to long (or perhaps found personally advantageous). Indeed, Freemasonry and the commercial community came to complement each other, even as they worked from different assumptions.

From its introduction in the eighteenth century, Freemasonry stressed a civic virtue that appealed particularly to the Founding Fathers, but the American Revolution transformed society and with it the Freemasons. Successful artisans and parvenus freely joined wealthy gentlemen in the rituals. American Freemasonry combined Jefferson's notion of an aristocracy of merit with a voluntary association of individuals bound by unselfish moral concern. Such ideals shifted on the frontier, where Masons strove to serve needs that were not being met or were being met rather badly. The Masons dispensed charity and established schools, and in a region lacking financial institutions and teeming with confidence men, membership in a lodge provided a good name and access to credit. In time, however, the Masons began moving away from universal benevolence toward giving preference to their own members. The Masons' secret rituals and willingness to assume leadership roles provoked outsiders' suspicions, and with the 1826 disappearance of William Morgan, an upstate New Yorker who had threatened to reveal the Freemasons' secrets, the fraternity came under public attack. During the early 1830s Freemasonry in Alabama suffered, and the state's Grand Lodge failed to meet in 1835 for lack of a quorum. The order responded by dispensing with many of its secret rituals, by stressing moral education, and by reexamining its social ideals.[15]

A lodge had been established in Greensboro even before some of the mainline Protestant denominations built sanctuaries. "Transient brethren are cordially invited," read an announcement in an 1823 edition of the *Greensboro Halcyon*. But Greensboro's Lafayette Lodge No. 26 languished in the face of a shifting population and national controversies. Membership, in fact, stayed at about a dozen during the 1820s and rose above thirty only once in its first fifteen years. But in 1839 the lodge doubled in size to fifty-four, a remarkable number for such a small place. The 1839 jump was too abrupt to have been merely a local push for members. More likely, the sudden growth in Greensboro's lodge reflected either self-interested attempts to establish cordial ties with potential litigants or a receptive ear to the Masonic message in a time of crisis—or some combination of the two.[16]

Conspicuous on the membership lists of Greensboro's Masons were the names of established, prosperous citizens involved in many facets of civic life. Some remained in the lodge for decades. But alongside these names were those of anonymous souls who remained on the rolls for only a few years or a few months.[17] For these men, membership in the Masons might provide an immediate ticket into business circles; when things looked better elsewhere, these members would move on. The conflict between the ideals of disinterested benevolence on the one hand and the reality of self-interest on the other thus seemed pronounced in the frontier lodges. Membership provided something larger than the individual, inclusion into a sacred fraternity that would serve—like families and churches—as a rock in the storm. And yet Masons seemed to be creating the very world from which they sought refuge.

Alabama Masons seldom recorded their visions of society, for their secrets were dispensed orally. From time to time, however, the veil was drawn back. At an 1847 meeting of the Grand Lodge of Alabama, a resolution passed directing all Masons to gather in order to hear addresses urging all unassociated Masons to affiliate themselves with their nearest lodge. The address given at Greensboro's Lafayette Lodge apparently did not survive, but Richard G. Earle kept the address he gave to Jacksonville's Hiram Lodge No. 42.[18] His object may have been to bring lapsed Masons back into the fold, but his speech dealt more with the fraternity's vision of community.

Earle began by drawing an analogy between natural bodies (such as organisms) and artificial bodies (such as Freemasonry). Both, he noted, obey the invincible natural law of self-preservation. Thus, societies, like individuals, should scrupulously attend to the health of their members. A diseased hand or foot disables the individual's body from the energetic discharge of his duties; likewise, he argued, an artificial body is weakened whenever one of its individual members is morally unfit for the duties society required. "Too much care can not be used in guarding . . . against the designs of the unworthy applicant . . . from without, and the cupidity of the mercenary from within." In all societies are found "those who hang like an incubus upon them, sucking of their vitals: imparting nothing in return but disease and if not arrested, death. This requires the most active energy, on the part of the virtuous and well meaning, to counteract it." Those guilty members should be expelled. Akin to the diseased members of society were those who loudly championed Masonry in good times but were the first to desert in times of trial. These sunnyday members were easily identified "by their cool selfishness, and the avidity with which they seek to find out what is popular with the brethren." These self-seekers diligently support "not the good of masonry but their own personal popularity, which when obtained, they immediately pervert to their own selfish ends." Like sponges afloat in the sea, they take all they can but never exert themselves for the benefit of the general good. "Such members are blights to any community, & more particularly that of ours."[19]

A healthy community, by contrast, is marked by honesty, moral rectitude, and an active benevolence. A prospective member of the fraternity of Masons must deliberately seek to join without self-interested motives: "He must apply freely and voluntarily; prompted alone by a desire of Knowledge and a sincere wish of being serviceable to his fellow creatures." Freemasonry cannot make good men out of bad, but it can provide the means of elevating and strengthening the virtuous. In sum, "Masonry stands upon the integrity of her sons." A Mason of weak moral character endangers the whole. Membership in such an artificial society means that one partakes in duties to himself and to the fraternity—that is, "all are equally and mutually bound to help in all the laudable and legitimate undertakings, of the fraternity," for "those who are not for us are against us." Even more, those who rule must be servants of all.[20]

Frontier Freemasonry tried to merge older concepts of community into American notions of individualism. Communities were voluntarily created, Earle argued, and thus artificial. Yet they were like natural bodies, where the infection of a single member with self-interest—like St. Matthew's offending hand—had to be cut out before it infected all. The fraternity tried to bridge this gap by employing rituals. Elaborate initiation ceremonies allowed disparate frontiersmen with virtually no sense of history to join a common past that claimed generations of adherents. Inheritance emerged from an act of will. Freemasonry was unequivocally exclusionary in a country where equal access was assumed. And where Masons expressed their ideals in charity and education, the frontier was devoid of such public institutions. Freemasonry, in sum, kept before the public eye an ideal of disinterested service, personal liberty, social responsibility, and natural community, an ideal that would recur during the 1860s.

★ ★ ★

Evangelical Christians, like the Masons, addressed the same problem of the unrestrained individual and used many of the same techniques. Both groups, for example, promoted moral order—particularly benevolence, temperance, piety, and personal discipline—as an alternative to an amoral market. Both groups, to greater or lesser degrees, were ritualistic.[21] And both Masons and Evangelicals restricted membership to those who voluntarily adopted the groups' programs to save the individual and ultimately humankind. The two certainly parted ways on matters of secrecy, extending membership to women, and specific creeds. But Masons and Christians both agreed that the world could be saved only by the transformation of individual character.

The churches arrived early in Greensboro. The first sermon was said to have been preached by a Methodist minister in 1818, before the town's incorporation. A Baptist preacher settled not long afterward and founded a church, and in 1823 the Baptist State Convention was formed at Salem Church, near Greensboro. The Presbyterians arrived about 1822. Although several Catholics and Jews lived in Greensboro, their numbers were never sufficient to warrant erecting their own buildings, so they met in homes or traveled to Demopolis or Tuscaloosa to worship. An outstanding feature of the earliest churches was their establishment through local initiatives that linked church building with community-building. A few months after sixty individuals professed their faith at an 1830 camp meeting at the county seat, for example, a letter appeared in the *Erie Gazette*. "A Citizen" urged that a general meeting be called to build a church for the little town. All that was required to begin, he argued, was for the citizens to work together. "Why should not we enjoy this blessing, as well as the citizens of other villages, and the thickly inhabited neighborhoods that surround us?"[22]

Only slowly did Greensborians come to agree on the proper relationships among church, community, and commerce. Watson, an Episcopalian, charged in

1834 that ministers were unpopular and no different from everyone else who was speculating, cheating, and fleecing: "This is no exaggeration. Even here many preachers, both among the Baptists, the Methodists & the Presbyterians, cultivate farms, trade in horses, by and sell negroes & do all ordinarily done by men of business & are not to be distinguished from other men except as on the Sabbath the men of the pulpit." His comments represented a variation on the troubling ambiguity of appearance and character on the frontier. Another observer reported during the height of the Flush Times that "religion is in a cold state here, . . . every ones heart is to much set upon money, it is the theme of the day."[23]

The Panic of 1837, however, gave a sudden boost to the churches, just as it had to the Masonic lodge, as individuals scrounged for safety during trying times. In 1839 a great revival broke out in Greensboro, led by the Methodist Reverend James M. Boatright. The Methodists soon bought a new lot and turned their old frame building over to their black members. The Episcopalians, who for several years had been meeting in a female academy, began to build St. Paul's shortly thereafter.[24]

William Scarborough was one of the converts of the late 1830s. He wrote from his new Greene County home to his astonished brother back in North Carolina confirming that he had joined "the despised Baptist church." Scarborough recounted that he and his wife had been baptized and were trying to serve God, aware that the Scriptures taught that the kingdom could be entered only by passing through much tribulation. He read the Bible prayerfully and attentively and tried by his own strength "till I thought every other man on earth had a better chance for heaven than myself." Finally, a feeling came over him that he was a child of God based on free grace alone and unmerited favor. Scarborough believed that Christians were to stand together as a bulwark against a grasping world—a force so insidious that it threatened the churches themselves. He complained of corrupted denominations that accepted wealthy men in order to get money and, nearly as bad, required their preachers to attend theological school before deeming them qualified. But Christ chose "the poor illiterate Fishermen to be his diciples and another scripture says god has chosen the weak things of this world to confound the mity I find these college fellows will not preach without a sallary of $500 to $1000." He reported rumors of a convention in Mississippi that wanted to rewrite the Scripture, which in its present form was too "Vulgar for the Refined minds of the present age. . . . all they want is power and they would take from us the blessed liberty which we at present enjoy." Scarborough's complaints were hardly unique. During the mid-1840s, another local charged that the "ministers are cotton planters. Elders, *usurers* loaning . . . their money at from *eighteen* to thirty six percent & that even to their own brethren in Christ."[25]

For their part, ministers of the Gospel found the demands they faced almost overwhelming. The Reverend E. V. LeVert wrote from Greensboro that thirty-five years' experience had shown him "the privations, & hardships to which a minister is subjected, who devotes all his time, & energies to his high & holy calling, & depends upon the voluntary contributions of his people for the bread that feeds his family. It is often the case, while they roll in luxury, he can barely supply the pressing wants of his family." With the great distances they traveled, "the ministers of the gospel may be likened to the camels crossing the desert, while loaded with the richest spices and perfumery, they must suffer with thirst, & feed very scantily upon the coarsest provender."[26]

Expectations that the church should stand apart seemed in time to fade. In their 1855 report to the Quarterly Conference, Greensboro's Methodists claimed good attendance at worship, but the report noted a "profound tranquillity . . . a tendency to gayety rather than to pensiveness and piety[,] a tendency to conformity to the world." Lines of distinction blurred. In the spring, for example, Greensboro's Presbyterians, Baptists, Methodists, and Episcopalians invited the town to join in a parade honoring Sabbath school students. Greensboro's militia companies met the procession of scholars and their teachers as they marched up Main Street from the Methodist to the Baptist church. There the crowd heard prayers, ministerial addresses, and hymns before retiring for a picnic. Greensboro's military, educational, and religious institutions could easily cooperate when they shared goals.[27]

The evangelical Christians were rigidly egalitarian among themselves, for membership, especially among the Baptists, was based on relationships with God too personal to be diluted by the assistance of others. An individual who sought conversion in order to avoid hell and reach heaven was acting out of self-interest. Yet he entered a Christian community—simultaneously local, ancient, and beyond place—that asked him to renounce self-interest. By losing one's life, one gained it. Churches and Masonic lodges had room for transients, the self-interested, and those longing for principled virtue, yet their communities were unavoidably elitist, as only those with special knowledge or revelation could join.

✳ ✳ ✳

Farm families pursued their activities in the county's outlying regions.[28] Mount Hebron Precinct, north of the Canebrake and far from Greensboro's influence, included both rich Tombigbee River bottomlands and red clay hills. The precinct was entirely rural, boasting only a doctor's office, a general store, a school, a post office, and a couple of churches. The nearest place of any size, Gainesville (about a third as big as Greensboro), lay across the Tombigbee in Sumter County.

Mount Hebron residents endured a numbing routine broken by regular ceremonies on Sunday mornings and irregular ones marking birth, marriage, and death. The weather and the seasons probably dominated conversations. Because these rural "plain folk," as they are known, left few written records, reconstructing the nature of their society often relies on demographic data and material culture. The survival of a single quilt from Greene County's hinterlands affords just such an opportunity.[29]

In 1858 some of the folk living around the little Sardis Methodist Church gathered to sew a quilt. The occasion may have been a fund-raiser for the church or school, or the occasion could have been the arrival of new individuals or families— a welcome novelty to lives attuned to the regularity of nature. Unlike the many Greensborians who came and went with alarming frequency, those living in Mount Hebron Precinct probably craved fresh faces. Whatever the motives, gathering to sew a quilt represented yet another voluntary community. The result celebrated both individuality (each block was signed by an individual) and cooperation (in pooling their individual efforts into a common product).

The Lanford Album Quilt, as it is known, contains forty-two separate blocks (each about 15 inches square, the whole quilt measuring approximately 90 by 104 inches) of separate appliquéd designs. More than half are stylized flowers, while the remainder are asymmetrical depictions of flowers and other plants. (Two blocks— a basket with flowers and an American flag—do not fit the pattern.) All of the plant designs that can be identified—such as the fig, sweet gum, and watermelon—are Southern. The blocks, signed with initials or names, are sewn together and quilted in a half-inch diamond pattern.[30]

The family name Lanford appears most frequently on the quilt, in ten or eleven blocks. The name Powers appears on seven blocks, Bibb on six, Smith on four or five, and Rogers and Stephens each on three. Various clues suggest that a few women sewed most of the blocks: many of the signed blocks include men's names; one is unsigned; and while each block is unique, similarities of design and technique are obvious. In all likelihood, those who were of limited dexterity with a needle sponsored blocks by paying someone else to sew them.

The quilt's signatures bespeak complex webs of family relationships. James I. Lanford, whose black-and-brown abstract design appears on the quilt's left-hand edge, in 1862 married Caroline Stephens, whose asymmetrical vine design is placed on the same row along the opposite edge. The names of both of James' parents, Elizabeth and Henry Lanford, appear on adjoining blocks, and the names of their other children are scattered across the quilt. The name of Caroline Stephens' brother, John L. Stephens, is found on a block with a primrose pattern. Six children of Mary and William Bibb sponsored blocks, and two of these siblings subsequently married other people whose names are on the quilt. Other family relationships can also be discovered.

It would be misleading to assume, however, that all these names formed a single whole. The most frequently named family, the Lanfords, had first purchased land in the precinct only weeks or months before the quilt was sewn in the fall of 1858, and other families were also new to the region. The precinct certainly did not suffer the emigration that Greensboro faced, but transience remained a problem. In other words, not all signers of the quilt were related by blood or by shared experiences; some may have known each other only casually.

Nor did these quilt signers all share the same economic status. The patriarch of the Lanford family, Henry, owned a farm of 180 acres, half improved, which he valued at $3,250 and on which he harvested twenty-eight bales of cotton as his cash crop in 1860. On the rest of his land he grew vegetables for his family's use along with six hundred bushels of corn, much of which went to feed the livestock he valued at $626. Lanford's farm implements were worth only $75. Although the census enumerator listed him as a planter, he would more accurately be considered a middling farmer who worked the fields along with his children. The two female slaves (one the mother of a small child) that he rented helped his wife, Elizabeth, with domestic chores.[31]

Some quilt signers did better than the Lanfords, others worse. William and Mary Bibb owned real estate valued at $2,000 and personal property (mostly slaves) valued at $11,000. The father of Caroline and John L. Stephens owned thirteen slaves. Anna Smith owned five. But James W. Rogers, born in 1841, was an overseer without prospects. Daniel W. W. Smith was an unattached young lawyer with time on his hands. And whereas all the Lanfords could read and write, the parents both of Smith and his siblings and of the Bibb children could not. Participation in the quilt thus was not distinguished by slave ownership or income; rather, participation was based on proximity, kinship, and probably membership in the local Methodist church.

The varied economic resources of the quilt signers closely mirror the economic spectrum of the precinct as a whole. On Mount Hebron's nearly sixty-six sections lived 345 white residents. While nearly half the families owned no slaves, a third owned eleven or more; slaves represented three times the white population. The average farm, 553 acres, was valued at nearly eight thousand dollars and annually produced 47 bales of cotton, 1,308 bushels of corn, and 55 swine. These impressive numbers, skewed by a few large plantations, nonetheless paled in comparison to German Creek Precinct in the heart of the Canebrake. There, on a slightly smaller area (fifty-eight and a half sections), lived fewer than 200 white individuals. While only a third of the families owned no slaves, a remarkable 44 percent owned eleven or more; slaves represented six times the white population, twice the Mount Hebron figure. The average farm, 957 acres, was valued at more than twenty-seven thousand dollars and produced 113 bales of cotton, 2,900 bushels of corn, and 105 swine.[32]

Maps, census records, and the Lanford quilt all suggest that farmers and planters in the Mount Hebron Precinct lived side by side and engaged in the same social and religious activities. By contrast, the German Creek landowners were significantly more involved in the marketplace. Plantations there often were owned in partnership or by absentee landlords, thus representing an investment rather than a homestead. Despite the contrast between the two precincts, however, the differences were of degree, not kind. The profits from participation in the marketplace by growing cotton and owning slaves were obvious to all and constituted a source of aspiration. Whatever culture may have emerged in Greene's outlying regions, the result was more generally rural than distinctively yeoman.

✦ ✦ ✦

A notice appeared in an 1847 edition of the *Beacon* under the heading "A CALL FOR A NEW ASSOCIATION." The author noted that Greensboro already had its Masons, Odd Fellows, and Christian societies. What the town now needed was an association called "Community." The author was referring particularly to providing coffins for the destitute, as high prices were an unreasonable burden, but he could have had in mind any of several benevolent causes. Indeed, only a month later Harvey issued a call in the *Beacon* for a public meeting to consider what could be done about the Irish famine. Ten prominent citizens (including the *Beacon* editor and three Masons) were designated as a committee to receive contributions. A plea was also sent out to the ladies. "There is a moral beauty in their ardent support of all efforts made in the name of suffering humanity," wrote a correspondent, "which elevates them in the sphere of being infinitely beyond our selfish sex." Within a week, Greensboro's citizens had contributed about seven hundred dollars in cash and nearly five hundred bushels of corn—a significant amount from such a small town. Greensboro soldiers then fighting in Mexico also contributed several thousand dollars to the cause.[33]

Reformers applied the same techniques they used in railroad building to character building. Leading citizens called for open meetings to address a particular concern, committees solicited donations or subscriptions, public addresses and newspaper articles kept the issue before the public, and voluntary associations agitated until the need was met. But while coffins for the poor and Irish relief had been discrete problems that soon ended, temperance would take decades to effect.

The formation of a temperance society was announced at an 1831 camp meeting in the Canebrake. Alongside newspaper columns reporting Nat Turner's rebellion and his subsequent confessions appeared editorials and public addresses advocating restraint from alcoholic beverages. Local temperance groups sprang up throughout Greene County, joining other reformers across the nation in championing the cause.[34]

The Greensboro Temperance Society was formally organized in March 1842. Its membership and enthusiasm wavered during the next few years, but in 1845 the society was thriving with 322 members (175 men and 147 women). With fewer than a thousand white citizens living within town limits, many of the members clearly came from the countryside; nevertheless, 332 still represented a large segment of the population. Harvey credited the temperance society with effecting a signal change: there was little drinking in Greensboro, "and we do not know a regular and hopeless drunkard in the town." Yet much was left to be done, Harvey noted, and citizens needed to engage openly and fearlessly in the cause.[35]

The antidrinking crusade took another step when Greensboro's residents organized a chapter of the Sons of Temperance in August 1848. The organization, begun six years earlier in New York City, demanded a pledge of total abstinence. Modeled somewhat after the Masons, the Sons built commitment through secret rituals and ornate regalia. The first ten officers in the Greensboro division were not distinguished by their wealth, but four of them were Masons, in keeping with the overlapping membership among all the town's voluntary associations. The Sons of Temperance presented a resolution for temperance reform that passed at the next annual session of the Alabama Methodists, which was held in Greensboro. And at the group's first anniversary celebration, which convened at an overflowing Greensboro Methodist Church, the Sons were presented with a banner in recognition of their success. The "grand affair" was so crowded that many could not get in to hear the speeches.[36]

The next year began with the *Beacon* devoting the entire front page of a January issue to printing "The Moral Dignity of the Temperance Reformation," an address to the Sons of Temperance by the Reverend C. F. Sturgis, the Baptist principal of the Greensboro Female Academy. Hardly memorable, the tone and arguments of temperance speeches nonetheless revealed how exalted the reformers believed their mission to be. Intemperance was a "river of death" that destroyed individuals and their innocent and unoffending families without regard to social or economic station. Intemperance not only robbed the purse of the individual and the nation but took away character, self-respect, and every comfort of body, mind, and estate. The greatness of the temperance movement, by contrast, lay in its moral dignity, both in the great ideals and in the unceasing labors those ideals activated. The crusade appealed to reason, humanity, patriotism, and religious principle. "Remember that you are engaged in a most glorious mission," Sturgis proclaimed, "recovery of your fellow-men, members of the great brotherhood of mankind."[37]

Temperance advocates, like Masons and evangelical Christians, found the root of society's problems in excessive self-regard. In an 1857 address to the Greensboro Temperance Association, Serano Watson, the younger brother of Henry Watson, labeled the intemperate man selfish, not only with regard to drink but also in striving for wealth, political power, and the pursuit of pleasure. And intemperance was everywhere—North and South, in the pulpit and on the bench, in city and country, in the streets and by the hearth, from the cradle to the coffin. Temperance, conversely, was self-control for the sake of others, a "godlike virtue" that exalted individuals to the condition that God expected for them. Indeed, all individuals had responsibilities beyond themselves, responsibilities that demanded that they reestablish an internal harmony in which the body became subject to the soul and the animalistic passions to the cultivated intellect. Watson called for citizens to apply their influence to remove "everything that can in any way prove a temptation & a snair to the young, the weak & the besotted."[38] That Serano Watson linked intemperance with selfishness and greed implied that many of the same problems manifested in the 1830s were still unresolved two decades later. His appeal to responsibilities represented a call for his fellow Greensborians to consider their town more than merely a place to make money.

Greensboro's temperance advocates eventually became prohibitionists, thereby stepping beyond voluntary cooperation. And they would succeed in removing liquor from Greensboro, but not until a coalition of town boosters, businessmen, religious leaders, and reformers joined forces on another project.

★ ★ ★

"The proper training and education of our children is the most important duty of our lives," wrote Henry Watson without a hint of hyperbole.[39] Building and keeping schools were particularly important—even acute—endeavors. Schools must train girls to resist and boys to confront this new grasping world; without established educational institutions to counter the unstable and selfish population, the prospects of social disintegration could not be lightly dismissed. Greensborians took on this challenge as they took on others—by soliciting voluntary cooperation.

In 1822 Israel Pickens reported "good schools" around Greensboro, with one having about sixty-five students enrolled. Pickens was an enterprising promoter, and thus his assessment was suspect. Others simply dismissed teachers as impostors, like horse doctors and miracle-cure salesmen. A fuller description came from the pen of Watson, who had once taught. By late 1830, he reported, Greensboro boasted five or six schools (including one run by the president of the temperance society). But this statistic was misleading, for the teachers were all "dunces and blockheads." Greensborians "think more of money here than of Education," Watson judged. Private tutors rarely received even $250 or $300 annual salary. Instead of an advanced classical education, frontiersmen wanted their children to be drilled in the basics of grammar, geography, arithmetic, reading, and writing.[40]

Some parents sent their children to be educated in New England, where the best schools were thought to be. An 1845 Beacon editorial entitled "Our Schools" noted that local schools had deteriorated, largely because of the prevailing view that "children cannot be well educated at home." Children scarcely ten years of age were being sent hundreds of miles away, the editor complained, an absence that "has the natural tendency to weaken the affection between the parent and the child."[41] Where social relations were already broken by frequent emigration, the Beacon's comments touched a nerve.

The problem with Greensboro's schools was not their absence: between 1845 and 1861, eighteen men announced schools for boys.[42] The problem lay in continuity and good teachers. Among all the schools and academies, two in particular succeeded where others did not, one by eliciting support from the town, the other through decades of selfless dedication by its founder.

Unlike temporary schools run by itinerant schoolmasters, the Greensboro Female Academy was established as a corporation. A board of trustees purchased land and subscribed five hundred dollars to buy scientific and chemical apparatus. The board procured assistant teachers, and 90 students were attending by 1834. Seven years later, when the trustees received formal incorporation from the Alabama

General Assembly, the enrollment had risen to 153, and in 1842 enrollment reached 161. The academy's trustees were generally town leaders who had actively involved themselves in other causes, such as building railroads and promoting temperance. Of those elected in 1853, for example, five were Masons and four were prominent members of the local volunteer militia company. The faculty they hired embraced educational reform. Christopher J. D. Pryor, for example (formerly of the Williamsburg Male and Female Academy, a preparatory school for William and Mary College), sought "to educate the understanding and reasoning faculties" rather than to require mere memorization. The academy was led in the 1850s by the Reverend William S. Barton, a Baptist minister who authored English textbooks and edited the *Southern Teacher.*[43]

Greensboro had far less success with its boys' schools, in part because of the presence in nearby Havanna (now spelled Havana), about fifteen miles north, of the renowned Greene Springs School for Boys. Greensborians routinely sent their sons to study under Greene Springs' founder, Henry Tutwiler, who had been among the first to earn a master's degree from the University of Virginia. When James G. Birney, a future antislavery presidential candidate, had traveled north in 1830 as a representative of the University of Alabama, he met Tutwiler and hired him as the university's first professor of ancient languages.[44] A few years later, discipline problems among the students forced some resignations, Tutwiler among them. The young teacher headed first to northwest Alabama and then to Greene Springs, where he established his school in 1847. There Tutwiler could implement his progressive ideas, which included allowing the student to select the subjects best adapted to his own peculiar talents and goals. In the school's first circular, he stated that "our ordinary system of education is defective [by] blunting, instead of stimulating that curiosity which is part of our nature." The result was that many people passed through life with an "imperfect knowledge of those sciences which have done so much to diffuse the comforts and luxuries of life among the great mass of mankind." Tutwiler conducted his school somewhat like a college, according to one student, alternating study and leisure in such ways that the boys were unable to get into mischief. The boys were required to be at prayers by daybreak and to say a lesson before breakfast. They then studied in their rooms and left for recitation when they heard the bell ring. In the evening Tutwiler delivered a lecture that put the topic in a broad, comprehensive context fully in keeping with his rejection of rote learning.[45]

Tutwiler at Greene Springs and Barton at the Greensboro Female Academy were part of a reform movement that focused on education as a means of tempering the ambition and greed that threatened the fabric of society. Scientific and technological achievements, these reformers conceded, had allowed humans to master nature. But humanity had used this power for selfish ends in the rapacious pursuit of lucre. Schools, the reformers maintained, should prepare individuals to be responsible citizens, capable of carrying on the great republican experiment—an experiment threatened by the selfish and ignorant. But not just any schools. Instead of places where students were forced to memorize an unchanging body of facts, schools should be educational sanctuaries where children could learn to master the world of progress rather than become its victims. Girls needed training in the cultivation of soothing feminine sensibilities that they would use to turn the home into a refuge for their families. Boys would one day have to confront the aggressive world of commerce and needed training to allow them both to succeed and to contribute. The classroom, like the family and the Masonic lodge, would become the means of reforming society and establishing community.[46]

By the 1850s the reformers' efforts came to focus on the public schools. The General Assembly had established a school system in 1823, but without enforcement clauses, the enterprise depended entirely on the vagaries of local initiative. Indeed, Greensboro had no public schools for its first three decades. But in 1854, at the prodding of reformers, the state established a modern system with a state superintendent, a means of overseeing local school districts, and finances directly based on taxation. The system was openly modeled on that of Massachusetts, devised by the renowned educator and antislavery reformer Horace Mann and generally considered the nation's most advanced school system. About 250 Greensboro children between the ages of five and eighteen were believed eligible for the free schools. Allen C. Jones, a planter and civic leader and candidate for the state senate, campaigned at the same time for election as the county's first commissioner of free schools. Harvey counseled his readers to reject another candidate who had voted against establishing the free school system, and the editor favored taxing the wealthiest in order "to extend the blessings of education to those who have not the means of educating themselves." Greensboro's public school was operating on a sound financial basis by 1859, thanks largely to the efforts of committed town leaders. Although the schoolhouse was primitive, especially by comparison to the Greensboro Female Academy, public schools were now operating under a dependable teacher, Miles Hassell Yerby, whose family would remain for decades prominent Greensboro teachers and newspaper editors.[47]

★ ★ ★

Greensboro's various voluntary communities—churches, commercial interests, temperance advocates, educational reformers, and town boosters—cooperated in the mid-1850s to take on the biggest project they had ever faced: enticing the Methodists to bring a proposed college to Greensboro. Some Greensborians remembered that the town had once been the site of a Baptist seminary. During the early 1830s, the denomination had selected Greensboro in large part because locals had subscribed thirty-six hundred dollars to help purchase about two hundred acres that the seminarians farmed to pay their fees. Despite broadening its curriculum beyond religion, the school was unable to survive either the Panic of 1837 or an unfortunate choice of faculty.[48] Nonetheless, Greensborians continued with their attempts to lure a denominational college.

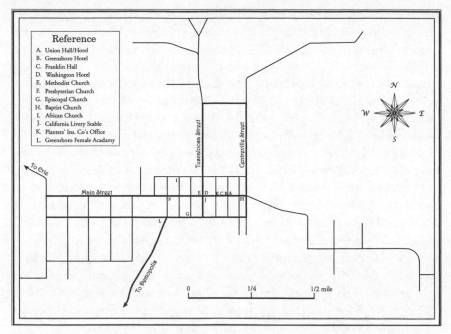

Greensboro, Alabama, from Snedecor's 1856 map of Greene County. (Drawn by Craig Remington, University of Alabama Cartographic Laboratory, Tuscaloosa)

When the Methodists convened the 1854 annual session of the Alabama Conference, the meeting was far from typical.[49] The Reverend Archelaus H. Mitchell, a leading educational reformer and president of the conference's Centenary Institute in Summerfield, delivered a strong sermon challenging the Methodists to build a college in central Alabama. The state university in Tuscaloosa already provided a general education to cultivate the intellect in the arts and sciences. What was needed were complementary institutions "that are not afraid to declare themselves full upon the side of God and religion. . . . no man is educated, however much he may know, who has a bad heart." Moral and religious instruction would try "to develop the latent capacities, to transform the helpless infant into a good and wise man, fitted to serve God and his generation on earth." Even as Mitchell spoke, the citizens of Auburn came forward with a proposal to establish a Methodist college there. The conference agreed to a college but left its location up to a committee to decide. The town that demonstrated its commitment by subscribing one hundred thousand dollars would win selection, almost like an auction.

Greensborians immediately recognized that this was an opportunity that could not be missed, and the *Alabama Beacon* announced a public meeting to consider how to proceed. But before any meetings could take place, writers to the newspaper were already stating their objections. Greensboro needed a college, yes, but one "for all christendom, free from every *sectarian* influence and tendency." The *Beacon*'s editor responded in the same issue, and his arguments revealed a great deal about his readers' character. He called for Greensboro's citizens to join the campaign as a means of furthering their own self-interests. The question at hand was not "What sort of a College shall we have?" but rather, "Would the prosperity of Greensboro', and vicinity, be promoted, by having a Methodist College located here?" His answer was unequivocal. A Methodist college in Greensboro "would very materially promote the prosperity of the place." And "all who feel a proper interest in this prosperity, should feel it a duty to co-operate in the effort." Harvey expanded on this theme of prudent self-interest in subsequent issues. Greensboro's citizens would be able to educate their children at home rather than sending them to Tuscaloosa; Charlottesville, Virginia; or even beyond. At home they would be under closer supervision and less likely to contract such bad habits as smoking, chewing, drinking, card playing, and swearing. Education in Greensboro would cost much less. The college would boost businesses, and property values would rise. Finally, the society would be improved by the college's mental culture. "Have we not public spirit enough in the place and vicinity," he posed, "to raise a sum sufficient to effect this object?"[50]

A February 1855 public meeting on the subject was well attended. John Erwin, who presided, delivered an opening speech reiterating the numerous advantages to the vicinity and chiding Greensborians about how little they had done for education by comparison to such nearby towns as Tuscaloosa (home of the University of Alabama) and Marion (home of the Baptists' Judson Female Institute and Howard College for young men.) Two very successful planters, Lucius Q. C. DeYampert (a Methodist) and John Nelson (a non-Methodist), then together pledged a quarter of the needed hundred thousand dollars. Erwin, John Walton, and Gideon Nelson—all prominent citizens—each pledged five thousand dollars. "Altogether, it was a proud day for Greensboro and its vicinity," wrote Harvey, adding almost as an afterthought, "as well as for the cause of education."[51]

Opposition to Greensboro came naturally enough from its cross-state rival, and a spirited squabble soon erupted between the *Alabama Beacon* and the *Auburn Gazette.* Many of the arguments were petty, with each side exaggerating the advantages of one site and the disastrous consequences of choosing the other. The wealth and intelligence of the citizens, accessibility by rail (or inaccessibility, in the case of Greensboro), future prospects, even the exact location of the town's boundaries—all were hashed and rehashed. The editor of the *Gazette* went so far as to take a census of the Auburn graveyard in order to "prove" Auburn's superior health.[52]

Amid all the silliness, one charge was taken seriously. Auburn residents were morally superior, the *Gazette* proclaimed in articles reprinted in the *Beacon*, because the village strictly prohibited the selling of liquor as a means of protecting the students at the town's male academy. The editor of the *Gazette* claimed never to have seen a drunken man on the streets and stated that "we have never known a single violation of law, order, conventional or social usage," including boisterous revelry, gambling, or desecration of the Sabbath. "Never was one of our citizens arraigned for high civil misdemeanors, or convicted of any crime against the state, or social body!!" By contrast, Greensboro, charged the *Gazette* editor, with a population of about 800 white citizens, had a dram shop for every 266 residents, male and female, young and old—in other words, exactly three liquor establishments. Further, the fact that Greensboro had laws against begging and public drunkenness proved the need to overcome its moral deficiencies.[53] Much of this argument surely was preposterous, but Greensborians could not afford to take a chance. Someone planned to counter the *Auburn Gazette*'s charges.

At the July 1855 Methodist conference in Summerfield, Greensboro's representatives arrived with 140 pledges adding up to $113,000 (the eight largest subscriptions totaled $59,700); Auburn pledged $100,000. The commission chose Greensboro. But unwilling to disappoint Auburn, the commissioners resolved that it, too, should have a college. The Greensboro contingent was disappointed, believing that two colleges would surely be weaker than one. With the next annual conference slated for December in nearby Eutaw, Greensboro called another town meeting and began raising even more subscriptions.[54] The annual conference in Eutaw spent three inconclusive days discussing the site. The Greensboro delegation arrived with pledges totaling $168,000, while the Auburn delegates had raised only $111,000. Greensboro was finally chosen the site of the new Methodist college. Townsmen, most likely members of the Greensboro Light Artillery Guards, fired cannon to celebrate the news.[55]

The Greensboro delegation was named to the board of trustees and charged with securing the necessary legal standing. A few months later, the General Assembly formally incorporated the institution as Southern University. The legislation, however, contained a corker. Efforts to secure the college had not rested solely with money, and Auburn's claim to a more temperate citizenry had clearly made its mark. Section 4 of the legislation decreed that from the first day of March 1857, no intoxicating beverages of any kind were to be sold within five miles of Greensboro. Druggists and physicians who prescribed alcohol for medicinal purposes were excluded.[56] Moral reform had been joined to self-interest.

"Greensboro sold to the Methodists," read a banner hung across Main Street on the first Saturday after the law went into effect. The incident was not reported in the newspaper; instead, the *Beacon*'s editor obliquely answered the charge by discoursing on the social contract. The promotion of the good of the whole, he argued, is the basis of all social organizations. In the savage state of nature, each individual protects his own rights of person, reputation, and property. But upon becoming a member of the social state, he surrenders certain personal rights and privileges that, if exercised without restraint, would conflict with the good of the whole. In this particular case, Greensborians had made a contract whereby the constituted authorities would enact laws calculated to promote the good of the whole. Greensborians were thus "under *moral,* as well as *legal* obligations" to observe those laws not in violation of the federal or state constitutions. Harvey had no doubt of the legislature's power to insert the provision prohibiting the sale of liquor. Now the people must obey.[57]

And they did. On a hot June day in 1857, three months after the law went into effect, a procession formed on Main Street about eleven in the morning. Militia general R. D. Huckabee and his staff led, followed by the Greensboro Light Artillery Guards in their new uniforms, the Odd Fellows, the Masons, and various dignitaries and citizens. The largest crowd ever assembled in the county (the newspaper estimated five thousand) met the procession east of town. Then the ceremony began. Standing on a platform and under an awning, the Reverend Dr. Thomas W. Dorman delivered a prayer, the band played, and then Grand Master McCaleb Wiley, representing the Alabama Masons, laid the cornerstone to Main Building. Into the block went various appropriate documents, including a Bible and the university's charter. After appropriate speeches, the group marched back to town, escorted by the Guards, and a memorable day in Greensboro's story was over. The ceremony marked a public recognition that Greensborians could collaborate to build together what their individual efforts could not have accomplished separately. This was something quite simple, something quite American, yet something quite noteworthy.[58] It had taken them a mere thirty-five years—less than two generations—to reach this point.

After construction of the first building was well under way, an unknown Greensborian decided to assess the advantages that Southern University had brought to the town. The remarkable wealth from cotton, he recognized, had created a crisis—a crisis of selfishness. Success now mandated that Greensboro's residents do something unselfish for "the further elevation of their own community, and the good of their fellows at large." Greensborians must respond, he continued, with a generous public spirit that overcame religious differences. And by late 1859, editor Harvey proudly reported that seven hundred donors had contributed enough to sponsor eight chairs at twenty-five thousand dollars each, to construct a sizable building, and to amass an endowment of more than one hundred thousand dollars, an enormous sum for the time. In return for this largesse, Greensboro's riches had grown. But just as important was the diffusion of intelligence, refinement of taste, and building of friendships. The university was bound to bring eminent people to Greensboro, the editor believed, and to fill the air with music and oratory. Greensborians had reason to be proud.[59]

Yet their town remained incomplete. In addition to placing the charter and Bible into the cornerstone, the officials also laid a history of Greensboro penned by John Erwin and a copy of V. Gayle Snedecor's 1856 *Directory of Greene County,* which included a few pages outlining the county's early settlement.[60] This new awareness that Greensboro had—or needed—a past was subtle yet nonetheless real. Many of the town's earliest residents had fled the attachments that held them back; Greensborians were now celebrating attachments and even inventing a few. Southern University's Main Building prominently displayed the crenellation and turrets of a

# LAYING OF THE
# CORNER STONE
## OF THE
## SOUTHERN UNIVERSITY,
### AT GREENSBORO, JUNE 11, 1857.

## ORDER OF PROCESSION.

The Masonic Fraternity will assemble at the Masonic Hall at 10 o'clock, a. m., and proceed thence to the place hereinafter designated for the formation of the line.

The Column will be formed in front of the Methodist Church at 11 a. m., by Maj. Gen. R. D. Huckabee, assisted by his Staff Officers.

1. Greensboro Light Artillery Guards.
2. Independent Order of Odd Fellows.
3. Masonic Fraternity.
4. Mayor and Council of Greensboro.
5. Professor and Trustees of Female Academy.
6. Trustees of the Centenary Institute.
7. Trustees of the Southern University.
8. Clergy.
9. Orators of the Day in Open Carriages.
10. Citizens.

### ORDER OF EXERCISES AT THE BUILDING.

1. Prayer by Rev. C. C. Callaway, Chaplain of Lafayette Lodge.
2. Music by the Band.
3. Ceremony of Laying the Corner Stone of the Southern University, by Past Master Rev. E. V. LeVert, assisted by the Officers of Lafayette Lodge.
4. Music by the Band.
5. Address by the Hon. H. W. Hilliard.
6. Music by the Band.
7. Address by the Rev. Bishop Pearce.
8. Music by the Band.
9. Benediction by Bishop Pearce.

After the exercises are closed the procession will be re-formed and march to the place of formation and be dismissed. The Independent Order of Odd Fellows and the Masonic Fraternity will be escorted to their respective Lodge Rooms by the Greensboro Light Artillery Guards. Persons will not be allowed in the procession on horse back or in carriages, excepting such as are designated in this programme.

By order of the Committee of Arrangements.

**R. D. HUCKABEE,**
Marshall of the Day.

Greensboro, Alabama, May 29, 1857.

"We would suggest to any of our friends in this section who contemplate building, that they would do well to see Mr. McCrary's house first," wrote John G. Harvey, editor of the *Greensboro Alabama Beacon*, in 1857. "The example set by Mr. McCrary . . . in erecting a mansion that does credit to the place, will be followed by many other of our wealthy citizens." The Reverend J. M. P. Otts also lived in this home. (Photograph by Frances Benjamin Johnston, Library of Congress)

university Gothic architecture developed centuries earlier on another continent. The many fine homes constructed in the 1850s all featured ornate embellishments—whether classical columns, Italianate brackets, or Gothic arches. Such gewgaws linked them with great achievements of the past—but only artificially.

By the late 1850s, Greensboro appeared settled and genteel. Its architecture rivaled any in the state. Its overlapping voluntary associations—characteristically American solutions to community-building—promoted commerce, maintained lodges and churches, and furthered moral and educational reforms. These miniature communities extended the reach of solitary individuals and held promise for creating a more encompassing community. But individualists they remained. Voluntary associations were more tools for realizing selfish purposes than products of selfless concern. Residents still complained of the disruption caused by thousands of people coming and going. Worse, seemingly settled families were apt to pick up and move to Texas, California, or some other spot that promised easy success. Hints at an underlying insecurity were voiced by the *Alabama Beacon*, which praised newly built homes for making Greensboro less easy to leave. A great home, like an ancient-looking college hall, signaled that someone intended to stay.[61]

# CHAPTER 4

# Guards and Slaves

**A perfect security against servile insurrection.**
★ John Hartwell Cocke, 1857

Like towns across the country, Greensboro had its militia companies. These were notoriously amateurish affairs. Often led by incompetent hacks, drills, when they occurred, might be conducted with brooms and umbrellas rather than muskets. The gatherings and paraphernalia resembled that of fraternal lodges as much as anything military. And local companies would disappear for years at a time as interest lagged, only to be resurrected when the populace felt threatened. In all these ways, Greensboro's militia companies were typical. Yet despite these shortcomings, one particular company—the Greensboro Light Artillery Guards—became an institution of singular significance for the town. Indeed, the Guards would eventually lead Greensboro away from its self-interested voluntarism and toward a community based on different premises.[1]

Postrevolutionary Americans believed that the militia would protect them from foreign invasion. Yet Greensboro's militiamen first went into battle against Alabama's Indians. Other dangers, even closer at hand, soon were alarming the town's white residents. Ever greater investments in land and slaves resulted in black bondsmen vastly outnumbering their white masters. The primary threat now seemed to come from slave revolts and race wars. When and if that threat materialized, Greensborians had a ready-made—if flawed—organization to deal with it: the Guards.[2]

The Guards also promoted community feelings. Indeed, the two issues of community and slavery could hardly be separated, for the readiness of Greensborians to pick up and move westward left those who remained behind more vulnerable to slave insurrections. Community-building involved more than voluntary associations to promote commerce, moral reform, and education. Community-building sought to draw self-interested individuals beyond themselves, creating the sort of mutual reliance and defense that would provide some protection against a race war.

The Greensboro Guards, then, stood at the center of the town's two critical problems. The Guards were expected to impart ideals of manliness, patriotism, camaraderie, and local pride. They formed the town's only institution capable of uniting everyone, because they had responsibility for protecting everyone. And by inviting all men to join, the Guards established a standard for inclusion in the community that cut across the financial, religious, or ideological differences that distinguished the town's other voluntary associations. But inclusion implied exclusion, and while protecting Greensboro, the Guards were also determining who would not be in their community. Here—in citizen protecting citizen, in exclusion and inclusion— were sources of Southern distinctiveness. Slaves, Guards, and community: none could untie this Greensborian knot.

The opening line of Alabama's 1819 constitution declared that all freemen were equal in rights under the social compact. As equals, they shared responsibility for the state's defense. Exemptions were made for judges, government officials, ministers, ferrymen, postmasters, millers, and the like, but otherwise, free white men between the ages of eighteen and forty-five were automatically enrolled. The constitution further instructed the General Assembly to organize the militia, producing a predictable hierarchy of divisions, brigades, regiments, and companies. Although divisions and brigades were routinely rearranged, the regiment, ideally containing ten companies of a hundred men each, stayed in a particular county. (Greensborians served in the Thirty-eighth Regiment throughout the antebellum decades.) As befitting this democracy of equally free men, each company elected its own officers. This unexceptional system was intended to augment the nation's tiny standing army. War was to be avoided, but if and when it came, the federal army planned to improvise with regulars until it could be augmented by state troops.[3]

The system that looked so neat on paper quickly fell apart in practice. By 1828 militia leaders in Greensboro reported to the governor that they were having difficulty retaining good officers. More importantly, they complained that the last legislature had halved the annual company musters to two and made no requirement that guns be carried. Because not one man in twenty was armed, drill thus presented what the leaders respectfully labeled an "awkward and unnatural appearance." And because noncommissioned officers were exempt from regimental drills, a full complement was seldom present. Company captains were not even compelled to wear uniforms.[4]

The problems of imposing a martial discipline on independent civilians was hardly limited to Greensboro. Augustus Baldwin Longstreet described a typical muster in his popular tale, "The Militia Company Drill." At the appointed hour only a third of the militiamen have arrived. As they stand in a crooked line, Captain Clodpole pulls out his book on drilling techniques. But first he asks his troops for their indulgence, inviting suggestions if he should not get things quite right. With preliminaries out of the way, drilling proceeds. Instead of heavy muskets, some march with open umbrellas that provide shade from the bright sun but also tend to

The general militia company musters. (From Longstreet, *Georgia Scenes*)

get in the way. After constant complaints of the heat and thirst, the captain sends for grog and decides to omit reading the military law. He resolves finally to order one last maneuver and call it a day. Wheeling right, however, is beyond the company's ability or patience, and the militia drill dissolves into anarchy. The humor turned, of course, on the immense contrast between the drill's reality and its expectations—a contrast that was all too familiar.[5]

To surmount the sort of inadequacies that Longstreet spoofed, state legislatures gradually adopted a two-tiered militia system. Alabama's 1837 reorganization formally sought to raise the general militia's effectiveness by shifting the primary role of defense to local volunteer companies, many of which had already organized spontaneously. The General Assembly encouraged these local efforts by formally incorporating many more. These remained attached to the general militia, with each regiment assigned up to three elite companies (light infantry or riflemen, cavalry, and light artillery); otherwise, the volunteer companies received considerable independence. Soon they indeed came to exhibit the esprit de corps that the general militia lacked, adopting striking winter and summer dress uniforms, often modeled on those used at West Point. The companies' drills became precise, their parades glorious, and their banners sewn by the prettiest girls. Many companies in the larger cities of Mobile and Montgomery rose to high social prominence.[6]

As early as 1823, one such militia company, the Greensboro Volunteer Artillery Company, distinguished itself. By styling themselves as "artillery," and later "guards," its members were staking claim to an elite status above the other militia companies. A light artillery unit was expected to support its regiment with small, horse-drawn cannon. By 1828, however, the Greensboro company still lacked any artillery and was petitioning the governor for a piece so that the unit might acquire skills in firing. The cavalrymen who formed the town's other volunteer company lacked sabers.[7] The general militia companies continued to form temporarily on the legally designated muster days.

The impetus behind starting Greensboro's volunteer companies seemed to arise out of the need for community-building more than the need for defense. The founding of the artillery company in the same year as the local Masonic lodge, for example, may have been more than coincidental. The ease with which individuals could shift their membership back and forth between the artillery and the cavalry, coupled with both companies' troubles in procuring arms, suggest that military threats did not loom large. And the volunteer companies took pride in joining public ceremonies. The artillery company marched in the 1830 procession carrying former Governor Israel Pickens' body to the Greensboro cemetery and regularly fired salutes at local Fourth of July and Washington's birthday celebrations.[8]

The centennial celebration of Washington's birth, 1832, was filled with special significance. About noon on February 22, the Greensboro Volunteer Artillery Company led the town's citizens to the Presbyterian church, where Washington's Farewell Address was read and appropriate remarks followed. Toward evening, the citizens sat for a great supper followed by a series of toasts: to the president; to the Union, the main edifice of real independence; to the day; to the Marquis de Lafayette, former presidents, and others. Each toast brought with it appropriate applause, cheering, and music and the firing of artillery (the company had by this time acquired or borrowed some sort of gun). Then followed a speech by Governor John Gayle, himself a Greensborian, touching on many of the issues of the day. When he finished, the celebrants resumed their toasting. According to the *Greene County Gazette,* "The company parted in great harmony and good feelings."[9]

The artillery company was raised to special prominence when, two years later, the General Assembly formally incorporated it "by the name and style of the light artillery guards." The Guards were but one of several volunteer companies incorporated during that session as the legislature moved to make the militia more professional. The terms of incorporation for the Greensborough Light Artillery Guards, as the group was formally but infrequently known, required membership to remain between thirty and one hundred, including a captain, one or two lieutenants, and at least one ensign (color-bearer). The Guards were further required to muster at least six times a year and to serve on slave patrols at least twenty-four nights. In return, members were exempted from serving on juries and from performing road or street duty, were allowed to select their own uniform, and otherwise were specifically held "wholly free and exempt from the order, co[n]trol or direction . . . of all other officers of the militia of this State, except when called into actual service." The Guards were explicitly left to report only to the governor—a source of friction with other militia leaders—and were implicitly expected to provide immediate leadership in case of crisis.[10]

The Greensboro Guards were starting to acquire the preeminence and visibility that the legislature had hoped its volunteers would attain. At the next commemoration of Washington's birthday, the Guards inducted several new members. The soldiers began acquiring gold lace, buttons, swords, and red silk sashes (at $15 each) for their uniforms. The captain spent the considerable sum of $70.99 for material alone.[11] Gaudy uniforms, the chance to march in parades, male camaraderie—many Greensborians certainly must have joined the Guards for a host of trivial reasons. Nonetheless, more serious considerations lay beneath the surface.

By 1836 the Guards numbered forty. Nothing is known of twelve of these men, but a fair bit has been uncovered about the other twenty-eight. Sixteen owned slaves (and many others probably belonged to slaveholding families), at least seventeen were married by 1840, twelve were Masons, and thirteen were still Guards in 1846. Only four listed their occupation as farmer or planter, a number that is surely low, because several others had too many slaves for simply domestic purposes. But the variety of other occupations is nonetheless striking: physician, bookkeeper, hotel owner, postmaster, druggist, sheriff, carpenter, laborer, merchant, professor, engineer, and an enigmatic "sportsman." These occupations, and the high number of Masons among the Guards, give evidence of success, prominence, and persistence. Equally significant is that most of the Guards' occupations were not solitary pursuits but involved services to Greensboro's residents, thereby suggesting that some individuals joined the Guards in order to participate more fully in civic life.[12]

Of course, the Guards' role included defense as well as community-building. Their formal incorporation and subsequent growth came as tensions were mounting between white Alabamians and their Indian neighbors. Greensborians had been rather insulated from such troubles for well over a decade. But on the state's periphery, Cherokees, Chickasaws, and Choctaws continued to live, with the Creeks in east Alabama holding roughly a fifth of the state's land. No wall separated Indian from white land; the Federal Road from Columbus, Georgia, to Montgomery ran through the middle of the Creek nation. Hungry Indians on occasion held up stages or stole livestock. White settlers hungered for more land. These elements would collide in the mid-1830s.

Following his inauguration in 1829, President Andrew Jackson encouraged treaties to remove the remaining Indian tribes to territory west of the Mississippi. Negotiations with Choctaws and Cherokees went relatively smoothly for the federal government. The 1832 Treaty of Cusseta with the Creeks, however, led to a war. Like the treaties with the other tribes, the Cusseta pact exchanged land for cash and annuities. Its critical point was the guarantee that no individual Creeks would be compelled to emigrate. After their territory had been surveyed and the Creeks had chosen their own lands, they could then keep the property and become citizens of

Alabama or sell it and remove to other lands farther west. Until then, white settlers were to stay out. But many Creeks, unfamiliar with legal notions, lost their certificates of ownership. Others sold their lands for nearly nothing after getting drunk on liquor generously provided by speculators. Still other Creeks sold lands that they did not even own or were pressured by the speculators into selling for nominal sums. Alabama's General Assembly sanctioned the skullduggery by dividing the Creek nation into nine counties before the Creeks had even chosen their land. President Jackson was enraged because the federal government, and not the state, had negotiated the treaty, and he threatened to expel those who had entered the lands illegally. Governor Gayle asserted Alabama's right to control its own affairs—a portent of future resistance to Washington. The two executives effected a compromise that expelled those who had moved into lands reserved for the Indians but permitted others to remain—a compromise so impossible to enforce that white settlers continued to pour into Creek lands. By 1835 the frauds had so inflamed the Creeks that white citizens nearby petitioned the governor for protection. The Creeks were also inspired by their relatives, the Seminoles, who had declared war in Florida. The resulting Creek War of 1836, a nearly forgotten affair, marked the first time that the state engaged its troops. The Greensboro Guards were among them, although just barely.[13]

Governor C. C. Clay received word in February 1836 that about twenty-five hundred poor Creeks, "desperate from starvation," had moved into Cherokee County. Fearing that "they would resort to plunder and rapine" or perhaps join the Seminoles, the governor began war preparations. He ordered each of the militia units to contribute at least thirty volunteers or conscripts for military service to the state, with the resulting regiment to meet March 10 at the federal arsenal in Vernon, Autuaga County.[14]

When the local militia major called for men in Greensboro, four times as many volunteered as the governor requested, and organizers were forced to hold a draft to determine who would *not* go. Unlike the Guards, the sixty-four members of Captain William Smith's volunteers comprised a virtually anonymous lot. Two and possibly a third were also Guards, and some of the surnames were familiar in Greene County. The others in Smith's ad hoc company were less prominent individuals with few lasting ties to Greensboro, a circumstance suggesting that they were motivated by a desire to acquire Creek lands in east Alabama.[15]

Some Greensborians denied that any threat existed. William Jeffreys wrote to his father in North Carolina that it was the greatest "foolishness" to send soldiers into the Creek nation where "a set of pore half starved deavles" were scared nearly to death by every white man they met; in fact, if a white man looked straight at an Indian, he would throw down his gun and walk off. Jeffreys was particularly disappointed that James Jeffreys (probably his brother) had joined the militia, leaving William alone to run the business. The "fools," as he called them, were pocketing eight dollars a month for little more than a chance to go out on an adventure.[16]

When Smith's volunteers reached Vernon, the arsenal's commander refused to arm them, citing a lack of authority. The troops were dismissed after four days. "The volunteers, most of them, went as if upon a frolic," wrote Henry Watson upon their return to Greensboro. "Weak puny, young fellows able to do nothing, expecting no fighting, or thinking it but boys sport. They have learned better. They all look miserably thin, sallow & cadaverous as if just from a bilious fever."[17]

At the same time, in the county seat of Erie, troops were being raised for the Texas War of Independence, and Captain Smith soon left to join that fighting. Watson lumped those going to Texas with those who had gone off to fight the Creeks. "The great body (the exceptions are few) are desperadoes & men without character & speculators in land, (land thieves, as Indians *would* say)."[18]

That spring the Creeks began attacking plantations and settlements in earnest. Word reached Greensboro on May 25 that a beloved townsman, the Reverend Daniel P. Bestor, had been killed while traveling by stage through the Creek nation. (The charge turned out to be false; Bestor returned to supervise the Greensboro Female Academy and to serve in the legislature.) There was more. Rumor had it that Creeks had "killed whole families, destroyed cattle and crops & burnt dwellings & in addition, attacked three or four stages, killed the passengers, destroyed the stages and scattered the mails." The commander of the arsenal at Vernon was blamed for not releasing arms in time to intimidate the Indians into remaining peaceable.[19]

Greensboro's Guards were enraged and frustrated. Twice during the week that Captain Smith was forming his company, the Guards had petitioned the governor to be accepted into service, yet Smith's volunteers left without the Guards. Now, following news of the Reverend Bestor, they could wait no longer. "The flame of Patriotism kindles in every breast to avenge the wrongs of our innocent murdered Citizens," wrote one anonymous Guard to the governor. "We are anxious to go into the service of our State. Give us a fair chance, and do not for God's sake, subject us any longer to the epithets of the base & the cowardly. . . . Treat us like *men*, respected governor, and not like children. We no longer wish to be 'fire-side solders.'"[20]

The force of the Guards' request prompted Governor Clay to order them to report to military headquarters in Montgomery, where they would be mustered into service. Because the Guards were not included in the militia divisions that the governor had already called up, they were attached as a mounted infantry company in the Second Alabama Mounted Volunteers. Not only did they lack such basic equipment as knapsacks and canteens, but as mounted volunteers the Guards had to buy saddles, spurs, stirrups, and the like for their horses. By June 3 they were ready, and forty men left with Captain Henry Webb in command. From Montgomery, the Guards probably traveled to Tuskegee to join the rest of the militia under Major General Benjamin Patterson. In fear of being sent to Florida after subduing the Creeks, the Guards extracted assurances from the governor before being mustered into federal service.[21]

Creek resistance quickly crumbled. More than 850 warriors and their families surrendered, and by July 1, the Creeks' leader, Chief Eufaula, was a prisoner. All that remained was to stop the holdouts from linking up with the Seminoles. This was accomplished a few weeks later by the Georgia militia, which defeated the Creeks in the only real, albeit minor, battle of the war. The citizen-soldiers declared victory and went home.

Stopping in Tuscaloosa along the Creeks' westward march out of the state, Chief Eufaula came to the Capitol to address the assembled legislature. He spoke in a room decorated with elaborate Greek embellishments: a semi-elliptical Ionic colonnade, an arched and ornamented ceiling, and an entablature with the words *Pro Patria* on its frieze. The irony of his words matched the irony of the occasion: "In time gone by," he was alleged to have spoken, "I have thought that the white man wanted to bring burden and ache of heart upon my people in driving them from their homes and yoking them with laws they did not understand. But I have now become satisfied that they are not unfriendly towards us, but that they wish us well." Politicians saw the advantage of proclaiming racial solidarity and holding out against federal authority. The governor delivered an address in the same room to the same audience, encouraging all Indians to leave as quickly as possible, concluding, "We shall never have tranquility whilst they remain amongst us."[22]

Not everyone felt that way. From Greensboro, Henry Watson wrote in August 1836 that "the Creek disturbances seem to be over; the mail runs regularly through and we hear of no disturbances of any kind." Nonetheless, he was not proud of his adopted state. "The Indians have been treated in a manner that is a disgrace to any country making pretensions to civilization," he complained privately. "One cannot find it in his heart to blame them for taking up arms. That they have rights as sacred as the rights of the white man cannot be questioned and were we to suffer but a thousandth part of the indignities they have suffered we should rise at once to resentment and revenge."[23]

Perhaps the cleverest reproach came from J. J. Hooper, who burlesqued the entire episode in his *Adventures of Captain Simon Suggs*. The unscrupulous Suggs has been among those bilking the Creeks of their land. When he hears that the Creeks have started a war, he rallies his fellow citizens into forming a military company they name the "Tallapoosy Vollantares." The scoundrel Suggs is elected their captain and promptly declares martial law in the two acres surrounding the storehouse he names Fort Suggs. The Vollantares finally get their chance to engage the enemy when they steal the horses and purse of two Indian towns competing at a ball game. The Indians want their property back and, in a reversal of roles, pursue the militiamen. "Kumpny form!" shouts Captain Suggs, "blaze away at the d———d old *hostile!*" When the smoke clears—literally—no Indians are in sight.[24]

The Suggs tale underscored the way in which avarice had driven the militiamen and personal advantage had driven the politicians. Alabamians cheated the Creeks of their land and then declared war when they resisted. Suggs turned those noble

Simon Suggs,
captain of the
"Tallapoosy
Vollantares." (From
Hooper, *Adventures
of Captain Simon
Suggs*)

aspirations that the volunteer companies supposedly represented into the debased tools of ambitious dissemblers. Greensborians were driven by the same calculations. War and military service often draw people closer, but not during the Creek War of 1836. In fact, the campaign had the opposite effect. A few rejected the war's principles altogether. Those who participated, however, discovered that the conflict opened new opportunities for private gain. If anything, the Creek War, fought for indefensibly selfish reasons, moved Greensborians further apart by indulging their rapacious natures. William Jeffreys, who had denounced his brother's foolishness in going after the Creeks, had no concern for the Indians; his objections were more self-serving: "I am not so fond of running the risk of my life and all for [no] profit," he wrote to his father, but "if I could get a fortune by going I would go it with a rush and kill ever last indian I could find."[25]

✳ ✳ ✳

Unease—but over slaves, not Indians—had been growing in the Canebrake since the first white immigrants had arrived in 1817. That hot summer, Frenchmen made their way up the Tombigbee River to four townships (nearly one hundred thousand acres) comprising the heart of the Canebrake and stretching from the Alabama

River north to within a mile of Greensboro. Congress had granted these settlers the land to cultivate grapes for wine and olives for their oil. The Vine and Olive Colony, as it came to be known, was to be a sanctuary for exiles from Napoleon Bonaparte's shattered empire. French immigrants were soon laying out streets at the confluence of the Black Warrior and Tombigbee Rivers for a town they named Demopolis (literally, the city of the people). Rude log cabins lined the streets when General Count Charles Lefebvre-Desnouettes, a close confidant of Napoleon and a veteran of Waterloo, arrived to take charge. He was joined by a host of other distinguished Napoleonic exiles, including members of the National Assembly who had voted to execute Louis XVI, a historian of the republic and prefect of police, distinguished military commanders, and the marchioness of Sinabaldi.[26]

The success of the colony could hardly rest on refined aristocrats such as these, and the Napoleonic exiles set out to attract more practical settlers. The leaders concocted fantastic accounts of a great venture, of an outpost of French culture with spacious public squares, and of their common commitment to cultivate the sciences, arts, and public virtues.[27] The invitations resulted in a second wave of refugees arriving in 1820, exiles not from Napoleonic France but from Santo Domingo. There, on the western half of Hispaniola, French planters had enriched themselves by exporting sugar and coffee cultivated by a massive number of African slaves. By the time of the French Revolution, bound laborers constituted more than 85 percent of the population. Prompted by the American Revolution and disorder in France, a general revolt broke out in 1791 led by Toussaint L'Ouverture. Thus began a descent into anarchy, disease, invasion, and retaliation. Former slaves declared an independent Haiti in 1804 and immediately turned to slaughtering their former owners. An estimated ten thousand refugees made their way first to such American ports as Charleston, New Orleans, and Philadelphia. Some of them, attracted by the Vine and Olive Colony's publicity, later came to Alabama.

The presence of Santo Domingan refugees was proof—if proof were needed—that slave uprisings were not just theoretical possibilities. Even as late as 1859 such Southern writers as George Fitzhugh were examining the degeneration of the black race in Haiti. The Santo Domingo uprising not only struck fear in white Southerners but also gave black bondsmen hope. When, in 1822, Denmark Vesey launched his insurrection in Charleston, he expected his confederates to escape to Haiti, and some admitted that they had tried to communicate with the Haitian government. To the Canebrake came exiles bringing cautionary tales of what happens when slaves rebel. Repeated, embellished, and convoluted with conflicting details and characters, these episodes became parables told and retold—one of the exiles was recounting her family story at age ninety-eight—until they took on the character of myth. Here were heroic accounts of a golden age overwhelmed by murderous black hordes. While the actual numbers of Santo Domingan refugees in the Canebrake and Greensboro may have been small, their stories carried disproportionate weight among the locals, convincing them to remain ever vigilant.[28]

Adele Bouttes d'Estival (1797–1881), for example, was born to a count and a countess on Santo Domingo, according to the embroidered version of her life that passed down. When former slaves came to murder their former master, her black nurse hid her under a large inverted wash pot. D'Estival was later smuggled out of Santo Domingo aboard a ship. She landed in Charleston, South Carolina, and then headed to France, where she was taken in a carriage for a ride with Napoleon. She eventually married Alexander Fournier, who took her with him to the French settlement in Alabama. A variant of the story holds that Adele's father was murdered and that she escaped Santo Domingo with her mother and sister. The mother eventually remarried a man named Bayol, who had been the one hidden under a large sugar kettle.[29]

Another tale concerned the family of Frederic Ravesies, who fled from Bordeaux to Santo Domingo when Napoleon came to power. The family involved itself heavily in the slave-based plantation economy. After witnessing the murder of his mother and sister, Ravesies escaped to Philadelphia with his father and from there journeyed to Alabama.[30]

Greensborians also heard the refugees recount the melodramatic story of a distinguished Santo Domingo lawyer, Jean Simon Coupery, and his wife, who were happy and prosperous in their "elegance and comfort." Their only child, Aimée François, was an infant when the slaves revolted. Madame de Coupery's loyal servant came to warn them that the powder magazine at Au Cape was about to be set on fire. They quickly gathered a bushel basket full of jewelry and silver and left with their daughter. Their lovely home was sacked and burned while they hid in the woods and in caves, eating only wild fruit. For several days they suffered "untold agony, fearing every moment they would be massacred by the negroes, who showed no mercy to women and children." The women and children were placed aboard French and American vessels with only the "thinnest clothing of the finest fabric with lisle thread hose and satin slippers, . . . their tender feet torn and bleeding." Jean Simon and his father were separated from the rest of the family, and news was finally received that they had been shot by the former slaves. The widow and her child both married into Greensboro's Stollenwerck family.[31]

The Vine and Olive Colony ultimately failed as an enterprise for several reasons. Bordeaux grapevines were unsuited for the Alabama summers, while olives could not survive the winters. The French were also beset by labor problems: imported German laborers proved unsuitable, and black slaves were not yet readily available. The terms of the congressional act gave no clear title to individuals until the entire four townships had been paid for, and by the time Congress remedied the problem in 1822, many colonists had already returned to France, where they were no longer considered a threat. Before long, signs of the colony were reduced to a few place-names. The Santo Domingan refugees largely remained in the Canebrake, however, having few ties to France and comfortable with a plantation economy. From time to time they gathered at the Eagle Hotel in Greensboro to toast, celebrate, and remember.[32]

The failed Vine and Olive Colony has frequently been dismissed as a mere romantic episode in Alabama's early history. This is a mistake, for its significance lay in the realm of imagination. The colony came first to represent an ideal of a high culture and sociability on a rude frontier. As early as 1834, correspondents were recounting the bold feats of exiles forced to abandon Caribbean luxury and refinement to start anew in Alabama: "They were men who had never wielded an axe or a hoe; the women were delicate & accomplished." The settlers used spades rather than plows and consequently nearly starved: "Their sufferings were almost incredible[.] Females who had never raised a finger by way of labor now turned out in homespun & barefooted and labored in the field"—more stuff of legends.[33] Their more crucial legacy, however, was to awaken Canebrakers to their own vulnerability.

Thereafter, word of rebellions alarmed Greensborians and prompted them to act. In 1830 the *Greene County Gazette* announced the discovery of a black conspiracy in Wilmington, North Carolina.[34] And then the next year came reports of mayhem in rural Southampton County, Virginia.

Nat Turner had been, by his own widely distributed account, the slave of a "kind master," Joseph Travis, who had "placed the greatest confidence" in Turner. But on the evening of August 21, 1831, Turner led his accomplices into his master's home and killed every member of the family, including an infant sleeping in his cradle. The Travis family was but the first of dozens of white county residents to die. Nearly half the dead were children, and more women than men were killed. Many were mutilated. Turner was clear about his mission: "'twas my object to carry terror and devastation wherever we went." A company of militia, fulfilling its duties, pursued the insurrectionists and arrested fifty-three. Twenty-one of those were acquitted, twelve exiled from the state, and twenty hanged. Turner managed to elude capture for two months by hiding in a pile of fence rails. Upon his arrest, Turner readily confessed and was then hanged, joining dozens of other slaves who had been killed immediately following the uprising.[35]

Turner represented a slave owner's worst fears, for he had been a model servant from all appearances. He was religious, once convincing a white man to cease his wicked behavior. Turner was responsible: his master had placed "the greatest confidence" in him. And he was literate, reading the Bible regularly. Turner admitted that he had no cause to complain. If Turner could turn on his master, were any white people safe? The rebellion immediately rekindled Southern fears, in large measure through interviews with him republished in Southern newspapers.

The rumors that swept through the South did not miss Greene County. Every casual word about a slave's misconduct was taken as part of a plan for insurrection and murder. Several women took sick from fear and were confined for three or four weeks. Greensborians read that insurrections had been discovered and put down in North Carolina and elsewhere in Virginia. The *Gazette* noted the distribution of "incendiary publications," most notoriously an abolitionist newspaper named *The*

## HORRID MASSACRE IN VIRGINIA·

The Scenes which the above Plate is designed to represent, are—Fig. 1, a Mother intreating for the lives of her children.—2, Mr. Travis, cruelly murdered by his own Slaves.—3, Mr. Barrow, who bravely defended himself until his wife escaped.—4, A comp. of mounted Dragoons in pursuit of the Blacks.

Local militia companies protected citizens against servile insurrections, especially following the Nat Turner rebellion. (From Samuel Warner, *Authentic and Impartial Narrative of the Tragical Scene Which Was Witnessed in Southampton County* [New York: Warner and West, 1831])

*Liberator:* "Any publication, whatever, having as its base the amelioration of the slaves *or* of free people of color of this country will be injurious . . . and perhaps lead to a general massacre." The *Gazette* insisted that a well-regulated slave patrol do its job but noted that if the South were forced to protect itself, then blood would flow freely. The paper also called on the federal government to concentrate its army in the slaveholding states. Citizens meeting in the Greene County Courthouse in Erie warned free blacks to leave. The newspaper commended the action, noting that throwing out the free blacks would break up haunts where slaves might congregate. The white citizens soon apprehended and interrogated a black man they suspected of insurrection but decided to acquit him.[36]

Greene County's 1831 fears came to a head one Saturday night at an autumn camp meeting. One white boy, probably bored and certainly bent on mischief, frightened a black boy so much that he bellowed. As soon as his cries were heard, the whole encampment was swept by confusion. The services stopped instantly, and the men began running. "Some left their camps without their clothes all on— some with boots on shoes—some without their wifes—turning neither to the right or left—over and through the fires—over girls and children." When word spread beyond the camp meeting, the men in the neighborhood loaded everything that would shoot and stood sentinel all night. The observer concluded that "such, Sir, is the conduct of a number of our Greene County men, a d——der set of cowards never breathed."[37]

On January 16, 1832, barely two months after Turner's execution, Alabama's General Assembly passed a more restrictive slave code that barred free blacks as well as slaves intended for sale from entering the state; the act further prohibited slaves from assembling, preaching, and being taught to read and write. Five days later, the legislature amended Greensboro's incorporation to provide for a stronger town government with authority to establish night watches and slave patrols. The intendant and town council were granted additional powers to suppress gaming and to regulate theatrical amusements, markets, and a number of heretofore unrestricted activities. The tightening of the law, it is important to note, had little effect on black slaves and a great deal more to do with prescribing white behavior. Only a determined and united front of virtuous white citizens could stave off anarchy and ensure the triumph of civil society.[38]

Vague rumors of slave insurrections continued through the rest of 1830s and into the 1840s. In late 1833, a number of slaves had reportedly been confined in Madison County, Alabama, on the Tennessee line, and suspicions were raised that the plot had extended to Greensboro. Townspeople established tighter patrols, vowing to kill any slave who showed the slightest evidence of hostile intentions. "There appears to be a spirit for freedom excited among them now in all quarters that will never be entirely suppressed," judged one Greensborian, "& sooner or later their end will be attained, I firmly believe." Greensboro's women were reported to be considerably alarmed.[39]

And again in 1835, events in Mississippi raised jittery nerves. Word that a slave insurrection had been suppressed in Clinton coincided with publications detailing the Murrell gang's nefarious slave-stealing exploits (the basis of W. Gilmore Simms' *Richard Hurdis*) and rumors of abolitionists arriving from the North. Greensboro's patrols were again warned to be more vigilant, especially after copies of *The Liberator* were found on the post office floor. Two preachers were arrested on suspicion of having dropped the newspaper there. Prudent citizens suggested that an investigation be held before lynching the two, who were fortunately found innocent and given a certificate to that effect. "The *law* imposes as a penalty the punishment of Death," explained a witness to the event, "but such is the excitement now that a mob would take the law into their own hands. . . . They are most of them respectable men, but are so excited on the subject as to be half mad."[40]

Another public meeting was held in Erie to address attempts by "misguided fanatics" to emancipate the slaves. The resulting race war, the citizens decided, would create "the bloodiest picture of human suffering which the pen of history has ever presented to man." Indeed, the slaves, whom the abolitionists wanted to help, "will be the victims of Southern vengeance." Appealing to the U.S. Constitution and claiming that slaves were contented and happy, the meeting adopted twelve resolutions condemning interference from Northern abolitionists. Significantly, the resolutions also established a Central Committee of Vigilance to try and then punish "all suspicious persons" who attempted to create insurrection among the slaves or to entice them to leave their owners. The committee asked the postmaster to turn over all inflammatory and insurrectionary publications he found. The crisis demanded that "the community shall assume the power and provide means to avert the impending danger."[41]

The rumors would not abate, and Greensboro seemed surrounded. The governor's office reported to militia leaders in late 1840 that slaves in the counties of Sumter, Marengo, and Pickens—all west of Greene—were conspiring to revolt during the Christmas holidays. *The Liberator* even printed rumors from Perry County, immediately east of Greene, that the slaves expected to be free either after Christmas or by March 4, the inauguration day of President William Henry Harrison.[42]

The Greensboro Guards knew their role in preventing slave insurrections. Not only did the company trace its beginnings to 1823, just after Vesey's plot to seize the Charleston, South Carolina, arsenal and liberate the slaves, but the group's members included several Santo Domingan refugees. The Greensboro Light Artillery Guards respectfully solicited the brass fieldpiece that the federal government had placed in Governor Joshua L. Martin's hands. "In no section of our state," they continued, "is there so great a demand for a well organized and an efficiently armed volunteer corps as in this immediate vicinity. With a sparse and decreasing white population we are in the midst of a large number of slaves. Even the apprehension of revolt from this class greatly disturbs the quiet & repose of many of our citizens." Governor Martin sent the Guards the fieldpiece they requested. But within two years they were again writing to the governor, this time asking for more accoutrements and an armory. Their letter noted that the company had, at its own expense, already amassed 210 muskets, forty pairs of cavalry pistols, forty cavalry swords, and thirty artillery swords—all of inferior quality. A state armory was a necessary precaution "for in the event of a disturbance among the black population in this Section it would most likely occur South of this place," that is, in the Canebrake. A state official summed up the situation in correspondence to the brigadier general over the Greensboro Guards. A public military presence was of vital importance to citizens of a state "possessing within its bosom a peculiar population, who can be kept in awe alone by a continual sense of superior physical power ready to act against them." The Guards' published constitutions divided the company into four squads to cover the twenty-four nights each year that the militiamen were required to furnish slave patrols. The Guards' participation in patrols and public parades thus had a direct role in intimidating would-be Nat Turners.[43]

★ ★ ★

Greensborians needed more than militiamen to protect themselves against slave revolts; they also needed ideas that explained and justified their peculiar institution. The philosophical defense did not come immediately but rather followed, at least logically, a series of debates over slavery's nature and future. Informal and unacknowledged, the Greensboro debates would mirror those occurring elsewhere in the South. And they would ultimately come to the same conclusion: the economic benefits of bound labor and—recalling Santo Domingo—the dangers of emancipation demanded that slavery continue, a decision crucial to the community being built.

Before Canebrake planters began to grow money from cotton stalks, public discussions of slavery usually concerned minor local problems and how to deal with them. An 1825 public meeting in Greensboro, for example, was called to consider thefts and disorders committed by slaves. Pointing out that bondsmen were selling goods to unwitting white citizens, the townspeople unanimously agreed to enforce the laws against trading with slaves.[44] When slaves were relatively few, such petty complaints could be addressed in small public meetings. But that changed with the arrival of each new coffle and each retelling of the Santo Domingan horrors. To assuage their fears, Greensborians took two complementary tacks: colonization and oppression.

The American Colonization Society, founded by such luminaries as James Madison, had been working since 1817 to effect the emigration of slaves from America to Liberia. Its proponents touted colonization to serve several purposes, including gradual emancipation, a softening of prejudice, and the chance to extend Christian benevolence to benighted peoples in Africa. The Alabama State Colonization Society had been in existence only a year and was starting auxiliary groups in various counties when word came of Nat Turner's rebellion. The news gave the reformers' efforts a certain urgency. "The subject of colonizing the free persons of color on the African Coast is rapidly gaining ground," approved the *Gazette*, Greene County's only newspaper; "its importance has enlisted the best men of our country." These included Alabama's future secessionist governor, Andrew B. Moore, who became a charter member of the nearby Perry County Colonization Society.[45]

Henry Tutwiler, head of the Greene Springs School for Boys, was another charter member. At the University of Virginia he had been exposed to such colonization leaders as James Madison, Thomas Jefferson, and John Hartwell Cocke. Tutwiler also corresponded about slavery with his friend James Gillespie Birney (who later resigned from the colonization movement, joined the antislavery crusade, and then ran unsuccessfully for president as the Liberty Party candidate). Slavery accounts for "almost all of the moral and political evil in our Country," wrote Tutwiler, "it exhausts our soil, corrupts our morals and is the chief cause of that diversity of interest which is fast tending to rend asunder our political fabric." Tutwiler claimed that he would willingly devote his whole life to the task of ending slavery if convinced that it could be achieved. Like so many others, Tutwiler could not end slavery by himself, so he continued to own slaves, recording thirty in 1861.[46]

The most tireless and consistent colonizationist in Greensboro—and the entire South, for that matter—was John Hartwell Cocke.[47] Cocke had the great fortune to have been born into one of the great landed Virginia families. He worked with Jefferson (who designed Cocke's plantation home, Bremo) to build the University of Virginia; he advocated agricultural reforms, especially the elimination of tobacco; and he favored temperance, serving in the mid-1830s as president of the American Temperance Union. Cocke's efforts to promote colonization were entirely consistent with his other reform interests.

Cocke had come to Greensboro in the late 1830s to confirm firsthand reports of the "incomparably" fertile Canebrake.[48] He soon resolved to establish a plantation, but Cocke's plantation would be like no other. He concluded that while slavery held in check the passions of the African race, it was nonetheless wrong. His solution was to treat slaves compassionately while encouraging responsible self-determination. He had already successfully done so with one slave family and paid their passage to Liberia. Now he was establishing Hopewell, a Canebrake plantation a few miles west of Greensboro, to secure him a profit while preparing his slaves for freedom. (Hopewell eventually included more than a thousand acres, while his nearby plantation, New Hope, measured nearly five hundred.)

One Sabbath morning in February 1841, Cocke formally called together "my people," as he and other planters routinely called their slaves. To those forty-nine at Hopewell he presented his plan: If they abided by four conditions—they had to earn their value, prove honest and fruitful, give up all strong drink, and keep secret the plan—then he would emancipate them and send them to Liberia. They all agreed and pledged themselves on a Bible. Cocke then added a few more ordinances. They were to pray daily, not to leave the plantation without a written pass, not to receive strange servants without a pass, not to fight, and not to provoke each other, and finally they were to submit themselves unconditionally to those authorities placed over them. After discussing the plan with his slaves for more than two hours, Cocke dismissed them "to enter upon the Experiment."[49]

Cocke returned to Virginia thinking all was on track. He employed his distant cousin (and Greensboro Guard) John Cocke as a steward, Elam Tanner as overseer, and George Skipwith (a slave) as driver. But Skipwith schemed to have Tanner removed, and when Tanner confessed to having fathered a child by one of the slaves, his authority evaporated. Skipwith stepped in to assume full day-to-day control of Hopewell in November 1846, but he in turn fell under the influence of drink and his own self-importance. When John Hartwell Cocke arrived from Bremo in early 1848, he discovered "a shocking state of moral depravity among the people of the place." Bastard mulatto children and venereal disease were rampant. Skipwith had forsaken his wife and ten children to live with a young girl, while two of his daughters were being kept as mistresses by "two of the young Southern Gentlemen of the vicinity." Cocke bitterly noted that "my school for ultimate Liberian freedom, had become a plantation Brothel headed by my Foreman."[50]

Despite these setbacks, Cocke added twenty more slaves from Virginia in 1851 and renewed his contract with his people. He did have a singular success with Lucy Skipwith, with whom the overseer had sired two children. Her conversion from Hopewell's "vilest sinner" to a sincere Christian produced a new person who could take responsibility for the plantation's moral equilibrium while Cocke was back in Virginia. In addition to cooking, sewing, and nursing, Lucy became the plantation's teacher. With help from a Greensboro teacher and distributor of religious tracts, Lucy taught the slave children to read, to write, and even to add, multiply, and subtract.[51]

For all his efforts, however, Cocke failed. As he saw it, with rare exceptions, the slaves proved incapable of restraining their passions. The same was true of white men. In an attempt to purify the plantation, he sent George's daughters to Mobile for sale. One was purchased by her lover (who had already fathered a child by her) for eight hundred dollars with the full knowledge and concurrence of his mother and brother. Cocke heard other reports of a Methodist who, while on parole in the neighborhood, sought to rape "young negroesses, threatening 'that he knew a negro's word was no evidence against a white man.'" Cocke bitterly admitted that "this last degree of infamous depravity can exist in no other state of civilized Society but under the circumstances of our 'Southern Institution.'"[52] Increasingly disillusioned with the prospects of emancipation, Cocke decided that slavery, while perhaps not a permanent condition, was nonetheless necessary for the time being.

Paternalistic slaveholders such as Tutwiler and Cocke were by far the exception, for slave life in the Canebrake had a reputation for being far more brutal, far more oppressive, than in the older eastern seaboard states. A contemporary account by an escaped slave furnishes an unusual confirmation from the slave's perspective. James Williams was twenty-eight, married, and a father when his master decided to send him from Virginia to work a newly acquired plantation in Greene County. In the summer of 1833, Williams arrived to serve as driver of field hands and to work closely under the overseer. The overseer's dwelling, where Williams also lived, was some three hundred yards from the slave quarters, log houses from twelve to fifteen feet square, each about fifty feet from the other. The workers, both men and women, were roused at dawn by the blowing of a horn and labored until dark in the fields, planting or clearing weeds. After supper, the men burned brush and the women spun and wove cotton for cloth.[53]

Discipline was rigid. When field hands ran away, Williams joined the overseer in pursuing them with five bloodhounds kept for the purpose. The dogs found one slave, Little John, hiding in a cane thicket and killed him before the overseers could intercede. Another runaway was whipped and put in stocks, where he died. When the overseer shot dead a particularly strong hand, the other slaves came to detest

James Williams, who escaped from a Canebrake plantation. (From James Williams, *Narrative*)

and fear the overseer. Williams claimed to have been ordered to whip other slaves, thereby serving the twin functions of instilling obedience and breaking down mutual trust among the slaves. In a form of punishment unique to the Canebrake, a runaway was placed in a cistern dug eight to ten feet deep out of the limestone. For more than twenty-four hours, he had to pump out the water as fast as it filled. Williams ultimately escaped, and by hiding during the day and traveling only at night, he eventually reached New York City on the first day of 1838. In fear of being returned as a fugitive slave, Williams boarded ship to Liverpool after some anti-slavery reformers paid his fare. The runaway never again saw the wife and children he left back in Virginia.[54]

Williams' tale is consistent with other accounts that suggest that the frontier was harsher for slaves than were the more settled areas of the Atlantic seaboard. Young Canebrake masters seemed intent on extracting all they could from their slaves' labor. Away from the constraints of family and a tradition-bound society, these rowdy entrepreneurs fashioned their plantations into cotton-growing machines. Israel Pickens, for example, allowed that he would willingly exchange lands for slaves—he had no attachment to either—but land prices around Greensboro in 1822 had been somewhat low and the price of slaves rather high. Twenty-five years later, little had changed in this regard. John Bell, a Canebrake overseer, sold a girl and child for seven hundred dollars. Added to some other money he had put away, he planned to acquire two boys or a woman with one or two children, or "Just what the money will buy." A family would be ideal; otherwise, he wrote, "let me have a Negro that Don't Let its foot Stay two Long in one place. I Rather Pay a good price for a Brisk lively Negro than to have a poke Slow give to me." Successful planters kept extensive and detailed accounts of each slave's production, ready to sell a particular slave at the most opportune moment.[55] Emotional indifference, of course, encouraged more level-headed business dealings.

The possibilities for great fortunes converted the doubters. Greensborians who had grown up in free states or countries did not hesitate to enter the ranks of slaveholders. Postmaster John Fife and merchant John Kerr, both native Scots, each owned a few slaves. Connecticut-born Amassa Dorman, mayor and prominent merchant, owned seventeen slaves in 1860. All were Greensboro Guards during the 1840s. Their Nova Scotia–born captain, Claudius Jones, owned seven slaves in 1840. Henry Watson particularly demonstrated the lure of profit. Watson left Connecticut for Greensboro with ambiguous views toward slavery. When deciding where his prospects for success were best, he factored in the costs of prime hands, yet he claimed to "abominate slavery," and several of his family certainly opposed it. Within a dozen years, however, Watson made his decision and never looked back. By 1850 he owned 81 slaves (7 in his Greensboro house and 74 on his Newbern plantation), and by 1860 the total had risen to 113.[56]

This Connecticut Yankee clearly displayed the cool calculation of a man of business accustomed to dealing with his chattel property. Writing to his mother, Watson described one of his domestic servants:

> Ellen continues to try my patience. It is very difficult to get a negro who understands good cooking. If they do ten to one they have some bad habits as bad temper & are not fit to be about. I have not succeeded in finding a cook & so have kept Ellen always determined to get one the first opportunity & dispose of her. Yet at times I think I can never be as well suited. Ellen is a *good milker*, a negro rarely is. She makes *good head[cheese]*, few can do it, or do do it. She makes excellent *coffee* this year better than when you were here. She cooks meats & vegetables well, but I might find others to do the same; I should have most excellent luck were I to find one who could milk, make good head & good coffee, all three.[57]

Ellen was disposable, and Watson was ready to exchange her if something better could be had at lower cost. Their relationship was not based on contract, for that would imply a rough equality based on services and payment, but on simple ownership. And so it was with Watson's other slaves. When he later purchased a black nurse for his newborn, Watson declared his intention to "dispense with her however as soon as the child gets old enough to go about." And if he treated domestic servants this way, his field hands probably fared much worse.[58]

Henry and Sophia Peck Watson. (Courtesy Forbes Library, Northampton, Massachusetts)

Oddly enough, Watson assumed that his slaves would be loyal to him. "She never goes off without permission," he noted approvingly of Ellen. And he considered himself like a loyal father to them. "Most people here feel an attachment to the servants, similar in some respects to that we feel for our children," he wrote to a cousin in the North. "We feed them, cloth them, nurse them when sick & in all things provide for them. How can we do this & not love them. . . . they look upon & to their masters with the same feelings of love & respect that a child looks to his father. It is a lovely trait in them." Despite his pleading, Watson's paternalistic metaphor could hardly be applied to a relationship where he would so readily sell his domestic servants.[59]

A striking contrast to Henry Watson's calculation is revealed in an episode described by his wife a few months later. "Patience is no more," Sophia Peck Watson began her letter. Word of her servant's impending death came late on Friday night:

I immediately went out, found her lying quiet but breathing differently from usual, her hands and feet were cold. . . . She was sensible until a few minutes before her death, and talked calmly with both Ma and Grandma about it. Said she felt no fear of death, that she felt prepared to meet her God. So soon as I found there was no hope of her recovery, I felt it my duty to ascertain her feelings and views on the subject of religion, and gave her what instructions I could. I found her very ignorant, more so than I supposed any one in this highly favored land could possibly be, even though a slave, but she seemed willing and anxious to talk on the subject and be instructed. I found myself a poor guide, but I could tell her of a Saviour (of whom she seemed never to have heard) and point her to Him as able and willing to save. . . . It seems scarcely possible that any one could die so calmly—full sensible too that they were dying—without feeling perfectly satisfied that they were prepared. If it was the means of her becoming a Christian her coming up here, I feel amply repaid for all care and anxiety that I suffered on her account.

The body was carried to the church, where a sermon was preached to an overflowing crowd. Many could not get seats and had to wait outside.[60]

While Henry Watson regarded Ellen as a commodity, Sophia Watson could not suppress her genuine concern for Patience. The actions of Sophia, Ma, and Grandma—their staying up with her, talking with her of Christianity, the funeral arrangements—bespeak a loyalty to which Henry seemed immune. These conflicting relationships within the same household support the claim that men and women interpreted their experiences in the Southwest differently. Young men on the make contracted with their peers out of self-interest; their slaves they owned. In both cases, the relationships were commercial. Women, conversely, seemed to value their domestic servants as a means of recalling the family ties that had been left behind. Living in Greensboro allowed women to socialize more readily, to re-create the community feelings they so longed for. Living in the Canebrake, however, seemed lonely and perhaps even dangerous among the vast numbers of anonymous field hands working under the watchful eyes of a few white overseers. For all that, this contrast between the ways that men and women dealt with slaves must be carefully qualified. Some female slaveholders certainly could be calculating, and some men could be compassionate and paternalistic.[61]

As Greensborians debated how to deal with their slaves, they also had to deal with an increasingly skeptical world. The task had started during the nervous days of 1835. "The Anti-Slavery Societies in the Northern & Middle States are doing all they can to destroy our domestic harmony," wrote a Greene County resident to his brother. The societies were "sending among us, pamphlets, tracts & newspapers—for the purpose of exciting dissatisfaction and insurrection among our slaves." At meetings held in Mobile, Montgomery, Greensboro, and Tuscaloosa, resolutions were adopted "denying the right of the Northern people to interfere in any manner, in our internal domestic concerns." After using slaves to cut down forests, cultivate lands, and make fortunes, Northerners had sold their bondsmen at great profit. And now they wanted to deny Southerners the same opportunities for wealth. But the Constitution guaranteed the right to own slaves. And further, "slavery is consistent both with the laws of God and man. Our slaves are better treated, better clothed and fed, and are required to labour fewer hours in the day, than the servants and labourers in the Northern States." This would become a common refrain, and eventually so would this correspondent's prescient conclusion: "It is my solemn opinion, that this question (to wit slavery) will ultimately bring about a dissolution of the Union of the States."[62]

The South was flooded by learned-sounding defenses of slavery resting on a tangle of biblical precedent, a pseudoscience of race, and the insistence that bondage was advantageous for slave and free alike. Greensboro was no exception. The *Alabama Beacon* noted in early 1847 the arrival in Greensboro of *A Defence of Negro Slavery, as It Exists in the United States,* written by Matthew Estes and published in Montgomery. The author was distributing the thousand copies that he had printed to the west Alabama towns between Montgomery and his own Columbus, Mississippi, as well as in Mobile and New Orleans. The *Beacon* liked Estes' work enough to excerpt his lengthy articles, the only proslavery work to receive such treatment.[63] His arguments hardly represent crucial or original insights (others expressed the same ideas better). The book's significance lies elsewhere. Written by a resident of another frontier town not that far away, *A Defence of Negro Slavery* tried to accommodate slavery into the same context that had engaged Greensborians for some time: the search for community.

Estes organized *A Defence* according to the benefits that the institution accrued to slave, master, and nation. Slaves, racially inferior beings, benefited from moral and religious teachings, from being happily free from responsibilities, and from being trained in the habits of industry and the arts of civilization. Slavery benefited masters by affording them the leisure time for intellectual and moral improvement and by training them in the habits of control. Finally, the nation benefited by having its wealth increased, its intelligence promoted, and its military security enhanced by allowing more men to shoulder arms. Estes then traced these features historically from ancient Israel to the contemporary South, concluding that superior races must retain control to avoid a race war.[64]

What, then, held Southern society together? Like the Masons, Estes turned to the distinction between natural and artificial societies. Natural relations (between husband and wife, for example, and parent and child) arose within families and were unaffected by time or circumstance—that is, they were found at all times among all peoples. By contrast, artificial relations (governments and voluntary associations, for example) could be amended, destroyed, or replaced according to varying conditions. "The institution of one age and nation, will not suit the people of a different age and nation: even the same nation, at different periods, requires very different institutions." Estes deemed slavery to be an artificial relation, for "though not the very best possible state of society for all people, and for all times, is much the best under particular circumstances." Slavery was a civil institution, and although beneficial to Hebrews and Southerners alike, it might one day cease to be so if environmental changes demanded it. Such a distinction was consistent with the slaves' role as commercial commodities. And self-interest drove masters to treat their slaves with proper food, clothing, lodging, and moral instruction—irrespective of principles of humanity or friendship.[65]

Yet the disinterested principles of natural relations also operated, for "the Master and the Slave form one family—they are frequently reared together—and of course must feel towards each other the kindly sympathies of our nature. This is natural." Masters treated their slaves the way a great patriarch treated his children. Thus, Estes concluded, "society may be compared to a great organism," where each member has different functions—some more intellectual, some more useful, some more honorable—but all necessary. "The Slave that performs his duties well may be as honorable and useful . . . as the proudest monarch that ever sat upon a throne." But if slaves aspired to equality, then "this kindly, paternal feeling gives way to a feeling of repulsive hate and jealousy."[66]

Like so many others, Estes tried to have it both ways. As commodities, slaves could be bought and sold, thus relegating them to the realm of the artificial, but as persons, they were expected to belong to some sort of organic social whole. That he failed to bridge the gap in the slaves' roles is hardly surprising, for the same disjunction seemed to exist among white people as well. Relations built on self-interest, as the example of Greensboro confirmed, were inherently commercial and temporary, whereas those within the family seemed natural, reliable, and able to accommodate changed circumstances. An organic civil community beyond the family remained a real, albeit frustratingly elusive, goal.

★ ★ ★

In this context of slavery and community, the Greensboro Light Artillery Guards faced the national events of the 1840s and '50s, beginning with the dispute over the annexation of Texas. Townspeople invited General Sam Houston, touring Alabama in 1845, to speak on the matter. The Guards were among those chosen to escort him into town. Citizens called on the Hero of San Jacinto at the Greensboro Hotel and the next day assembled at the Baptist church to hear him recount the history of Texas and its struggles with Mexico. He outlined the difficulties encountered in his own repeated efforts to have the Republic of Texas annexed to the United States. Houston was said to have impressed many, especially women, with the desire to visit his beautiful land of "sunshine and chivalry." He predicted that annexation would not precipitate war between Mexico and the United States.[67]

Houston was wrong. A few months after his visit, skirmishing broke out in disputed territory between Texas and Mexico, and by May 1846 the two countries were at war. Congress organized a Volunteer Corps, and Alabamians petitioned the governor to form a regiment for the war. The governor responded immediately with a call for volunteers.[68]

Jesse J. Melton had just ridden into Greensboro when he heard the roll of drums calling for enlistees. He signed his name sixth on the muster roll of the Greensborough Independent Volunteers. Nearly one hundred men followed Melton's example, electing as their captain Andrew L. Pickens, son of former governor Israel Pickens, and selecting green worsted frock suits for their uniforms. On the designated day, they marched out "with buoyant hearts sustaining our name as 'Independent Volunteers' & fondly anticipating the day when we shall plant our standard triumphantly upon the banks of the Rio Grande." After boarding a steamboat at Demopolis, they became the first company to arrive in Mobile and thus were designated Company A, First Regiment of Alabama [Infantry] Volunteers and mustered into U.S. service for twelve months. The second company to arrive was the Eutaw Rangers.[69]

Greensboro's Independent Volunteers sailed from Mobile with the Alabama Regiment at the end of June.[70] For half a year they suffered from dysentery, diarrhea, measles, and boredom in Matamoros and Camargo along the Rio Grande. Some were sent home, and some died. Finally, forty-eight of the ninety-three Greensborians received orders to sail for Tampico, along Mexico's coast, where they landed on December 17. Besides throwing up breastworks to defend against attack, the Alabamians did little more in Tampico than they had along the Rio Grande other than raise two or three thousand dollars to send for relief of the Irish famine.

General Winfield Scott, they learned, was preparing to attack Vera Cruz. In fine spirits at the prospect of finally getting into battle, the Greensborians boarded yet another steamship on March 6, 1847, and set out. Three days later, they could see the imposing castle of San Juan de Ulua, a four-sided bastion of 128 guns located on a coral island about a thousand yards from Vera Cruz. The Alabamians were among the last troops to land, leaving their ship just as the sun was setting behind the snow-capped peaks to the west. They bivouacked on the beach without tents. The battle finally commenced on March 22; a week later, seven thousand Mexican troops marched out, stacked their guns, and surrendered. On April 9, the army began its advance on Mexico City, the Alabama Regiment pulling up the rear. The march was a great adventure, as the soldiers toured Santa Anna's wrecked and deserted hacienda, camped at the splendidly arched National Bridge, walked among the dead on the Cerro Gordo battleground, and saw for the first time the snow-capped extinct volcano Orizaba. "It was the grandest sight ever beheld. It baffles all description," wrote the Eutaw Rangers' captain, Sydenham Moore, in his journal. At Jalapa the men from Alabama dined on coffee, oranges, and pineapples and wondered at the magnificent cathedral.

Then, expecting to continue on to the capital, the Alabamians received orders to disband. With the Alabama Regiment's twelve-month enlistment drawing to a close, the men had been asked to reenlist for the duration of the war. They countered with an offer to serve three months or until Mexico City was taken, but the regulars sent the volunteers packing nonetheless. The Alabamians quickly struck out for Vera Cruz, boarded the *Virginia,* and landed in New Orleans. There they bathed, shaved, and threw out their louse-infested old uniforms—producing a change so dramatic that the veterans had to be introduced to each other on the streets. The Alabamians boarded passage for Mobile, where they spent a day, and then took the first boat up the Black Warrior. Just above Demopolis, the boat ran aground. The Rangers turned northwest toward Eutaw, and the Independent Volunteers headed for Greensboro.

The Volunteers had been gone a year. All had suffered from heat and thirst; some had contracted diseases; a few died. When Lieutenant John L. May succumbed to a violent fever, his funeral attracted one of the largest crowds in Greensboro's history. The Greensboro Guards and the Greensboro Cavalry, the Odd Fellows' lodge, and many citizens conveyed the corpse two miles to the grave. Greensboro's church bells all tolled, and the stores were closed for the day.[71] His death had a certain glory to it, but all in all, the Mexican War seemed more of an escapade than a bitter struggle. The Volunteers had seen exotic locales and unimagined mountain vistas. The enemy had been defeated with unexpected ease. Greensborians had fallen to disease but not to enemy fire. Their first military adventures against the Creeks and the Mexicans had involved little sacrifice, largely because no one was truly threatened.

The Mexican War had not interested the Greensboro Guards enough to go (with the exception of three individuals). The company's decision was not specifically spelled out, but clues are numerous. First and most obvious, the Guards were chartered by the state for its defense, not for a war that did not directly threaten Alabama and certainly did not threaten Greensboro—that threat came from the vast numbers of slaves tilling the Canebrake. Further, the Independent Volunteers were an ad hoc organization formed for a specific purpose, while dozens of strings tied the Guards to their town.[72] Those who volunteered for Mexico were the same sort of eager young men who had first come to the Canebrake. The war offered opportunities for adventure, for glory perhaps, and for economic advancement. The newly opened lands would serve—as the Canebrake had for the parents of these men— as new opportunities to make one's own fortune, to make one's own way.

Like the Creek War of 1836, the annexation of Texas and defeat of the Mexicans, by stimulating cupidity and migration, added to the problems Greensborians already faced. "The Churches in all this region," wrote a Greensboro minister, "are almost ruined by the love of money, the root of all evil." Some attributed the attitude to the war with Mexico, and the minister noted a change for the worse since its declaration. "Every one here seems willing to sell out & *remove*—and even in this new country our churches are suffering from removals." Such examples could be multiplied manyfold. A farmer from Boligee wrote that if worms again ate the cotton, he would be leaving for Texas. A few years later, he and his family were still thinking of going: "I would be in my glory if we were all settled down comfortably in Texas."[73]

Even while Greensborians in Mexico cast covetous eyes on the land, even while

Greensborians at home read Estes' *Defence of Negro Slavery,* an obscure freshman Democrat from Pennsylvania introduced an amendment to a congressional appropriations bill. The Wilmot Proviso would prohibit slavery in any lands obtained from Mexico. The response was immediate. "I seriously begin to think," wrote Andrew Pickens Calhoun from his Canebrake plantation to his father, John C. Calhoun, that "dissolution will be the only remedy to preserve *life liberty* or *honor.*" The South, he believed, must close its ports to any state that allowed antislavery doctrines to be voiced. The *Beacon* reprinted from the *Charleston Mercury* an article proclaiming that the "whole united people of the South" would resist the proposed "insulting and tyrannous legislation" to exclude slavery from any land acquired from Mexico. The *Montgomery Flag and Advertiser* published an article, also reprinted in the *Beacon,* declaring that neither Congress nor the people, "except in their sovereign capacity," were constitutionally capable of limiting slavery in either the District of Columbia or the new territories. And the following week, readers learned that the French had abolished slavery in Martinique.[74]

Some thought that the 1848 election would put an end to the political posturing. Whig presidential candidate Zachary Taylor carried the county, as he did most of the Black Belt. His opponents included Lewis Cass, a Democrat from Michigan, and former President Martin Van Buren, running as head of the Free Soil Party and supporting the proviso. But Taylor's victory did not quell the uproar. Even before he took office, the Guards reorganized themselves with a determination to bring the company back to what it was in its "palmiest days." And the *Beacon*'s editor, John Harvey, railed against the "*fool-hardy* course" of those Northern agitators who threatened the Union's very existence. "Let us alone!" he noted, had become the South's warning to the North.[75]

Meetings were announced in Alabama's larger slaveholding counties to discuss what action to take in the event that Congress tried to abolish slavery in either the territories or the District of Columbia. Greene County's meeting convened on April 9, 1849, in Eutaw (the county seat since 1838). The participants, regardless of political affiliation, resolved that the territories represented the common property of all the states; thus, Congress could not constitutionally forbid slave owners from taking their property there. More to the point, the meeting's attendees proclaimed that the South had long submitted without retaliation to the systematic assault on its constitutional right to own slaves. In sum, "*aggression upon our rights has reached beyond which* IT SHALL NOT GO." Those at the meeting instead backed an extension of the Missouri Compromise line westward "by way of *conciliation and to preserve the Union.*" A year later, these resolutions were reaffirmed as John Erwin, Greensboro's longtime lawyer and politician, prepared to depart for the Nashville Convention of nine slave states. Delegates there heard fire-eating oratory proclaiming the virtue of a Southern nation pledged to slavery. They backed away, however, from outright secession. In Alabama, public meetings in Perry and Sumter Counties adopted the most proslavery resolutions of the Nashville Convention and declared that the people of the South should hold conventions to decide their fate should Congress restrict slavery. An editorialist ironically signing himself "A Lover of the Union," published in the *Beacon* a call for nonintercourse with the North. If Southerners lived within themselves, self-sufficient in food and raiment, and built their own cotton and wool factories, then "the North will rue the day she ever interfered with Southern interests." The South had every resource for securing perfect independence.[76] Ten years later, the argument would again be heard.

In Washington, Senator Stephen A. Douglas of Illinois was pushing through Henry Clay's proposal for a great compromise: California was to enter as a free state with New Mexico and Utah as territories; a new federal Fugitive Slave Act, biased toward Southerners, would be enacted; and the sale of slaves would be banned in the District of Columbia. Yet another public meeting was held in Eutaw on October 7, 1850, with perhaps as many as 500 people attending. After an acrimonious debate, Erwin called for the sense of the crowd: 75 favored the compromise and 110 opposed it.[77] Greensborians were still willing to allow a diversity of opinions.

Samuel Pickens, a wealthy planter, despaired that the chance to settle the slavery question to the South's advantage had passed. More discussion would not cause the North to cease its agitation for abolition: "the only thing that will move them to do us justice is the fear of dissolution. . . . In my opinion, all that will be necessary for us to do is to show an undivided front & to declare that in the event of any further encroachments on our rights, that we will in a body withdraw from the Union." Northerners, he was certain, would always back down. "They will yield us any thing we wish rather than the union should be broken up. But to produce this effect on them, we must all stand up like men."[78]

The underlying issue of sovereignty was the subject of a series of published debates between "Common Sense" and John Harvey from the fall of 1851 into the spring of 1852.[79] The editor, who had recently declared his intention of keeping the *Beacon* politically neutral, claimed that the federal government had limited powers and therefore could not be sovereign. His proof rested in the Tenth Amendment, which reserved all undelegated powers to the states and the people and thus implied that the federal government's powers were limited. Common Sense, supporting the federal Constitution, responded by taking Harvey's point to absurdity. If the federal government possessed limited powers that prevented its being sovereign, then the state government's powers must be unlimited. And what was to prevent carrying the idea even further? If the power to make and enforce laws was the test of sovereignty, then Greensboro, which had recently enacted an ordinance to prevent the burning of coal kilns within the town, should claim its position alongside the nations of the earth. Eventually, someone would contend that citizens were sovereign and owed no allegiance at all. His tone was sarcastic, yet this was a crucial problem for individualists. One day they would be forced to ponder the question, To whom must we be loyal?

Most of Harvey's responses to Common Sense hinged on petty issues of interpretation. But one argument—from origins—did not. The editor argued that the states were originally sovereign and then delegated certain powers to the federal government. The preamble to the Constitution of Alabama, in obvious parallel to the federal Constitution, stated that "to establish justice, ensure tranquility . . . and to secure to ourselves and our posterity the *rights of life, liberty, and property,*" the people of the Alabama territory mutually agreed with each other to form themselves into the "free and independent" state of Alabama. Moreover, the 1819 constitution included the "Declaration of Rights," the second section of which declared that "All political power is inherent in the people, and all free governments are founded on their authority." In sum, "the States composing this Confederacy are Sovereignties."

Common Sense, anticipating Abraham Lincoln's argument, pointed out that if the states delegated their powers to the federal government to be resumed at will, then the social compact was meaningless. Eight months of charges and countercharges moved the argument little beyond this point. No matter, the articles raised other issues. Their language, for example, drew heavily from the realm of commerce. Was authority a contract or a loan? Either way, it was not natural but, like civil society, artificial. Harvey ended with the stronger argument if the criterion for judgment was general acceptance. Greensborians would give their allegiance to the government or institution that would protect their peculiar interests and ease their fears.

Those fears only grew. Greensboro's charter was specifically amended in 1850 to authorize officials to arrest and jail any slaves suspected of having committed a crime or even any slaves found without a permit—the first change in the town's slave ordinances since the aftermath of the Nat Turner rebellion. The publication of *Uncle Tom's Cabin* could be ignored in the Canebrake or its distribution in the South suppressed, but letters from relatives told of the great noise it was making, even in Paris. The French translation, a "most infamous tissue of falsehood," was making the South detested by the whole of Europe.[80]

And then in early 1854, Senator Douglas reopened the question of slavery in the territories by introducing the Nebraska Bill in Congress. To gain needed support from Southerners for a proposed transcontinental railroad, Douglas amended his bill to include a popular-sovereignty clause specifying that the residents of each potential state would decide whether to allow slavery. While its democratic elements gave the bill a superficial appeal, Douglas had failed to gauge the depth of antislavery feelings. The North screamed with indignation, and a coalition opposed to the spread of slavery into the territories began a new political party, the Republicans. After Douglas' bill became law, Kansas turned into bitter and bloody battleground as pro- and antislavery groups contended for domination.

In Greensboro, the *Beacon* devoted a series of articles to "the Kansas question," concluding that the passage of the Kansas-Nebraska Act, which repealed the Missouri Compromise and opened the territories to slavery if residents approved, represented the "*most important,* recognition of the Constitutional rights of the South, that has ever been made by Congress." But others criticized Douglas for unnecessarily reopening a settled question in order to gain personal political advantage. "The whole Kansas quarrell is humbuggery & nonsense," wrote Watson to his mother. No one in Greensboro ever supposed that Kansas would be a slave state, and not one in a thousand cared. Watson recounted that Jefferson Buford from Barbour County had sold his property and raised a company of half-crazy men to invade Kansas, but they scattered as soon as they got there, and Buford returned home ten thousand dollars poorer. In Greensboro, however, no excitement could be gotten up. In this climate, Watson decided, immediate "*emancipation* is *impossible.*" Slavery could not be abolished, and besides, the Constitution guaranteed the right of ownership. If the North were to understand these two problems and leave the South alone, "there would be nothing between us." But "there never were two people who so little understood each other as those of the north & the south," wrote the former Connecticut Yankee. The sport of aspiring politicians and the caprice of raving fanatics were causing the South and the North "to cordially *hate* each other."[81] From the Wilmot Proviso through the Compromise of 1850, the Kansas-Nebraska Act, and bleeding Kansas—issues thoroughly reported in the *Beacon*—came an ever-encroaching threat. Where once Greensborians had feared only those slaves who would be free, they now feared those who would make the slaves free.

Greensboro's Guards prepared for that eventuality. As the 1857 Washington's birthday celebrations approached, a notice appeared in the *Beacon*. The Light Artillery Guards, which for several years had not been active, planned to march in a Saturday parade (a day early because February 22 fell on a Sunday) and then to elect officers. The anonymous correspondent urged all members to turn out and to bring with them any suggestions for inducing others to join the unit. He also used the announcement as an opportunity to consider the salutary effects of a volunteer military company on its community. A company certainly provides security in times of excitement, danger, or lawless violence. And the regular militia system of Alabama—and most, if not all, of the other states—had proven woefully inadequate, a "mere *burlesque* on the military." But a volunteer company, like the Guards, fostered a military spirit among the people, a particular value in a land that depended on its citizen-soldiers for "its defence, the vindication of its rights, and the preservation of its liberties." Finally, the correspondent noted that a volunteer military company promoted a valuable public spirit that "prompts the good citizen to lend his countenance to whatever is likely to be of service to the community in which he lives." He ended by inviting his fellow citizens to join the Guards or at least to contribute financially; the company needed its own armory, for example.[82]

The Guards celebrated Washington's birthday, elected their officers, and were gratified that the turnout was larger than for any previous parade. The next week they marched in the procession to lay the Southern University cornerstone. Greensborians also contributed financially, raising enough money over the next couple of months to purchase fifteen or sixteen uniforms for men unable to afford their own.[83]

John Hartwell Cocke, reformer and proponent of colonization, also wrote an open letter to the newspaper. He had become committed to the Guards' success because they, as the other correspondent noted, contributed to Greensboro's moral and intellectual resources. Cocke challenged the Guards to include total abstinence in their constitution and promised to contribute one thousand dollars if the company could enlist one hundred men who would take such a pledge. A temperate volunteer company, he believed, would raise the village into a town and the town into a city, and the city would enlighten the whole South. But that was not all. Cocke, who hoped one day to see the end of slavery, noted that a volunteer military company like the Greensboro Guards served as "a perfect security against servile insurrection."[84]

Here lay the crux of the matter. The Guards contributed by promoting standards of personal character and engaging in civic life. But the militiamen also stood sentinel, guarding against a more immediate threat in the nearby Canebrake. In the thirty-five years of its existence, the company had emerged from its former position as merely one of Greensboro's many voluntary associations to become the institution that represented and protected the townspeople.

PART III

# Guarding Greensboro

# CHAPTER 5

# One Voice

**We all feel like Brothers.**
★ Jules Honoré Bayol, 1861

White Greensborians had just cause to feel proud. Their elegant columned mansions, imposing Southern University, and the hustle and bustle of daily life testified to their success. As their cotton grew, so did their prosperity. Yet so did their fears. A master's wealth increased with every newborn black slave, certainly, but the growth in the bound population capable of bloody rebellion easily outstripped the growth in the free population. Compounding white fears was the continuing problem of loosely tied individualists who hardly hesitated to leave Greensboro and head west. And in the late 1850s Southerners faced a new threat: the prospect of losing control of the national government to a political party they charged with being apostate, sectional, and inimical to slavery, willing to let white Americans into the West but not their black slaves. Nat Turner's little band had killed only a few dozen, after all. Much more was now at stake if the Northern states were to put their political will beyond stopping slavery's spread to abolishing slavery outright. Greensborians would then lose an enormous financial investment and might even have to fight a race war, as the Santo Domingan exiles had done decades earlier. With Lincoln's victory in 1860, Greensborians moved overwhelmingly toward secession.

Self-interest could no longer sustain their society. Greensborians called out not for voluntary cooperation but for unanimity—through persuasion if possible, through compulsion if necessary—to end this threat. The Guards showed the way. At first the little company had seemed little different from the other voluntary associations that townsmen could join. But now the moment had come. After years of patriotically celebrating the Fourth of July, Washington's birthday, and Jackson's victory at New Orleans, the Guards took up arms against others who observed the same holidays. Greensborians rallied behind their soldiers as never before, melding themselves into a single community based on mutual dependence and constancy.

As their young men guarded Greensboro by donning uniforms and departing for battlefields, the population was split between Alabama and Virginia. But unlike emigration, this geographical separation strengthened community-building efforts by establishing a standard of inclusion based on who was—and who was not—willing to protect the townspeople. When Guards took sick, fell from Yankee bullets, lost limbs to the surgeon's knife, entered prison camps, or died, those left behind redoubled their efforts lest those losses be in vain. Gathering to sew quilts became more than a social occasion for women, more even than an effort to keep their soldiers warm, for into every quilt the women sewed commitment. All were in the war. Duty, self-sacrifice, a common cause, enemy, and past: this was the stuff of loyalty—to the Confederacy, yes, but even more so to each other.

A loyal community emerged not only from shared purposes and sacrifices but also from the nature of the war. As Greensborians were forced to weigh the significance of national events and to contribute toward changing their course, individual lives assumed a dramatic quality that they themselves recognized. Many of the Guards began diaries in which they identified heroes and villains, recorded courageous actions, and poured out their grief. With the end of the fighting came the end of their diaries, as if a book had ended. By recounting their struggles against a backdrop of the land, the enemy, and events beyond their control, the Guards were not merely listing a sequence of unrelated events. They were imparting a unity and meaning to lives that had heretofore lacked both the shared sense of crisis and the need for mutual reliance that strengthen relationships.

The Guards' story was their community's as well. Autonomous Greensborians had previously cooperated with each other in order to promote personal advantage. But the Civil War raised cooperation to an entirely different level. People died for each other. The conflict tempered their individualism, and Greensborians began to exhibit new qualities. This war became a tale of shared hopes, shared sacrifices, and shared loss. As the Guards recorded confessions and anecdotes in diaries, letters, and the Greensboro newspaper, as years later they published reminiscences, and as they justified their decisions both to themselves and to succeeding generations, they were merging their many experiences into a single story with many actors.[1] They were not engaged, either during the conflict or for years afterward, in writing a dispassionate history of America's Civil War. They were instead developing a creation myth that would define white Greensborians as a community, a creation myth that the following five chapters seek to reconstruct.

★ ★ ★

Two days before the celebrations of 1857's glorious Fourth of July, the Guards assembled in full summer uniform to march from their armory to the Greensboro Female Academy. Miss Helen C. May was there to present the Guards with a banner—a Star Spangled Banner—that she and her fellow students had sewn. "I am about to present to you a Flag," she began, "for the defence of our homes and common country." Her brief speech implored Providence to avert from their happy country the horrors of war. But if a foreign foe were to invade the land, "then fling the banner to the breeze." Other threats lay closer at hand. "Should wild fanaticism, which hangs like a threatening cloud o'er the Northern horizon, seek by force to trample on the rights of our beloved South," then "may your watchword ever be, 'We defend our rights.'"[2]

Orderly Sergeant Edwin Lafayette Hobson accepted the flag on behalf of the company. Feelings of patriotism had prompted the Guards to reorganize themselves, "to serve, without pay, rewarded only by the consciousness of discharging a duty to our beloved South." Should the Guards ever be called to suppress an insurrection or to resist "the mad fanatics of the North," then he promised to unfurl the flag and proclaim it "the Banner of resistance to all encroachments." Should the abolitionists persist in their mad attempts to undermine the South's institutions, then "we will help to raise the banner of Southern Rights . . . and firmly placing it on the Mason's & Dixon's line, say to them, 'Thus far shalt thou come but no further . . . equality in the Union or independence out of it.'" And, of course, the Guards vowed to safeguard the academy's students and others of the fairer sex from all possible dangers.[3]

Their cause defined, their flag before them, the Guards became honored guests at every patriotic occasion thereafter. Alfred Hatch invited them especially for the Fourth of July celebrations at his plantation along the Black Warrior. With a handsome new cannon, the company paraded before seven to eight hundred celebrants. The Declaration of Independence was then read from a podium flanked by two large paintings of George Washington. In February 1858 the Guards, their numbers reaching nearly seventy, marched through Greensboro to celebrate Washington's birthday and their eventful past year. They listened to a reading of Washington's Farewell Address and a suitable oration denouncing such filibustering expeditions as the invasion of Nicaragua by William Walker (who would soon be speaking to an unsympathetic Greensboro). The Guards raised $15.76 to present to the Mount Vernon Association before Mary A. Terry, a teacher at the Greensboro Female Academy, closed the ceremonies by playing her own composition, the "Light Artillery Guards' March." At the 1858 Fourth of July festivities, the Guards turned out to hear a strong patriotic appeal for the Union "that had cost our forefathers so much blood and treasure,—and for whose destruction, many of the descendents of those revolutionary heroes are now laboring." The Guards continued to parade—at the Battle of New Orleans commemoration, at the May Day celebration of the Methodist Sabbath School, and even at the Demopolis Fair.[4]

Not only the Guards but all the volunteer companies were becoming more visible in the late 1850s. A call went out to reactivate the Guards' counterpart, the Greensboro Cavalry. Like the Guards, the Cavalry had formerly been quite visible; indeed, cavalry units were generally regarded as the most elite of the volunteer companies. And like the Guards, the Cavalry was touted as an honor to the town. (Bad riders, the *Alabama Beacon* admonished, detract from the effect; only skillful riders with fine horses should apply.) The Cavalry, too, received a banner sewn by the students of the Greensboro Female Academy. But despite the fancy words, new banners, and official recognition by the General Assembly, military efficiency remained embarrassingly poor. One Guard attending a general muster of the Thirty-eighth Militia Regiment, which included both Greensboro companies, mused that he had never seen a "more complete farce," a "magnificent humbug" directed by officers with no knowledge of military tactics. The newspaper, ever positive, boasted of the same citizen-soldiers' handsome display and particularly of the officers' fine appearance and military bearing.[5]

Complacency vanished when Alabamians learned of John Brown's 1859 raid on Harper's Ferry. Brown's explicit admission that he intended to start a slave rebellion reignited Greensborians' worst fears. "The subject of raising Volunteer Companies throughout the State, is now engaging public attention," noted the *Beacon* on December 2, the day of Brown's execution. The nefarious attempt to create a slave insurrection had failed this time, warned editor John G. Harvey, but the South must prepare for the next such incident, and "the cheapest and most efficient plan for accomplishing this object, *is to organize efficient Volunteer Companies.*" Harvey, a West Point graduate, appealed to his fellow townspeople to bolster their cavalry company through contributions to defray the cost of uniforms for those who could not afford them.[6]

In response to Brown's raid and growing tensions, Alabama's General Assembly reorganized the militia system. By March 1860, Greensborians were reading of a new law to provide an efficient military organization for the state. Acting on recommendations by the Joint Military Committee (which included Greensboro's Allen C. Jones, state senator and captain of the Guards) the legislators elevated the volunteer companies to the main defense of the state. The proposed Volunteer Corps of the State of Alabama was to enroll no more than eight thousand men into companies of between forty-four and eighty men. Each captain would drill his company twelve times a year with arms and accoutrements supplied by the governor, who, along with his aides, would also designate a state flag and uniform. To implement the act's provisions, the legislature promised to appropriate two hundred thousand dollars, to be raised by new taxes. In another act passed during the same session, the legislature turned the University of Alabama into a military academy. Such saber rattling elicited the first signs of reticence on the part of Harvey, who had earlier supported volunteer companies. The *Beacon*'s editor saw no need for such military preparations, believing that the assembly's acts only encouraged Disunionists. "Alabama is at peace with all the world—Abolitiondom included."[7]

Military preparations were but one sign of heightened anxiety over political developments. A plethora of public meetings were called and resolutions were debated to prepare citizens for the November 1860 presidential election. Several Greensborians rode to a typical meeting held in nearby Marion. There Governor Andrew B.

Moore, a former colonizationist, pressed for a boycott of any article purchased or manufactured in any of the Northern states. The resolutions also encouraged citizens not to patronize any Southern school taught by Northern teachers or to send Southern children to Northern schools, with the single exception of West Point. Vacationing in the free states was condemned. Finally, the resolutions urged the state government to establish arsenals and arms factories and to convene a convention for defense and general welfare—a euphemism for secession. As expected, the Marion audience adopted the resolutions. A few Greensborians dissented, however. Editor Harvey, shying from the proposed boycott's secessionist implications, labeled it impractical. But a *Beacon* correspondent, "Southern Independence," argued that boycotts did not go far enough. He urged Southerners to purchase shares in Southern manufactures and steamship lines. "The patriotism which would prompt to such an effort, would consecrate the self-interest of it," he noted, making an appeal that Greensborians readily understood. "Such a principle, *all* contributing a *mite*, would form a *Lever* that would move *any* people, out of *any* difficulty." Slavery had been forced on the South, he continued, diverting its capital from the shipping, manufactures, and trade that made the North great and prosperous. But a concerted action born from self-interest and patriotism could effect independence. "Let *all* unite in *small* contributions."[8]

Greensborians were following a typical pattern. At public meetings, citizens would solicit cooperation to effect a particular plan of action. Resolutions would be advanced, debated, and (almost invariably) adopted. Leaders would then carry the message to hamlets in the hinterlands and appeal to more gatherings of the citizenry.[9] These local political meetings seemed to manifest the same spirit that had been used to form voluntary communities. But subtle differences set the two impulses apart. Greensborians were comfortable cooperating together to establish railroad companies, promote temperance, and most recently to secure Southern University. They did not attach political labels, however, to such efforts. If a railroad were to come to the Canebrake, then Whig and Democratic planters alike would benefit by being able to transport their cotton bales more easily to the markets. Schools served the children of both Whigs and Democrats. When individuals split politically, it was not over local issues but over state and national matters. Indeed, partisanship impeded community-building, but when directed against a single external foe, political activity could have the opposite effect.

Whether an individual voted Democrat or Whig largely resulted from his conception of freedom and the role of government. Both Democrats and Whigs embraced freedom, certainly, but each understood the term differently.[10] For Democrats, freedom meant independence, a right to be left alone. Its opposite was dependence and governance by others, a sort of slavery among those lacking the economic resources to stand apart. Conspiracies of powerful individuals and corporations, Democrats believed, were constantly endangering personal freedom and equality by using tricks to exploit the citizens' vulnerability. Democrats consequently tended to remain skeptical of most cooperative endeavors, even reform movements, that might threaten individual autonomy. As might be expected, those regions of Alabama populated by self-sufficient farmers tended to vote for Democrats.

Whigs, conversely, understood freedom as an ideal requiring constant effort, the reward for education, sacrifice, cooperation, and hard work. Independence was not a synonym for freedom but rather a natural condition that made freedom all the harder to achieve. The solution lay in self-government and in cooperating together to build institutions—schools, railroads, and banks, for example—that would allow individualists to succeed in an increasingly competitive and commercial world. Whiggery was most popular among planters and lawyers, those whose lives were most tied to contract and commerce.

Democrats and Whigs naturally assigned to government contrasting roles. Democrats wanted a sort of "trade union of the electorate" to shield ordinary citizens from special interests and wealthy citizens—to protect freedom, in other words. Publicly funded universities, hospitals for the insane, and railroads were deemed either elitist or sources of indoctrination. Whigs instead wanted to model government along the lines of a religious denomination or reform group, in which initiatives could be advanced to deliver individuals from the bonds of poverty, ignorance, and moral depravity. Whigs wanted their government to create freedom and promote a person's capacity to govern himself.[11]

Greensboro's commercially minded individualists, those who came seeking to make their fortunes in the Canebrake, urged citizens and the government to build plank roads and railroads that would link the plantations to international markets. These people founded schools and Southern University, formed committees to press for moral reform, and, not surprisingly, voted Whig. Alabamians could count on Greene to be one of the state's strongest Whig counties; either Whigs or their successors, the Know-Nothings, consistently had carried the county's popular vote in every presidential election since 1840. Of course Greene's attraction to Whiggish ideas did not mean that Democrats were nowhere to be found within the county.

Local conditions invariably created exceptions to the usual party distinctions. In Greensboro, for example, the most prominent politician was John Erwin, one of the first lawyers to arrive, a man of considerable wealth and prestige, and a fierce Democrat. He served in the state legislature beginning in 1831 and presided over the Democratic National Conventions in 1852 and 1860. When agitating for programs and institutions that improved Greensboro, however, his views were indistinguishable from those of the Whigs. Many men entered one political party because the other was already filled with capable candidates. Perhaps adding to Erwin's decision was that in a state such as Alabama, where Democrats outnumbered Whigs, those with state or national aspirations were well advised to become Democrats. Erwin's son-in-law and captain of the Greensboro Guards, Allen C. Jones, was also a promi-

Lawyer and politician John Erwin. (Courtesy Alabama Department of Archives and History, Montgomery)

nent Democrat, but whether from conviction or from the influence of his wife's dominating father, it would be impossible to say.

Similar anomalies could be found throughout the county. In the 1848 presidential election, the Whig candidate, Mexican War hero Zachary Taylor, comfortably carried Greene County, receiving 714 votes to Democrat Franklin Pierce's 587. (The fire-eaters' candidate, George M. Troup, received 10 votes.) But Pierce carried several of the plantation precincts most involved in the market economy and thus likely to vote Whig, and some less market oriented precincts voted for Taylor.[12] The discrepancies probably resulted from the influence of local personalities.

In keeping with their different views of freedom, both Whigs and Democrats supported slavery but for different reasons. Democrats believed that slaves in the fields allowed independent small farmers to keep their freedom, avoiding the curse of having to work for capitalist planters. Further, owning slaves offered small farmers the prospect of economic security and social equality. Southern Whigs also believed that slavery was linked to white freedom, but in the sense of being yet another institution that allowed individualists to achieve more. Slavery guaranteed prosperity and white freedom. Abolition, both parties agreed, would contradict fundamental American values.[13]

And both Whigs and Democrats knew that Alabama voters insisted on preserving white freedom by preserving black bondage. Beginning with the Nullification Crisis (which in Alabama's case referred to the federal government's assertion of jurisdiction over Indian lands) and continuing through the blazing debates over banks, tariffs, and internal improvements, Alabama politicians expressed their support of slavery through other surrogate issues—manufactured vehicles to be ridden to political victory.

Every election found Democrats and Whigs pushing the extremes of what would resonate among the electorate until 1849, when Democrats began calling for all Southerners, regardless of party, to defend slavery by uniting against its common foes. The collapse of the national Whig Party added to this blurring of party lines and gave a certain legitimacy to the Democrats' claim of conspiracy. "I shall vote for them," wrote a former Whig of the 1856 Democratic presidential ticket, "the destruction of the Whig Party . . . having left me as it were without a party." The Democratic platform, which argued for congressional noninterference, contained what he called "the true doctrine on the Slavery." Just a step beyond lay the fire-eaters, who promised the simplest of solutions to the voters' confusion: secession.[14]

The crucial 1860 presidential election was the culmination of this ever-spiraling game. Under Erwin's chairmanship, the Alabama Democratic Party's Committee on the Platform declared the unqualified right of slaveholders to have their property protected everywhere—in the states, in the territories, and in any unorganized wilderness—thereby explicitly rejecting the Republican Party's position. But Erwin's committee went even further, instructing Alabama's delegates to the national Democratic Convention in April to withdraw should the party fail to adopt a platform recognizing the uncompromisable Southern rights the committee had listed.[15] When the Democrats met in Charleston, William Lowndes Yancey, true to his word, led the Alabama delegation and those from seven other slave states out of the convention hall. The remaining National Democrats agreed to reassemble in Baltimore on June 18, where they nominated Senator Stephen A. Douglas of Illinois. The dissenting Southerners reconvened first in Richmond, where Erwin presided, and then in Baltimore. There, on June 28, they nominated Vice President John C. Breckinridge of Kentucky to head their ticket. The rival National and Southern Democrats would face two opponents. The remnants of the Whig and Know-Nothing Parties united in early May to form the Constitutional Union Party, vaguely pledged to supporting the Constitution and to condemning sectional parties; their presidential nominee was Senator John Bell of Tennessee. That same month, the Republicans met in Chicago and nominated Abraham Lincoln.

Greene County's Whigs, especially those self-made men engaged in commercial agriculture, saw Bell as an attractive candidate. The Constitutional Union Party thus had an edge from the start, especially when respected Greensboro lawyer J. D. Webb ran as a presidential elector pledged to Bell and maintaining the Union. The National Democrats were fortunate to have Harvey as their spokesman, pushing hard in his columns for Douglas' election. Breckinridge was the favored candidate of the most vocal Democrats and secessionists; in addition to Erwin, Guards' Captain Jones and Orderly Sergeant Hobson both openly backed Breckinridge.[16]

But virtually all Greensborians—no matter what their party—agreed on certain principles: opposition to Lincoln and support for Southerners' right to take slaves into the West. The decision came to hinge less on party differences than on which candidate had the most realistic chance of beating Lincoln and securing slave property. Douglas advocated popular sovereignty as a matter of practicality and, at least for Harvey, preservation of the Union. Bell backers in Alabama, unlike other states, came out so stridently for federal protection of slavery that Breckinridge supporters charged theft. The latter also announced simply that the election of Lincoln would be sufficient cause for secession. Here was the only issue in which the Breckinridge Democrats genuinely parted company from the other two parties. In central Alabama at least, a vote for Breckinridge was a vote to secede.[17]

As in other times of crisis, the presidential election raised afresh Greensborians' long-standing fears of slave insurrections. One Sunday morning in June, a domestic servant named Henry shot a visitor at the Uniontown home of a Mr. Nicolson. Thus, Greensborians were ready to believe vague reports of problems in Selma and Talladega. Railroad hands and nearby slaves were about to start a "rising," someone said. Greensboro's regular and volunteer slave patrols went out and performed their duties adequately. The crisis culminated when the patrols caught a slave away from his plantation without a pass—spending the night in bed with his wife.[18] Everyone rested easier.

Election day passed quietly. True to its Whig tradition, Greene County gave the majority of its vote to Bell, who received 765 votes to Breckinridge's 696 and Douglas' 157. In Greensboro, the majority was even stronger: 203 for Bell, 122 for Breckinridge, and 60 for Douglas. The Mount Hebron Precinct recorded 21 votes for Bell, 26 for Breckinridge, and 5 for Douglas, while Newbern, deep in the Canebrake, recorded 5, 18, and 4, respectively.[19] Such a trend suggests (but by no means proves) that rural areas with fewer institutions and large majorities of slaves were more attracted to Breckinridge's unambiguous message than was Greensboro, a commercial center. Of course, a few hundred votes in Greensboro, Alabama, mattered not at all to Lincoln, who won the presidency with the support of almost two million Americans. But Greensboro's votes and who cast them mattered a great deal to Greensborians.

Rashly reacting to Senator Douglas' defeat, Harvey precipitated a confrontation. His editorials in the *Beacon* blamed those Southern Democrats, led by Yancey and Erwin, who had broken up the convention at Charleston, divided the party, and allowed the Republicans to win. Now these same Southern Democrats, he charged, were breaking up the Union by declaring that the mere election of Lincoln was sufficient cause to secede. As if to prove his point, the *Beacon*'s columns printed the presidential election results alongside calls for a state convention whose sole task would be to decide Alabama's future relationship with the United States. Aghast, the editor continued his charges in the next week's issue. Under the headline "Is the Election of Lincoln Good Cause for a Dissolution of the Union?" Harvey vowed to oppose "with all the energy that we can bring to bear" any movement toward secession. Two columns away, the editor printed a letter written by "Brush Creek," who claimed devotion to the South's interests in every particular but also confessed alarm at those who supported immediate and unqualified resistance. Brush Creek understood, as few others did, that the Southern states would lose their moral authority by seceding and thus violating the Constitution they claimed to uphold. He counseled patience: "Should we not look at the thing calmly and dispassionately?—count well the cost? Consider whether it will add to or detract from our liberty, happiness or prosperity? . . . Do we not need time to cool off?" The *Beacon* was becoming a Unionist mouthpiece. Harvey invited all those who believed the Union worth preserving to convene on the following Saturday, November 17. He had gone too far.[20]

Instead of rallying the Unionists, the editor's call incited the Disunionists. Handbills announcing the meeting were torn down, some by Erwin. And when the Unionists finally met, the outcome was hardly as Harvey had planned. After the group came to order, Judge Sydenham Moore immediately asked for the floor. This respected and well-educated U.S. congressman had led the Eutaw Rangers to Mexico and was well tied to Greensboro, having married Guard E. L. Hobson's sister. Judge Moore stressed the importance of the South's speaking with one voice. He then proposed that the question of disunion be deferred until a public meeting could be held. Harvey replied that the difference of opinion and purpose was too wide and alluded to the gulf between his feelings and those of the judge. Moore responded that he would further widen the breach by stating publicly his supreme contempt for Harvey. The bickering continued until the formerly moderate Webb led the Disunionists out from what they termed a "nest of black republicans." Speech making continued in the street.[21]

The Disunionists began canceling their subscriptions to the *Beacon* and taking steps to publish their own newspaper. They contacted William Henry Fowler, a former state legislator at various times associated with the *Eutaw Whig* and the *Tuscaloosa Monitor*, about establishing a Southern-rights press in Greensboro. Fowler had joined the Greensboro Guards during the 1840s. He responded with an open letter, published in the *Beacon*, detailing how he and the other Constitutional Unionists who had voted for the moderate Bell were now ready to respond to the North's fanaticism with action. "In the masses of our people, with slight exception, there seems to be but one voice." The people demand resistance, he explained, the only question being whether to wait for the combined action of all the Southern states or whether Alabamians should secede immediately and unilaterally. Fowler prudently declined to state which he preferred. But Greensborians must act, for "if we falter now," he declared, "shall we not deserve the contempt of those who have been our friends, and of all mankind?"[22]

The same issue of the *Beacon* contained a personal notice from Harvey announcing that after seventeen years as proprietor and editor, he had sold his newspaper to Fowler, a regrettable circumstance forced by his subscribers' strong antagonism to his Unionist principles. In order to distance himself from his painful decision, Harvey began referring to himself in the third person: "Without a sacrifice of his honest convictions, he could not shape the course of the Beacon so as to make it acceptable to many of its oldest patrons. . . . he must act as the emergency demands.—To sacrifice his principles, on the alt[a]r of expediency, or to change his opinions merely because he finds them unpopular with his readers,—is a course the undersigned has never yet pursued,—nor will self-respect allow him to do so now."[23]

The editorial policy of the newspaper decided, the Disunionists met on the following Saturday, November 24, in Dorman Hall, with Captain Jones presiding. Judge Moore introduced for consideration the Mobile Resolutions, which stated bluntly that Lincoln's election, "a virtual overthrow of the Constitution and of the equal rights of the States," required Alabama to "withdraw from the Federal Union without any further delay." The resolutions passed.[24]

"This people is apparently gone crazy," concluded Unionist Serano Watson; "I do not know how to account for it & have no idea what will be the end of it." He complained of a campaign to "browbeat & bully into silence those whom they cannot persuade to go with them & so to make it appear that there is but one opinion throughout the South." A few Unionists may indeed have been forcibly silenced. Dr. William T. Blackford self-righteously boasted a decade later that he had been placed on trial for his Unionist sympathies by a vigilance committee that spared his life only after friends intervened. But Harvey's prominence as a Unionist newspaper editor makes it easy to exaggerate such incidents. While some firebrands were indeed outraged, other Greensborians wrote of a deep sense of gloom. Then sentiment began to coalesce. Douglas, Bell, and Breckinridge supporters alike loudly proclaimed their refusal to submit to a Lincoln administration, a position that left them nowhere to turn but secession. A "great many who before the election professed to be Union men," wrote Serano Watson, moved "more or less completely" to join the Disunionists. Serano's brother, Henry, observed that within a few weeks, Greensboro's gloom had been replaced by a calm demeanor that signaled a "unanimity of sentiment." Residents had been convinced, not coerced. Serano Watson advised his friends in the North that the people were now secessionists almost to a man. What few Union supporters were left could now only advise delaying until enough states seceded together to form a respectable government with cooler heads to run it. "I have ceased to expect that Reason will resume her sway," wrote Serano Watson, and blood, he was now sure, would be shed: "From my knowledge of this people I know they are not to be *conquered*, they may possibly be *annihilated*." All were ready to resist Lincoln's disposition to interfere with slavery. Not even a constitutional amendment guaranteeing the institution would satisfy them. One could as easily dam the Mississippi.[25]

Governor Moore took the first formal step toward resisting Lincoln when he called a December 24 election for delegates to a secession convention. The opposing factions quickly split between Cooperationists and Immediate Secessionists. Cooperationists in certain mountainous counties of Alabama may have opposed secession altogether, but in Greene County, as in the rest of the Black Belt, Cooperationists favored secession and disagreed with their Immediatist opponents only over the tactics to achieve independence, arguing instead for a combined action of all the Southern states. Immediatists, as their name implied, counseled Alabama to "resume" its independence unilaterally and immediately; the new republic might— and probably would—subsequently unite with other former states to form a larger country. The decision to secede would not follow traditional Whig-Democrat divisions.[26]

Two delegates from each county would be elected to the convention. The Cooperationists nominated William P. Webb from the county seat, Eutaw, and Algernon Sydney Jeffries from Greensboro; the Immediatists nominated Thomas Hord Herndon from Eutaw and J. D. Webb from Greensboro. The two Webbs were brothers, lawyers, and members of Greensboro's Masonic lodge, although one was a Cooperationist and the other an Immediatist. All four were well-educated slaveholders. Indeed, nothing in the backgrounds of Greene County's four candidates distinguished one from another.[27] The candidates chosen, the campaign began. But no matter which side was speaking, the mantra was unity, unity, unity.

"We are *one people* in interest, suffering and destiny—let us be but *one people* in maintaining our rights and redressing our grievances," proclaimed local Methodist minister J. J. Hutchinson in an address commissioned by thirty-nine Greensborians, seventeen of them Guards. "Let us be united," the Reverend Hutchinson continued. "Unite here to-day,—unite with the people of Greensboro—unite throughout Greene county—unite throughout Alabama—unite throughout the South." He stressed that the people's unity grew from commonly suffered wrongs and from the resolve to redress the slander. The only divisions concerned the timing and manner of withdrawal from the Union. But once the choice was made, all individual preferences must be relinquished: "Let us present a firm and undivided phalanx to a common foe." The determined sacrifices, calm, and courage of the Founding Fathers had produced a glorious union of states, but those advantages and memories lay in the past. "In the *present state of things* we will disrupt these bonds of Union once so dear, now a badge of shame and degradation." On the whole, however, Hutchinson counseled Greensborians to act with deliberation. Immediate secession might result in the loss of arsenals, forts, arms, and vast western territories and could even precipitate a war. But Southerners held a lever that could move the world: "COTTON IS KING," indeed, "KING OF THE WORLD!" The South should lock up its warehouses and "defy the world!" Northern laborers would be thrown out of employment; England and France would be humbled; the convulsion would shake the world from the hills of Caledonia to the mines of Australia. All must act together. "Union! union! not in the Federal compact, but among ourselves, is the great object now to be effected."[28]

Immediatist candidate J. D. Webb penned an open letter generally echoing Hutchinson's sentiments but calling for the South to waste no more time. The mere election of Mr. Lincoln, the former Bell supporter declared, was sufficient cause for secession. His address, like so many others, was replete with stock phrases asserting the state government's responsibilities. These included taking measures to secure "the blessings of government" as well as Alabamians' "rights to their property in a manner consistent with their honor and safety as free men." And if anyone failed to understand which property he meant, Webb laid it out: "we cannot and will not consent to continue under a government, the powers of which are to be wielded by those who are hostile in feeling and in sentiment to negro slavery and are to be arraigned in antagonism to so large and valuable a property interest as we own in slaves." He concluded that secession, "with all its consequences is not only inevitable but desirable."[29]

The *Beacon*'s new editor, William Henry Fowler, added more coals to the fire by reprinting his own lengthy address entitled "The Times and Our Duty." The first part of his speech included the usual denunciations of the fanatical North as having grown "fat with wealth and impudent with power" by electing a sectional president determined to destroy slavery and now primed to destroy the republic. Then Fowler revealed himself as an Immediatist, denouncing moderation, for under its cloak the Black Republicans had subverted the Constitution. The South's salvation lay in its own hands. The South was strong, blessed with fertile and diverse soil, enterprising citizens, undeveloped resources, and above all else the institution of slavery. Bound labor had given the South the staples of commerce and industry that kept English looms running and millions from revolting. The presence of slaves in the South had held back the tide of vandal immigrants who would call out for a communal property. But most important, expanding on ideas of inclusion and exclusion, slavery had created "a common bond of perpetual fraternity, . . . the deep foundation stone of Republican liberty." Slavery had created a homogeneous white Republic of the South, "bound together by inalienable ties of sympathy and love and resistance to a common oppression." This was worth fighting for.[30]

Elections for the Alabama Convention were held on Christmas Eve. Greene County as a whole recorded 638 votes for Immediate Secessionist candidates J. D. Webb and Herndon; 470 voted for the Cooperationist candidates Jeffries and William P. Webb. (These results were consistent with those of Alabama's other Black Belt counties, all of which elected Immediatists.) The town of Greensboro recorded 203 votes for the Immediatists and 132 for the Cooperationists. J. D. Webb and Herndon left for the Alabama Convention in Montgomery, where, on January 11, they voted with the majority to remove Alabama's star from the Stars and Stripes and to fly it alone. The next day Webb sat down to write to his wife in Greensboro. The events of the day before, when Alabama formally withdrew from the Union, remained vividly on his mind. Some of the delegates had refused to vote for the Ordinance of Secession because of prior pledges to their constituents. But times had changed, and now the delegates felt vindicated before the world. They vowed their loyalty to the sovereign Republic of Alabama, pledging (in an allusion to the Declaration of Independence) their lives, their fortunes, and their sacred honor to the newly independent state.[31]

Serano Watson was writing a letter to his young niece when word of Alabama's independence reached him in Greensboro. He inquired if she understood that several Southern states had left the Union and had taken over all federal properties within their borders except Fort Sumter in Charleston Harbor and Fort Pickens in Pensacola Bay. Even before the state seceded, Alabama's governor had ordered state troops to seize the U.S. arsenal at Mount Vernon, less than thirty miles north of Mobile, and the two forts guarding the mouth of Mobile Bay. Watson fully appreciated the irony of his fellow townspeople celebrating their social solidarity newly forged out of secession. "We are no longer one people," he concluded privately, even as Greensborians were noisily proclaiming that they had at last become one people.[32]

★ ★ ★

While the convention deliberated, the Greensboro Guards received orders to join the garrison at Fort Morgan, the larger of Alabama's two newly appropriated forts. With only two days' notice, the Guards were having to leave their families and businesses. No one knew how long the company would be gone. Learning that the families of some of the Guards would suffer during their absence, Captain Jones called a town meeting that raised fourteen hundred dollars from forty-three contributors for the families' aid. After a sad parting, fifty-seven Guards headed out of Greensboro on Sunday morning, January 13, 1861. At Eastport along the Black Warrior River, a gentleman of some seventy years approached the captain to enlist his only son and two grandsons in the Guards. Unable to restrain his tears, the old man confessed that he did not cry because his boys were going but because he was too old to go himself. The Guards boarded the steamer *Cherokee* for Mobile, where correspondents from the Mobile newspapers described the group as "picked men, the flower of the lusty youth and stallwart manhood." In their ranks were to be found wealthy planters, merchants, professional men, and skilled artisans—"worthy representatives of the most useful classes in a civilized community." The correspondent estimated that the company members had a combined worth of more than a million dollars. Their merit, however, lay not in their wealth but in their "sense of honor and fine moral character." Of particular note was their black drummer, London Dufphey, who was said to be almost as well known in the state as any white man. "Old Lon" had pounded his huge blue drum during the War of 1812, during the Creek War of 1836, and for the Greensboro Volunteers in Mexico.[33]

The honor and moral character of the Guards is not the material of measurement, but the Mobile correspondents' description of the Guards' vocations and wealth is. Most of the Guards, whose average age was twenty-three, were artisans or professionals. Only about a quarter of the company lived on farms or plantations. The Guards were distinguished not only by their prosperity but also by their immediate ties to slavery: at least half came from slaveholding families. In general, those Guards who left for Fort Morgan in January 1861 were settled and successful citizens of Greensboro.[34]

The Guards reached Fort Morgan on Tuesday, January 15. They enjoyed splendid weather and a constant sea breeze. During the day, the men strolled along the beach, and at night they gathered to sing. One of the Guards set "My Green[e] County Home" to the tune of "Old Virginia." Before they could finish singing the song, however, about half the company stopped to wipe tears from their eyes. Another night, about a hundred soldiers went up on the ramparts to watch the moon rise above the Gulf of Mexico. With guitars accompanying, they again sang: "when the base joyned in I could feel a cold chill creap all over me," wrote Jules Honoré Bayol to his mother; "we all feel like Brothers here."[35]

The Guards did more than just swim and sing, of course; they stood watch—and hated it. Six sentinels alternated between two hours walking and four hours resting. After twenty-four hours, the sentinels were relieved of duty, but the boredom continued. The officers instituted dress parades to add variety, but one correspondent confessed that he had not learned any new ideas about military precision from observing these maneuvers. Every day the soldiers observed boats loaded with armed men on their way eastward to the siege of Fort Pickens; the Mississippians looked particularly rough. While reclining around the fire one evening, the Guards heard the roar of what sounded like a cannon from about a mile off, followed by two more blasts and finally the sound of a bursting shell. The sentinels immediately fired their weapons, the long roll was beaten, and the cry "To arms" sounded. In five minutes

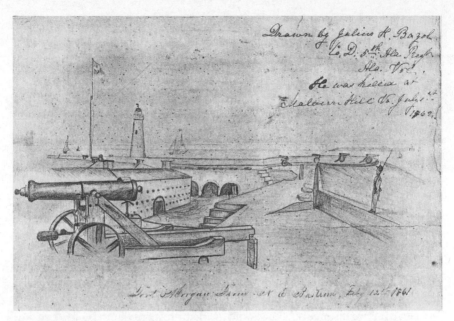

"Fort Morgan From N E Bastion, Feby 12th 1861," by Guard Jules Honoré Bayol. (Courtesy Alabama Department of Archives and History, Montgomery)

the troops were on the parapet, ready to meet the enemy. The attack turned out to have been the production of some officers who thought that the troops' readiness for duty needed testing. They stood the test well.[36]

While the Guards wasted weeks at Fort Morgan, delegates from the southernmost states met in Montgomery to construct their new nation. The Provisional Confederate Congress organized on February 4 and four days later approved the new constitution (modeled on the 1789 U.S. Constitution but with stronger protection of slave ownership and a few other anomalies). The delegates elected the provisional vice president and president the next day, and on February 18, with a band playing "Dixie," Jefferson Davis was inaugurated as president of the Confederate States of America on Alabama's statehouse portico.

The Guards missed all this excitement, but just barely, receiving orders to pack up their bags within days of the inauguration. Greensborians expected their soldiers to arrive home on the morning of February 22—appropriately for the Guards, George Washington's birthday. Businesses closed that Friday, and the townspeople gathered at the west end of Main Street. Many sent wagons and carriages to the landing at Eastport for the Guards' convenience, but when a messenger came up the road bringing word that the company's arrival would not occur before evening, all went home disappointed. Fanny Erwin, wife of Guard George W. Erwin (John Erwin's son), was ready to sit down to dinner when she heard the firing of a cannon, signaling the Guards' approach. So off she flew, "with hurried step and beating heart," along with everyone else, from Main Street to the most remote corners of town. The excitement grew as the rattle of the drum came louder and as the Guards' escort, the Greensboro Cavalry, first came into sight. The cheers and huzzahs could not be restrained. Amid reverberating booms and clouds of smoke, the cannon roared "Welcome Home" to the returning company. "Ladies, negroes, & children—such a motley crowd you never saw," wrote Fanny Erwin. Captain Jones (related to Fanny Erwin by both blood and marriage) marched the Guards up to the speaker's stand, where J. D. Webb delivered a handsome short speech. The crowd cheered, and the captain responded with appropriate words about how such a manifestation of support would steel their hearts in times of danger. The entire town then formed a procession and paraded up the street, making "the noise of as many armies as could be raked & scraped up, the firing of cannon, & ringing of all the bells in town. I was not so excited in all my life," confessed Fanny Erwin, "it was as much as I could do to keep myself from crying & screaming out." The *Beacon* was nearly as effusive: "Greensboro ne'er saw such another sight."[37]

The celebrations honoring the Guards did not end with the parade and speeches. The next day the ladies began preparing for a supper, which expanded into a grand soiree by the time it was held on March 5. An immense crowd of townspeople gathered at the newly opened Southern University, joined by citizens from Eutaw, Newbern, Demopolis, and the Canebrake. The Guards headed out to meet the Marion Rifles, who had also been at Fort Morgan, and escorted them to the armory. That evening the two companies assembled as a battalion and performed military maneuvers for the assembled crowd. Then came the supper honoring the citizen-soldiers. Afterward, many couples moved on to the town hall, where they danced to fiddle tunes far into the night.[38]

The weeks in Fort Morgan had been delightful if boring, the return glorious. If secession was about bathing in the gulf and parties in Greensboro, then the South should have taken these steps earlier. Yet few believed that the process could be this easy. The uncertainty of the times had already convinced some people to stop buying slaves. And, as if the cause needed a defense, the *Beacon*'s new editor continued his bluster: "In the maintenance of our rights and all that is dear to us, we will show to the world that we are freemen," wrote Fowler after the Guards' return. "Our citizens will make themselves soldiers, and beat their plow-shares into swords, and the pruning-hooks into spears, as weapons of defence—we will teach despots that all freedom is not a dream." He jabbed at the "miserable croakers" who had warned that the wealthy would not shoulder arms in defense of an independent Alabama. There were privates in the Guards, he boasted, who would not seek higher rank and who owned more slaves than all the croakers put together. "And, if need be, their negroes will follow them to the field in defence of Southern honor—*and make better and more reliable soldiers, too, by all odds, than the North can raise!*"[39] These were heady times. Doubts had been replaced by the joyous conviction that the people were—at last—one.

CHAPTER 6

# Greene County's Still

I have united my destiny with the company.

★ J. D. Webb, 1861

March 4, 1861. In Washington, Abraham Lincoln stood on the Capitol steps to deliver his inaugural address. He avowed his intention not to interfere with the institution of slavery where it already existed, declared the Union perpetual and incapable of division, and appealed to all Americans to remember the "mystic chords of memory" that linked them all. ("Very warlike" judged Greensborians.) In Montgomery, the Confederate Congress hoisted a new flag, while Greensboro's J. D. Webb called on President Jefferson Davis and pronounced him an affable conversationalist. In the Canebrake, planter Philip Henry Pitts recorded the day in his diary just as he did any other: "The day Lincoln was inaugurated—I paid Deason's two accounts to see Terrell, one Dental account for $53.00 and Dray account for $16.$^{\underline{59}}$ making 69$^{\underline{59}}$." And in Greensboro, "the 4 March has come & passed and we see no change here," wrote Henry Watson to his mother in Connecticut. "All things go on in the old way."[1]

And yet new breezes were blowing. Despite repeated declarations that he feared neither slaves nor war, Watson began to think about closing the Planter's Insurance Company, Greensboro's only bank, for the collection of debts had almost ceased. (The final closure would, nonetheless, take several more years.) Income from his plantation had fallen off by thousands of dollars. The editorship of the *Alabama Beacon* was also changing. William Henry Fowler resigned to take a brief appointment in the militia before joining Tuscaloosa's Warrior Guards, with whom he had already served at Fort Morgan. His rather surprising replacement was John G. Harvey. The former editor explained that his earlier opposition to secession had arisen not from a lack of devotion to the South but from the conviction that disunion was not in the South's best interest. But the past was decided. Loyal citizens such as he were now obligated to recognize and support this new Confederate government. With this brief apology, Harvey asked to take leave of the subject.[2]

While Greensborians could ignore Lincoln's inauguration, his actions commanded their attention. President Lincoln was determined that both Fort Pickens and Fort Sumter remain in Union hands, while President Davis was equally determined that these symbols of Federal authority should fall. The Union forces at Fort Pickens could be reinforced, but Fort Sumter was in a much more precarious position. With relief ships nearing and Union Major Robert Anderson still refusing to surrender, the Confederate artillery batteries opened fire at 4:30 on the morning of Friday, April 12.

The news reached Greensboro the next day. One Southern University student walked off into the woods to pray. Fifty-one other young men immediately joined the Greensboro Guards.[3]

Within a short time, the Guards reached their full strength of a hundred (an additional thirty others had applied unsuccessfully). The *Beacon* proudly observed that these new Guards (all but twenty-five of whom had not been to Fort Morgan) included men of all professions, ages, and political opinions (before secession, of course). Robert Jeffries, whose father had run unsuccessfully as Greensboro's Co-operationist candidate for the secession convention, had been among the first to sign up. One father joined with his two sons. Three brothers marched side by side. Only sixteen Guards can be directly linked to farming or planting. Most were, like the Fort Morgan Guards, artisans or professionals: thirteen clerks, seven in the healing arts, five merchants, and two lawyers. The negative information is even more revealing. Only three of the fifty-three Fort Morgan Guards failed to leave their names in the census or elsewhere, but fifteen of the seventy-five new Guards left no records. The occupations of only fifteen of the Fort Morgan Guards were unrecorded, but a remarkably large fifty-five of the new Guards did not list what they did. Twenty-four of the fifty-three Fort Morgan Guards were married in 1860, but only fourteen new Guards were married, and fifty were living with their parents. Whereas half the Fort Morgan Guards had come from slaveholding families, the figure fell to less than 40 percent of those Guards who went to Virginia—a figure suggesting that the earlier group was wealthier and more closely tied to planting. Those who entered Confederate service included fewer town leaders, heads of households, and men with permanent occupations. In short, going to war was another opportunity—for glory, for exhilaration, for a future—that young, unattached men might have found attractive. They were headed off to prove themselves, as their fathers had set off for the Alabama frontier.[4]

After Captain Allen C. Jones formally tendered the Greensboro Guards to the state's service, the company set up camp north of town and prepared for the governor's response. While waiting, many Guards began writing journals and letters in which they reported their activities and examined their motives. These records were often the products of well-educated individuals (a half dozen had studied at the University of Virginia and at least that many practiced in medical professions) and thus exhibited a certain literary quality.[5]

The first words of John H. Cowin's diary were straightforward enough: "After the election of Abraham Lincoln to the presidency of the United States by the abolitionists of the North it became evident to the people of the South that their rights would not be respected, and that every thing would be done to break down the peculiar institutions of the South, they therefore determined to separate themselves from a government so inimical to their interests." The Alabama-born Cowin had earned a medical degree from Jefferson University in Philadelphia, one of the country's most prestigious medical schools, not long before he chose to return to the South. He knew that by joining the Guards he was embarking on a new and dramatic chapter in his life. Dr. Cowin continued his account by listing the events—from South Carolina's withdrawal to Fort Sumter's bombardment to Lincoln's call for troops—that led up to April 22, when the reorganized Greensboro Guards went into camp and elected their officers.[6]

J. D. Webb, a former delegate to the Alabama Convention, also joined the Guards. Marching around camp in a little blue jacket and gray pants, he was deemed the jolliest man in the company. But he turned serious when writing to his wife. Webb instructed Justina to tell their children that he had not chosen to fight but was off to defend the honor of his country and preserve for them "the blessings of civil liberty [and] the equal rights of all free white men." From the beginning, he

The Selma Blues, later Company D of the Eighth Alabama. (Courtesy Alabama Department of Archives and History, Montgomery)

and those like him linked slavery to personal rights, expressing the constitutional right to own slaves as "the equal rights of all free white men." Because slaves were neither free nor white, the phrase conveniently defended racial slavery without mentioning the term. And because white citizens enjoyed a multiplicity of rights, such appeals raised slave ownership to a par with the Bill of Rights and the right of free people to establish their own government.[7] Webb would return to the problem of justifying the war, and with each reconsideration, the defense of slavery would recede while broad (and increasingly vague) ideas of liberty grew. He was hardly unique. Over the course of the next four years, and indeed for decades thereafter, Greensborians would pause to reflect on why they had gone to war. But in the winter and spring of 1861, the issues were unclouded by doubt.

Captain Jones received the orders the Guards anticipated, and on Sunday morning, May 5, they broke camp, said their good-byes, and set off for Montgomery. Devoted mothers and loving sisters shed tears. Indulgent fathers gave advice. Friends wished the Guards safe passage. All asked God for protection. Then the citizens of Greensboro conveyed their soldiers by carriage or wagon to Newbern, where the company drilled for the locals before spending the night. The next morning, the Guards stood beneath the new Confederate flag at the Newbern depot. Again, mothers cried as their beardless boys stepped onto the train. Many a "God bless you" was heard. One woman penned a poem for the occasion.

> God's blessings on our noble "Guards,"
>    In *life* or *death*, we shrine them now
> Within the temple of our hearts,
>    And weave love's chaplet round each brow,
> And pledge success with glad huzzahs,
> To their proud flag of Stars and Bars

The people raised three hearty cheers in anticipation of the Guards' return, the conductor called "All aboard!" and the soldiers found seats in the open car. As the train moved out, the men gave out three cheers for Newbern and three more for the ladies. Captain Jones proposed three more cheers for "the old county of Greene" (as if it had been founded four centuries before and not four decades). The hearty response came both from those sons born on Greene's soil and from those who had chosen the county as their home. "With care thrown to the winds," they moved off. Families at the depot watched, waved, and listened until the huzzahs and singing gradually faded.[8] The adventure was under way.

Two hours later, after stopping in Uniontown, the company reached Selma, where smiling citizens greeted the soldiers with more cheering. A half dozen young men there approached Captain Jones, asked to join the company, and were accepted. The Phoenix Fire Company and the Selma Blues then escorted their Greensboro comrades to a cotton warehouse overlooking the Alabama River that would serve as quarters. The Tuscaloosa Warrior Guards and the Livingston Rifles joined the boys from Greene, and together they drilled for several days. Early Wednesday morning, the three companies boarded the steamboat *Southern Republic,* where they found already on board the Grove Hill Guards and the Cahaba Rifles. The boat was so crowded with about 460 soldiers that the Guards had to eat on the lower deck with the horses. Arriving in Montgomery late in the day, the troops marched to Camp Jeff. Davis at the fairgrounds and pitched their tents. Alabama's adjutant general ordered the troops to organize themselves by electing field officers. From the four companies aboard the *Southern Republic* and six others, the Fifth Alabama Infantry Regiment was established:

Company A—Grove Hill Guards (Captain Josephus M. Hall)
Company B—Livingston Rifles (Captain John Hubbard Dent)
Company C—Pickensville Blues (Captain Sampson Noland Ferguson)
Company D—Monroe Guards (Captain Giles Goode)
Company E—Talladega Artillery (Captain Charles Miller Shelley)
Company F—Sumter Rifle Guard (Captain Robert P. Blount)
Company G—Cahaba Rifles (Captain John Tyler Morgan/Christopher Claudius Pegues)
Company H—Warrior Guards (Captain Robert E. Rodes/William Henry Fowler)
Company I—Greensboro Guards (Captain Allen C. Jones/Edwin Lafayette Hobson)
Company K—Mobile Continental State Artillery (Captain William H. Ketchum)[9]

This would be the last time the regiment could field its full strength of one thousand.

The Fifth Alabama elected Robert Emmett Rodes as its first colonel, and Fowler, the former *Beacon* editor, succeeded Rodes as captain of Tuscaloosa's Warrior Guards. Rodes had graduated from the Virginia Military Institute before coming to Alabama as a civil engineer for the Northeast and Southwest Railroad. Greensboro's Jones was elected lieutenant colonel, and Edwin Lafayette Hobson took over as captain of the Greensboro Guards. Rodes appointed Webb regimental quartermaster. "I have united my destiny with the company," he wrote to his wife.[10]

Once organized, the Fifth Alabama left by rail to join the siege of Fort Pickens. Florida's governor, following the examples of South Carolina and Alabama, ordered his troops to take the defenses around Pensacola Bay. Before that could happen, however, Union soldiers and sailors abandoned all the forts except Fort Pickens on Santa Rosa Island, at the same time destroying more than twenty thousand pounds of powder and spiking the guns at the other forts. The Floridians laid siege and asked for help from neighboring states. Louisiana, Mississippi, Georgia, and Alabama troops poured into the area, occupying the forts and batteries that the Federal forces had abandoned. Because Fort Pickens was accessible from the gulf, the Federal troops were able to hold out, and that was how the situation stood when the Greensboro Guards arrived at daybreak on May 13. The men set up camp about a quarter mile from town and some two hundred yards from the bay. The next day they cleared the ground for drilling. "So here commences our campaign in earnest," wrote Dr. Cowin.[11]

The Guards found Pensacola unimpressive. The town was dirty, and its inhabitants—exotic combinations of French, Spanish, and African—all lived in low-built houses. The laborers and tradesmen, with a few exceptions, cared nothing for the soldiers except as a source of profit. The boredom of camp life only increased the Alabamians' exasperation. They bathed in the bay before breakfast. During the day they drilled awkwardly in the sand before dress parade at six. After supper, some of the boys would break out their banjos, violins, and flutes to accompany the others in singing. Tattoo was set for nine o'clock.[12]

The sight of the Union flag flying above Fort Pickens a mile across the bay irked like a hangnail. The soldiers had arrived expecting to attack but found themselves merely waiting and watching their frustration grow.

> Just let Col Rodes take the 5th Regt down
> And we'll give the Yankees one good round
> We'll soon force 'em out, and then you'll hear 'em cry
> Good bye Fort Pickens we've got to root hog or die.
>
> The Greensboro boys are anxious for a fight
> With Hobson in the lead and Dedman all right
> We'll soon show the Yankees if we'll only try
> How quick we can learn 'em to sing, root hog or die.

Such doggerel helped to pass the time, but everyone knew that nothing was going on in Pensacola and that everything seemed to be happening in Virginia.[13]

Rejoicing and mass disorder erupted when orders were read out transferring the regiment to Virginia. The Guards immediately struck their tents and gathered up the sick. Leaving the Continental Artillery behind, the nine remaining companies left the hot sands of Pensacola on June 2. After a day in Montgomery, they boarded tightly packed boxcars for the long journey northward. Pretty ladies greeted the soldiers at depots, waving flags; offering cakes, sweetmeats, and other delicacies; and throwing flowers or bits of poetry. One Georgia beauty told Bill Britton that she would never marry a man whose face had not been tanned by the sun in fighting for his country. The crowd cheered and waved handkerchiefs. North of Dalton, the railroad kept mostly in the valleys, now and then creeping along the side of a mountain or through a tunnel. Horses, herds of Devon and Durham cattle, and flocks of sheep grazed in the clover and bluegrass. "My eyes never beheld such a country before," wrote Sergeant Joseph Borden to his wife, Fannie. "Switzerland it seems to me cannot surpass it." At Knoxville, the soldiers heard former presidential candidate John Bell speak in favor of secession. They saw the Stars and Stripes a few miles later at Strawberry Plains, and before the day was over Unionists fired at the Confederates. But on the whole, this was a promising start. The country they were to defend was beautiful, and with minor exceptions, the people were hailing the soldiers as heroes—before they had fired a shot. That seven Guards had to be left along the way, sick with measles, boded other unanticipated misfortunes.[14]

A week and a day after breaking camp in Pensacola, the regiment reached Richmond. The men quickly found a church and collapsed in sleep. With no food to be found and with citizens suspicious of the ten or twelve thousand soldiers stationed in their midst, the men found themselves unwelcome—a decided contrast from their receptions in Selma and other towns. The Guards could hardly be special among untold other companies. The Fifth Alabama was first given a camp at an unshaded racetrack a mile and a half from the city; then, on June 18, they boarded railroad cars once again. The train headed north until it stopped late that night and the soldiers got off and started walking. The weather remained hot; the roads were rough, broken, and dusty; and the ground was far from level. After about seven miles, the Alabamians finally pitched their tents. The Guards were unsure of their location. They were told vaguely that they were at "a place called Stony bridge on Bull Run creek."[15]

The Guards' only concern was for food and drink, each in short supply. Good water was at least a mile away and food another mile beyond. Some men could not be bothered and simply took what they needed from the farmer on whose land they were encamped, an old Unionist who grumbled that they had drunk twenty gallons of his milk and eaten all of his butter. This site would not do, and the Fifth Alabama was soon ordered back some thirteen miles east, toward Fairfax Court House. At their new camp at Farr's Cross Roads along the Orange and Alexandria Railroad, the regiment added an infantry company from Barbour County, Captain Eugene Blackford's Barbour Greys (Company K), to fill the place of the Mobile artillery company left at Pensacola.[16]

The troops once again settled into a routine designed to make citizens into soldiers. They drilled hard in an old field full of stumps, stones, briers, and ditches. They built breastworks. And they started keeping irksome records of each man's comings and goings. At the end of each day they talked to each other about the news, sang, and wrote letters home. "I feel somewhat at a loss what to write you," Sergeant Borden disclosed to his wife, "locked up in the woods with nothing but the days work to occupy our mind." The men had been ordered to reduce baggage and dispose of books, although reading of the Bible continued and officers boned up on their military tactics. "The truth is a good soldier is a machine," Borden concluded, "worked at the option of the superior officers, and not always allowed to exercise the brain, like a clock when it has run down rests perfectly quiet."[17]

Everyone knew that a battle loomed, perhaps the one that would establish Southern independence once and for all. Northern artillery announced the Fourth of July, but not a Southern gun fired. After months of waiting, every Guard was anxious to fight and was getting more so every day. Jittery sentinels nearly fired on their own men. The Rebels read Washington newspapers reporting a Union advance. Once the Rebels were overrun, one paper boasted, it would be "On to Richmond."[18]

The Guards' initial encounter with Yankees was not, however, a great battle. On the morning of July 17, the Guards on picket duty engaged an advance party of

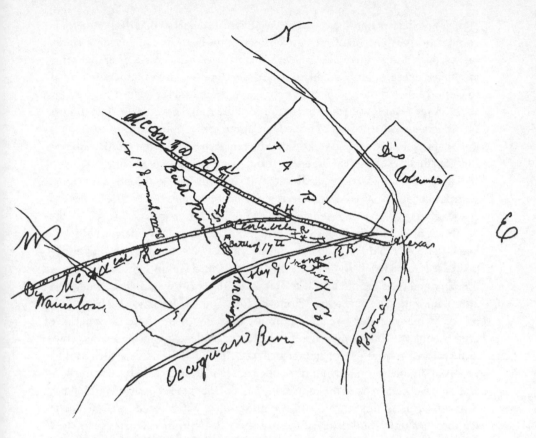

Guard Joseph Borden's sketch of Fairfax County, Virginia. He marked the Guards' camp near the railroad bridge with an asterisk. (Courtesy Winifred Borden)

Union troops and fired what the Confederates falsely believed were the first shots of the engagement. W. L. Kennedy stood in an open road and calmly pulled the trigger five times, killing two men, he believed, and wounding two others. (It was an audacious display that prompted Colonel Rodes to appoint Kennedy corporal and part of the color-bearer staff; thenceforth, the Greensboro Guards would carry the regiment's banner.) The enemy took eight shots at Kennedy and all missed. Joe Wright also stood and fired, bringing down one. And George Nutting refused to budge, even though his gun failed him. Such foolhardiness could be dismissed as youthful inexperience or perhaps the confidence of an individualist determined to control his own fate. Either way, such courage, if that be the word, would not keep men alive through the war. Scouts raced back to camp with warnings. Tents were struck, wagons loaded, and balls soon began whistling through the air. A couple of men from other companies were slightly wounded. Colonel Rodes was ready to stand and fight, but he had orders to pull the Fifth Alabama back. The soldiers reluctantly left the breastworks, as doing so was giving the enemy weeks of work.

Some Confederates hoped to be overtaken by the Federals so that the Southerners could stand and fight. Many men broke down in the heat and caught rides in passing wagons. Clothes, knapsacks, and even blankets were discarded. After two hours at Wilmer McLean's Ford on Bull Run, the order came to march another three miles to Union Mills, a station along the Orange and Alexandria Railroad.[19]

There the Guards waited. Artillery fire continued all the next day, while rumors spread of a great battle in which vastly outnumbered Confederate forces had repulsed the Union army. The Guards huddled in bushes where the railroad crossed Bull Run in order to prevent the enemy from gaining control of the line.[20]

The great confrontation finally came during breakfast on Sunday morning, July 21, when the Guards began to hear the boom of cannon two or three miles off. A courier arrived ordering General Richard B. Ewell to march his brigade to the north side of Bull Run near the Stone Bridge. As part of that brigade, the Fifth Alabama started a rapid forced march, but the order was countermanded, and they proceeded immediately to the battlefield. They passed within sight of the Fourth Alabama and their commander, General Barnard Bee (he would die that day, just after bestowing the appellation "Stonewall" on Thomas J. Jackson). The Guards passed by the wounded returning from the field, and their desire for vengeance grew. About one o'clock they finally reached the battlefield, only to see the "cowardly villains" retreating. But that incident was not the whole battle, which continued until late afternoon, when fresh Confederate forces arrived and struck the Federal right flank and rear; in the confusion, Yankee troops raced back to Washington. Rumors spread of duplicitous Yankees luring unwary Rebels with a Confederate flag and then unleashing artillery and musketry at short range. Other reports told of an enemy advance on the Fifth Alabama's former position at Union Mills, and the regiment was ordered back. About ten o'clock that night, the Guards arrived, having marched twenty miles. They fell onto their blankets and into a deep sleep.[21]

The day after the battle, Dr. Cowin rose so tired and sore that he could scarcely walk. He felt better after breakfast and decided to set out to see the battle's aftermath. The sight was shocking, even to a medical doctor. Many soldiers lay dead, with bullet holes in every part of their bodies. The wounded were being taken to the Union Mills depot, where many more would die. But the Confederates had seized a great trove of equipment: seventy-one pieces of artillery (including one particularly large gun they called Long Tom), two hundred wagons, horses, ambulances, blankets, much-needed minié muskets—"in short, every thing." More reports came in of Yankee troops who would not stop running until they got to Washington, of troops firing on their comrades to get them to stop running, of captured congressmen.[22]

The calculation of prisoners and materiel soon yielded to calculations of a different sort. "It was a great victory," wrote Sergeant Borden to Fannie, "but they had to yeald to the indomitable courage of our troops." The Yankees were probably not satisfied, and their return was expected. "I would to God they would become satisfied and . . . let the people go home and attend to various occupations and peace reign throughout the land." Notwithstanding his earlier jingoistic oratory, J. D. Webb was shaken. "I saw wounded men of our side every where it was terrible to be sure. I saw occasionally friends bearing off the body of a deceased comrade." Webb's secessionist colleague, Sydenham Moore, admitted to his wife that a great many of his friends and acquaintances from Alabama and elsewhere had been killed or wounded: "The dead lie thick on the ground."[23]

Encounters with enemy prisoners were puzzling. Webb's "blood c[o]ursed warm" when he looked on Union men who were so wicked as to attack and "attempt to reduce to their subjection a people who desire only to be freemen & the equals of freemen." Dr. Cowin found four or five hundred Yankee prisoners confined in a large pen, many of them immigrants for whom he had great distaste. As they passed by Cowin's tent, one prisoner remarked, "Good bye boys I left home to go to Richmond and by ——— I am going." Sergeant Borden asked the prisoners why they fought, and many responded that they were fighting to uphold their flag and preserve the Union. But others, perhaps trying to tell their captors what they wanted to hear, reported being deceived into going to war. A few prisoners said that they had nothing to do at home and had joined the army to keep from starving and that they had nothing against the South. One man asked if there were any paper mills in the South where he could find employment.[24]

Such expressions prodded Borden to reconsider the nature of the conflict and to conclude that "the Rulers consider the war as a means of employing those that are idle, to prevent disturbances at home." The Union should instead have used the money spent on prosecuting the war to relieve the poor. And Northerners might again try to reconcile with the South, "to whom they are indebted for their prosperity, and the loss of which has driven them to such desperation. Fanaticism rules the day," he judged. Borden's speculations hinged on his inability to believe that most Union citizens would object to the South's going its own way. He could surmise only that secession had left the North without an economic base, vulnerable to dictators who robbed the people's liberties. The South, conversely, "will be able to stand it, fight it out, and not only sustain our own independence, but perhaps give it to them that now know not what it is." And then he added a curious statement: "I am every day more conscious that negro slavery is only the ostensible object for which this war is waged."[25] What had been so simple back in Greensboro seemed less so on the battlefield.

✭ ✭ ✭

The citizens back in Greene County swelled with pride and confidence. In Concord the Reverend T. S. Winn gave a rousing sermon to his Presbyterian congregation that likened the Confederate victory at Manassas to David and the Israelites' victory over Goliath and the Philistines. A Greensboro town father observed that he "never saw the community more orderly & law abiding." Greensborians were busily assisting their young men in uniform. Financial contributions spontaneously began flowing in even before the Guards reached Montgomery, and citizens meeting at the town hall soon formally established a fund for the Guards' benefit. After sixty-six individuals donated a total of nearly three thousand dollars, the meeting adjourned with the resolution that "the citizens of Greensboro will consider the Light Artillery Guards under their care during their absence, and will most cheerfully respond to any call they may make upon them."[26]

Virtually every week the *Beacon* reported new efforts to benefit the Guards. The ladies of Newbern advertised plans for a fund-raising concert and tableaux of amateur talent. Not to be outdone, the young ladies of Greensboro presented their own show. Charging $1 for adults and $.50 for children, this event raised $268.80 for the Guards after expenses were deducted. Such presentations continued throughout the war. Typical were the concerts presented for the soldiers' benefit on summer evenings in 1863. Young people who used the occasions to stay out late could enjoy charades and various combinations of violin, piano, and voice in Southern University's elegant chapel. The results: rapturous applause and $500. In the smaller outlying villages, where entertainments were rarer, support came through open solicitation. Thomas K. Carson, who had belonged to the Guards during the 1840s, announced that he would receive contributions for the soldiers, box them, and get them to the Guards as soon as possible. He appealed to those women who could furnish socks, drawers, undershirts, neckties, or anything else to make the soldiers comfortable, and he suggested that men donate good shoes—stout, high-quartered, with thick soles, sizes six to ten. Harvey, the *Beacon*'s editor, endorsed the governor's suggestion that each lady in Alabama knit a pair of woolen socks and deposit them with the probate judge to be forwarded to the front. But skepticism met the *Eutaw Whig*'s suggestion that young ladies present their jewelry to the government to be melted down for funds.[27]

The Reverend J. J. Hutchinson and his family often coordinated these supportive measures. Hutchinson came to Greensboro from Georgia during the Flush Times, married, fathered seven children, and began practicing law. After his conversion at an 1845 revival, he gave up law to begin a new life as a Methodist minister. Hutchinson spent most of his time in Greensboro and used his influence to pick his hometown when he served on the committee to choose the site of Southern University. His five sons all shouldered rifles, one as a Greensboro Guard. During July and August 1861, the family directed at least four separate efforts to support the troops. Typical was a sermon of thanksgiving that the Reverend Hutchinson conducted at Wesley Chapel, near Greensboro. After the service he asked for contributions to aid wounded Confederate soldiers in Virginia and collected $163.75 in cash. He also traveled throughout the county with others, soliciting loans in cotton to the Confederacy. Following speeches and a splendid basket dinner, 417 bales were subscribed at Havanna, and at Newbern, 195 bales were subscribed. In all, Greene County east of the Black Warrior pledged more than 4,300 bales of cotton and thousands of dollars. The wealthy were not the only ones to commit. Even poor folk who cultivated cotton with their own hands tendered from two-thirds to four-fifths of their crop to the new nation, and some subscribed their entire crop. At Flat Woods, one elderly lady stated to the gathering that she had no income but would knit socks for the soldiers during the war. A youth arose from the audience and pledged to give himself to the country by joining the first and nearest company of volunteers. Those at a Madison's Mills meeting promised 150 pairs of socks within a month, and other meetings were equally productive. One of those who volunteered to fight remarked, "I have now signed three of the papers. I have subscribed all my cotton, given five dollars to the soldiers, volunteered for the war, and I'll now go home and get my wife to sign the subscription for socks."[28] These efforts, extensively reported in the *Beacon,* did more than support the soldiers: such works cemented ties that included everyone—men and women, rich and poor—in a community of loyal citizens. Even more, these efforts added to the people's new sense of themselves.

That October, the Reverend Hutchinson traveled to Virginia to deliver the provisions to the Guards; not to be outdone, his wife, Mary Adelaide Hutchinson, served as president of the Greensboro Soldiers' Aid Society. Such societies had formed spontaneously all over the South during the summer of 1861; by fall, Governor Moore stepped in to establish a system whereby the government would furnish sewing circles with raw materials, and within a few months more than a hundred ladies' aid societies were listed with the governor. Havanna's aid society was especially energetic in supporting its soldiers, several of whom served in the Greensboro Guards. The announcement of the Greensboro Society's founding reported that the group was already busy making clothing, knitting socks, and providing old linen for the soldiers who had already left or were soon going. Visitors to a meeting of the society held in a large room in the Dorman building saw a number of ladies, several servants, and even ten or twelve little girls, all industriously moving their needles. In ten days, participants made up thirty-six comforters for the soldiers without spending a dollar. Mrs. Hutchinson made it clear that donations of every piece of cloth could be used for the soldiers' comfort. A list of participating women was dominated, as might be expected, by those with sons or husbands in the Guards and other local companies.[29]

Greensboro's aid society also participated in an unusual project to build ironclads. Learning of the css *Virginia*'s successful attack on the Union fleet at Hampton Roads, Virginia, and its subsequent battle with the uss *Monitor,* Southern women began raising funds to build what came to be known as ladies' gunboats. The *Beacon*'s editor challenged Alabama's women to build the first one, and funds were started in some thirty-six Alabama towns. Again, the women presented fundraising concerts and donated their money and jewelry. Men contributed, too, and officers and common soldiers at the front set aside part of their pay to go to the gunboat fund. The most unusual contribution came from Martha Jane Hatter, a widow from Greensboro with two sons in the army, who sewed incomparable quilts to be raffled off. The first featured a large woolen floral bouquet appliquéd in the center of a square of chocolate-brown silk taffeta, along with smaller bouquets in each corner. The Reverend Hutchinson auctioned the quilt in Marion for one hundred dollars; the purchaser kept it briefly and then returned it to be auctioned again, this time in Tuscaloosa for another hundred dollars, with all the money going directly into the gunboat fund. In reporting this news, Hutchinson gleefully announced that Mrs. Hatter had placed in his hands an even more richly crafted quilt to be auctioned for the gunboat. This second quilt, a child's, also featured a central floral design but with strawberries, nine birds, and four butterflies; along the edge twenty-one bouquets alternated with triangular patterns. Hutchinson auctioned off this second quilt twice in Tuscaloosa (once for five hundred dollars), once in Summerfield, and once in Selma. In the end, the money raised by the Alabama's ladies' aid societies—perhaps ten thousand dollars—fell considerably short of the eighty thousand dollars needed for an ironclad, and the funds were applied to soldiers' hospitals.[30]

While the women took up their needles, the men took up their guns. The first companies to march out from Greene County had been the long-standing Greensboro Guards and the Eutaw Rangers. (The Greensboro Cavalry had more trouble organizing and remained part of the local Thirty-eighth Regiment of the Alabama Militia.)[31] The Rangers, led by Judge Moore, were assigned to the Eleventh Alabama Infantry Regiment, which frequently fought alongside the Fifth.

Those who could not get into the older companies quickly began their own, and before the first battle at Manassas, a half dozen or so volunteer companies were already drilling. The Greensboro Home Guards, which organized in June, included among its officers Greensboro Guards who had served at Fort Morgan but were too old to travel to Virginia. When thirty or forty ardent Home Guards wanted to drill more frequently, they organized themselves into the Dixie Guards. Mathematics Professor Thomas A. Gatch taught military tactics to a company of Southern University students who, with some old scrounged muskets, offered to defend Greensboro's citizens. A company of Greensboro youths between the ages of twelve and eighteen spontaneously formed the Young Rebels. For uniforms they chose red flannel shirts and white pants, both trimmed in green; for weapons they carried shotguns. "Nothing would please them better than to get a shot at some of Lincoln's mercenaries," noted the *Beacon*. Every weekday afternoon at six, all stores and businesses closed for militia drill on the campus. "We have all turned soldiers," wrote Dr. John H. Parrish from Greensboro.[32]

Even more companies formed after Manassas, when people realized that this would not be a one-battle war. Each of the county's seventeen precincts organized militia companies, and John Gideon Harris, a former Greensboro Guard, organized his own company from east Greene, committed to serving for the duration of the war. "The time is come," he proclaimed, for "all that we hold dear and sacred is involved in this contest." The Planters' Guards, as they called themselves, served in the West and would become the only company to approach the Greensboro Guards in the town's affections.[33] New companies continued to crop up until the constant drain forced Greensborians to consider other sources of manpower.

In the first years of the war, soldiers retained close ties to home, in large part through the activities of civilians at the front. While the Guards were still in Pensacola, Anne Locke Kerr arrived to nurse the ill. A young widow with two sons, she had married William Kerr, a native of Scotland, major general in the Alabama militia, former captain of the Greensboro Cavalry, and successful merchant and farmer. When Mrs. Kerr arrived in the Guards' camp, perhaps on a visit to James W. Locke, her son, she sensed a need and immediately rented rooms to be used as a hospital. With towels and other items sent by Greensboro's women, she nursed sick soldiers. They responded immediately to her, expressing gratitude for her efforts in letter after letter. "Too much cannot be said in honor of her," wrote J. D. Webb. "She has given up the luxuries and endearments of home to take her place by the rude straw bed of the suffering soldier." Visitors to the little hospital found Mrs. Kerr moving from room to room "like a thing of life." Either she or one of her four or five assistants would stop at an unconscious soldier and bend over where he lay on a straw bed on the floor. With her own hands she would bathe his feet in a hot mustard bath. And at night she would stand by his bed "wiping the death-dew from his brow." When the camp commander would not allow Mrs. Kerr to pass through the navy yard, the Guards informed him that Mrs. Kerr was a soldier of the Fifth Alabama, and she was promptly granted the army's highest privileges, including permission to go where she needed. Mrs. Kerr followed the Guards to Virginia, setting up her hospital at Culpeper Court House along the Orange and Alexandria Railroad. Within ten days she had taken the train to Manassas Junction. With her carpetbag filled with medicine and sitting on her hatbox, she rode in a wagon out to the Guards' camp and immediately began preparing teas for the ailing. The Guards eventually sent her back to Culpeper Court House because they expected an attack. "Who, of all our friends at home will ever forget the devotion of this dear lady to our citizen soldiery and to her country?" wrote a Guard in an open letter published in the *Beacon,* "*Brave* and *patriotic* men *might* learn a lesson from her."[34]

Young men together—away from home, sharing food, with no understanding of germs—got sick. Otherwise minor childhood ailments became deadly afflictions. Seven of the Guards had been left in Knoxville with measles, among them Samuel J. Dorroh. Then about twenty-one years of age, Dorroh successfully farmed near the former county seat of Erie, where his family had been among the first to settle. When he felt better, Dorroh made his way to Richmond and then to Manassas. He finally struggled into camp on July 5, but lasted only a week before he and several others were ordered to Mrs. Kerr's hospital in Culpeper. A few weeks later Dorroh and another Guard entered camp again, looking fat and healthy and bragging that they had enjoyed themselves finely with the ladies. But Dorroh's respite proved short. By the middle of August he was jaundiced and retired to the country for ten days to recover. In September he was sick again with chills, fever, and sweats.

Dr. Cowin, who had grown up with Dorroh, received permission to attend to him and to two others who were also frail. Mrs. Kerr came and bathed Dorroh's head and hands. Some days he would improve and lose his fever, only to decline the next day. He became delirious, and Cowin grew apprehensive. On the morning of September 25, Dorroh appeared considerably revived, but a fever set in again and he began to sink more rapidly than any patient Dr. Cowin had ever seen: "I knew his case was hopeless." Late that morning, Dorroh prayed and grasped his friend's hand with the warmth of gratitude and attachment. "Thus died one of my best friends and messmates in the army, and nearest neighbor at home," wrote Cowin in his diary. "May his soul have winged its way to heaven. How sad to behold the cold and lifeless corpse of one who but a few months since presented the embodiment of health. Strong, active and brave, cheerfully performing every duty imposed upon him. A warm and devoted friend, a bold and chivalrous soldier."[35]

The next morning Dr. Cowin sent up to the courthouse for a coffin. The Guards expected to send Dorroh's body home to Greensboro but were denied the privilege. They blamed the refusal on the fact that Dorroh was a mere private; after all, Captain Giles Goode of the Monroe Guards had died the night before, and his body had been sent home with an escort. So the Guards dug Dorroh's grave. Cowin assisted in placing his friend in the coffin, noticing that he was terribly disfigured with gangrene of the bowels. The cause of death was listed as typhoid fever. Samuel J. Dorroh was buried with military honors on a bleak, rainy day. More would follow, but the first deaths always carried the greatest effect. A week later another neighbor, William H. Willingham, died of typhoid pneumonia. A large and healthy man, no one believed that he could succumb to disease, yet "death makes no distinctions," observed Cowin sadly, "but seizes upon all alike." Willingham was buried next to Dorroh.[36]

The bodies of Dorroh and Willingham were exhumed in November by Greensboro's Dr. William T. Blackford. He placed the two soldiers in coffins sealed with pitch and took them home for reburial in the town cemetery. For that selfless act "he certainly deserves great credit," wrote another doctor, John H. Cowin. A double funeral was held in Greensboro's Methodist church. Lieutenant Marcus L. Dedman, formerly of the Guards, then led a profession to the public graveyard, where the Reverend Hutchinson conducted the services with military honors.[37] Linking gratitude, loss, God, and community, the ritual elevated the men's deaths from tragedy to a glorious sacrificial act. The bodies of the two brothers in arms were then placed in the same grave to rest together until the final resurrection.

★ ★ ★

While Greensborians mourned, the Guards were settling into their new home near Sangster's Crossroads, about nine miles east of Bull Run. They were amused to read articles in the *Beacon* reporting their suffering. In fact, their only annoyance came from the huge flies that tried to take over the tents. Some Guards even worried about what they would do with the overabundance of clothing that the folks back home promised to send. "I never felt better in my life," wrote James L. Boardman to his father, a prominent Greensboro jeweler. When writing to his sister, however, Boardman was careful to express the Guards' gratitude for the packages.[38]

The Guards adjusted to more than just new quarters. In October 1861, Rodes received command of General Ewell's former brigade. This promotion caused a vacancy at the top of the Fifth Alabama, which was filled by promoting Allen C. Jones to colonel. Son of a prominent family from Hillsborough, North Carolina, Jones had moved to Greensboro about 1835, made a successful living from planting, and married John Erwin's daughter. Jones told the 1860 census enumerator that his real estate was worth thirty thousand dollars and his personal estate was valued at seventy-eight thousand dollars. Jones had sought or served in various civic capacities, including the local commissioner of free schools, but the Guards knew him as the driving force behind the company's 1857 reorganization and as its captain until they reached Montgomery. They naturally preferred the big-hearted Jones to the rather cold and distant Rodes, although they readily admitted that the latter was more the military man. Those from other companies were not quite as indulgent: "any one more unfit to command could scarcely be conceived," judged Captain Blackford of the Barbour Greys. At age forty-nine (although he looked sixty), Jones was a jovial fellow, with perfectly white hair and beard and a face of deep red, except for a purple nose; he would allow anyone with a little tact to do exactly as he pleased. At dress parade or on a Sunday inspection when the officers were expected to look neater than usual, "the old gentleman comes out in a full Confederate suit, and furnishes the whole corps a rich treat in witnessing the drawing of his sword. So much does he enlarge upon these occasions that he could not draw it were he confined to a room as large as any in our house, altho' he has done it every evening since his promotion, . . . the men never fail to laugh, and in such a manner that the officers cannot check it."[39] Jones would not last.

Comfortably situated at Camp Masked Battery, as Rodes named it, the Guards' thoughts turned to food. The Bayol brothers, Jules and Ned, went as far as the Blue Ridge on a detail to find beef. They supped at the home of an old widow, found some cattle, and the next day drove the herd back through the valleys and over the hills. At one point they could see twenty miles each way, including a full view of the thousands of soldiers drilling on the Manassas battleground. "Oh! Pa," wrote Jules, "I do wish you all at home could see the beautiful sight . . . the grandest and most magnificent sight on earth, no artist could paint it or pensman could describe it to do it justice." After returning to camp, the Bayols dined on biscuits, corn bread, fried chicken, corn, stewed tomatoes, molasses, and apple tart that they had acquired from the neighborhood. In the distance, an entire brigade was drilling. They were "purfectly enchanted with the sight."[40]

The men occasionally had to make do with tough beef and a half-done biscuit, but food around Manassas Junction was generally both plentiful and tasty in the fall

Guard Francis Edward ("Ned") Bayol, c. August 1861. (Courtesy Sara Bayol Taylor)

of 1861. One Sunday morning after washing all their clothes, the Bayol brothers feasted on cabbage flavored with a piece of shoulder meat, corn bread, and fritters and molasses for dessert. A good cigar topped off the feast. Dr. Cowin and his father, Samuel C. Cowin, also a Guard, dined in relative opulence at Manassas Junction on oysters that they purchased for eighty cents a quart, some cheese for fifty cents a pound, and coffee. Indeed, Manassas Junction was more like a city than a railroad stop, with seven stores and many warehouses. One evening, the Bayol brothers went to the junction and bought a keg of molasses, a large bologna sausage, a quart of oysters, a pound of soda, a cigar box full of peanuts and chestnuts, and even a pound of candy. For breakfast they had fried oysters, sausage, fat meat, molasses, and good coffee. By October, however, servants were having to spend much of their time scrounging for their masters, and prices escalated. Butter went for forty cents a pound, and two dozen eggs could be had for thirty-seven and a half cents. "We spend our months wages in a few days buying provisions," wrote Dr. Cowin. Sutlers were demanding three times the usual price for pens, ink, and tobacco.[41]

After food, the Guards directed their attention to shelter, especially as the Virginia winter approached. The Fifth Alabama moved twice more before finally establishing winter quarters on the Dumfries road about five miles below Manassas Junction. There each mess began to fell logs for its own cabin. In three hours, four men could cut as many as fifty pines into fourteen- or sixteen-foot logs. The logs were then notched and fit together. With a rough roof and bunks at one end, the men were snugly situated before the ground had frozen.[42]

Camp life that winter alternated among boredom, false alarms, drilling, and more boredom. One typical evening, the men sat around their camp fires, some playing cards, others amusing themselves in various ways. Jules Bayol was spinning yarns to about twenty other men. Suddenly, orders came for an immediate march. The men quickly donned their knapsacks and ran to the color line, where they were told to stack their arms, hold themselves ready, and then take a nap. No sooner had they laid down, however, than the order came to prepare to set off. They waited until two in the morning without further directions and then returned to their fires and their napping. At daybreak they were ordered back to their quarters, the entire night wasted. Another evening, the men were doing little when one of the sentries shot a hog. The sound of the musket aroused Lon Dufphey, the Guards' drummer. Thinking that the sentry was shooting at Yankees, Dufphey beat the long roll. The regiment sprang up, grabbed its weapons, and was soon ready for action—only to discover that Dufphey had sounded a false alarm. Rodes sent for the drummer and reprimanded him severely. "Well, dats de way we done in Mexico," replied Dufphey, and he never beat his drum again.[43] Here again was the stuff of myth: the faithful servant.

The men continued to drill hard in camp, sometimes on the double-quick. Every evening was dress parade, when the band would play. Its leader was Charles von Badenhausen, a six-foot German-born teacher from Faunsdale plantation who had joined the Guards in Selma. And the soldiers built fortifications and bridges. The work was tough, but the reward might be a barrel of whiskey. When the snow finally fell, the Guards' captain, E. L. Hobson, ordered the men out for a snowball fight. The Pickensville Blues' captain ordered his company out and challenged the Guards to a game they called "foot-ball." While the two hundred men were racing after the ball, "kicking & nocking each other down on the snow in every direction," the balance of the Fifth Alabama attacked both companies with snowballs. The resulting pitched battle was quite a sight as five or six hundred men created a tremendous storm of snowballs. The yelling was almost frightful. For a little while, the men almost forgot that they were in the same army.[44]

As the Virginia winter deepened, the Guards lost some of the distinguishing signs that identified them with Greensboro. For example, the company was increasingly known by its military designation—Company I, Fifth Alabama—rather than as the Greensboro Guards. The men also changed uniforms. In Greensboro they had paraded in a standard militia dress uniform, but by the battle of Manassas, they knew that a new uniform was needed. The citizens of Greensboro soon supplied its sons with comfortable red flannel shirts and kersey pants. This, too, did not last. In October, one of the lieutenants received unlimited furlough to find gray cloth for a Confederate uniform. The men also received a new flag, the Stars and Bars being too easily confused with the Stars and Stripes. On the last day of October, dress parade was held early so that a new battle flag, the Southern Cross, could be presented to the regiment.[45]

The army tried to set soldiers apart. Physically removing them from home, imposing rigid discipline, submitting to authority, and even the wearing of distinctive clothing encouraged men to learn to fight together as soldiers rather than separately as citizens.[46] Doing so required a readiness to sacrifice themselves individually for the good of the whole. Leadership in an army where companies elected their own officers required finesse, particularly in the case of the Guards, whose privates included many of Greensboro's best-educated and wealthiest young men. In this sort of reverse honor, serving in the lowest rank made it easier to exhibit the care, sacrifice, and courage that expressed civic virtue. Reverse honor elevated common soldiers above the self-interested contractual relationships that had so often marked civilian life. Soldiers would elevate ordinary farmers who exhibited such qualities. Good soldiers were not distinguished by wealth or rank but by an eagerness to serve.

The army tried to set soldiers apart, but the Guards remained Greensborians. Financial support, Mrs. Kerr's nursing, socks and parcels brought by the Reverend Hutchinson, and furloughs home all reinforced those links. The strongest ties were probably private letters. Husbands would give advice on crops and business, wives would confess their devotion, and sons would report on younger brothers. Public letters describing the Guards' activities were regularly written by one of the officers for prominent inclusion on the *Beacon*'s pages. The community was no longer confined to a few streets on the northern edge of the Canebrake; it now stretched to battlefields and campgrounds in Virginia. Moreover, the soldiers, not those who remained behind, were living out the community's ideals. As they waited for the first battle of Manassas to begin, the Guards had even advanced two of their own for the state legislature. Robert Perrin and J. M. Jack addressed their fellow citizens in an open letter. "Our friends are your friends," they proclaimed, "our interests are your interests." The two candidates admitted that they might be unavoidably detained for some time defending their country, "yet we are Greene County's still."[47]

CHAPTER 7

# Beyond a Simple Calculus

**To avenge the blood of comrades slain.**
★ John M. P. Otts, 1862

"When I hear people talk about our Volunteers," wrote Justina Webb to her husband, "I feel as if I have an interest in them all." J. D. Webb and the other Guards were then in Pensacola, but rumors already had started of staying beyond their twelve-month commitment. If it came to that, Justina was ready to draft every man who had not signed up.[1] Despite complaints, however, few of Greensboro's men needed to be drafted. Most flocked to the colors. Voluntary enlistment proved commitment—even moral superiority—and would establish a standard of inclusion in the community. Ironically, conscription would also work to strengthen community ties by disallowing the dissent that avoiding service implied. Either way, military service was changing the nature of common ties.

Before resorting to conscription, Southerners first tried to retain and reinforce the old companies. Pressures mounted after the battle at Manassas for the men to reenlist for the war. In August, when Captain Edwin Lafayette Hobson wrote back to Greensboro asking for up to twenty recruits, fifteen joined. But those sorts of ad hoc measures, even if every company had succeeded, were not enough. So in late 1861 the Confederate Congress began to offer inducements for veterans to sign up for three years or for the war, including a fifty dollar bonus, sixty-day furlough, and permission to join a new regiment if desired. A few Guards took the bait, probably less for the money (many of the wealthier men were already in uniform) than for the chance to go back home. Sergeant Thomas C. Hill, for example, reenlisted for the war in early January and immediately left on furlough for his Newbern plantation. Those without families were thought especially likely to sign on because of their fewer responsibilities at home.[2]

Such expectations proved wide of the mark. When no crisis appeared after Manassas, drilling seemed pointless and remaining in the army lost some of its charm. Personal interests loomed over duty. James L. Boardman wrote to his sister that he anxiously awaited discharge so that he could hurry home—unless he heard that a certain romantic rival had supplanted him as a suitor, in which case he would en-

Guard David Barnum posing in his immaculately tailored uniform before the Guards' April 1862 reorganization. (Courtesy Carlisle Barracks)

list for the war or commit some other "much-to-be-lamented act." John F. Christian, a veteran of Fort Morgan, advised others not to join the company, for eight and a half months in uniform was enough to completely satisfy a soldier. The Bayol brothers promised their father that they would not reenlist before going home or before giving those who stayed at home a chance to take their places. The Bayols admitted to feeling a sense of duty to fight, but it was not right for them to reenlist for the war when able men had done nothing but enjoy the comforts and luxuries of home. "Let them come & try it a while, *then; (and not until then)* we will talk about coming again, & that is about the popular sentiment of this company." Many of the twelve-month men were simply willing to wait until their enlistments ran out in April and then go home. Lieutenant Samuel Cowin (father of Dr. John H. Cowin) was soon heading back to Greensboro to see if he could entice some new men into joining the Guards.[3]

Sergeant Joseph Borden stumbled over his words in denouncing those who hesitated to reenlist, whom he saw as selfish individuals who were giving up "their country and liberties to a fanatical despotism for the sake of an opportunity to gratify their avarice or for the comfort and pleasures of home." The problem became critical as recruiting trips back home yielded uncertain and uneven results. By February, officers in the Fifth Alabama wrote confidently of the regiment's disbanding. Their opinions were strengthened when Captain William Henry Fowler of the Warrior Guards decided to form an artillery company under his own name and persuaded fifty-two Tuscaloosans to go with him.[4]

Unwillingness to join was only one problem, and not even the main one for a town such as Greensboro. Established volunteer companies had long traditions that made advancement unlikely for newcomers. An easier path for those who desired to rise in the ranks was to start their own units—an occurrence that happened with amazing frequency. The same issue of the *Alabama Beacon* that reported Lieutenant Cowin's recruiting trip also contained announcements of three new volunteer companies being raised in west Greene; of the chartering of the Greene County Reserve and Volunteers' Relief Society for home defense and support of the needy; of a recruiting trip from the Canebrake Legion; of the election of officers (including one of the Reverend J. J. Hutchinson's sons) to Captain James A. Wemyss' new company, the Greensboro Confederates (later Company C of the Thirty-sixth Alabama); and of still other companies being raised. As Lieutenant Cowin returned to the front a few weeks later with about twenty new Guards, even Henry Tutwiler's assistant at the Greene Springs School was trying to form a new company.[5]

The *Beacon* reviewed the volunteer companies that had been raised in Greene County by early April. West Greene had gathered a total of six companies for the duration of the war. East Greene supplied three full companies (the Greensboro Guards, the Planters' Guards, and Captain Wemyss' company) and had contributed enough men to other units raised from the Canebrake regions of Marengo and Perry Counties to make about four and a half companies. When those enrolled in the ninety-day volunteer companies (one each from east and west Greene) were added to the other soldiers scattered about, the total of Greene County volunteers equaled the voting population—about sixteen hundred men. Justina Webb now had a different reason to complain. "The town looks thin of men," she wrote to her husband.[6]

For the rest of the South, however, reenlistment bonuses, recruiting trips, and new companies simply left too much to chance. Confederate leaders realized that they could not rely on voluntarism to decide their fate in the face of an enemy amassing huge armies for spring offensives. With the twelve-month enlistments due to expire shortly for some 150 regiments, the Confederate Congress passed the first conscription law in American history. All men between the ages of eighteen and thirty-five were to serve for three years. Exemptions were allowed for such essential workers as ferrymen, ironworkers, printers, druggists, teachers, and certain government officials. And a drafted man could hire a substitute—a potential source of abuse and social division. The twelve-monthers were required to remain in service for an additional two years, but they were allowed to reorganize themselves, elect new officers, and fill up their diminished ranks. Many individuals took the opportunity to change their situations. Regimental Quartermaster J. D. Webb, for example, tendered his resignation and went home. In August he and John T. Morgan, a former major in the Fifth Alabama and future senator, established the Fifty-first Alabama Mounted Infantry. Lieutenant Samuel Cowin, in his late forties, resigned because of poor health, having spent most of his year of service in a frustrating search for recruits and supplies.[7]

Sunday, April 27, was the day set for reorganization, even as the Army of the Potomac was trying to march through the Confederate forces up the Peninsula. The men took a swig of whiskey when it passed and went to the polls to elect new officers of "the conscripted 5th Ala. Regt.," as one Guard derisively put it. The kindly but unmilitary Allen C. Jones was replaced as colonel by Captain Christopher C. Pegues, Captain Josephus M. Hall took over as lieutenant colonel, and the Greensboro Guards' captain, Edwin Lafayette Hobson, became the regiment's major. The Guards also selected new officers. J. W. Williams moved up from second lieutenant to captain, a position he occupied until nearly the end of the war; his subordinates each moved up a rank.[8]

Not just the personnel but the entire structure of the Fifth Alabama changed. The twenty-one Warrior Guards who had not departed with Captain Fowler chose to join the Greensboro Guards. The Warrior Guards' place was filled by the Haymouth Guards of Lowndes County. The letter designations of the companies were also changed to the order they would retain for the rest of the war:

Company A—Barbour Greys (formerly Company K)
Company B—Talladega Artillery (formerly Company E)
Company C—Monroe Guards (formerly Company D)

Company D—Greensboro Guards (formerly Company I)
Company E—Sumter Rifle Guard (formerly Company F)
Company F—Cahaba Rifles (formerly Company G)
Company G—Livingston Rifles (formerly Company B)
Company H—Pickensville Blues (formerly Company C)
Company I—Grove Hill Guards (formerly Company A)
Company K—Haymouth Guards (added April 27)

The Fifth Alabama remained part of Rodes' brigade, assigned to General D. H. Hill's division during the ensuing campaign against General George B. McClellan's huge army pushing toward Richmond.[9]

The Guards, now Company D, certainly differed from the group that had marched off from Greensboro a year earlier. Their fatherly first captain had effectively been sent packing, and other company officers were now giving orders. More than twenty new members from Tuscaloosa had entered the ranks; they were not fellow Greensborians, despite being from a town only forty miles away. Some Guards had died of sickness, but the others were harder men than they had once been. Some might have thought their bonds to the little town on the northern edge of the Canebrake to be strained or even broken.

In fact, however, the unprecedented trials that the Guards would face over the next six months would draw them closer, not only to each other but also to their homes. From the Virginia Peninsula to the mountains of western Maryland, they would march without knowing the reason or the destination. Lacking maps, they would give the wrong names to terrain they crossed. They would inflate the importance of minor skirmishes and fail to understand the significance of critical battles. Common soldiers knew little of their role in the larger picture, and the collective wisdom of the company was hardly better. They would learn that the blue-jacketed Yankees were dangerous if enigmatic foes. But even as the enemy came close to annihilating the Guards, they were creating something: an example of commitment on which to build a new type of community.

★ ★ ★

General Joseph E. Johnston had to move his men quickly. His Union opponent, McClellan, was in the opening moves of a plan to end the war in one dramatic sweep. He had already landed his Army of the Potomac, numbering more than fifty thousand men, at the end of the Peninsula and was preparing to advance northwest on Richmond. A mere thirteen thousand Confederates encamped at Yorktown opposed him. They were hopelessly outmanned, but their commander, John Bankhead Magruder, determined to delay the Federals by a display worthy of the theater he so loved. Magruder sent his men marching back and forth constantly until McClellan believed that he faced an army far larger than it actually was. The delay gave Johnston the chance to bolster Magruder's slim forces and to assume overall responsibility for the defense of Richmond.

The Guards left their winter quarters on April 7, boarded trains, arrived in Richmond, and immediately set out for Yorktown. The problems began immediately on disembarking, because rain had made a mess of everything. "Mud, slop, Rain, holes of water to a farewell &c &c." Men stumbled and fell as every drop seemed to add ten pounds to their blankets. Stopping at the camp of the hospitable Fifth Louisiana, each Guard received a most welcome two cups of coffee. By April 9, the Guards finally made it to the battlefield and camped in a piney woods on Minor's Farm, about a mile from Yorktown and within sight of Yankees. The Guards soon moved closer to the enemy, near the monument commemorating the surrender of Cornwallis and the end of the first American Revolution. "A feeling sometimes comes over me," wrote the captain of the Barbour Greys, "that mayhap Providence may intend to achieve the independence of this new republic on the same spot where that of the first was established."[10] The Confederacy's independence, however, would not hinge on such feelings.

Life around Yorktown was hardly pleasant. Some of the men ventured into town, only to find houses shelled or burned. Other dwellings had been pulled down to prevent them from catching fire as a result of heated shot from enemy cannons. Food, although scarce, could be had in the houses left intact, now serving as commissary storehouses. It was also possible to get a drink there, as Charles von Badenhausen and Dick Adams were fond of doing. On Sundays, complained John S. Tucker, one of the newly recruited Guards, instead of resting and listening to church bells, "we hear nothing but the Roar of artillery & rattle of Musketry & see nothing but large squads of men at almost every imaginable army work & duty." He was also chagrined to discover off-duty soldiers playing poker, singing vulgar songs, and cursing. At other times, the men would amuse themselves by seeing who could tell the biggest lie. "3 years camp life with nothing to do will ruin any man," observed Adams. The rain turned to snow, and the snow turned back to rain. The men, who sometimes slept directly on the wet ground under overcoats with guns and accoutrements for pillows, were soaked. Sergeant Borden did not pull off his clothes for two weeks. The rain continued.[11]

And the tensions continued. Yankee sharpshooters hidden in a neighboring orchard annoyed the Confederates until two regiments drove the snipers out and cut down the trees. Unfortunately, cutting down the trees afforded the sharpshooters even better cover, and they resumed their deadly task the next day. The Twenty-fourth Virginia was ordered to whittle the trees down further. Two Yankees asleep in a rifle pit awoke and, pretending to be Confederates, put a rifle against a Confederate captain's head and pulled the trigger. Meanwhile, fire from gunboats and some land batteries began to tax the Confederates' nerves. The awful screams from the heavy guns started from a mile and a half away and grew more indescribably unnerving as they approached. Slumbering soldiers awoke with a start on May 1 when the Yankees began heavy firing on the picket lines. The Rebels responded with their largest guns. Many of the men were certain that the battle had finally commenced, and General Johnston apparently reached the same conclusion. Realizing that his men were about to be overwhelmed, he ordered the wagon train to move out with the commissary stores and officers' baggage. Adams, who was detailed to guard the supplies, was upset. "I have a hankering for a more active life. Afraid the Regt will get in a little fracas & I not be in it." Once started, the train formed a continuous line for the twelve miles to Williamsburg. The drivers popped their whips, cursed, and hollered at the horses to move. The artillery bogged down in the mud. From nine at night until three in the morning, the train traveled only two miles.[12]

The rest of Rodes' brigade, still in Yorktown, prepared three days' rations. The men spiked the cannon that had to be left behind, burned tents, and destroyed everything else that could not be carried. At eight o'clock on Saturday night, May 3, the whole army quickly moved out in perfect silence, every man holding his canteen to prevent rattling. Captain Blackford's Barbour Greys remained behind to support the pickets; when they left about 10:30, the last Confederate was gone.[13]

The Guards moved through an open plain the next day and could see nothing but troops, artillery, cavalry, wagons, and ambulances plodding westward. About noon, the Guards passed through Williamsburg, "a nice but old-looking town." The buildings were crowded with citizens whose faces betrayed sadness and regret as they anticipated the desolation of their homes and towns. The Guards reached their bivouac a couple of miles beyond Williamsburg and stopped. Federal troops had already entered the Yorktown defenses and were beginning to harass the Confederates' rear guard.[14]

Shortly after noon on Monday, General Robert E. Rodes ordered his brigade to double-quick back for two miles. Reaching Williamsburg again, they piled their knapsacks and overcoats. The Barbour Greys' captain described the scene: "Have you ever heard the expression 'the light of battle,' this was plainly visible upon the face of every man as the ladies would wave their handkerchief's & address encouraging words to the men. . . . Some women were upon their knees, some waving han[d]kerchiefs, while most of them were giving water to the poor wounded fellows who were coming from the fight." The encouragement of Williamsburg's "noble ladies" impressed Adams: "Who could not help fighting when he had such ladies to cheer them on as we did and give such words of sympathy."[15] Threatened citizens were appreciative citizens.

On the soldiers plodded through the mud and water until they reached the battle late in the afternoon. They were ready to fight, convinced that the fate of the war was about to be decided in their favor. Rodes drew his brigade up in line and ordered it to the left, where firing had broken out. But the Guards, like everyone else, were forced to stand ankle deep in mud, exposed all the while to a cold wet wind. And thus the Battle of Williamsburg ended for the Guards like Manassas had—without engaging the enemy. And again like Manassas, the Confederates could boast that they had inflicted more casualties (twenty-two hundred) than they had suffered (seventeen hundred)—although given the Union's significantly greater numbers, this hardly represented victory.[16] Unlike Manassas, however, this time it was the Confederates who were retreating to defend their capital.

The Fifth Alabama was ordered to move out after midnight, despite the fact that nearly everyone had broken down from fatigue, hunger, and lack of sleep. The Guards made their third passage through Williamsburg knee-deep in mud. Blankets, clothing, knapsacks, cooking utensils, and the sick were strewn for five miles. The men marched until five that evening, when they stopped at a place appropriately named Ordinary. Having had nothing to eat, they consumed corn, collard stalks, turnips, beets, and anything else they could find. The next day, they marched until two in the afternoon, when they reached Liberty Church. They briefly rested and then took up the march again, not stopping until two in the morning. At one point they had been on their feet for twenty-six hours but had covered only thirteen miles. They continued marching, with only brief respites, until Friday, May 9, when they camped on a commanding eminence guarding a bridge over the Chickahominy River about twenty miles from Richmond. The enemy waited on the opposite bank. The Guards killed some cattle and washed themselves of "the best part of the soil of the Peninsula." They stopped there for only a couple of days, using the time to drill. Under the strict orders of their new captain, Williams, the Guards were better disciplined than ever. When they started moving again, at only four miles or so a day, they did not stop until they were about two miles from Richmond.[17]

The Guards knew only mud, fatigue, hunger, and orders issued and rescinded. They were confused, and not for the last time. Some claimed that the enemy was advancing and that a fight might begin any hour. Others reported McClellan's forces falling back.[18] In fact, McClellan had moved his massive army up the Peninsula toward Richmond until he had three corps north of and two corps south of the Chickahominy, a swampy stream that meandered southeastward from north of Richmond until it entered into the James River upstream from Williamsburg. The recent rain, while hated by the men who had to slog through it, presented Johnston with an opportunity to isolate and crush the two Federal corps south of the Chickahominy before McClellan could cross the swollen river, whose bridges had been washed out, and reunite his forces. General Johnston selected as the point of attack a crossroads called Seven Pines.

"Another wonderful & eventful day in the history of our country," began Dick Adams' diary on May 31. "Called from our wet & damp beds, we buckled on our armor to advance against the enemy. Now the time had come." The Guards were finally about to taste enemy fire. The twenty-two hundred men in Rodes' brigade were stationed on the Charles City Road about three and a half miles southeast of the village of Seven Pines. The soldiers began the day with a short meal and packed a two-day ration of hard bread before moving out toward the fighting. Rain had washed away a bridge, and some of the men were forced to wade up to their waists; others became completely submerged. To make up for the delay, the men double-quicked to the Williamsburg Road, where they turned east toward Seven Pines.

Even so, when the signal to attack was given, only two regiments (the Sixth Alabama and the Twelfth Mississippi) and a line of skirmishers were in position. The rest, including the Fifth Alabama, were at least fifteen minutes behind. But the attack would not be delayed, and on the men pressed.[19]

Rodes ordered his brigade up to the line, but thick undergrowth and marshy ground frustrated military order. When the Fifth Alabama emerged from the thick woods along the Williamsburg Road, heavy fire from both artillery and muskets poured in on them. They were, in fact, directly facing the enemy's camp. About a quarter of a mile away, a redoubt bristling with a battery of guns commanded the field from the center of a long line of breastworks and rifle pits. In front of that the Yankees had erected a nearly impassable abatis of thickly felled timber. The Fifth Alabama split into two wings, the first, under command of Hobson, now a major, moved to the left of the Twelfth Mississippi, which had moved forward into the abatis; the second wing formed to the right of the Twelfth Mississippi and linked up with other troops. Misunderstanding an order from Rodes and eager to engage the enemy, Hobson moved his wing forward beyond the abatis into the field. Heavy artillery and musket fire trained on the advancing Rebels, dismembering them with shot and canister. When Hobson's horse was shot from under him, he coolly dismounted and continued on foot. But his men could not remain long under such conditions and fell back with the rest of the brigade. With his line now complete and with the enemy beginning to falter from the effects of accurate Confederate artillery fire, Rodes personally ordered his entire brigade to advance. Through three feet of water, down ditches, and over embankments the men charged. In the confusion, the Guards and two other companies fell in with the Sixth and Twelfth Alabama. Chris Shelden was hit from a ball fired out of the redoubt. "Thick as hail fell the shot around us," Adams wrote in his diary, "more different tunes than were ever heard to them. Some burst as they struck, others a fluttering noise & then the keen whistle of the minnie ball."[20]

Recalling the battles years later, the Guards sometimes interjected anecdotes that heightened the drama by contrasting humor and carnage. Typical was the incident between von Badenhausen, the regimental bandmaster and former lieutenant in the Austrian army, and David Barnum, a small and underage soldier. The two had gone into the battle nursing a feud. A few days before, Barnum had even drawn a knife on von Badenhausen, who patted the young soldier on the shoulder, admonishing him to "be quiet: keep cool, oderwise I draws my knife on you." As the battle raged and the men lay flat, not knowing who would die first, Adams shouted, "Barnum, keep cool, oderwise I draws my knife on you." Von Badenhausen quietly replied, "Adams, dis is no dime for such tam foolishness."[21]

The Guards charged into the redoubt with other members of the regiment, capturing the battery of six or seven guns and immediately turning them on the fleeing Yankees. In their hurry, the enemy troops left behind horses, their colors, quartermaster's supplies, medical stores, fruit, a wagon and team, and baggage. Rodes ordered his men out, through the Yankee camp, and drawn up in line in order to hold their position until reinforcements came. Federal infantry soon approached, threatening Rodes' brigade from two directions, but Confederate artillery broke the enemy column, and reinforcements arrived. Rodes ordered his men to renew the attack, but the second advance was far costlier than the first. The Fifth Alabama moved into an open field, where it remained under fire for an hour and a half. And when other Confederate troops moved in front of them, the soldiers of the Fifth were unable to fire for fear of shooting their comrades in the back. Here the regiment suffered the most, losing more than a hundred killed and wounded.[22]

Several Guards numbered among the casualties. "There it was I . . . bled in my country's cause," recounted Dick Adams. "When the ball struck me I rolled over in the mud, but got up & staggered back a little to where Carter [his brother] had placed Lonnie Coleman, who was also wounded. We went back behind a pile of wood where we found Haden wounded." Adams cut loose a horse from a Yankee artillery limber and took Haden off the battlefield. "Of all the sights, that field beat all. Wounded & dying. Night coming on darkened the scene. The moon & stars abashed, refused to look upon such a heart rending scene."[23]

The men had been under fire for five and a half hours before they were ordered to fall back about sixty paces to the cover of a woodpile. That night, the Confederates slept on the field in the Yankees' tents and exchanged their old weapons and canteens for better ones. The attack was renewed the next morning, but Rodes' brigade spent the rest of the battle in the woods without loss.[24]

"With the exception of Shiloh," a captain in the Fifth Alabama wrote to his father, "the battle of Saturday is by far the greatest ever fought upon this continent, and among the bloodiest in history." The toll was indeed chilling. Rodes' brigade had entered the action with about twenty-two hundred men; half were now either missing or dead. Rodes himself was injured and had to relinquish command to a subordinate. ("He has no fear," wrote a Guard who saw him hit.) Rodes was expected to report his brigade unfit for duty but decided not to do so. One company in the Sixth Alabama had forty-four casualties out of its fifty-five who fought. Even the Confederates' commanding general, Johnston, was among the wounded; President Jefferson Davis immediately replaced Johnston with Robert E. Lee. The entire Confederate casualties amounted to more than sixty-one hundred; the Union lost more than five thousand. All of this to gain a bit of swampland.[25]

Although the Guards lost fewer men than did some companies, their first day of battle claimed its share. At least seventeen were wounded. Two were dead—the first to die at the enemy's hand. Gus Moore, a young physician in his mid-twenties, died carrying the flag as Rodes' brigade charged the redoubt; Alonzo Chapman, a recent arrival in Greensboro, fell beyond the redoubt. Both men were buried on the battlefield, and a map was drawn so that their bodies might later be taken home for reburial in the Greensboro cemetery.[26]

Along with the rest of their regiment, the Guards were ordered back about a mile

Map of the Seven Pines
battlefield by Guard Jules
Honoré Bayol. (Courtesy
Alabama Department of
Archives and History,
Montgomery)

The position of our brigade at 4. o'clock.
  " 13. 12th Miss. Reg.
  " 14. 5th Ala
  " 15. 12th Ala
  " 16. 6th Ala

  " 17. 18. 19. Yankee Encampments
  " 20. Yankee Troops
  " 21. a pile of cord wood
  " 22. Yankee redout
  " 23. Yankee breastworks
  " 24. Old barn used by the Yanks as a
brigade Commissary house
  " 25. General Casey's Hd.Quarters (Yank)

  " 26. Where our Men are buried

[Note no number 12 and redoubt misspelled
in original; have silently added apostrophes
to avoid ambiguity]

**[Legend to] Battle Field of 31st of May & 1st June 62**

No. 1. Where Gus Moore was killed
  " 2.    "    Chapman was    "
  " 3.    "    Alfred Ward was wounded
  " 4.    "    Gus & Chapman are buried
  " 5. Carter's battery
  " 6. Left Wing of 5th Ala
  " 7. 12th Mississippi Regt
  " 8. Right Wing of 5th Ala
  " 9. 4th Va battalion
  " 10. 12th Ala Regiment
  " 11. 6th   "    "

in the rear of the battlefield while the two great armies glared at each other. "Nothing has occurred of interest," James Boardman wrote to his father, "except a very daring reconnaissance of Gen J. E. B. Stewart."[27] Lee could hardly be expected to defend Richmond without adequate knowledge of the enemy's positions and strength, and so he ordered J. E. B. Stuart to assess the Union right flank north of the Chickahominy. Stuart led his twelve hundred cavalrymen out on June 12, crossed the river, turned east, and kept going. They galloped—capturing soldiers, supplies, and accolades—until a hundred miles and four days later they returned, having encircled the Union forces. The Confederacy had a hero, and Lee had a battle plan. Stonewall Jackson and his army were secretly brought from the Shenandoah Valley to attack the Union's exposed right; meanwhile, Lee ordered three divisions guarding Richmond to cross the Chickahominy and join Jackson's men.

On June 25 a minor fight broke out in the middle of the lines at King's School House (some called it the Oak Grove) near the Williamsburg Road, an inauspicious start to one of the war's bloodiest weeks, the Seven Days' Battles. The next day, Rodes' brigade (now including the Third Alabama and the Twenty-sixth Alabama in place of the Twelfth Mississippi) joined the other brigades under Major General D. H. Hill and began marching to the Mechanicsville turnpike. There they stayed until late in the afternoon, while Union forces at Mechanicsville inflicted four times as many casualties on the Confederates as they suffered. Later, the brigade crossed the Chickahominy and bivouacked in an open field.[28]

Another Union general might have used the Mechanicsville victory as an opportunity to take the offensive, but not McClellan. He knew that Jackson's men were not far off and instead ordered a strategic retreat to a new base on the north shore of the James River, where his supplies could be brought by steamers under protection of Union gunboats. During the night, the Union troops at Mechanicsville fell back a few miles to high ground near a gristmill belonging to a doctor named Gaines.

The Guards would pay a heavy price again, this time at the Battle of Gaines' Mill. Hill's division set out on the morning of June 27 and stopped at Old Cold Harbor, a couple of miles east of Gaines' Mill. The enemy opened artillery fire, smashing into the head of the Guards' Lieutenant Matthew S. Ramsey, a "gallant officer and high-toned gentleman." The Confederates resumed their march. To get at the enemy, the Southern forces first had to cross a dense swamp with tangled underbrush, where their carefully planned order of advance became confused. The men pushed on under heavy artillery fire from shell and canister. In this action, Colonel C. C. Pegues, commander of the Fifth, fell wounded in the shoulder. (A month later, he would be dead.) Pegues called out to Major Hobson, former captain of the Guards, who was next in command. The Fifth, Pegues told Hobson, had always been in the advance, and his last wish was for his regiment to proceed and let no other pass it. Hobson did as requested. When Rodes' brigade formed a line of battle, the Fifth and Twenty-sixth Alabama regiments led the others toward four Union regiments flanked by artillery and infantry. As the Union troops gave way, Hobson wheeled the Fifth to the left and ordered them to double-quick. They met the enemy troops headed directly at them and drove them back. Orders then came to join Stonewall Jackson's men for a general assault.[29]

Rodes' brigade now found itself on the edge of a wooded swamp with the enemy fortifying a hill beyond an open field that stretched before them. The hour was late. Yet the Confederates attacked. A Union battery gave way, then Union troops fell back. Confederate soldiers all along the line began to break through. With the sun now setting, the Confederates congratulated themselves on routing the enemy and driving them south across the Chickahominy "with great slaughter." But in the attack George Price and William Ellison joined Lieutenant Ramsey in death. Ten other Guards lay wounded.[30]

The next day, a Saturday, McClellan's army continued to shift men, cattle, and supplies south toward the James River. Some of the Guards picked up abandoned materiel, including Yankee stationery that made its way back to Greensboro. The Southerners also collected enemy stragglers, cared for the wounded, and buried the dead. The battle had cost the Confederates dearly: more than eighty-seven hundred killed and wounded. (The Union lost less than half that many, plus twenty-eight hundred taken prisoner.) The Fifth Alabama lost fifteen killed and about fifty-eight wounded, many of whom later died of their injuries.[31]

The Fifth Alabama was not involved in the next of the Seven Days' Battles, Savage's Station. Instead, the Confederates again crossed the Chickahominy as part of Lee's plan to bring his armies together at Glendale and crush the Yankees there. Jackson led his troops across the York River Railroad and down the Charles City Road to the White Oak Swamp, but the bridge had been burned by retreating Federals, some of whom could be seen waiting across the creek. Artillerists cleared out the Federals, and the Confederates crossed. But the delay prevented the Fifth Alabama from reaching Glendale. The fight there was bloody, with the Rebels suffering twice as many casualties as their enemy. The day was arguably the most decisive of the campaign, for Lee lost his opportunity to crush McClellan.[32]

The Union general moved his Army of the Potomac back to a strategic position atop Malvern Hill, some three miles south of Glendale, near the James River. McClellan had chosen well. The 150-foot rise was easily defended, approached by a broad field flanked by natural ravines. The comment of the Greensborians' division commander, D. H. Hill, should have been heeded: "If General McClellan is there in force, we had better let him alone." And the Union general was indeed "there in force," with 100 well-placed guns in several lines and 150 more in reserve.[33] But the testy Lee, whose patience had worn thin, was determined to drive the Union army from the gates of Richmond, no matter what the cost.

Hill led his division southward, linking up with the rest of Lee's army a few miles from Malvern Hill. The combined forces then pressed forward until they came within range of Yankee artillery. Rodes' brigade advanced with the others across an open meadow, raked by enemy canister and musketry. The Confederates forded a creek and began to climb the hill under cover of woods. A low rise, in sight of the enemy's batteries, provided more protection, and the Southern forces paused to await orders. Hill described the scene before him: "The Yankees were found to be strongly posted on a commanding hill, all the approaches to which could be swept by [their] artillery, and were guarded by swarms of infantry securely sheltered by fences, ditches, and ravines. Tier after tier of batteries were grimly visible on the plateau, rising in the form of an amphitheater. One flank was protected by Turkey Creek and the other by gunboats."[34] Hill expressed his reservations to Lee, but to no avail.

About two in the afternoon of July 1, Hill received orders to lead his division as part of a general assault. A shout was to signal the men to storm the Yankees' position with fixed bayonets. Hill arranged his division so that Rodes' brigade was on the right, thus placing the Fifth Alabama near the center of the Confederate attack. The general's orders noted that artillery would be brought up to silence the enemy's cannon. But a few Confederate batteries were no match for a hundred Yankee guns.

While the officers talked among themselves and sundown approached, they heard shouting followed by the roar of musketry. General Hill and his officers agreed that this must be the signal. "We advanced alone," he noted in his official report. Rodes' brigade headed for the Yankee artillery batteries immediately in front and seven or eight hundred yards away. With no Confederate artillery to fear, the Yankees aimed their guns directly at the approaching infantry. Federal muskets added to the deadly discharge. "They moved on under this terrible fire," Hill continued, "breaking and driving off the first line of infantry, until within a little over 200 yards of the batteries. Here the canister and musketry mowed down my already thinned ranks so rapidly that it became impossible to advance without support." The men were ordered to lie down and fire. Another brigade was sent forward to help but never reached the desperate men. "It seemed as if nothing could live," wrote one soldier. Troops from another division had already been repulsed and refused to rally. With half the men killed or wounded, only about six hundred of Rodes' soldiers were left to load and fire. Colonel John B. Gordon, commanding, ordered the men to fall back. "The dead of this brigade marked a line nearer the batteries than any other," he boasted. The battle, concluded General Hill, "was not war—it was murder." His observation certainly applied to the Guards: in the aftermath of Malvern Hill, only seven were capable of continuing the fight.[35]

Greensborians later came to see Gaines' Mill and Malvern Hill as a turning point in the war. At the time, however, the Guards knew only that the Army of the Potomac was continuing its retreat to Harrison's Landing on the James River. Lee made no plans to renew the attack. The citizens of Richmond rejoiced.

Certainly no Greensborian (and few Americans, for that matter) had ever endured such desperate struggles as the Guards faced defending Richmond. They described their experiences in letters back home and in their diaries. But that was hardly the end of the matter. Years later, the Guards' captain, J. W. Williams, published a series of reminiscences in Greensboro newspapers. The old captain claimed that he wanted to show the suffering of the old soldiers and consequently stressed the hardships they endured in the army.[36] While he had little need to exaggerate, Williams certainly described the Guards' engagements as little dramas, complete unto themselves. During any particular campaign, the soldiers may have been befuddled, but by the time he wrote, years later, their actions possessed unity, direction, and purpose. This adjustment suggests more than a reconstruction, more than just reflection; it suggests that the soldiers came to form their experiences into patterns and narratives that expressed who they were. Such is clearly seen in Williams' account of the Guards' next campaign, Lee's foray into Maryland.

The Army of the Potomac withdrew its last troops from near Richmond on August 16. That would ordinarily have been good news, but the Guards soon learned that all their requests for furloughs were denied, no matter what the circumstances.[37] Something big had to be brewing. The enemy's new commander, General John Pope, was putting together a force outside of Washington at Manassas Junction.

The Guards were awakened early on August 19 and by daybreak were already marching. As they passed through Richmond, a correspondent from the *Mobile Advertiser and Register* noticed that some of the soldiers were barefoot. They continued northward along dusty roads through picturesque country with plenty to eat—including corn, apples, peaches, melons, chickens, eggs, and cider—until they got to Hanover Junction, twenty miles from Richmond, where they camped for five days.[38]

Then started what Captain Williams later recalled as the hardest march the Greensboro Guards ever endured.[39] They continued in close column, without straggling, for fifty minutes and then rested for ten before starting out again. On the first day, D. H. Hill's division led, followed by the wagon and artillery trains, with McLaws' division bringing up the rear. That day the Guards were among the first to get to the wells and had plenty of fresh water to drink. They marched into the night and bivouacked. The next day was a different matter. McLaws' division, they learned, would take Hill's place in front, and Hill's division would bring up the rear in the August heat. The Guards became thirsty before they had gone far, but the wells had been drunk dry by the time the Greensborians' turn arrived. Instead of drinking water, they ate dust. The first sight of the Blue Ridge elicited rousing cheers from the army, but that was no compensation for the lack of water. "Our lips were blistered and our tongues so dry and parched," Williams recalled, that "we could scarcely talk." The captain told those who were suffering the most to hide in the woods where the provost guard would not find them and then to come into camp after dark. The army stretched for three or four miles and could be seen for quite a distance merely by its clouds of red dust, which combined with the heat to torment the soldiers in the rear. To worsen matters, by the time the front column had rested its allotted ten minutes, the rear had not caught up and thus was not allowed a rest. Late in the evening, the Guards finally reached a cool stream at the foot of a mountain. Williams did not allow his men to drink immediately but made the company sit by the road, ordered two men to fill a couple of canteens, and permitted each soldier only six swallows of water. The captain drank last. The remainder of the water he poured on the men's wrists. He repeated the ritual twice more at five-minute intervals until the soldiers were cool enough to drink all they wanted. "Although Co. 'D' was mad enough with me to have killed me," he recounted, "they all afterwards agreed that I was right." Before long, they could hear screams up and down the line from soldiers who had quickly swallowed too much cool water while hot. Rumors spread that seven men in the division had even died. The Guards, however, were refreshed and were able to continue their march when they received the order to fall in. At Warrenton Springs, they crossed the Rappahannock and bivouacked. This minor episode, certainly enhanced, clearly put Williams in a good light, but more to the point, it also showed that prudence and a selfless concern for all benefited all.

The next day the Guards reached the plains of Manassas, just three days after the end of the second great battle there. "Went all over the Battle Field and never saw as many dead Yankees on a field before," commented one Guard, Sergeant John S. Tucker, who served as regimental commissary clerk.[40] The Confederates were putting their Yankee prisoners to the task of burying the dead. In the hot sun, hundreds of swollen bodies had blackened beyond recognition.

The Guards had little time to contemplate the gruesome scale of the Confederate victory, for Lee planned to resume the offensive. The next day, September 3, they took up the march eastward, but after only a mile they turned to the north. They reached Leesburg that night under a brightly shining moon. Citizens crowded the sidewalks to cheer the troops. The ladies seemed "perfectly delighted to see us," reported Tucker, "which was duely appreciated judging from the deafening yells that went up from each regt. as they filed by."[41]

The troops continued their march north, singing "Maryland, My Maryland," for they now knew where they were headed. At the Potomac River, just below Point of Rocks, they brought up several dozen cannon and shelled the woods on the other side of the river in hopes of hitting a few Yankee pickets. Instead, a Maryland civilian ran out into an open field, and the Confederates immediately trained their guns on him. "At times the poor scared fellow would be literally lost from view by the dust made by the explosion of the shells, but when the dust settled he would be in sight again and our soldiers would yell and holl[er] 'shoot him! shoot him!' It was a miracle that he escaped unhurt." Captain Williams joked that "marbles could have been playing on his coat tail," because it stretched straight out behind him as he ran. Firing at innocent civilians was hardly an auspicious beginning to the Maryland campaign. Colonel Gordon of the Sixth Alabama was called on to address Rodes' brigade with a few appropriate remarks as the men prepared to leave

Virginia. After spending that night and the next day wrecking the Chesapeake and Ohio Canal (although the stone aqueduct at the Monocacy resisted their efforts) the army moved on toward Frederick.[42]

The Guards crowded together with the rest of the Fifth Alabama when they bivouacked in dense woods about four miles south of town. The little ground they occupied looked like a giant patchwork of blankets. No sooner had they laid down when one of the Pickensville Blues jumped up, yelling that something was moving under his blanket. It turned out to be a large snake. The excitement eventually died down, but then little David Barnum complained that a rock under his blanket was keeping him awake. A closer examination found nothing, either under his blanket or in his pocket. At last the "rock" was traced to a minié ball that had hit him at Seven Pines and that surgeons had been unable to locate. During the day some of the Guards ventured into Frederick. Sergeant Tucker received a free dinner, talked with the ladies, and read Yankee newspapers. Others were not as fortunate. When Ned Bayol reached town, he found that many stores were closed, Unionists refused to take his Confederate money, and Confederate sympathizers had already emptied the shelves. Not surprisingly, most of Frederick's citizens viewed the dirty and hungry soldiers not as liberators but invaders. Some of the Southern ladies suggested that the Confederates open all the stores and take what they needed, but Lee had expressly forbidden such actions.[43]

The army left Frederick heading not toward Baltimore, as the Guards expected, but westward along the National Road.[44] They crossed South Mountain at Turner's Gap and halted while General Hill called for three companies from the Fifth Alabama to take picket duty. Companies C (the Monroe Guards), D (the Greensboro Guards), and E (the Sumter Rifle Guard) came forward. Captain Williams was placed in charge and reported his men ready for duty. General Hill issued the orders, and Williams led the three companies west over the mountain for about four miles until they reached a stream. Above the road stood a large mill and below it the miller's residence. The creek's name was Antietam. About a mile farther, the road reached the little town of Sharpsburg.

One company established its picket along a road north of the mill, another company was stationed to the south, and Captain Williams selected the mill itself for his Greensboro Guards. The old miller, who had never seen soldiers, ran out and asked what general commanded their army. While the captain gave instructions to Companies C and E, Alex McCall pulled the miller to one side and whispered that Williams was second or third in command behind the great General Robert E. Lee, who had never given an order without first consulting Williams. The Guards feasted sumptuously for two days on meals provided by the credulous miller and his good wife. The couple was preparing an elegant Sunday morning breakfast for them when a courier brought orders for the three companies to hurry back to their regiment.

Unbeknownst to the Guards, the Union army had happened upon a tremendous piece of good luck that could destroy its enemy: Lee's marching orders, dropped by an officer who had used them as a wrapper for his cigars. If General McClellan, reinstated as head of the Army of the Potomac, acted quickly, he could destroy Lee's widely dispersed army one piece at a time. But the cautious McClellan waited until the next morning, Sunday, September 14, to move. By this time Lee had learned of McClellan's discovery and was struggling to rein in his troops. He ordered D. H. Hill to take his division back to the gaps through South Mountain to slow McClellan's approaching army.[45]

As the Guards and the other two companies walked briskly back along the Old Sharpsburg Road, they heard thunder in a cloudless sky—the roar of distant artillery. They chatted breezily about their fine time at the mill in an attempt to disguise their fears that by day's end some would be lying cold and stiff. The officers buoyed the companies' spirits and hurried them along.

When the three companies reached the crest at Fox's Gap, a grand yet awful sight lay in the valley before them: a Yankee line of battle extending for miles on either side of the road and a second line three hundred yards behind the first. As both lines advanced deliberately straight up the mountain at the Southerners, perhaps a half dozen artillery batteries fired away at the Confederate defenders. Four more lines of battle lay some two miles beyond, advancing apace. The Guards believed that they were facing eighty thousand bluecoats.[46] Brigadier General Samuel Garland (brother of the University of Alabama's president) commanded the defenses at Fox's Gap. When Williams asked Garland if he knew where Rodes' brigade was, Garland pointed toward Turner's Gap, the northernmost gap, where the National Road crossed South Mountain. But as they spoke, a minié ball hit Garland in the hip; he turned, and a second ball hit his chest, throwing him from his saddle to writhe in pain as the life seeped out of him.

The three companies filed to their left, Williams gave the order to double-quick, and after about a mile they reached Rodes' brigade. All the field officers were on foot because their horses could not negotiate the mountainous terrain. Rodes decided to prevent the Yankees from flanking his men by extending his line north along the ridge of the mountain as far as the twelve hundred men remaining in his brigade would stretch.[47] Hobson began moving his Fifth Alabama up and down the mountain crest for hours without rest. Many of the men broke down from fatigue. As usual, they had little idea of why they were moving about. They later decided that Rodes and Hobson were re-creating General Magruder's tactics at Yorktown, gaining time by pretending to be a larger force. About three in the afternoon, a dozen or so artillery batteries opened fire on the Confederates, and two of the Federal lines began their assault, followed closely by the other lines. The Fifth was in a lonely position. No Confederate regiment lay closer than three hundred yards. And as if that were not enough, Hobson approached Williams with a sobering order: "John, take the three first companies, halt here, and keep them in check as long as possible." They were to hold off the Army of the Potomac so that the rest of the Confederates could escape. As the other companies in the Fifth Alabama passed out of sight to their rear, the Greensboro Guards, Pickensville Blues, and Haymouth Guards looked around. To their right along the mountain's ridge, not a soldier could be seen or heard. Behind them were some large rocks, so Williams ordered the three companies to set up their defense there. For faster loading, the men lined up their cartridges and caps in front of them on the rocks. They began murmuring, as much to themselves as to each other, "here they come, be ready." When the first Yankee skirmishers came within 300 yards, the three companies opened fire and stopped the advance. Then the first line of infantry came up and halted about 150 yards away, fell behind rocks and trees, and returned fire. "The balls would hit those rocks," recounted Captain Williams, "and it sounded like heavy hail." Three or four of the men lay dead, including Guard W. B. Moorman, all shot through the head.[48] "In a short time they began to fire into us from the rear," according to Williams, "and also from above us." The three companies crawled up under the rocks as best they could to protect themselves from the enemy's fire, now coming from both the front and the rear. Captain T. C. Belsher of the Pickensville Blues, whose company was on the left, nearest to the enemy, called out, asking what to do. Williams told him to find something white, tie it to a ramrod, and wave it high in the air.

Hearing Williams' call for surrender, Alex McCall jumped up, threw down his gun and cartridge box, and declared, "You all can stay here, but I am going out." Although his fellow Guards warned him that he would be killed, he started running anyway. The two enemy lines were now so close that by firing at McCall, they risked shooting each other, so they called out, "Halt." But the Rebel kept running. He got beyond the lines, and what seemed like eight hundred or a thousand men opened fire. Not a ball touched him. Ned Bayol also managed to escape.[49]

The Yankees were surprised when only thirty-two Confederates surrendered, between nine and thirteen of them Greensboro Guards. Captain Williams first handed his sword to one of the Union sergeants, then drew it back and demanded to give it only to an officer of equal or higher rank. The sergeant referred Williams to a lieutenant, who used words inappropriate for Sunday school. When a colonel rode up, the impetuous lieutenant declared, "There d——n you is an officer who is your superior in rank, surrender your sword to him." Satisfied, the captain delivered his sword to the colonel. The officer admired Williams' pluck and promised that after the war he could get his sword back by writing to Colonel Fisher of the Fifth Pennsylvania Reserves.[50]

With the sword problem settled, the Union sergeant gathered a detail of six from his company to escort the Confederates back. Two of the prisoners helped along Samuel Willingham of Sawyerville, west of Greensboro, who had suffered a severe wound to the head. As the group moved back through the lines, some of the Yankee soldiers yelled, "let me shoot the d——n rebels." Captain Williams could hardly let that pass. He told them that he had run across their kind in the Confederate army—those who are brave two or three miles behind the battle line. At division headquarters, the prisoners were turned over to the provost guard. One of the sentinels gave Williams a blanket and kept a hot fire burning at his feet all night. The next morning Williams discovered that in addition, some big-hearted fellow had thrown an overcoat over the prisoner. The captors' kindness did not end there. Breakfast began with real coffee, the Guards' first since Williamsburg.

While the prisoners waited, a battle raged just a few miles west. Thanks in part to the delaying actions at South Mountain, Lee had united his widely separated forces along Antietam Creek. On Wednesday, September 17, the Army of Northern Virginia met the Army of the Potomac in the bloodiest single day of the Civil War. By nightfall, the Battle of Sharpsburg, as the Confederates called it, had resulted in the wounding or death of twenty-three thousand Union and Confederate soldiers. The remnants of Rodes' brigade defended "Bloody Lane"; among four companies of the Sixth Alabama, which fought alongside the remnants of the Fifth, only two men remained unharmed.[51] On Thursday evening, the Confederate forces withdrew back to Virginia. And a few days later, on September 22, President Lincoln called his cabinet into session to announce that he would issue an emancipation proclamation.

The Guards knew none of this. About noon on Friday, they were marching off among a group of approximately 150 prisoners captured at South Mountain and about 350 more captured at Sharpsburg. By noon on the next day, September 20, they had reached the railroad five miles beyond Frederick, having eaten nothing except what their captors had shared of their own rations. At the depot the Confederates found the Union's real assets: acres covered with barrels of pickled pork, hardtack, sugar, coffee, and other food. The colonel told the men to help themselves. The prisoners took a little of the coffee, sugar, and hardtack, but the pickled pork was another matter. With forked sticks, they stabbed fifteen- to twenty-pound pieces stuffed in barrels. Several hundred men sat on the ground, gorging themselves. They then traveled by train to Baltimore, where they walked through the city in a careless, indifferent fashion. Thousands came to gawk at the sight of the dirty, ragged soldiers holding chunks of pork on sticks. Some of the ladies began to cry and tried unsuccessfully to give packages to the prisoners, who responded by lining up in fours, lifting their heads, and marching in perfect step. They could hear the ladies say that even "if they are ragged, they can march." At the wharf, Captain Belsher made the secret Masonic sign to a Yankee colonel, who replied, "I see you are a Mason, what can I do for you?" Belsher asked where they were going and was told that their destination was Fort Delaware, a massive fortification recently completed on Pea Patch Island in the Delaware River. The colonel added that he would send some clothing and blankets by the next boat, a promise he kept. The captured Confederates boarded a steamer that evening and reached Fort Delaware about noon the next day.

The officers were separated from the enlisted men, isolating Captain Williams from his fellow Greensborians. After seven weeks, three large ocean steamers cast anchor in front of the fort, and the prisoners were told to gather their things. They quickly formed into ranks, the officers boarding first. Williams stood at the entrance to one of the ships, anxious to see if all the Guards were still alive because he had heard that many men had died. A thousand soldiers passed by, but no Guards. Williams went up to the colonel in charge, explained that his company was among the prisoners, and requested that he be allowed to go on another boat with his men. The colonel replied that a boat with better accommodations had been selected for the officers, but Williams wanted to be with his men. "Come on," said the colonel, and together they found the Guards, all together and well.

The reunited Greensborians stuck close together as they left Fort Delaware and headed for exchange. The steamer at last made its way up the James River, and the Guards were the first off when it docked twelve miles below Richmond. They quickly headed up the bluff and began walking toward the city when a Yankee sentinel ordered them to go no further. All prisoners were first to be taken to Camp Winder and kept there until exchanges were arranged. The Guards noticed that in the calm and very dry conditions, the dust from passing horses might conceal them in a huge cloud. When some cavalrymen came galloping by, the Guards jumped into the road behind them, adding to the confusion by kicking up even more dust. They had not gone far before yet another Yankee soldier confronted them, demanding to know if they were escaping prisoners. When they told him that they were not, he laughed and warned them to leave the road and head due west if they wanted to avoid capture. They followed his advice, and after a day spent wading creeks and keeping the sun in their faces, they reached Richmond just at dark.

The Guards turned up a street that took them by the Capitol Square and made for Mrs. Barnes' boardinghouse, located on Franklin Street about three hundred yards from the square, where the Guards had boarded while in Richmond and where they had left their extra baggage when orders came to march. (Henry Beck once left in her care several hundred dollars in gold, and when he called for it after the war she paid him every cent.) The beloved Mrs. Barnes put the men in her quietest room. They bathed and found fresh clothes—their first change in three months—from among those left the previous spring. After eating a good supper, they returned to their room.

At ten o'clock the next morning, Captain Williams went up to the Capitol and sought out Alabama Senator C. C. Clay, whose wife was related to Williams' mother. Clay heard Williams' story and found North Carolina Senator William T. Dortch, whose wife was also related to Williams, and the two senators approached Secretary of War George Randolph. "Captain, where is your company?" asked the secretary. To avoid undermining the system for exchanging Union and Confederate prisoners, Williams lied and said that the men were at Camp Winder. The men received thirty-day furloughs, orders for transportation, and back pay. With some tobacco, pipes, and cards to occupy them during the trip, the Guards left for home.

Greensboro welcomed its returning heroes. The town looked as it always did in late fall, when only a few leaves still clung to their branches. Together once more, the Greensboro community could look forward to Christmas.

★ ★ ★

Back in the late spring, when the Guards had been facing McClellan's army on the Peninsula, Greensborians waited with "breathless anxiety" to hear which Guards were injured, taken prisoner, or even dead. "I was so excited [I] could scarcely read the names thinking all the while yours might be the next," wrote Fannie Borden to her husband, Joseph. "Would that this war was ended. My heart grows sick at the thought of so much suffering."[52]

Southerners had indeed paid dearly to purchase Richmond's salvation. General Lee lost nearly 20,000 of his Army of Northern Virginia killed or wounded. Rodes' brigade reported 662 killed and wounded from the battles of Gaines' Mill and Malvern Hill alone. A year earlier, the Fifth Alabama had numbered 800; after Malvern Hill, the regiment was down to 133.[53]

The Guards emerged from that battle with only seven effectives. Joseph Borden, now a lieutenant, had been wounded in the shoulder. Orderly Sergeant E. Pompey Jones received painful wounds in his right hand and right side. Corporal Shelby Chadwick had been hit in his right hand, and Paul Lavender had been wounded in his leg. Jim Jack's leg had to be taken off below the knee. Robert Jeffries had his foot removed and then, in a second operation, his leg. James Ezra Wilson was in critical condition with a broken thigh. Charles von Badenhausen lost his left arm and a finger of his right hand. William L. Kennedy, who had been appointed the color-bearer after Gus Moore's death, was also among the wounded.[54]

These and the other injured were taken to Richmond, where Captain Williams came looking for them.[55] He went to the largest hospital, the Chimborazo, which had about thirty wards, each about twice as large as any church in Greensboro. The head surgeon recognized the Masonic sign that Williams made and summoned a clerk to serve as an escort. In what was called the "dead house," where thirty or forty soldiers lay cold and stiff, a black servant sat by his dead master, waiting for a wagon to take the body home.

Four Guards lay not in the dead house but buried on the battlefields east of Richmond.

Dr. Augustus H. Moore, a young physician, had been among the first to enlist when the Guards reorganized in April 1861. The son of a prominent planter, Gus served alongside two or three of his brothers. The Guards reported that he died "with his face to the enemy, nobly carrying the flag of his country" as Rodes' brigade charged the redoubt at Seven Pines. His extensive obituary notice in the *Beacon*, written by "A Friend," spared no compliments. "Tears will flow that this brave young hero of but 26 years, whose heart was full of benevolence and affection, is another martyr to this unholy war; yet though the genius of sorrow broods over his grave, the pen of the historian will weave a laurel wreath for his brow, for from the tombs of such martyrs a nation will be generated." Dr. Moore's life had purpose beyond the grave. "There is a memory of his noble soul which will drive the blood in boiling currents through the veins of his surviving companions, encouraging them not to falter—not to fear!—And the flag which was bathed in the blood of this gallant soldier, will be a symbol of new life, which must fan the flame of war, until that flag will cease to be a figure of speech, but an empowered and recognized reality." Months later, his death was memorialized in a thirty-line poem entitled "Brave Alabamians":

> Still weary and wan he blessed his sweet child,
> Then rushed to the battle so fierce and so wild.
> They ask not for "furlough," they ask but to fight
> For country and "flag," for God and the "Right."

The poem was signed "Yadkin," after a river in North Carolina.[56]

Alonzo B. Chapman, age twenty-two, had joined the Guards the same day as Dr. Moore. Chapman's extensive obituary notice following his death at Seven Pines, also written by "A Friend," mentioned nothing of Chapman's profession, as he had only recently moved to Greensboro from Dallas County, Alabama. Instead, the notice mentioned Chapman's cheerful nature, liberality, bravery, and "patriotic love for the cause of constitutional liberty"—qualities that had caused his superiors to love him as a younger brother. "He considered it a privilege to be permitted to lay down his life in defence of his country."[57]

Dr. Matthew S. Ramsey, the Guards' first lieutenant, was also counted among the four killed "in defending the rights and honor of the South in the great conflict waged against her by the Vandals of the North." The *Beacon*'s editor noted that Ramsey's father was an honored resident of adjacent Sumter County and that his brother had recently pastored Greensboro's Methodist church. Ramsey, like Chapman, had settled in Greensboro only a few weeks before joining the Guards and setting off for Pensacola and Virginia. His death had occurred during the battle of Gaines' Mill, as Hill's division slowly moved forward toward the main battle. The newspaper did not mention that a Yankee cannonball had carried off the young doctor's head.[58]

The *Beacon*'s announcement of Jules Honoré Bayol's death was probably written by the Reverend J. J. Hutchinson, who effusively described Bayol as having a "warm-hearted, generous and affectionate . . . countenance beaming with smiles and intelligence." The youngest son, "at the threshold of manhood and usefulness," his family idolized him. "Gifted, genial and loving, many aching hearts attest his virtue and lament their sad bereavement." Jules fell a true patriot, "driving a ruthless invader from the consecrated soil of his native land" in this "inhuman and diabolical war of Yankee greed and vengeance." The ball that cut him down at Seven Pines came from the "cruel shaft of Northern hate." The Reverend Hutchinson did not explain that both of Jules' parents had fled as children from the slave uprisings in Santo Domingo and had arrived in the French grant in the early 1820s or that the family still sang the *Marseillaise*. Jules' father, Edward, had been a prominent member of the Greensboro Guards during the 1830s and '40s. Jules and his older brother, Ned, followed in their father's footsteps, joining the Guards together in August 1861. Jules' last letter to his parents had been penned two miles beyond the Gaines' Mill battlefield. It read, "in *hot pursuit* of the *enemy*, . . . Safe & sound after having been through the most bloody battle imaginable." Three days later, he lay dead on the field below Malvern Hill.[59]

The deaths of Moore, Chapman, Ramsey, and Bayol—the first Greensborians ever to die in battle—seemed to demand justification. Had they died in vain? The *Beacon*'s notices, with their ritualistic tones and phrases, could hardly have denied the suggestion more emphatically. But personal letters back and forth from the front and home divulge a profound reexamination of both the meaning of their ultimate sacrifice and the reasons for continuing the fight. Every death certainly prompts survivors to question over and again the causes of the tragic event. But in Greensboro's case, the question was loaded with implications for the town's social structure. The struggle to understand would move Greensborians beyond the glib self-assurance of a year earlier, beyond the simple calculus that deemed the preservation of slavery worth going to war. The answers they submitted—often vague and inconsistent—ultimately said more about what they were becoming than the cause for which they fought.

Bayol's death was a blow to his parents, of course, but also to Fannie Borden, the Bayol family's neighbor. Fannie's correspondence with her husband dwelled heavily on death and separation. Joseph had prepared his wife for bad news during the battle of Gaines' Mill. "You must nerve yourself to hear what ever takes place, if my life is spared it will be through the mercy of God alone. For our men are slayed on all sides." He then listed some of the wounded Guards and revealed that a cannonball had decapitated Dr. Ramsey.[60] Although Joseph Borden survived, Bayol's death started Fannie down a path to near obsession.

"Mr and Mrs Bayol are almost heartbroken and the girls too are in deep distress," Fannie reported. "They all looked up to Jules and I think he was the pet of the whole family." In the middle of her lengthy letter, she delicately asked her wounded husband to come home if at all possible, adding that his father agreed. But by the end of her letter, Fannie discarded the delicacy. "Oh!, how I long to have you back there with us! . . . Oh! would that all this trouble was ended—that all our dear friends might return and we be happy once more."[61]

Fannie's distress was only just beginning. Within a week her letters declared, "I have been so long hoping to see you that I now almost despair of ever seeing you." She had been bedridden and had lost her appetite. "The anxiety and excitement of the past month was too much for me and many sleepless nights have I passed, have fallen off at least 10 or 20 pounds, which makes considerable difference in my appearance as well as in feelings." Every week she sent Joseph a letter more ardent than the last. "Oh! why didn't you come home? I thought now while so many of the company are absent on furlough, would be the time for you also to leave—and night after night we would hear of different ones of the G. Guards coming. I couldn't help looking for you too, but alas! another disappointment!" Then she appealed to his responsibilities as a father. "Do *come—come home.* I'm afraid the children will forget you, although I try to keep you ever in their hearts—and they often ask why Pa don't come home too, as so many others are daily arriving." Alternating with her petitions came descriptions of the daily routines of home life: thirty acres of late cotton would yield well if it rained; Mr. Oaks was sick; his father had gone to see about a ditch to drain a field; and the six spinners under Fannie's supervision had woven a total of about 180 yards of homespun in the past three months. But all this was largely filler for an increasingly desperate wife and mother.[62]

Fannie feared for her husband, but that did not mean that she no longer supported the Confederacy, "for we all know there is still much hard fighting and many precious lives yet to be lost before our independence will be acknowledged." She prayed for battlefield successes that would make the enemy realize the error of attempting to subjugate the South. Fannie's attitudes were common enough. When skirmishing returned near Malvern Hill, she urged that every effort be made to keep the enemy from reaching Richmond. "We have already had too much precious blood poured out to secure those places and ought (it seems to me) [to] use every exertion to still hold them." The use of "we" to describe the Confederate forces may in the end mean little, but it does suggest that Fannie had identified her destiny with the army's. Her assertion that too much blood had already been spilled to back down would be echoed by her husband, recovering from his injuries at Bremo, the home of John Hartwell Cocke. Joseph had never desired to settle the differences between North and South by arms, he claimed, yet "if such should be the case we will have to fight until the last man is slain. We cannot yield."[63] The point would be repeated time and time again, even after Lee's surrender at Appomattox. To yield was to render the deaths and sacrifices meaningless.

Fannie seemed to calm herself over the next few months. Then came word in December that her brother, Ruffin Gray, had been killed during the fighting at Fredericksburg, his skull fractured by an enemy shell. Although sick and looking feeble, Ruffin had ignored advice to return to the rear, instead choosing to remain at his post and sacrifice his life. Joseph Borden arranged for the body either to be placed in a coffin and brought to Richmond or be buried at some well-marked spot. The family suggested that he be buried next to Jules Bayol.[64]

Beyond consolation, Fannie declared her brother "too faithful to his country. . . . Oh! how horrible to think of! dying among strangers with no dear friend or relative near." She did not miss the opportunity to insist that Joseph now return. "If not for your sake, for *mine* and our *dear children,* don't sacrifice your life and health—but come home and stay at least till Spring. We have already lost one so dear to us—who Father and Ma had looked upon as a support in their declining years, and if you should be taken, just think of the many little ones with no one to look to."[65]

When Gray's servant, Ellick, brought the grieving family a lock of Gray's hair, they were surprised to see that it had turned gray. The body came to Newbern by rail, and on January 6, 1863, the family laid him to rest at the foot of his father's grave. Gray's mother grieved that his last days had been spent suffering for need of the clothes she had made but he had not received. His family also pondered whether he had prepared his soul for death, having never made an open profession of faith.[66]

Her brother's funeral elicited Fannie's most impassioned response yet. She alluded to the health of her husband and herself. As a last resort, she pleaded for Joseph to resign. By March, Fannie was accusing her husband of being "*too honest* to come home—if you would only put *on* a *little more* you might get off. Now I don't believe in that way of getting off, but must admit it would be a great inducement to me to *prevaricate* just a *little.*" Fannie at last had her way. Near the end of 1863, Lieutenant Joseph Borden tendered his resignation; the surgeon for the Fifth Alabama certified that he had been unable to perform any duty for eight months due to a "serious & protracted rheumatism" that left him enfeebled.[67]

The Bordens' reactions were probably typical. They both agreed that the Confederacy must keep up the fight; the only question was the role of a single individual in that fight. In a superficial sense, Fannie's responses were self-interested, but another interpretation would describe Fannie's loyalty to those closest to her as having precedence over her commitments to a political entity but a year or two old. Despite creating more burdens on widows and soldiers' families, the Civil War deepened and broadened bonds of loyalty among individuals. "I could not fully appreciate having you with us 'til since our separation," wrote Fannie to Joseph, "but can now set full value on you." These ties would hold their community together long after the Confederate States of America had ceased to be.[68]

What, then, kept Greensborians going? They had marched out from their town explicitly avowing their intention to prevent the destruction of slavery. But they were soon phrasing their apologies in terms of the liberties of free white men. When he met his first Yankee prisoners, Joseph Borden found that he no longer believed slavery to be at the root of the conflict but rather only an "ostensible object" by the North to prevent anarchy at home. Although he had studied in Philadelphia, Dr. John H. Cowin found his reason to fight in the Yankees themselves, "descended below the brute creation in the scale of human degredation—men who would reduce to ashes our cities and towns, devastate our fields, murder and outrage the fair daughters of the South, and bend our necks beneath the galling yoke of slavery." As a white Southerner, Yankees and black slaves gave Cowin, and probably many like him, an essential component of his identity—an antithesis. If slaves were black, then free men were white, and if Yankees were evil, then Confederates must be good. Former Guard John Gideon Harris tried to cover all bases, declaring that "patriotism, love of country, love of home, love of family, and love of *constitutional freedom, protected by constitutional law,* demands our untiring energy and zeal." And if that were not enough, "Christianity in all its varied relations" demands action, and "humanity cries to us for assistance." As the war continued, fewer would find such uncharted abstractions compelling.[69]

Other reasons to fight lay cold in the Greensboro cemetery. If the deaths of Moore, Chapman, Ramsey, and Bayol were to be redeemed—if this drama were not to end as tragedy—then only one course lay open. The Reverend John M. P. Otts, pastor of Greensboro's Presbyterian church, composed a poem dedicated to those convalescing after the Peninsula campaign:

**To the Wounded of the Greensboro Guards.**

Soldiers, nobly death you have braved;
Thanks to God your lives were saved;
You fought,—on Him depending,
You fought,—your rights defending,
You bled—but live to bleed again;
Avenge the blood of comrades slain.

Hail ye soldiers, welcome home;
Short your stay—but welcome come,
From the battle field all gory,
Come with honor and glory.
When wounds shall heal go back again
To avenge the blood of comrades slain.

Yes, back! You, we can not detain,
Our country bleeds in every vein;
Go stand amid the battle
And brave the cannon's rattle.
Brave men—be brave again,
Avenge the blood of comrades slain

We know you are brave and bold and true:
Know you and can depend on you.
Your country boasts no braver,
Go ye then bleed to save her
Rush onward to the battle plain
Avenge the blood of comrades slain

Farewell ye men of holy cause,
Battling for rights & holy laws
Ye go, our prayers attend you;

May heaven's guards defend you;
In peace may you return again;
When ye revenge the noble slain

Greensboro, Ala. Aug. 20th 1862 M. P.[70]

While the women fretted, the Guards returned to the front. As much as to achieve independence and preserve slavery, they now fought for revenge and to avert the tragedy of wasted lives. The dead were now commanding.

# CHAPTER 8

# Confidence and Despair

How sudden & heart-rending the change.
★ John S. Tucker, 1863

General Robert E. Lee's army had retreated into Virginia following the battles at South Mountain and Sharpsburg and was now defending the heights above Fredericksburg from the Army of the Potomac, headed yet again toward Richmond and under the command of a new leader, Ambrose Burnside. D. H. Hill's division was camped east of Fredericksburg near Rappahannock Academy, along the river about five miles above Port Royal, and there the Guards returning from their furloughs found the Fifth Alabama. With new recruits, the company now boasted at least a respectable sixty soldiers.[1]

The company's complexion had changed since its first year. True, some of the new Guards were from the county's oldest and wealthiest families. Sam Pickens, for example, was the son of Samuel Pickens, a planter, and belonged to a prominent Greene County family that included Governor Israel Pickens, Captain Andrew Pickens (commander of the Greensboro Volunteers in Mexico), and Colonel Samuel B. Pickens (commander of the Twelfth Alabama). Sam's widowed mother reported real estate valued at $209,000 and personal estate (slaves) worth $250,000 to the 1860 census enumerator. But the Guards also now included for the first time some soldiers with no known connection to Greene County or the Canebrake: for example, John C. Ray came from Tallapoosa County in east-central Alabama; J. C. Roberts enlisted in Choctaw County, southwest of Greene; and J. D. Sellers enlisted in Pike County, a poor region in southeast Alabama. These newcomers, all signed by different recruiters, probably remained outsiders, for they elicited few comments in the diaries and letters of the other Guards, seldom if ever received promotions, and demonstrated no conspicuous bravery in battle.

The Guards, both veterans and new recruits, were roused before daylight on December 11, 1862, to go on picket. They quickly reached the river, where their Federal counterparts, standing picket on the opposite bank, bragged that the massive Army of the Potomac was crossing at Fredericksburg. The Union troops continued across the next day, while the Guards, still on picket, listened to cannonading coming from

"Uncle John" (c. 1887), who accompanied his master, Samuel Pickens, to war. (Courtesy John McCall)

Fredericksburg above them and from Port Royal below. They received orders to return just before evening, but their camp had moved, and by the time they got back, the Guards thought they had marched twenty miles in the dark.[2]

Famished from not having eaten the night before, the Guards made breakfast of broiled pork and corn bread. The pounding of artillery soon started again from Fredericksburg, and D. H. Hill's division moved off toward it. After two or three miles, the men stopped out of sight under a hill. Shot and shell began to hiss and whistle overhead. Other shells fell in a meadow in front of them, throwing up mud and grass as high as trees. The wounded—some walking on their own, others on litters—began passing by on their way back to the hospital. Rodes' brigade was ordered to the right to repulse an anticipated attack. The Confederate forces had to pass through an open field with shells and shot continuing over their heads before reaching the edge of some woods, where they formed a line and loaded their muskets. But the attack did not occur, and the men moved back. A ball struck and bent a man's gun in the company ahead of the Guards, yet no one was touched. The Guards passed squads of Union prisoners on the way to the rear. That evening, the brigade went back into the woods, formed a line, and stayed as reserves until General Stonewall Jackson ordered an advance on the enemy. The Guards started marching, then double-quicking, but in the dark they became confused. A Union artillery battery opened fire, and the men hit the ground. Shell and canister whizzed just over their heads, cutting bushes and saplings. No one was hit. When the firing ended, the Guards were ordered to turn around and march silently back to camp. They made fires, shared their food, and went to sleep.[3]

Sunday passed quietly. When the flags of truce began waving, Confederates entered the battlefields in search of plunder. Bloated and blackened bodies filled the fields below Marye's Heights, where Union forces had launched a futile assault on a well-protected Confederate line. Nearly thirteen hundred Union soldiers lay dead, as well as about half that many Confederates, among them Ruffin Gray, Fannie Borden's brother. The day ended with hard, freezing rain.

After the Confederate victory at Fredericksburg, the Guards wintered with the rest of the Army of Northern Virginia, glaring at the enemy across the Rappahannock. Rain and snow bogged the two armies in mud well into April. "It is not my purpose to give to the readers of the Beacon the news of a great battle fought and glorious victory won," wrote Dr. John H. Cowin in a letter printed in the *Alabama Beacon*'s March 27, 1863, edition. He merely wanted Greensboro to know that its Guards were "in fine health and spirits, . . . ever ready and willing to fight a great battle and win a glorious victory when that time arrives, the time that 'tries men's souls.'" The war's end was uppermost in everyone's mind. "Some have allowed themselves to be deluded with the thought that peace will dawn upon us at an early day," but he could see no reason to believe it himself. The Northern states, with their determination to crush at all costs the gigantic armed rebellion, could hardly be expected to let their former states go in peace. And because Southerners could never pledge obedience to such a despot, they would wade through "seas of blood such as have never yet been recorded on the pages of time" before peace came to the now saddened homes of the South. Cowin called on the newspaper's readers to nerve themselves for the coming struggle, confident that in the end victory bright and glorious would be theirs, "for right is might and will prevail."[4] Within only a few months, few Confederates could believe such an equation.

The Fifth Alabama was better off than it had been in a year, recovered veterans and new recruits raising the rolls to about seven hundred men (approximately fifty-five of them Guards). General Robert E. Rodes would soon assume command of D. H. Hill's division, and Colonel Edward A. O'Neal of the Twenty-sixth Alabama would move up to command the brigade. General Lee was itching to get the army moving. In March he ordered excess baggage reduced and a day set aside for fasting and prayer. But another month would pass without a move. The Guards regularly saw Yankee observation balloons, but otherwise camp life continued a routine of standing picket, games of town ball, harvesting wild onions, and pipe smoking.[5]

The long-anticipated confrontation began early Wednesday morning, April 29. Sam Pickens was getting ready to go on picket when he learned that the Yankees were crossing the Rappahannock. The Guards were soon marching west. They passed a pine thicket near Hamilton's Crossing where Yankee batteries again fired shells over their heads. That night they slept fitfully in a drizzle, bivouacking without fires (lest they reveal their position) and speculating on what would happen the next day.[6]

The Guards were roused before sunup and began a terrible march in the rain. Men fell out along the muddy roads to rest in muddy rifle pits. Cannon fired all day, sending shells to the right and left of the Confederates but at least this time not over their heads. They spent a second night in a forest, grateful to be allowed to make fires and dry their clothes. There Captain J. W. Williams received three orders: send all baggage and sick to the rear, see that every man had forty rounds of ammunition and a bayonet, and have the men cook three days' rations and be ready to move at a moment's notice. The men obeyed, and by nine o'clock that evening they were prepared.

In the early hours of May 1, a drumroll yanked the Guards from sleep and sent them running to the regimental battle line forming at the edge of the woods. Edwin Lafayette Hobson, the Guards' former captain who had recently been promoted to lieutenant colonel, shouted out the orders: "Battalion right face, countermarch by file left, march!" The regiment headed up the river by way of wet and slippery roads. At Hamilton's Crossing they were detained by a seemingly endless line of troops headed in the same direction. The wagons in front of them stopped frequently. A dense fog that left them without bearings was soon burned off by a hot sun. They passed deserted winter camps before stopping about noon to eat, rest, and fill their canteens. Sam Pickens felt sick and faint from the marching. He passed his uncle, Colonel Samuel B. Pickens of the Twelfth Alabama; the two shook hands and wished each other a safe battle. All the time they could hear cannon firing.

The soldiers continued to a plank road between Culpeper Court House and Fredericksburg. As they piled their knapsacks, General Lee rode by, followed by his aides and couriers. Sam Pickens described him as "a well set venerable looking man with white hair & beard," although his expression was hard to fathom. "He passed in silence—no cheering. All who knew him was inspired with the utmost confidence & gazed attentively upon him."

Continuing their march westward, the Guards were unsure where they were going. Thick woods broke up their line. They passed wounded left behind in the yards of private homes. The men pressed forward and then had to retrace their steps. In the evening, they made a large circuit past several battle lines before finally stopping at a breastworks on the edge of a woods. There they washed and lay down for an hour or so. Troops and artillery continued to pass by at a good clip. The Guards marched another couple of miles up the plank road until they halted in a field and orchard. The men were completely broken down. Pickens had only a biscuit left to eat—the wagon trains had failed to keep up—and decided to keep it for breakfast.[7]

Lee was launching his most audacious attack yet, dividing his army and striking an enemy that outnumbered his own by two to one. He had directed Jubal Early to leave his ten thousand troops at Fredericksburg to keep the Union forces there occupied. At the same time, the rest of the infantry headed west toward Chancellorsville, where General Joseph Hooker, the latest commander of the Army of the Potomac, had stopped his Union forces. That night, while their troops rested, Jackson and Lee discussed the situation over a campfire. J. E. B. Stuart had brought them valuable information that Hooker's right wing was vulnerable. The two decided that Lee's fifteen thousand men would remain facing the enemy at Chancellorsville, while Jackson's thirty thousand soldiers marched west in a wide flanking movement. If all went well, the Union's right would be caught unawares. Stuart's cavalry would serve as a screen to keep Jackson's men from being detected. It was a daring and brilliant maneuver.

The next morning, May 2, the Guards were allowed to sleep past daybreak. After refreshing themselves by washing in the stream, they started marching. O'Neal's Alabamians led the entire thirty thousand–man movement, paced by the Greensboro Guards, who, as the Fifth Alabama's color company, carried the flag. The column occasionally would stop while the men shared biscuits, crackers, and scrap meat. At one point word passed down the lines to give way to the left "& there came glorious old Stonewall at a sweeping gallop—hat in hand on his sorrel horse followed by aids & couriers." All along the line, the troops waved their hats and cheered long and loud. "I cant describe my feelings at thus seeing him suddenly for 1st time," Pickens recorded in his diary, "but my breast swelled with emotions of pride & gratification, & all must have felt confident of success when we shd. meet enemy. Could only see he was a younger lookg man than I expected to see & not so stout but apparently well made—blk hair & beard & a little bald spot on back head that showed plainly after passing." The marching resumed. Heavy skirmishing echoed to the right. About four in the afternoon, the men came to the plank road and marched on it toward the river. They reached some trees that the Yankees had cut to block the road. General Jackson declared, "These trees must be moved," and Rodes ordered the Fifth and Sixth Alabama to do so. Jackson continued down the road and returned just as the Alabamians were finishing their job. He came up to Rodes and spoke a few words, and then Rodes went over to the Guards' captain at the head of the column: "Williams, file to the left, and march as near as you can at a right angle to this road until the order is passed down the line to halt; then you will front, and dress on the right." When the Fifth Alabama had covered about a half mile through dense undergrowth, the order to halt sounded.

Jackson and Rodes had moved the men so far to the west that the Guards were in the rear of the Union forces. The Confederates formed a battle line in the woods and lay down in a deathlike silence while two other lines formed behind them. Then came the order to load, and ten thousand ramrods dropped into ten thousand guns. The men shifted their cap and cartridge boxes around from their backs in order to load as fast as possible. Then they rested their hands on their gun muzzles, waiting for the other divisions to get into position. Captain Williams claimed that no one felt a tremor of fear; indeed, "every one was as cheerful as if going on a dress parade." The men mocked each other playfully: "John," one would whisper, "when you are killed this evening I will send Miss ———'s picture and letters back to her, with one of your beautiful curls enclosed." Another would joke, "Old fellow, I'll be on the detail to bury you to-night."

Stonewall Jackson sat awkwardly on his horse as he looked first down his line of ragged soldiers and then up the road toward the enemy. "Are you ready?" he asked General Rodes. "Yes sir." "Then move forward sir."[8] The time was late—about 5:15 in the evening—so late that the soldiers had thought the attack might be delayed until morning. But the men advanced nonetheless. Random shots from the sharpshooters came crackling through the thick woods. The Confederates began to double-quick. On the right came terrific musket fire. Excited with anticipation, men began firing at anything they thought they saw. Sam Pickens caught the contagion and blazed away at an imagined blue line on a pine-covered hillside. Captain Williams immediately ordered the firing stopped until there was something to shoot at. The Confederates reloaded, and the bluecoats soon started "running like turkeys." More than twenty thousand muskets and twelve pieces of artillery rang out. Above that noise, the Rebel yell pierced the air. The earth seemed to quiver. Confederates began racing after the Yankees as fast as they could. "The quiet woods was now changed into a mighty roar, as if all the demons in the lower regions were turned loose."

The next few minutes felt like hours of glorious confusion. The Union soldiers who had been busy cooking supper ran off, leaving their guns still stacked. They stopped when they got behind a hill or breastwork, but as soon as the Rebels came upon the Northerners, they would be off and running again. The bluecoats "might as well have tried to stop a cyclone," commented Captain Williams. Pickens saw a Yankee shot down, but when approached, he jumped up and fired until he was shot down again. Another Yankee fell and put the butt of his gun up to signify surrender. Lieutenant Colonel Hobson told him to drop his gun and lie down if he did not want to be killed; he was then sent to the rear as a prisoner. Hundreds surrendered, since running seemed to guarantee death. Yet run they did. Some of the Confederates—perhaps from overeagerness, perhaps in a vain attempt to reach the retreating enemy—began firing wildly in the air without aiming. The Guards, in the front, feared being killed by their own men. Pickens noticed minié balls striking the ground in front of him, and several times he prevented men from firing at friends either by screaming at them or by pushing their gun barrels into the air just as they fired. The Guards were running so fast that they had to wait for the rest of the regiment to catch up. Pickens got separated from the company but saw Lieutenant Colonel Hobson waving his sword and leading the charge and stuck close to him. The Confederates advanced on an artillery redoubt that threw canister like hail, lay down for a minute or two at the edge of a pine thicket, then jumped up with a shout. The Yankees started running again. Pickens spied a large Newfoundland dog dying from a ball that had gone through him. Yankee officers on horseback tried vainly to rally the troops. As the Confederates continued their push, Hobson found a lone horse standing. He called to some men to catch it for him but was shot in the flesh of his leg before getting his mount. A wounded Yankee lieutenant called out, and Pickens offered the man water. The lieutenant asked for a surgeon and for Pickens' name and regiment, promising something about being ever mindful. Pickens left him and headed for the color-bearer, who had become separated from the majority of the regiment. He finally found Ed Hutchinson, Charles Hafner, John H. Cowin, and Jim Arrington. The five Guards stayed together. Exhaustion and darkness overtook them, and they lay down among some pines.

But the fight that day was not over. A Union battery began shelling the woods. The five men lay close to the ground as an artillery barrage cut the trees around and above them. When the shelling let up, they joined a squad of men taking prisoners to the rear. The Guards were very hungry. Pickens and Arrington shared a cracker taken from a Yankee haversack. The men began culling the fields for plunder and rations, but other troops had already cleaned up. The five Guards finally found the brigade. Handshakes and congratulations were passed around. Only five Guards had been wounded, and Hobson had merely been slowed by his flesh wound. The Confederates stacked their arms, made fires, and finished the Yankees' suppers.

The Confederates had driven the enemy a mile and a half or perhaps two and had captured thousands of weapons, large stores of provisions, and the guns from three artillery batteries. The Guards boasted trophies from the well-provisioned Army of the Potomac: food, oilcloths, blankets, canteens, and haversacks. After supper, the men moved up the road to some breastworks near the hospital. They bivouacked there, about a mile and a half south of Chancellorsville, on a road running north and south.

The night was bright. About ten o'clock, they heard heavy firing and grabbed their weapons. Some soldiers passed by, bearing a wounded man on a litter. The Guards asked who he was. "Only a soldier," was the reply. The soldier, they discovered later, was their beloved Stonewall. With Jackson mortally injured, command passed first to A. P. Hill, who was also wounded, and then to Robert E. Rodes, former captain of the Warrior Guards, colonel of the Fifth Alabama, brigadier, and now divisional commander. But Rodes soon deferred to J. E. B. Stuart, whose high reputation was more likely to rally the troops.

The Guards awakened Sunday morning to artillery firing. By six o'clock they had prepared for battle, still believing that they would lead the attack as they had the day before. When the order came for Rodes' division to move forward, however, the Guards found themselves in the third line, behind two other divisions that had come up during the night. The Guards pressed forward with their brigade, which was placed on the extreme left of the division, with the Fifth Alabama on the inside. The men moved rapidly over a mile through the open but dense woods that bordered Chancellorsville. "The air was alive with the roar of musketry," reported Shelby Chadwick to the *Beacon*, "the boom of cannon, the bursting of bombs, the unearthly whizzing of shot and grape, and the confused din of strife."[9] Despite Yankee shells striking about twice a minute, no one paused. Nothing was heard but the order to "Close up, men," or "Steady, men, steady," when a cannonball came too near. A single shell exploded about ten steps to the Guards' right, and thirteen of the Fifth Alabama lay in a heap. Four or five others were forced to the rear with their wounds. Men screamed in pain as shells exploded and fragments hissed.

The Guards' line closed to fill in the gaps. When the two lines ahead of them became hotly engaged and lay down to fire, Rodes' division passed over them and once again led the attack. The men moved up rapidly to take out the Yankees' terrible artillery fire, driving the enemy back about three hundred yards to a little ridge in the southwest corner of the field around the Chancellorsville house that served as General Hooker's headquarters. Northeast of this little ridge was yet another ridge on which the enemy had erected breastworks during the night. An open ravine ran from west to east between the two ridges. As O'Neal's brigade reached the first ridge, it faced strong batteries, supported by heavy columns of infantry, on the second ridge. The Southerners halted, and the Fifth Alabama was ordered to lie down and fire at the Yankee artillerymen.[10]

The Confederates had not been long on the ridge—maybe fifteen or twenty minutes—before another enemy artillery battery opened up from the left, enfilading them in a deadly crossfire. Dr. Cowin was hit in his femoral artery. He directed Captain Williams and another man to apply a tourniquet with an old canteen strap, a technique he may have learned in medical school. As they prepared to move him, Cowin whispered to a comrade, "I am sinking very fast, I think. If I die, tell my father that I fell near the colors, and in the discharge of my duty."[11] Despite all efforts, this well-educated young man, the hope of his family, bled to death on a Virginia field far from the Greensboro his passing would help to define.

The battle would hardly stop while soldiers pondered such matters. As the crossfire slackened, orders barked out to charge the Yankee artillery at the ridge. Not everyone heard, but those who did—without protection or support, without flinching, and without delay—moved forward. "We did so in dashing style," wrote the romantic Chadwick home to the *Beacon*. George Nutting waved the flag and cried out again, "Come on, boys!" Within ten minutes the Confederates had captured the redoubts above Chancellorsville and driven the enemy out. Nutting proudly planted the colors on the ridge.[12]

From atop the second ridge, the Guards saw another line of battle engaged to the south. To the right a heavy column of Union infantry stretched from one ridge to the other. And a terrible fire opened at the regiment from the left. The call was made to evacuate, but not everyone heard the order. Captain Williams sat in the breastworks gathering his strength and talking quietly with Jim Arrington, Williams' warm friend and relative and a former Warrior Guard. Near them a dead Yankee lay on the ground. Suddenly and without warning, Yankee soldiers surrounded them. As Captain Williams was marched off, once again a prisoner, he looked around, and Arrington was gone, Williams thought, perhaps killed by the shots coming from every quarter. Rather than surrender, Nutting grabbed the colors and ran straight into the 111th Pennsylvania Volunteers. He refused to give up the flag even after the enemy threatened to shoot and the other Guards begged him to comply. Instead, Nutting threw it into the woods as far as he could. "There is not a d——n Yankee living that I would hand that flag to," he vowed.[13]

The battle was essentially over, despite a few skirmishes over the next couple of days. Taking advantage of a rainstorm, Hooker consolidated his forces. The Union had suffered 17,000 casualties and the Confederates 13,000—a fifth of their forces. The Fifth Alabama lost 24 men killed and 254 wounded or missing.[14] Fourteen Greensboro Guards had been taken prisoner, seventeen lay wounded, and perhaps as many as four had received fatal wounds. The Guards' experiences at Chancellorsville mirrored on a small scale those of the South. The little company had led the glorious assault against a larger foe and, as part of Lee's army, triumphed. But in this, the South's greatest victory, also lay its greatest losses: Dr. Cowin for the Guards and Stonewall Jackson for the South.

A few days later, the thirty-five remaining Guards in the regiment selected one of their members for inscription on the Roll of Honor, the only recognition of bravery that the Confederacy bestowed. Dr. Cowin was the men's unanimous choice. "Another of the flower and hope of our country," wrote Chadwick to the *Beacon*, "is added to the long list of those who have given their heart's best blood in defence of her rights and her sacred soil." The correspondent pointed out that the well-educated Cowin, like many others in the company, was certainly qualified for promotion but had chosen to remain in the ranks. Several men commented that over the last several months he had borne a "quiet, courteous, and strictly moral deportment."[15]

The captured Guards were again sent north, this time to the Old Capitol prison in Washington, D.C. Life there was dreary but not unbearable. The Alabamians joined 740 men crammed into five rooms. The prisoners were divided into squads of fifty, with two cooks to a room. As each man's name was called, he drew four crackers, a slice of meat, and a cup of coffee. Sutlers sold fruit, cakes of cheese, and pies. The prisoners received paper, envelopes, and stamps for two letters.[16]

Sam Pickens tried to buy a tin cup from one of his captors. When he presented a Confederate dollar, the Yankee looked at it curiously and handed it back, filling the cup with soup and adding a piece of bread, careful that no officer observed. "I thanked him and told him if he should ever be in the South under same circumsts. I'd be glad to do him any favor." Pickens was forced to admit that the Union soldiers treated their Confederate prisoners better than the reverse. "But that is natural for we consider them invaders trying to subjug. & rob of everythg. we hold dear on earth. While many of them are only in army for a living & take no fighti[n]g in self defense on our own territory."[17]

On Monday, May 11—a week and a day after their capture—the prisoners were ordered to answer the roll call. As each man's name was read out, he walked between two lines of Union soldiers. The prisoners then marched down Pennsylvania Avenue. Crowds of citizens lined the streets to see the Southerners, with Union officers forbidding the hurling of insults. The Capitol's new dome dominated the skyline. After a fatiguing walk in the hot sun, seven hundred men set off aboard the crowded *State of Maine*. The next day the ship stopped opposite the heavily guarded Fortress Monroe on the tip of the Peninsula—a familiar sight to the Guards who had been captured after South Mountain—and the prisoners boarded another boat for the trip upriver. They passed where the *Monitor* and the *Virginia* battled. They passed the wreck of the *Cumberland*. They passed the scattered chimneys and few brick walls that marked the ruins of Jamestown. And finally they arrived at City Point late in the evening, delighted to see a Confederate banner floating atop the hill. The Guards boarded a train the next day, reached Petersburg about noon, and marched through town up to the camp of paroled prisoners two miles beyond.[18]

Pickens and Nutting slipped off to Petersburg. A friend offered to introduce them to some ladies who were partial to Alabamians. The men drank iced mint juleps, played tenpins, then returned to their hotel and went to bed—a nice day for paroled prisoners. The next day, five thousand Yankee prisoners marched by on their way to exchange. Pickens thought them "a dirty filthy low lived set" of foreigners. The two returned to the parole camp and left on a train that afternoon, arriving in Richmond about sundown. Like the Guards paroled after South Mountain, the parolees slipped off and headed for Mrs. Barnes' boardinghouse. That night, they went to the Broad Street Theater to watch a performance of *The Jewess*.[19]

The parolees had quite the life for the next week. They visited their wounded comrades in the Third Alabama Hospital, run by a beloved nurse from Alabama, Julia Ann Hopkins. Ned Bayol was recovering there from a ball in the hip; he would never again go into battle. Bill Britton had a severe injury to his lung. Sam Jackson's toe had nearly been shot off, and Bob Price had a ball in his leg. Heavy bleeding from a leg wound had reduced Lieutenant Colonel Hobson to a wan and thin imitation of himself; some thought his condition critical. With those obligations met, the parolees went to playing billiards in earnest. Then there were the letters to write, dinner with Mrs. Barnes, and another performance at the Broad Street Theater. They bathed, changed clothes, and had their boots blacked and their hair shampooed and trimmed. On Sunday they attended services at St. Paul's (where Generals Lee, Ewell, and Ramseur were worshiping) and then tried to hear Stonewall Jackson's memorial sermon at the Presbyterian church; the great crowd, however, rendered that impossible. The rest of the week was taken up with more billiards, cake and ice cream ("how nice & refreshing"), Sam Pickens' first shave ("cooler"), shopping (a new hat, paper, pens, toothbrush, and comb), and still more theater.[20]

The parolees boarded a train on May 21 and headed back to their regiment. (Their exchanges may finally have been approved or they may have simply decided to leave.) They got off at Guiney's Station and walked the five or six miles to camp. A week later, Captain Williams arrived. The first Guard to meet Williams was Arrington. Williams thought that Arrington had been killed at the ridge and asked how he had escaped alive. "Don't you remember seeing a dead Yankee lying near us at the breast works?" replied Arrington. "I thought I would feign death, so I took up a handful of his blood, and deluged my neck and face, and lay down. A Yankee passed by, gave me a kick and remarked 'he is dead,' and passed on. In a few minutes Ramse[ur]'s N.C. brigade came up and recaptured the works, and I got up and went to fighting."[21]

The exchanged Guards had barely returned to camp before Rodes, now a major general, drew his troops up for a grand review at a field on the road to Hamilton's Crossing. The bands played occasionally as the brigades were drawn out in line of battle, each behind the other. General Lee galloped up on Traveller accompanied by Generals Longstreet, A. P. Hill, and Rodes. The officers passed between the rows, examining each soldier. The men's confidence and the generals' pride were so palpable as to need no words. When the generals stopped in the front of a brigade, the men presented their arms and the flag bearers lowered their banners; General Lee returned their honors by doffing his hat. The long day was fatiguing, lasting from about ten until five, but it ended with a welcome bath in a creek to wash off the dust.[22]

These exercises had more than a few uses. Banners waving, men marching, and brass bands blaring—such rituals raised the pride of an army already convinced of its supremacy. The sight and approbation of General Lee, especially now that Stonewall Jackson was gone, reassured the men. But Lee also needed reassurance. Even before the Battle of Fredericksburg, he had been planning to take his army north again. A renewed invasion would, he hoped, confound the enemy's plans, ease Union pressure on the western armies, perhaps persuade foreign nations to recognize the Confederacy, and relieve Virginia farmers from the demands of feeding tens of thousands of troops. Lee needed his men in top form.

The Army of Northern Virginia began moving north on June 3, 1863. Rodes' division left the next day about two in the morning. The men passed through Spotsylvania Court House, camped a mile beyond, and the next morning were again marching before daylight. The Blue Ridge stood outlined on their left. Evening rains relieved the day's heat and dust. The Guards crossed the Rapidan and passed through Culpeper Court House, which Pickens called "a very old town in a poor, worn out country." On June 9 the division was ordered out to help Stuart's cavalry in an engagement at Brandy Station, a railroad stop a few miles northeast of Culpeper Court House, but the men were not ordered forward. Continuing through rich clover pastures and splendid fields of wheat, the farther north they marched, the better the lands looked. "They must swim in milk & butter all thro' this country," observed Pickens. Every hour the column would rest for ten minutes, but the going was tough even when the Guards marched at the head of the division. Pickens' feet, like those of others, were badly blistered, partly from crossing streams while wearing shoes and socks, which the men were not allowed to remove.[23]

Picturesque villages sustained the men with cheers and food. At Flint Hill, David Barnum managed to get some hot corn bread, fresh butter, and his canteen filled with milk. The people of Front Royal expressed delight that the Union soldiers who had been raiding them would finally be stopped. At Millwood, the citizens reported that Yankee cavalry had passed not an hour ahead. Two lovely young ladies brought buckets of water to soldiers waiting at a fence. "It was excellent water, too, cold as ice," judged Pickens. The Confederates marched to within a mile or two of Berryville and formed a line of battle. But the enemy had left quickly in confusion. The Rebels helped themselves not only to food left cooking on fires but also to other abundant stores: lemons, sugar, coffee, soap, boots, clothing, nearly new haversacks, and writing paper. One Smithfield woman poured buttermilk in the Southerners' cups and passed out slices of buttered bread. The troops cheered, the ladies waved handkerchiefs, and the bands played on during these confident, abundant, and heady days.

On June 19, the Alabamians finally reached the Potomac, across from Williamsport. They took off their pants and drawers and waded across the two hundred yards of a swift and clear river. Back in Maryland. Six miles further, the soldiers marched through Hagerstown, singing "The Bonnie Blue Flag" to more ladies waving handkerchiefs and Confederate flags. The Guards camped on Antietam Creek, a few miles from the site of their battle nine months earlier.

After a few days' rest, the men marched back through Hagerstown on the road to Chambersburg, Pennsylvania. They gathered all the horses and cattle they could find, driving them along as a commissary on hoof. The cherries on the trees were large and juicy, the springs cold and clear. Indeed, Pennsylvania's prosperity astonished the intruders. The soldiers were issued molasses, cigars, chewing tobacco, and maple sugar. David Barnum set off to investigate Chambersburg's houses and returned with a canteen of milk, a cup of creamery butter, and the first apple butter that Sam Pickens had ever tasted ("very nice"). Surrounding fields teemed with oats, rye, barley, clover, and hay. The Germans' large stone or brick barns, complete with glazed windows, were kept nearly as well as their homes and were better kept than many Southern homes.

Lee's soldiers resumed their march, passing through a series of small towns— Shippensburg, Leesburg, Centreville, and others—until they reached the edge of Carlisle. For a few days, the Guards again enjoyed the pleasures of the Pennsylvania countryside. But then on the last day of June, they marched as far as Heidlersburg, where they camped. The next day they continued on, unaware of their ultimate destination. But when they began to hear cannon fire ahead of them, the Guards suspected that they would soon see action. About two miles ahead lay a crossroads town called Gettysburg.

In his first test as a division commander, Rodes had before him an unequaled opportunity. By arriving in force, his men could send the enemy running. Rodes ordered his division to form a line of battle and advance. Because the Fifth Alabama was on the left of O'Neal's brigade as it turned a right wheel, the regiment had to move very rapidly—even run—to stay in line. The Alabamians came through fields of fully grown wheat, over plowed ground, through orchards and gardens, over wood and stone fences. Sam Pickens claimed never to have suffered so much from heat and fatigue. Many fell out. Some fainted. Five hundred yards from the enemy, the brigade halted and lay down to rest. O'Neal sent four regiments forward, holding the Fifth Alabama in reserve to fill a hole between his brigade and another. The Fifth could see artillery batteries firing at each other from 150 yards apart. The Confederate gunners soon broke off the duel, leaving five or six dead horses and a couple of broken carriages. The regiment was then ordered to rejoin the brigade and attack the enemy, which consisted of two heavy lines of infantry and a line of sharpshooters supported by artillery. Most of the Fifth reached the brigade, but the Guards were split off and sent to help some North Carolinian sharpshooters who had exhausted their ammunition and were holed up in a barn. Yankees hiding behind a fence in the woods felled William Stokes as he ran, and Joe Brown was wounded after they reached the structure. The brigade passed, and the Guards ran out of the barn to rejoin their regiment. The bullets were thick. "I never saw troops so scattered & in such confusion," wrote Pickens. Caught in a crossfire from their front and left, they fell back to a fence where O'Neal and Rodes were rallying the brigade.[24]

Paul Lavender had been shot, and Pickens and three members of the ambulance corps carried him to the surgeon, about a mile away. After the ball was extracted, they waited in vain all evening for an ambulance. Pickens finally set out and found one and helped his friend reach the hospital late that night. Pickens was shocked: "The scenes about the Hospital were the most horrible I ever beheld. There were the poor wounded men lying all over the yard, moaning & groaning, while in the barn the terrible work of amputating limbs was going on, and the pallid limbs lying around presented a most disagreeable sight."

While Pickens tended to Lavender, the remaining Guards helped drive the Yankees through the town of Gettysburg. O'Neal's brigade re-formed and took its position northwest of town on an unfinished railroad line. In contrast to the larger success that Lee's army enjoyed in driving Yankees back, the first day ended badly for the Guards. George Nutting—a company favorite and Pickens' close friend and messmate—fell with the flag and died on the field shortly thereafter. His last words—"Come on boys!"—were identical to those uttered by his predecessor. John S. Tucker learned that his younger brother, Tun, had also been killed. "Never shall I forget my feelings when I got to him & found him lifeless," he recorded in his diary. "How sudden & heart-rending the change. Had parted with him only a few hours before in perfect health & fine spirits, never dreaming that it was the last & final interview."[25]

The next morning, July 2, began quietly. The Federals had established their position on Cemetery Ridge—the most defensible position in the area—anchored by Culp's Hill in the north and Little Round Top to the south. To the Union's north and west, the Confederates occupied Gettysburg itself (where every large building had been turned into a hospital filled largely by Union wounded) and Seminary Ridge, which paralleled the Yankee defenses less than a mile away. The Guards were altogether unaware of the broad outlines of the battle. Gilliam James brought word to his fellow Guards that the Confederates were amassing eighty pieces of artillery along the ridge. These guns finally opened fire late in the afternoon. According to Pickens, "the cannonading was terrific: almost as rapid as musketry," but the shooting was largely a demonstration in the center of the lines to keep the Union occupied; the main thrust came at the enemy's flanks. At the southern end, the Confederate plan was frustrated by an uncooperative James Longstreet and a Union corps' unauthorized movement out from its position on Little Round Top. The result was a most confused and bloody engagement as the Confederates pushed the bluecoats out of Devil's Den, the Wheatfield, and the Peach Orchard to their former positions. The assault on the Union right came later in the evening. Rodes' division moved forward in line of battle against a heavily fortified Cemetery Hill. The division was down significantly in numbers. The Fifth Alabama, with 226 casualties the day before, could field only about 380 men. But many of those fell out of the ranks, and by the time they reached their objective, as few as 300 remained in the regiment. They stayed in a field for a while and then, without being engaged, returned in complete darkness to sleep along one of Gettysburg's streets.

Early the next morning—the third and climactic day of the battle—O'Neal's brigade was again sent out to attack Culp's Hill. The Fifth Alabama, however, stayed behind to hold Gettysburg. The Greensboro Guards were designated sharpshooters and sent to the edge of town, where they erected breastworks and remained until evening. A minié ball occasionally whistled over their heads or a shell passed through a neighboring stable or crib and exploded. The sun was intense and the shade dear. But the most remarkable event of the day—arguably, of the entire war—escaped the Guards' notice.

With the previous attacks on the Union flanks unsuccessful, Lee ordered an assault on the center of the Union lines to be spearheaded by George Pickett's three brigades. Lee believed that a heavy artillery barrage would soften the center for three divisions to split the Union line and defeat the Army of the Potomac in one glorious charge. Perhaps this time the South could win the war. A little after one in the afternoon, 150 Confederate guns began the greatest artillery duel on American soil. For two hours the cannoneers aimed shot after shot at the Union line on Cemetery Ridge, but to little effect: they overshot their targets, which were safely hidden behind stone walls on slightly higher ground. Thirteen thousand Confederates then moved forward. The heat and the distance—nearly a mile—took their toll. But on the Southerners came, nearing their objective. Then the Union guns—which had remained silent to save ammunition and fool the Confederates—then those guns thundered, and Yankee Springfields joined the clamor. Pickett's charge faltered and then collapsed. Perhaps half of his men made it back to Seminary Ridge. Of these events, the Guards knew nothing. Wrote Pickens, "A heavy cannonading was kept up—a great many shells passing over us—and some from our own batteries exploded over our line & killed men in Doles', Ramseur's &, I think, Iverson's brigades. It was either very inferior ammunition or great carelessness on the part of the gunners."

After midnight, the Guards were roused and ordered back to higher ground. The air smelled of dead soldiers and horses. Rain started the following noon, and the men put up tents. Late that night, the early hours of July 5, the Guards joined the march back to Virginia. By that time, the roads had turned into sloppy troughs where men could hardly stay on their feet. Wagon wheels sunk in the mud and blocked the road. But the march nonetheless continued past sunrise, with the wagon trains on the roads and the troops trudging through the fields and woods on either side. Union cavalry caught up at Fairfield and started firing, but without any effect.

Lee's army eventually took a strong defensive position north of the Potomac. Then, on July 13, the army moved out quietly and deliberately. Campfires were left burning and a single regiment from each brigade stayed behind to protect the others as they pulled back. The remaining regiments then followed, covered by sharpshooters and a few cavalrymen. Union forces discovered the retreat and charged with a double line of skirmishers, but the sharpshooters held off the enemy. Finally, the last Confederates snuck out in a light rain. Because the road down to the river was blocked by troops, the Guards stood for an hour or so in ankle-deep mud and water. The column began to move, but every few yards it would halt. At daybreak on July 14, the Guards were finally able to begin wading across the swollen Potomac, now waist deep and very wide. They hung their cartridge boxes around their necks to keep them dry. Everything else—clothes, blankets, and haversacks—became wet and heavy. The men held onto each other to avoid falling. The muddy banks on the far side were steep and slippery, but the Guards were safely in Virginia.[26]

✯ ✯ ✯

Families back in Greensboro waited impatiently for particulars. A third of Lee's seventy-five thousand–man army were casualties, including three missing Guards who were presumed captured. Five Guards lay wounded, including two known to be taken prisoner. George Nutting's death, the company's third fallen color-bearer, commanded special attention in a public letter written by Lieutenant E. Pompey Jones (whose father had served as the Guards' captain during the 1840s): "I know of no one in the Company who would have been missed more and talked of as much as he; in fact, he was the life of the Company, always in a good humor, full of fun, and as brave as a lion." Jones claimed that the Guards felt the loss not only of a brave soldier but also of "a *friend* whose place cannot be filled." One of Nutting's brothers-in-law, John S. Tucker, was a Guard, and another, Dr. William T. Black-ford, had served as the Guards' unofficial surgeon. In addition, Nutting's brother, Ed-win, had also served as a Guard until his discharge in December 1862. When Nut-ting's mother heard of her son's death, it affected her so deeply that according to her obituary, written fifty years later, she never fully recovered.[27]

Nutting was not the last Guard to die that season. A few weeks after Joe Wright arrived back home on furlough, he succumbed to undefined chills. At the time he was visiting his aunt, Bettie or Belinda Dorroh, the bereaved mother of Sam Dor-roh. Wright was buried in the Greensboro cemetery with full military honors. Like all Greensboro's sons, he was deemed "an estimable young man, of moral and ex-emplary deportment, much respected in this community, and a particular favorite with his comrades in arms." And in October came word that William W. Stokes, who had been taken prisoner at Gettysburg, had died of measles. "He was a kind husband and affectionate father," noted the *Beacon,* "and leaves a devoted wife and four small children, father and mother, brothers and sisters."[28] Words of criticism, of course, were never spoken of a Guard who died in service.

The events of July forced Greensborians to examine their war yet again. They deemed the loss of Vicksburg crucial and would not understand the significance of Gettysburg until much later. Yet sobered Greensborians knew that the self-assured days when the Guards had marched off to preserve the peculiar institution lay far behind them. Now more than just slavery was imperiled. Confidence sagged; re-solve needed stiffening. In August, the *Beacon* announced a series of open meetings and barbecues to consider the Eutaw Resolutions, which had been passed on Au-gust 15 by citizens gathered at the county seat. The six resolutions declared that the war must be vigorously prosecuted until independence was acknowledged and peace secured; that every citizen's duty was to cooperate zealously, even to the point of sacrificing property and life in order to forestall subjugation; that reconstruction was morally and politically impossible and to think otherwise was treasonous; and that the governments of the Confederacy and of Alabama should promptly bring into service every available man capable of bearing arms.[29]

These first four resolutions were not particularly controversial, for they merely reaffirmed the oft-repeated claims that the war could be won with more zeal and sacrifice. *Beacon* editor John G. Harvey, however, refused to concede that reconstruction was impossible. Nor, he claimed, should those who charged higher prices be branded "extortioners" or "enemies of the country," as the sixth resolution charged. Specie was simply unavailable, he pointed out, and higher prices reflected economic realities. Moreover, the editor was objecting to the singleness of mind that several of the Eutaw Resolutions demanded: "We are not prepared to brand as 'traitors,' those who may think differently."[30] (Harvey of course had almost been thrown out of town during the secession crisis as a result of his Unionist views.) Once more, a crisis had raised the problem of exclusion—as it would again.

The indictment of those who charged high prices was the sixth and last of the resolutions, but it was not the most important. That distinction belonged to the fifth: "That the North having armed a portion of our slaves to fight against us, we, in turn, should arm enough of them to at least counterbalance the force of the insurgent blacks arrayed against us." In the late summer of 1863, months before General Patrick Cleburne's celebrated proposal, the heart of the plantation South was seriously considering the idea of arming slaves.[31]

When the *Montgomery Mail* took up the question the next week, the entire state joined the debate. In an article entitled "Employment of Negroes in the Army," the *Mail* appealed first to necessity: "We must either employ the negroes ourselves, or the enemy will employ them against us." At least six hundred thousand slaves could be capable of bearing arms, and at least fifty thousand blacks were already doing so—in Federal ranks. Two weeks after Gettysburg, the Fifty-fourth Massachusetts Colored Infantry had assaulted Battery Wagner in Charleston Harbor, suffering high casualties but proving the worth of black soldiers in combat. Lincoln now proposed expanding the program, the *Mail* continued, and the Confederate government must forestall his scheme: "Let them be declared free, placed in the ranks, and told to fight for their homes and country." The *Mail* admitted that emancipation would have far-reaching effects beyond the battlefield. Black soldiers would prove to the Europeans, whose recognition might still come, "that it is not a war exclusively for the privilege of holding negroes in bondage . . . but a war for the most sacred of all principles, for the dearest of all rights—the right to govern ourselves."[32]

The most significant aspect of the argument was not so much its origins from the disappointment of 1863 but rather its tacit admission that fighting entailed freedom. Slaves might be compelled to work in fields, but they could not be compelled to die to keep themselves in bondage. A man who shouldered arms entered a fraternity of equals. Therein lay the rub.

Harvey admitted as much when he argued for using black slaves as teamsters, cooks, and axmen but not in the ranks. Slaves were already engaged in such auxiliary work under the direction of individual masters, a situation that was consistent with blacks' subordinate roles in Southern society. Captain Williams estimated years later that altogether perhaps thirty Guards' servants accompanied their masters at various times during the war. Williams, from whom service in the war invariably invoked praise, was careful to applaud the "faithful servant" at every turn. The body servant's main task, he noted, was to anticipate his master's every want: foraging, carrying knapsacks, minding personal effects, and cooking food. The Guards sometimes would have been out tramping through snow on the firing line after midnight, according to Williams, and twenty or thirty servants would bring cooked supper to their masters. Servants marched by day at the company's side, laughing and talking with the soldiers, and at night the slaves sat among the soldiers around the campfires. The Guards certainly came to depend on their servants. Before his death at Chancellorsville, Dr. Cowin had lamented that his Seve's illness had left his mess without a cook. "Am in hopes he will soon recover," Cowin wrote, "for when he gets sick we are in a bad fix." Although some slaves were purchased (one captain in the Fifth Alabama even bought a native African in late 1864), they were more commonly sent from home. James Boardman, for example, requested that his father send him a new servant: "You have no idea how I miss Caesar. Its a great pity the rascals dont know how highly they are prized!!" Editor Harvey urged that slaves continue to serve in these capacities. They could not be relied upon as soldiers, he claimed, because they lacked courage and would likely desert to the enemy. Further, at the end of the war they would be valueless as slaves, for their service would require their emancipation. White soldiers would feel humiliated. And finally, "the effect of our adopting such a policy would, we think, be most damaging to the institution of slavery."[33] Precisely. The faithful servant entered the mythology of Greensborians' Civil War but did so neither as a partner nor as an individual.

The arguments for and against arming slaves raged through 1864 and early '65. In neighboring Sumter County, which had supplied two companies to the Fifth Alabama, the editor of the *Gainesville Independent* railed against the idea. The war was for "the liberty and right of the States to maintain and protect the institution of slavery," one of his correspondents proclaimed. And in a simple but curious summation, the paper stated, "Southern slavery is *Liberty*. Northern *freedom* is the abomination of slavery." The *Beacon* reprinted articles that C. C. Langdon had originally written for his *Mobile Advertiser and Register* and then gathered into a pamphlet entitled *The Question of Employing the Negro as a Soldier! The Impolicy and Impracticability of the Proposed Measure Discussed*. Langdon listed several objections to the idea, all of them reducible to one problem: making soldiers of slaves and teaching them the art of war would mean the destruction of slavery. In time, Harvey dropped his reticence to putting slaves in uniform and declaring them free. "In the solidity of the institution of slavery exists, in our humble judgment, the glory and stability of this Southern Confederacy, but come weal, come woe, we are first and always for the separate independence of the South . . . and if the negro stands in the way of this independence, let him go." Placing slaves in the army might risk desertion, but leaving them on the farms ensured their emancipation when the Yankee armies arrived. Still, critics were not convinced. "What is the proposition?" asked an unnamed *Beacon* correspondent. "To elevate the negro to the position of a free man and a soldier, and when our independence is secured turn him loose in our midst, where his wife and children are in bondage! It requires no prophetic vision to foresee the consequence. There must be emancipation, or we may expect to see the horrid tragedy of San Domingo re-enacted," a potent vision among Greensborians.[34]

Greensboro's soldiers at first resisted the idea. "As we expected," reported the *Beacon* in late 1864, "the brave men who fight our battles have no confidence in the negro as a soldier. Nor are they willing to submit to the associations which would result from carrying this most short-sighted scheme into effect." But within a few months, the Guards were willing to share the bloodletting. "Soldier" wrote back home in support of the idea, observing that one hundred thousand slaves in the field could make quite a difference, as Union armies had demonstrated. By mid-February officers of the Fifth Alabama were discussing whether slaves would be more effective placed in segregated companies or in existing ones. The men still did not like the idea, reported the captains. Nevertheless, "anything rather than subjagation by the Yankees, & they are willing to submit to any measures deemed necessary to prevent it." Greensborians had gone off to war to prevent a slave insurrection. Now they were desperate, prepared to arm the same slaves they feared if doing so would stave off defeat. Harvey put it correctly: "we have no alternative but to *fight, whatever may be the fate of slavery.*"[35]

In no extant letter, in no extant diary, did a Greensboro Guard ever question the morality of owning another person; indeed, despite claims that body servants were held in high regard, their names seldom even appeared. The debate over arming slaves did not signal any change in Greensborians' belief in the innate inferiority of black people. Nor did the debate represent an affirmation of a Confederate nationalism that existed apart from slavery—at least not to the townsfolk in Greensboro.[36] The final decision would be imposed by the government in Richmond in the war's waning days, not by townspeople in an increasingly isolated area of central Alabama. Rather, the question of whether to arm and emancipate slaves—like the war itself—showed that desperate Greensborians were willing to make common decisions that encroached on individual autonomy—in this case, property rights that had once been held nearly sacred.

The gloom that settled on Greensboro following Gettysburg and Vicksburg was deepened by a falling economy. The prospects had looked good after Fort Sumter. When a vast number of Greene County planters instructed their factors in Mobile to pay the proceeds of their cotton sales in twenty-year government bonds, everyone applauded this sign of faith. But within only six months, business in Greensboro was "almost suspended" because of high prices and a scarcity of goods. A great many firms had closed up entirely, while the rest operated on a cash-only basis. The slump forced Greensboro's only bank, the Planters Insurance Company, to close its doors. Planters were expected to plant grain instead of cotton, to raise meat stock, to spin their own cloth and sew their own clothes, and to make their own shoes. One planter tried to put the best face on these changes by claiming that the new grasses, clover, and stock would rest the lands, improve the farms, and beautify the Canebrake. The shift of Canebrake lands from cotton to grain and pasture intensified through the war.[37]

Planter John Haywood's experiences may have been typical. He met the tax collector in late 1862 but "had not a dime" and so paid nothing. A few months later, the tax assessor required Haywood and the other planters to hand over all corn and cotton harvested in 1861 and 1862—a rather steep tax. When Haywood tried to raise cash by selling a certificate of deposit, he could not interest two of the most substantial neighboring planters, for they had no money. Another planter asked Haywood to accept Confederate currency in payment for debts, an option that he was loath to accept, although public sentiment forced it on him. Haywood's "near naked" slaves were suffering, subsisting on milk and bread. Yet he had received an order from the impressment agent for two good hands, each with thirty-five pounds of good bacon, an axe, a shovel, two suits of clothing, bedding, and cooking utensils. For this he was to receive a dollar a day per hand and sixty cents a pound for the bacon. Some of the slaves he furnished died from the work. A few days after the battle at Gettysburg, Haywood wrote to his brother that he had paid the Confederate agent in Greensboro thirty-seven hundred dollars in place of the thirty bales of cotton the Haywoods had subscribed when the first Confederate bonds were offered. He reported in the same letter that over his vehement protests, an impressment agent from Demopolis had selected a fine young steer and a yearling from their herd of two steers, two bulls, and five yearlings. The agent showed official orders for those he took plus another hundred. By the beginning of 1864, Haywood was complaining to his brother and business partner that they had purchased no provisions, clothes, or shoes. People were withholding provisions from the government agent, who was offering $1.50 a bushel for the corn that now covered the Canebrake. Those living in Greensboro could not hire wagons, as the teamsters charged $10 to $15 a day. Coarse cloth for slaves was selling for $3.50 a yard in stores, while cloth made with any wool fetched $15 to $20 a yard. Mules were selling for $500, and land was $50 per acre. On two nearby plantations lived no whites at all. In February 1864, the impressment agent took the only wagon and team left on the Haywoods' plantation. And in June, an artillery company tried to impress a mule. Furthermore, cholera killed eighty-four of the Haywoods' hogs. "If our bad luck increases we will have to quit the business of farming."[38]

That some felt cheated by soaring prices was inevitable. Justina Webb complained bitterly about selling the family's mansion for Confederate dollars of diminished worth, although she felt duty bound. The Bordens paid twenty dollars in the summer of 1862 for a half sack of Clarke County salt, a price they blamed on extortionists, whom Fannie labeled "certainly our worst enemies." At the Episcopalians' annual state council, held in Greensboro in May 1863, the bishop stated that "this is no proper time for any man to meditate upon schemes of self-aggrandizement."[39] The Eutaw Resolutions, too, protested against the supposed extortioners and thereby backed restrictions on individual autonomy.

"Justice" wrote a letter to the *Beacon* after the summer of 1863 alerting the populace to a new enemy. Men of means had been accustomed to borrowing large amounts of money to invest in land, slaves, and merchandise. These investors had often borrowed from moderate men who, by their personal industry and economy, had managed to save a small surplus. At the beginning of the war, the well-off had availed themselves of certain laws, enacted for the benefit of the soldiers and the poor, and refused to pay their debts or even the interest they owed. But after the 1863 reverses, some of the wealthy had lost confidence and were anxious to pay their debts. One planter who had borrowed in gold and silver announced that he would repay in Confederate bonds and notes. "But I suppose this will make no difference," he cleverly added, "as you are a *hopeful, trustful, loyal* man, and a *soldier,* and *all soldiers* are pleased to get all the Confederate money they can." Hiding behind a pretense of patriotism, the debtor was unloading his inflated Confederate money on the hapless creditor. "Justice" asked that the legislature allow debts to continue until one year after peace.[40] He made no claim for a conspiracy, but he did resent individuals furthering their own self-interests at the expense of the whole, a complaint that the preceding generation had not voiced. Even more than a protest against high prices and profiteering, his letter bespeaks a shift away from the interests of the individual in favor of those of the community.

A week after the Eutaw Resolutions were reported, in the same issue that reported Joseph Wright's death, an article appeared on the front page of the *Beacon* with the simple title "Home." "Those only who have been forced to bid adieu to scenes of their earliest years," Harvey began his essay, "are fully prepared to test the truth that 'life's choicest blessings centre all at home.'" The editor compared the family circle to a desert oasis, making the native land appear more beautiful than the finest landscape. "The love of home has led the warrior forth to fight the invaders of his country, and at the moment of conflict has nerved his arm with increasing strength. It has won the weeping prodigal back to his father's door, and reclaimed him from the depths of vice and misery." The specter of death in a far-off land made the security and familiarity of home even dearer. If a brother fell in defense of his country, the pleasure of his family would be severed until all were rejoined forever in their heavenly home. "O! who can realize the joys of that meeting?" Harvey asked.[41]

Home was becoming dearer to Greensborians. But where was home? Before the war, *home* usually referred to the location of one's birth. But now *home*—especially for the Guards in Virginia—meant their little town on the northern edge of the Canebrake. The constant dangers and battlefield deaths were elevating Greensboro to a sanctuary for the wounded, the object of sweet memories, and the final resting place for the dead. Families lived there. But the Guards had become a sort of family, too. They were not simply individual soldiers fighting in some distant land but brothers depending on each other for their very lives.

CHAPTER 9

# Defying the Machine

**What I did was in the discharge of my duty
& not to gain any fame or to render myself
conspicuous.** ★ Edwin Lafayette Hobson, 1864

Even as the wheels of war ground inexorably on, civic life in the little town on the
Canebrake's northern edge seemed to stand still. Correspondents noted the change
only a year after the conflict began: "There are few people in the neighborhood,"
wrote James Pickens to his brother, Sam, in the Guards, "& it is only occasionally
that any one is seen passing on the road." The small congregations that assembled
to hear the Reverend J. J. Hutchinson preach at Wesley Chapel contrasted strikingly
with the crowds he had addressed a few years earlier. Greensboro's only newspaper
printed virtually no local news, for precious little was happening; gone too were
newspapers from other locales, formerly supplied by steamboat. As early as January 1862, the Union blockade and the demands of war had virtually stopped business transactions in the formerly bustling Greensboro. Frustration and weariness
were palpable. And as 1863 turned to 1864 and then to 1865, Greensborians could
bring themselves to launch no new civic projects. The young men who might have
led such endeavors had long since joined the military and left for the front. In their
hands rested the town's fate and its story.[1]

"Writing," Sam Pickens told his mother, "is the only way in which I can now hold
sweet communion with those nearest and dearest."[2] Greensborians were at the
mercy of smudged pencil marks on scraps of paper. Some of these letters, usually
penned by a junior officer or first sergeant, continued to be sent for printing in the
*Alabama Beacon*. Such public correspondence did more than inform and reassure:
publication tied the company's fate ever closer to the town's. After several writers
were killed in action, the task fell in 1863 to Shelby Chadwick, whose unfailingly
positive letters never touched on the soldiers' desperate situation.

Thus, not until much later did Greensborians learn of the Guards' trials during
the war's last two years, one of the circumstances that prodded Captain J. W.
Williams to publish his reminiscences at the turn of the century. Williams stressed

Edwin Lafayette Hobson, former Greensboro Guard who commanded the Fifth Alabama for much of the war. (Courtesy Alabama Department of Archives and History, Montgomery)

the horrors of the campaigns, particularly in the Wilderness, openly admitting that he wanted his readers to understand the suffering that his generation had endured. He sometimes allowed details—some of which verged on the trivial—to take over his narrative, but at the time he wrote, many of the Guards (and certainly their family names) remained familiar to Greensborians. The cumulative effect was to rekindle the war's immediacy for some and to convey it for the first time to a younger generation.

Greensboro had become emotionally united even as it was geographically divided. The stresses of war cemented the commitment between hometown and front line.[3] It had been easy enough to head for Virginia after the company's pleasant sojourn at Fort Morgan, when prospects for a glorious and short war were bright. But now the Guards were acting from a sense of duty. What had started as an adventure was now a drama, and some men began to wonder if it might in fact end as tragedy.

★ ★ ★

After Gettysburg, the Army of Northern Virginia continued its retreat south through Winchester and Front Royal, pursued by General George Meade's Army of the Potomac. At Manassas Gap, the Guards were sent up the mountain to prevent the Yankees from flanking the Confederates. From this safe position, the Guards could see the enemy charge, only to retreat when one or two small pieces of Confederate artillery sent them scurrying. Later that evening General Robert E. Lee's army marched out. The day was extremely hard—twenty-eight or thirty miles of marching—but the Southerners had left behind their antagonists and were not bothered again before reaching their camp east of Orange Court House.[4]

"Never, perhaps, were the armies of Northern Virginia and the Potomac more quiescent than at present," wrote Chadwick in a letter intended for publication in the *Beacon*. "Nothing worthy of record disturbs the unbroken tranquility that reigns supreme." In contrast to the despair that had settled over Greensboro, the Guards were encouraged, he insisted. The recent reverses had not disheartened the Guards in the least; on the contrary, Gettysburg and Vicksburg had aroused latent energies and made the men more determined never to abandon the struggle. "The lo[u]d huzzas and ringing laughs that resound through the encampment, the cheerful looks and confident words of the troops all testify to this. No words of despondency are heard from, no clouds of gloom rest upon our gallant army."[5]

But Chadwick's sanguine words to Greensboro were contradicted by diary entries privately admitting "an over abundance of Sorrow grief and loneliness." And the soldiers' actions denied Chadwick's words as well. By the end of July some twenty thousand men were gone from Confederate rolls, many of them deserters. Lee acknowledged as much when he issued a general order for absentees to return: "To remain at home in this, the hour of your country's need, is unworthy the manhood of a Southern soldier. . . . let it not be said that you deserted your comrades in a contest in which everything you hold dear is at stake." Desertions were occurring en masse and were presumed to be by conscripts from regions with few slaves; in fact, however, many of the desertions came from regiments with distinguished battle records. To alleviate the shortage of men, all soldiers on detached service (including such Guards as Commissary Clerk John S. Tucker, Ordnance Officer Jim E. Webb, and Wagon Master J. E. Griggs) were ordered to return to their companies in mid-August, their former positions to be filled by disabled soldiers.[6]

A sign of trouble came on August 13, when twenty-one of thirty-two members of a company in the Twelfth Alabama departed with their arms and accoutrements. This desertion particularly alarmed the Guards, for the Twelfth was in Rodes' old brigade and was commanded by Colonel Samuel B. Pickens, who was related to some of the Guards. Two squads left in pursuit with instructions to take the deserters alive if possible, dead if necessary. Three days later, General Lee announced a system of furloughs by which two exemplary soldiers out of every hundred were granted thirty-day furloughs; upon their return, one from every hundred would be allowed a pass. Six men from the Fifth Alabama were the first to go. At the same time, a general pardon was offered except for those men who had deserted more than once. To enforce compliance, Lee reinstituted the death sentence for deserters, and every division was ordered to organize a general court-martial to try offenders. General Rodes appointed the Guards' J. W. Williams to the thirteen-member court, the only captain among the majors, colonels, and brigadiers. At least five panel members, according to Williams' reminiscences, understood their duty differently and tried to prevent executions.[7]

Desertions continued nonetheless. On September 5, news spread through the army that ten from Johnson's division had been executed; not only had they deserted, but they had killed several of the troops sent to catch them. And on September 16, Rodes' division was taken out to see the execution of a North Carolina deserter from Ramseur's brigade. Each regiment marched by the dead soldier to make the message abundantly clear. In January 1864, the division was again drawn up to witness the execution of twelve deserters from Daniels' North Carolina brigade.

Executions were described vividly. Different Guards employed the same phrases, as if reciting together a liturgy. Their accounts typically began with broad descriptions of the weather: "The day was a beautiful, balmy spring-like one. The ground was covered in a winding-sheet of snow, and the brilliant rays of the sun shining upon it were reflected back in a myriad of sparkling beams." The focus then narrowed to the troops assembled in three sides of a square. The doomed men were brought into the center and tied to stakes. A chaplain said a prayer and spoke a personal word to each. Bandages were then placed over their eyes and the firing squad brought in line. "The sharp click of the fire[lo]cks was heard—a momentary pause, and the word 'Aim' followed." Seamlessly and unconsciously, the descriptions would slip from the past to the present tense. "The muskets are leveled at the breasts of the poor fellows, and in another moment the fatal command, 'Fire!' is given. A volley is emptied into their bosoms—a compulsive shudder shakes their bodies as they gradually sink to the earth, and as the smoke clears away an attendant surgeon hastens up and examines their pulses. Finding the vital spark had not yet fled, he withdraws, the soldiery reload their pieces, and another volley is fired at their prostrate forms." With death now final, the writers returned to the past tense. "I felt the moment after the volley was fired, an indescribable & mixed sensation of sickness & horror at the sight." The troops were then dismissed and returned to camp to ponder the event and its lesson. The summary: a "magnificently grand but terrible spectacle."[8]

Camped on the Rapidan River in central Virginia, the soldiers had little else to concern them. Meade's army had followed Lee's and had set up camp across the river so close that the Guards sometimes heard the sound of the enemy's cannon. The cavalry would rush off and the infantry would form lines of battle, but little came of it. Typical was an instance in mid-September when the Guards were called out to Morton's Ford for an expected attack by the enemy, thought to be assembling just across the river. The men labored hard all day and into the night to build breastworks, but instead of waking up the next morning to the roar of cannon aimed at them, they found a quiet, serene, and delightful day.[9]

Lee searched for an opportunity to strike at his opponent and perhaps redeem some of what had been lost in Pennsylvania, but he had to act before the winter winds ended the year's fighting.[10] The Guards, as part of the Fifth Alabama, left camp on October 9, heading west and north, until they reached Jeffersonton a few days later. The village was held by a large force of Yankee cavalry, but Rodes sent his men straight at the enemy, who streamed out of the woods toward Rebel skirmishers lying in wait. A hundred bluecoats were taken prisoner. The Confederates continued on in pursuit of the Federals as they fled to the safety of Warrenton Springs (sometimes known as Sulphur Springs). Rodes ordered the Guards and two other companies to deploy as skirmishers. The men crossed the Rappahannock but after about an hour of fighting were left stranded for the rest of the night. "No one but those that have experienced it," recalled Captain Williams in typical hyperbole, "can tell the suffering we underwent that night." The men never dried out after wading the river, and they could not light fires, despite the night's freezing temperatures, for fear of alerting the enemy.

About nine the next morning, the Guards were ordered to rejoin the Fifth Alabama, which had gone ahead. They overtook the regiment on the outskirts of Warrenton. To their surprise, they found General Lee walking among their brigade, scanning the countryside with his field glasses in expectation of finding Meade's army in retreat. Even on foot, he remained "the grandest specimen of humanity" Williams had ever seen. J. E. B. Stuart stood nearby with "a bevy of Ladies" vying for his attention.

The two armies continued skirmishing off and on for the rest of October and into November. On one occasion, the Guards were ordered to move across a treeless and level field. As they moved in a line, the Yankees began firing from rifle pits on the opposite side of the river. Williams again use the superlative to describe the experience as the most trying fire the Guards encountered. They were without cover as the minié balls began zipping over and around them. Word soon came to lie down in the field's waist-high weeds. The soil was sand, and using their hands and tin plates, the men dug holes for themselves. After learning that General Meade had ordered his troops back, Williams led the companies back to the safety of Pony Mountain, near Culpeper.

Rodes' division remained in the vicinity for only a short time before moving to its old camp across the Rapidan, near Raccoon Ford. During the last week in November, Meade sent sixty-five thousand troops against Lee's right flank south of the Rapidan along Mine Run. Along with their brigade (now led by Cullen A. Battle, who had replaced Edward A. O'Neal after Gettysburg), the Guards rushed to the fighting, hastily digging breastworks of poles and earth by loosening the dirt with anything they could find: sharpened oak poles, bayonets, tin plates, cups, and even their bare hands.[11] The Confederate defenses withstood the Yankee shelling, and shortly thereafter the enemy retreated, this time for good. Both armies went into winter quarters, with the Yankees occupying some of those that the Confederates had made for themselves.

★ ★ ★

"Unbroken quiet reigns over the two hostile hosts now calmly reposing and gathering strength for the coming spring," reported an upbeat Chadwick in his letter to the *Beacon* in February 1864. The winter was proving severe, he continued, but the army's camp—about five miles from Orange Court House near Raccoon Ford—was convenient to the railroad, which brought them such treats as genuine coffee, sugar, lard, rice, peas, and dried fruit. The "loving mothers and fair daughters of noble old Greene" had contributed to the Guards' Christmas and New Year's celebrations by sending an abundance of such delicacies as turkey, ham, oysters, sweet potatoes, and even wine. The men collected around their blazing hearths to converse and sing: "Could you have heard the ringing laughter, the joyous words, and the snatches of songs that pealed forth in rich melodious tones from the festive groups, you would scarcely have thought them to be soldiers of the gallant 'Army of Northern Virginia'—veterans of a three years' war—inured to and acquainted with all the hardships, dangers and fatigue incidental to campaigning in Northern and Eastern Virginia."[12]

Chadwick's next letter back to the *Beacon* was again full of cheerful confidence. He boasted that no year had started "under brighter and more favorable auspices for us than the year 1864." By late March, when he penned the letter, Chadwick claimed that the North had suffered a host of setbacks that boded well for the Confederacy. On land, a recent Union raid on Richmond had been thwarted; General William T. Sherman's campaign to destroy the railroads and armies in Mississippi had come to naught, and his army now cowered inside the fortifications of Vicksburg; and General William S. Rosecrans' army had been halted at Chickamauga and driven back to Chattanooga. On the water, the *Hunley* became the first submarine to sink an enemy ship, the *Housatonic,* in Charleston Harbor, and Admiral David Glasgow Farragut's fleet was stymied outside Mobile Bay and rumored to be withdrawing. Union troops were despondent, Chadwick claimed, veterans were not rejoining, and the Canadas were swarming with Union deserters that another generation would label draft dodgers.[13]

Chadwick insisted that the Confederacy had men eager to replenish the ranks, unlike Lincolndom, and that nearly every regiment had voluntarily tendered its services for the duration of the war. The Greensboro Guards took credit for initiating this movement when they reenlisted on January 25, with Chadwick composing the pledge in appropriate, flowery language. And the Union blockade had converted the Confederacy into "one immense workshop" for the manufacture of everything from armaments to household items. In short, the South "will enter the spring campaign with veteran armies, victorious on scores of bloody fields and buoyant with hope." With renewed exertion, victory was within grasp. "Awake, then, from your lethargy!"[14]

Lethargy was hardly the problem. Like the dying Dr. Cowin, the South was simply being drained of its lifeblood. Just two weeks after Chadwick's letter appeared in the *Beacon*, the paper printed solicitations asking Greensborians to aid Calhoun County soldiers' families who lacked bread, corn, or money to buy food. The gallant and selfless fighting men had a right to expect their families to be provided for in their absence. One writer counseled those with a spare bushel of corn to part with it; others should donate money. By the last September of the war, the probate judge reported to the governor that Greene County contained 252 indigent families (904 individuals). Two years earlier, the judge had reported only 64 indigent families (173 individuals).[15] With the town's economic base jeopardized and with most local leaders in uniform by 1864, Greensboro's civic life had come to a virtual halt.

Nor could the military situation be accurately described in Chadwick's hopeful terms. The Yankee juggernaut seemed to press forward on all fronts: The Army of the Potomac lay just across the Rapidan from the Army of Northern Virginia; Sherman would lead a successful assault on Atlanta before the year's end; and Nathaniel Banks had been ordered to seize parts of Louisiana and then head toward Mobile while the blockade strangled the Southern ports. Lee's committed and seasoned veterans certainly were as good as could be had, but deserters were still being shot. In need of more troops, the Confederate Congress had been forced to restrict exemptions and substitutes, and men over age seventeen and under fifty were now subject to the draft.

The Guards knew firsthand the limitations of the new recruits. During that spring the Alabama legislature petitioned to have the Twenty-sixth infantry, which had served with the Fifth since June 1862, removed from Battle's brigade and sent back to Alabama, where it could replenish its badly thinned ranks. (The Twenty-sixth instead ended up in Dalton, Georgia.) In its place went the Sixty-first Alabama, a regiment made up of boys and older men who had been drafted under the February 1864 conscription act.[16] The veterans found this outfit laughable, but the Sixty-first would prove itself in the Wilderness.

Some of the Guards' new soldiers, such as James Pickens, also raised eyebrows. Sam Pickens knew that his brother was neither physically nor mentally suited to join the company. A headache had sent Jamie to bed on his first night away from home—not the best start to soldiering.[17] The younger Pickens, who was about twenty-one when he arrived in camp, was an unusual soul in the Army of Northern Virginia. His chronic inability to fight allowed him the time to write candidly of camp life and of his longing to go home. Other diarists and correspondents, especially early in the war, raged about defeating the Yankees, but Jamie's innocent diary reveals an attachment to home others may have deemed unmanly.

Only two weeks after leaving Umbria, his home in Sawyerville, Jamie felt that he had been away for ages. "Would that there were no war, that peace would be proclaimed & that Sam, Tom & I were all united at dear old home, sweet home, with our dear mother, sisters & brothers & those we love." Jamie looked to God to end this bitter war and to restore peace and happiness to the land, a plea he repeated in his diary every few days: "Would to God that no cruel war were raging in our land & that man, too, would cease from strife with his fellow-man, & learning a lesson from the little birds, praise his maker in songs of thanksgiving, for sending springtime & harvest upon the earth again! God grant that ere many days have passed, we may welcome the return of peace & praise His holy name in crowning our arms with signal triumph, securing independence & nationality to our country & immunity & safety from the hands of our foes, to our country!" Peace, however, could not come without independence. When rumors spread through camp that Presidents Davis and Lincoln were arranging a treaty of peace, Jamie noted that any news of this sort excited hopes for peace, but "not however with out the free & full recognition of every right & institution of the Confederacy & a restoration of all the territory which belongs to it as a separate and independent nation!" Jamie recorded in his diary on April 12 that it was the third anniversary of the day that the Yankees had inaugurated the war by firing on Fort Sumter. This well-educated young man (he had studied at the University of Virginia and spent his days as a Guard reading biographies of obscure Reformation figures) knew that it had been the South Carolinians who had opened fire on Union troops in Fort Sumter, and not the other way around. Yet he had allowed his commitments to displace reasonable judgments. Jamie's last diary entry was written in the middle of May. It read, "Oh Lord grant that I may soon be restored to my dear mother, sisters & brothers to guard, help & protect them."[18] He would soon be sent home on a medical discharge, never having fired his weapon. Jamie Pickens was not much of a soldier, yet he too would one day be honored as a veteran.

★ ★ ★

On the morning of May 4, the Guards awoke hours before daylight. They ate their breakfast of broiled ham and corn bread and were marching by seven. Winter camp was behind them, and the fourth season of fighting lay ahead.[19] At the same time, Lieutenant General Ulysses S. Grant was putting into effect his plan to keep the Southern armies from combining their forces. One Union army under Major General Benjamin Butler was to echo McClellan's 1862 strategy by advancing along the James toward Richmond. Major General Franz Sigel was to lead a second army up the Valley to pressure Lee's left flank, cutting his communication and supply lines. (Neither Butler nor Sigel would succeed.) Meanwhile, Meade's Army of the Potomac, where Grant established his mobile headquarters, was to head south to turn the right flank of Lee's Army of the Northern Virginia. "Wherever Lee goes," Grant instructed Meade, "there will you go also."

General Lee, of course, had his own strategy. As the Yankees headed south, he sent two of his three corps directly at them from the west. The Confederates would be outmanned nearly two to one, but Lee hoped that fighting in the Wilderness, a poor land of second-growth oaks and pines, would minimize the Union's superior strength. If the soldiers under Richard S. Ewell and A. P. Hill could hold the Union forces for a day, then James Longstreet's corps, recently returned from Georgia and Tennessee, would have time to smash the Union army's southern flank.

What would be known as the Battle of the Wilderness thus began with the Union forces marching south toward the Wilderness Tavern as the Confederates were converging from the west. The Fifth Alabama marched with Battle's brigade (Rodes' division, Ewell's corps) along a plank road toward Raccoon Ford on the Rapidan, which they reached about eleven o'clock. Receiving word that the enemy had already crossed the river downstream, the Confederates started east along the old turnpike between Orange Court House and Fredericksburg. After six or seven miles, they halted and went into camp, as they were considerably ahead of Hill's corps, which was marching along a parallel road. That night, Sam and Jamie Pickens lay down under a tree with one blanket on the ground and one above them. Neither slept well amid the bustle of preparing for the impending fight.[20]

Battle's brigade was aroused early the next morning, May 5. By daylight they were eating breakfast, and by midmorning they were continuing their march along the turnpike. The Sixty-first Alabama stood out from the rest of the troops. The grizzled men and fair-haired boys who composed the regiment had old quilts strapped across their shoulders and carried old-fashioned canteens, while the veterans were outfitted with nearly new provisions taken from dead Yankees. "What have you got that mattress on your back for?" jibed the seasoned troops. But as they neared the enemy, the jokes turned to sober warnings about making final arrangements for their impending deaths.[21]

About one or two in the afternoon, the sound of artillery could be heard ahead. Orders came to close up, for soon the men would be in battle. Along a ridge on either side of the turnpike, Ewell spread his brigades—John M. Jones', Cullen Battle's, and John B. Gordon's—one behind the other. The four generals consulted within earshot of the Guards. "If Jones gives way," Rodes and Ewell instructed Battle, "move up your brigade and retake the ridge." Jones' Virginians quickly repulsed two Yankee charges, but the stream of stragglers and wounded emerging from the dense pine thicket convinced Battle that Jones' brigade was giving way. Battle ordered his men forward. When they reached the front, however, they found Jones' brigade still holding its position, so they moved up into the Virginians' line and were ordered to lie down.[22]

The firing was so intense that Captain Williams did not raise his head for a while. When he did, he saw no one down the line—not even any Virginians—except the wounded and one other Guard, his friend Ed Hutchinson. The two hurriedly turned around and ran down the hill. Hutchinson was bitter, swearing that he never would have joined had he known that his regiment would disgrace itself by running. The two soon came upon a man trying to get his badly wounded brother off the field. The Guards stopped to help, but they had not gone far when the injured man asked them to put him down and let him die. They did as asked. When Williams and Hutchinson reached the original line of battle, they found Brigadier Jones trying to rally some fifty men by declaring his intention to die before giving up another inch. An enemy bullet quickly fulfilled Jones' vow. Hutchinson and Williams kept moving back until they reached Gordon's Georgians, still formed in a perfect line. When the Yankees started shouting "Hip, hip, hooray!" the general commanded his brigade to advance. Striking his horse with his hat, he galloped up and down the line, urging the counterattack. The Confederates were soon driving the Federals back to their first line, then their second, and even their third until five battle lines had merged into a solid mass.

The two lost Guards continued back until they finally met the rest of their company some distance in the rear. Everyone was laughing and trying to explain why they had retreated. Some claimed that those in Jones' brigade believed that Battle's troops had relieved them. But the more likely explanation was less complimentary. Other regiments claimed that Jones' panic-stricken Virginians had indeed stampeded and confused the Alabamians, who retreated with them. Pick Moore, an original member of the company who was then serving as a courier for General Rodes, placed his hands on Captain Williams' shoulders and laughed. "John, what was the matter with us?" he asked. "We came down that hill like a lot of thoroughbreds pulling on their bits." Williams also learned what had happened to the rest of the brigade. While the Fifth and the Third Alabama Regiments followed Jones' brigade to the rear, the Sixth and the untested Sixty-first Alabama Regiments had been left to face the Yankees. After some furious fighting, the Confederates charged and the Yankee line broke. Captain Williams was forced to admit that the young and elderly soldiers of the Sixty-first, whom he had ridiculed, had stood their ground and fought "like tigers." They had captured two cannon and caissons with all the horses. And instead of quilts, they now could sleep under Union-issue blankets.[23]

Once regrouped, the Fifth Alabama was ordered back to the front line. The Guards passed a Yankee soldier suffering so intensely from a wound in the bowels that he begged them to kill him. Henry Childress stopped, handed the injured man a canteen, and resumed the march. (Later that evening, some of the Guards went back to find the Yankee soldier dead. He had taken the toothed blade of his case knife and sawed his throat until he reached the carotid artery. General Rodes had the man buried and his grave concealed with pine straw lest the enemy believe that the Confederates had killed him.) The regiment finally reached the same ridge it had fled earlier in the day. There, the captains ordered half of each company to remain in line with their weapons ready while the other half put up breastworks of logs, dirt, and anything they could find—even Yankee knapsacks—that would protect them from an assault. The Yankees charged once or twice as the Confederates worked, but Major Eugene Blackford's sharpshooters drove the attackers back. By day's end, four Guards (D. E. Bayley, J. A. Farrier, D. J. Bridges, and Lewis Elias) had been wounded, and three more (Thomas R. Ward Sr., Edward Thomas Martin, and John L. Youngblood) had been wounded and captured.[24]

While the Fifth Alabama lay safely behind its breastworks, at dawn the next day, May 6, the Federals launched a massive attack a few miles south.[25] Grant was still attempting to turn the Confederates' right wing and place the Union army between Lee's men and Richmond. A. P. Hill's corps collapsed and ran to the rear. General Lee personally was attempting to rally his troops when Longstreet arrived with fresh men, who counterattacked and drove the Federals from the field.

As night fell, the captains received orders to bury the dead Yankees if prudent, because the smell of rotting corpses was overwhelming. Captain Williams delegated the task to Corporal Paul Lavender, who in turn chose some privates. When they returned, Williams asked for details. "I did it well," responded Lavender, "but buried them all North and South, so they would not face the East at the Resurrection." Another of the Guards set out to see what valuables he could recover while his comrades were burying the bodies. Sure enough, he found a dead Yankee still wearing a splendid pair of boots. After tugging hard to get them off the soldier's badly swollen feet, he returned to camp with his prize. He traded the boots to a fellow soldier who put his hand down one of the boots and pulled out thirty-five or forty dollars in Union greenbacks. A spirited argument quickly arose as to whom the money belonged to, and the claimants turned to Williams for a decision. The Solomonic captain advised them to divide the money equally, and they did.

The dawn found the two armies staring at each other. The outnumbered Confederates were strongly positioned on high ground behind formidable log and earthen barricades. While the enemy made demonstrations as if to attack, sharpshooters kept the Confederates' nerves on edge. The commander of artillery for Ewell's corps was standing among the Guards looking at the enemy through his field glasses. A shot rang out, striking a pine limb about thirty feet above him. As the limb fell, it turned downward and passed directly through his head. The cries of the wounded on the field in front of the Guards continued throughout the day and night. Two days of fighting had cost perhaps 11,000 Confederate casualties; the Fifth Alabama alone counted 5 killed, 28 wounded, and 48 missing. The Yankees officially listed their casualties at 17,666, but even this underestimate represented more men than the North had lost at the Chancellorsville debacle.[26]

Realizing that attacking Lee directly might be disastrous, Grant decided to force the Confederates out by moving his army southward. Not long after dark on May 7, Grant and Meade mounted their horses and turned them toward Richmond. The Army of the Potomac responded—despite the soldiers' wounds, despite their weariness, despite their many defeats—and cheers echoed through the forest.

Grant quieted the men down lest the noise alert the Confederates. The Federals were headed first to Spotsylvania Court House. The Confederates, too, raced to Spotsylvania, unbeknownst to the Federals, along a parallel road. Lee figured that Grant would either move his army to Fredericksburg and regroup or head south toward Richmond. Either way, the crossroads at Spotsylvania was a strategic location that Lee needed to hold; the fate of the entire campaign might well hang on which army first reached the village. Throughout the night, the Confederates hurriedly erected log barricades across the road at Laurel Hill, where the Yankees were expected. At the same time, General Richard H. Anderson, who had replaced the injured Longstreet, moved his corps south along another route parallel to the Yankees. At sunup, just as the cavalry was giving way to the vast numbers of Union troops, Anderson's men arrived to throw back a Yankee assault.

Reinforcements from both sides quickly moved to the new battle site. Approaching late on the evening of May 8 and having left at dawn, Rodes ordered his division to halt and close up into a battle line. Once his men were in order, he rode down the line giving encouragement. When he reached the Fifth Alabama, his old regiment, he said to Captain Williams and his Guards, "Boys, you played hell the other evening; now, when the order is given I want you to run over those Yankees in front." Rodes brought his division up to stop the Union armies from flanking Anderson's corps. As the Southern forces moved across a level field, skirmishers ahead started to fire. Then the order passed down the line to double-quick forward. The Confederates came to within 150 yards of some woods despite Yankee minié balls and continued over fences and across fields until they reached a pine forest "so dense that you could scarcely see the sky above you."

The enemy was driven back until darkness ended the fighting. Bunk Butler walked about, trying to find the Guards of the Fifth Alabama. After a while he heard a welcome sound: "Here is the flag of the Fifth Alabama." He walked right over and said, "Boys, you were damned hard to find," and a half dozen voices ordered, "Throw that gun down, Johnnie, we have got you." Butler was not seen again until after the war's end, because Grant refused to exchange prisoners. Hutchinson was wounded in the head, although not seriously. Charlie Briggs was wounded. And Lieutenant Colonel Edwin Lafayette Hobson had been shot in the thigh.[27]

The Guards spent May 9 digging trenches only a few hundred yards behind the main line. General Lee had finally learned that good defensive works could compensate for his army's ever-diminishing numbers. Orders were issued that no man could take off his accoutrements—night or day—and that weapons must be within reach. Jamie Pickens set his gun down along the way and lost his cartridge box at a hospital, leaving him only a cap box and ramrod. "I have seen enough of battle," he decided.[28]

Grant intended for his troops to assault the entire Confederate line on the afternoon of May 10, but various problems delayed his plan. About six o'clock, however, twelve select regiments led by Colonel Emory Upton were ready to attack the Mule

Shoe, a half-mile-long protrusion along the Confederate line about three hundred yards from the Guards. Upton assembled his troops at the edge of the woods across from Ewell's corps and instructed the men to charge with fixed bayonets, running without pausing even to fire. Once the bluecoats had breached the Confederate defenses, they were to spread right and left through the trenches to widen the gap, through which the rest of the troops would follow.

The Guards heard some fighting on their right. Rodes galloped up and ordered Battle's brigade to move forward—and quickly. The Guards, who were on the brigade's extreme right, ran forward without taking time to form into lines. Briggs threw his bayonet in the bushes, vowing, "I'm not going to get close enough to a Yankee to stick him with that thing, or let one get close enough to stick me." The Guards came out into the open fields. "Which way, general?" one asked. "Into the pine thicket and retake those works." Upton's attack was under way. The Fifth Alabama crossed a small creek and met artillerymen waving their red caps and yelling, "Charge them, Alabamians, charge them!" The Guards were now in front of the entire brigade. They passed through the pine thicket, not more than thirty yards wide, and confronted three thousand Yankees about eighty yards in front of them. The Guards fired first.

The fighting was relentless, according to Captain Williams. "We asked no favors, and granted none. We returned shot for shot, yell for yell. As the regiment was being thinned out, men from the brigade would push forward and take their places." Best friends were shot down, yet the survivors continued pressing nearer and nearer to the Yankees. The roar of muskets and the cheering of the men in the rear was deafening, so deafening that some Guards never heard the twenty cannon exchanging shots.

Lieutenant E. Pompey Jones of the Guards was standing with a squad of twenty men on special detail when he saw his comrades wade into the pine thicket. At that moment, General Lee rode up to Jones and asked, "Lieutenant, what are you doing here? Take your men in, those people MUST be driven back!" When Jones reached the scene, the soldiers were already packed twenty deep, and in the crush he could only stand at their backs.

At the front line Captain Williams heard an awful blow strike the head of a man beside him. He turned to see one of the Cahaba Rifles trying to kill a prisoner. "What in the world are you treating that prisoner so for?" asked Williams. The man responded, "Captain, he was just in the act of shooting you." The Guards moved on, and when the Pickensville Blues came up behind, the prisoner raised himself up and shot a lieutenant. Nine bayonets instantly pierced his body.

The soldiers gradually moved closer until the two lines were less than twenty-five yards apart, still firing away. Some Yankee soldiers captured a battery of four guns but could not turn them around in the dense crowd. A cloud of smoke from the gunpowder came to rest over them. When it lifted, the Guards could see the Yankees going back over the breastworks much faster than they had come in. With a wild yell, the Fifth Alabama rushed at them, and about 150 of the enemy threw down their guns and surrendered. Another 50 Yankees decided not to recross the open field and crawled back over and surrendered. The fighting had taken about twenty minutes.

Suddenly, it seemed that all was silent save for the groans of the wounded. In less than an acre, the Guards saw more dead Yankees than they had seen in battlefields twenty times larger. Some had fallen wounded only to be smothered beneath still others. Confederates rolled dead bodies off the wounded to save their lives.

Williams asked Briggs if he had missed the bayonet he had cast in the woods. He had but decided instead to use the butt end of his gun for all it was worth. One of the officers remarked, "A humming bird could not have lived at the edge of that little field in the rear."[29]

Back at the field hospital, Jamie Pickens watched the casualties come in. Colonel Josephus M. Hall, commanding the Fifth Alabama, was severely wounded (the next morning his right arm would be amputated below the shoulder). Rodes immediately went to see and thank Hall: "Colonel, you and your regiment saved Lee's army this evening, for his center was broken and nothing but your quick work saved it." The Guards were fortunate: none had been killed, and only four were missing. Among the handful of injured Guards, Captain Williams had been struck and stunned by a ball (he would soon leave for a Richmond hospital). Lieutenant Colonel Hobson had not yet recovered from his wound.[30]

Grant decided again to try Colonel Upton's attack on the Mule Shoe two days later, on May 12. This initial assault netted the Union four thousand prisoners. Lee called for his troops, including the Fifth Alabama, to strike back, and the battle turned into another hand-to-hand struggle at what came to be known as the Bloody Angle. Men again lay in heaps. After about twenty hours of fighting, the Confederates retreated to a new and more defensible line. Each side had little to show for this, the most savage fight of the entire war, except for hundreds of dead piled on each other. Grant lost perhaps nine thousand men that day and Lee about eight thousand.[31]

The Union army continued trying to outflank Lee's improved defensive positions. On May 19, the day after yet another unsuccessful Yankee attack on the Bloody Angle, General Lee ordered Ewell's corps to reconnoiter, suspecting that the enemy had pulled out. The men despised this job, which they called a "feeling expedition." At Harris Farm, a couple of miles north, Rodes' and Gordon's divisions engaged the Federals and added more casualties to the ever-growing total.

Grant sent his men racing south again, and Lee's army pulled out of its defenses at Spotsylvania and moved quickly to establish a new position along the North Anna River at Hanover Junction.[32] The Confederates arrived on May 22, ahead of the enemy, and quickly began building breastworks. The Union forces attacked and suffered for it. The pattern was becoming predictable.

Yet again, Grant ordered his army to move south around Lee's right flank, and again Lee raced south with his army to stop the Union forces before they reached Richmond. On May 29, Lee established a defensive line along the small Totopotomoy Creek. Rodes' division went forward on another feeling expedition eastward toward Bethesda Church. After only about a half mile the men were halted, put in line, and ordered forward. Two hundred yards in front a line of Yankees waited behind a deadly abatis of sharpened old field pines. As Captain Williams looked at the defenses, his heart stood still and his throat tightened.

"Charge!" came the order. The Alabamians held their guns tightly, crossed a small ravine, and shouted out the Rebel yell with whatever courage they had left. The Yankees fired but hit surprisingly few men. When the Confederates came within a hundred yards of the defenses, the enemy broke. The Confederates continued on until they reached the second line. Again the order to charge was shouted. The Fifth and Sixth Alabama led the drive. A third time they were ordered to charge, and the two regiments occupied the Yankees' third line—the only Confederates to do so.

The sky was now dark, the men exhausted. As they sat talking softly among themselves, one of the Guards looked up to see numerous Yankee campfires. In the glow he could see regiment after regiment double-quicking to reinforce their comrades. General Rodes approached on horseback and called for Captain T. J. Riley, who was commanding the Fifth Alabama in place of the wounded Hobson. But Riley had been wounded, leaving Captain Williams in charge. "Williams," Rodes ordered, "wheel the 5th at a right angle to the works letting your right rest on the inside of the works, and when I give the order to the 6th 'to wheel to the left,' . . . you move, and clear the works of those Yankees." Williams responded, "General they have been throwing reinforcements in there for the last half hour." Rodes dismounted, and by lying flat on the ground, he could see the enemy backlit by the campfires. He decided on prudence and ordered Williams to move the Fifth back with the Sixth to the captured defenses in the rear.

When daylight came, the Yankees occupied the defenses that the Confederates had left the night before. Throughout the day, the two lines fired at each other, stopped, smoked pipes, told a few jokes, and then started firing again. A Confederate artillery officer presently arrived. Through his field glasses he could see an enemy artillery battery seven hundred yards away, at the edge of the field. He requested that Captain Williams move the Fifth Alabama out of the way. Two batteries (eight guns) soon opened fire on the Yankee guns, which immediately returned the compliment. At seven hundred yards, the muzzles were not elevated an inch. The duel did not go well for the Confederates. Too many artillerymen were killed to manage even three guns, and too many horses were killed to pull the guns from the field. In the end, Rodes' division abandoned its position, and Lieutenant Colonel Hobson returned to take command of the Fifth Alabama.

While Rodes' division was engaging the Yankees at Bethesda Church, General Lee had his troops building more defenses. Grant ordered a massive assault at Cold Harbor, only ten miles from Richmond and familiar ground to those who had fought in the Seven Days' battles of 1862. Fifty thousand Union soldiers, many with their names and addresses pinned to their uniforms so that their bodies could be identified, headed straight for the Confederates at dawn on June 3. In short order the Union lost six thousand men and the Confederates perhaps a quarter of that number.[33] Grant called off the attack. Frontal assaults on entrenched infantry and artillery were simply too costly. The Northern public would not approve.

The spring offensive had launched a new kind of war. Instead of fighting a single major battle and retiring across a river to recover, the armies had been engaged for a month of unrelieved fighting. The Union counted about forty-four thousand casualties and the Confederacy twenty-five thousand. And privates were not the only ones who suffered. Lee had remained sick for a week, and Jubal Early replaced Ewell as head of the Second Corps, a change that would directly affect the Fifth Alabama and the Greensboro Guards.

★ ★ ★

Among those fatally wounded during the May 12 assault on the Bloody Angle was Lieutenant James Hutchinson, aide-de-camp to General Rodes and brother of Greensboro Guard Ed Hutchinson. Their father, the Reverend J. J. Hutchinson, made his way to the Spotsylvania battlefield, accompanied by the lieutenant's servant, George, and a Confederate soldier named Lloyd. They came to bring the minister's eldest son back to Greensboro, where he would be laid to rest beside his brother, Joe. Stories of journeying to the front to retrieve a dead son's body were all too common, yet this was not just any story. The newspaper that published the account some years later identified it as an extract from the Reverend Hutchinson's diary. The article's polished and precise conversations, however, reflect extensive editing in order to create a minor drama of defiance, redemption, and even reconciliation—another contribution to Greensboro's collective memory.[34]

Union cavalry under General Philip Sheridan captured the Reverend Hutchinson and his party as they were returning with the lieutenant's body and brought the men in for questioning. The colonel in charge decided to send them on. But before departing, Hutchinson saw a detail of soldiers with shovels about to rebury his son. He protested and demanded to be taken to a higher authority. About eleven o'clock at night he stood at the tent of General Henry Eugene Davies. As the general reclined on his blankets, his face lit by a lantern, he seemed interested only in how the Reverend Hutchinson had passed through Union lines without a permit. "I knew nothing of your lines. I was in my own country returning from where my boy was slain with his dead body when you arrested me," protested Hutchinson.

Davies was unimpressed. "You carry a high head, old man. Do you know who you are talking to?"

"No sir," replied the minister, "I do not, but I can tell you to whom you are talking, for though I came before you a suppliant with my dead child in my arms, yet as sure as you live you are talking to a man." Hutchinson then asked the general to send the burial detail away and to allow him to bury his son in the morning and to mark the spot.

"You may think yourself well off to have your son's body buried," the general responded icily. "How many of our brave fellows as good as he have been left on the ground to be eaten by dogs and crows?"

Hutchinson explained that he had never been guilty of an act of inhumanity in his life and that if others were, it was no reflection on either of them.

The general then disclosed that the minister would be set at liberty in a few days but could not expect to carry home either his son's body or his black servant. Hutchinson asked to be taken to someone of even higher authority, so he was taken to Ross Smith, who, although only a colonel, was provost marshal of Sheridan's corps. At six the next morning, the minister stood before a handsome and superbly dressed man who introduced himself. After hearing Hutchinson's account, the colonel spoke. "Ah, sir, I sympathize with you. There are many hearts agonized by this bloody war."

Hutchinson thanked him and explained that this was his second son buried on a battlefield that he had disinterred with his own hands.

"Indeed sir," said the colonel, "you have had your share of blood and suffering. Where are your other three sons?"

"All in the Confederate army."

"Were they volunteers or conscripts?"

"All volunteers."

"Did you encourage them to volunteer?"

"No sir; they needed no encouragement from me or anyone; they followed their own patriotic impulses. Colonel, I feel assured I address a gentleman; let us understand each other. I put no obstacle in the way of my son volunteering, though I felt as a father on seeing them go to the field of danger and death. They never knew how heavy my heart was in parting from them. Every throb of my heart, Colonel, is Southern. I have no sympathy with your cause. We are enemies. Anything you do for me must be done on the basis of our common humanity. I was bearing the body of my first born, cut down in the full vigor of his young manhood, to a grave where his mother and sisters might weep over the dust that covers him, when your men arrested me."

Colonel Smith interrupted the minister. "You shall carry your brave boy home, sir. I will give you the public property. Your servant, too, if he wills, can drive you to Richmond." The Confederate soldier, Lloyd, however, would have to be retained as a prisoner of war.

Hutchinson was appreciative, of course. "Colonel, you have started a noble, generous action, not surpassed for magnanimity by any in this cruel war. I have no words to thank you or express my sense of obligation, but Colonel, you are a kind and generous gentleman. Do not blur a noble deed; let your generosity be full and free; let me, when I rehearse this among the stories of this cruel war, have no drawback, no discount to make; let it be worthy of you, Colonel." And, pointing to Lloyd, Hutchinson said, "send this poor broken-legged boy home too. He has a poor widowed mother in North Carolina. He can never do you harm. Though in the Confederate service, it is in detail for menial service. He came with me out of sympathy and hoping to make by the trip a few dollars to send to that indigent mother. I never intended to disappoint him, and you, Colonel, who certainly are a kind-hearted gentleman, don't you do it."

Colonel Ross was touched. "Well, sir he shall go home, too. I'll parole him." He then asked the minister on his honor to reveal nothing and sent the three of them on their way. For the second time, the Reverend Hutchinson buried a son in the Greensboro cemetery. Nowhere else would do.

★ ★ ★

After the Union's disastrous June 3 assault at Cold Harbor, the armies dug their trenches and warily posted watch. Every other night, half of the Guards stood picket. Soldiers continued to wear their accoutrements at all times.[35] Still outnumbered two-to-one, Lee was not about to risk annihilation by attacking, although it no doubt pained him to sit and wait. The next move would be up to Grant. While the bulk of his army made a fast dash toward Petersburg, the key confluence of railroads that supplied Richmond and Lee's army, Grant ordered Union forces under General Sheridan to despoil the Shenandoah Valley. The fertile Valley was essential to keeping Virginians fed, a problem even more pressing than keeping soldiers armed. When Lee learned that Sheridan's men had occupied Staunton, burned the Virginia Military Institute and the governor's personal home in Lexington, and were threatening worse, he dispatched the Second Corps under Jubal Early to repulse the invaders.

The Guards set out on June 13, about two in the morning. Lee was gambling again, this time that Grant would not learn just how thinly the Confederate forces were spread. But as Early's corps marched west, Grant was secretly moving his army from Cold Harbor to Petersburg. Consistent with previous campaigns, the Guards could only guess where they were going. Near Charlottesville, General Early learned that Union forces were threatening Lynchburg, about thirty miles to the southwest. The troops boarded every bit of rolling stock that Early could requisition and headed out to meet the enemy. The Federals attacked on the afternoon of June 18 and were easily repulsed. The next morning Early struck hard, but the Yankees had retreated during the night. Strangely, they had gone west, and Early now had before him the entire Shenandoah Valley, with no army in his way. At Lexington, Rodes diverted his division from the main column. As a regimental band played a funeral dirge, the men solemnly marched with arms reversed by Stonewall Jackson's grave, covered with flowers.[36]

Down the Valley Pike the Guards tramped to Staunton, where Early reorganized his corps into the Army of the Valley. More an army in name than in numbers,

Early's four divisions totaled perhaps ten thousand infantry, and his cavalry numbered about four thousand. Some of the brigades were no larger than full regiments, some of the regiments were no larger than companies, and many of the companies were commanded by corporals. Of the twelve brigadiers in Rodes' division, only Battle (in whose brigade the Fifth Alabama served) was still commanding the same troops as he had at the beginning of the spring campaign.[37]

The troops left Staunton on June 28, heading north along the Valley turnpike and making good time. They passed through New Market, Woodstock, and Winchester on successive days. Marching usually commenced at 3:45 A.M., and by noon the men had covered fifteen miles. After an hour's rest, they would march for another five or six miles before setting up camp for the night. On several days they covered twenty-seven or twenty-eight miles. A year before, they had felt themselves on the verge of winning the war. Now a vastly reduced army thought mostly of revenge. Independence Day was spent at Charlestown, the site of John Brown's hanging. After dark and a skirmish with the enemy, Battle took his brigade into Harpers Ferry, where they heartily pillaged Federal property all night.[38]

After resting for a day and a half, the Army of the Valley marched to Shepherdstown and waded across the Potomac into Maryland. This foray lacked the sense of anticipation and hope that had marked the previous two. At Sharpsburg, men bathed once again in Antietam Creek. Early levied a "contribution" from the residents of Frederick: forty-five hundred suits of clothing, four thousand pairs of shoes, bacon, and flour, in addition to a considerable financial tax. Just south, along the Monocacy River, the army was delayed a day while fighting inexperienced Union troops under Lew Wallace. The Confederates resumed marching—twenty-five miles under a hot sun through Urbana, Hyattstown, Clarksburg, and Rockville—until midafternoon on Monday, July 11, when they came in sight of the greatest prize: the seat of the U.S. government. The brigade stopped near the home of Postmaster General Montgomery Blair, while the Fifth Alabama stood picket near Fort Stevens. From there, along Washington's northern outskirts, the Guards could plainly see the dome of the Capitol. Throughout the night they heard trains and the whistle of transports filled with Union troops coming to defend the city. The Yankees fired large shells over the Confederates during the late afternoon of July 12, and the Fifth Alabama fought for two hours, with the Guards' William H. McCrary among the wounded.[39]

Washington seemed to lie in the Southerners' grasp, just as it had after First Manassas. But Early recognized that Washington's heavy fortifications, now manned by two corps of veterans brought up from the Army of the Potomac, could not be taken. Early's reduced forces started back for Virginia that night, their way illuminated by the flames consuming the Blair mansion. The raid lifted the spirits of a depressed South: the three thousand horses and twenty-five hundred head of beef cattle that the soldiers claimed to have captured (probably an exaggeration) would be welcome back in Virginia, and Lincoln's reelection chances surely had dimmed.[40] But the Confederates overestimated the raid's importance. Washington had not been significantly damaged, and the siege of Petersburg continued.

The little army moved back into the Valley, annoyed the whole way by enemy cavalry. Several Guards were wounded or taken prisoner at Berryville, Virginia, but an engagement at Kernstown resulted in a complete rout of the Yankees, at least according to a public letter written by Chadwick. At Winchester, smiling ladies, children, and servants stood on the porches and sidewalks, offering tempting food and pitchers of cool water. The Guards camped at Bunker Hill and marched through Smithfield, skirmished with Yankees at Charlestown, and then marched back to Shepherdstown, where the ladies again waved handkerchiefs and proffered kind words. The soldiers marched up and down the Valley Pike so often that one Alabamian claimed to know every house, fence, spring, and shade tree as well as the names of the area's husbands, wives, and children. But marching wore on the men. One of the largest companies in the Twelfth Alabama counted fewer than thirty soldiers, and Battle's entire brigade numbered fewer than a thousand.[41]

After Early's cavalry burned Chambersburg, Pennsylvania, Grant ordered General Sheridan after the annoying Confederates. The Yankees harassed their opponents and then stopped them a few miles north of Winchester, Virginia. Early on the morning of September 19, the Guards were still in camp a few miles south of Bunker Hill when they heard cannon fire in the distance. By nine o'clock the men were on the march, but instead of Yankees, it was retreating Confederates that the Guards first met. General Early ordered Battle's brigade forward, and the Alabamians "hurled back the blue tide of the enemy," according to Sam Pickens, "pouring in a fire which strowed the field with their dead and wounded." The Guards joined the other Rebels in a woods, repelling several Yankee attacks with musketry and artillery. But late in the afternoon, with the cavalry to the left giving way and the enemy about to reach in the rear, the brigade beat a hasty retreat toward Winchester. As the chief of artillery stopped a battery and opened on the Yankees, General Gordon galloped up with hat in hand and called on the Alabamians to rally. Four or five Guards stopped, fired their last cartridges, and continued retreating. Union shot and shell poured on the Confederates. The hospital, a substantial building in Winchester, was directly hit. Scattered troops were soon fleeing through the town in total disorder and confusion. Upon hearing women exclaim that the Yankees were in the town, Guard Henry Beck mounted his horse and witnessed "the grandest stampede I ever saw in my life" as "panic seized the troops" and the whole army gave way. By evening, Sheridan's troops held all of Winchester.[42]

Sam Pickens was stunned when a shell fragment struck his head; he would recuperate in a Richmond hospital. Major General Rodes had also been hit by a shell fragment. But instead of retiring to a doctor's care, the former captain of the Warrior Guards, first colonel of the Fifth Alabama, brigade and then division commander—among the greatest of Lee's lieutenants—lay dead. His body would be returned to Tuscaloosa for burial.[43]

Sheridan could not quite stop Early at Winchester, so the Union general tried again at Cedar Creek on October 19. General Battle gave his last command, "move steadily forward and sweep every thing before you. Close in on the coons and then cut their fur." The wounded Battle then relinquished command of the brigade to Hobson, who attacked an artillery battery that was firing at the Southerners. "Forward!" came the command, clear and shrill, and the Confederates bounded with a deafening Rebel yell. One of the Guards described the scene: "Under the guidance of our gallant Lieutenant-Colonel, E. L. Hobson, they drove every thing before them. Wherever the shell and shot fell thickest he could be seen on his dashing charger, hat in hand, cheering on his victorious troops." And then the correspondent turned to the present tense. "Now . . . the fighting grows more stubborn. Galloping down the lines Col. Hobson orders a charge, and amid a storm of bullets leads the brigade to more successes. Riding coolly amid the storm of leaden hail and bursting bombs he seems to bear a charmed life." Hobson's men responded to his leadership and soon found themselves demanding the surrender of the artillery battery that had been firing at them. Those Yankees who refused to give up were either shot or, in at least one case, cut down by a sword.[44]

Despite retreating that morning, the Yankees returned late in the afternoon under General Sheridan's personal command. Hobson's men received the brunt of the Yankee advance and managed to hurl the enemy back. The troops on the left, however, were not as successful. The Alabamians soon saw Kershaw's and Gordon's men fleeing to the rear. Others followed until finally the entire brigade, disorganized by the fleeing troops, collapsed. "They did not heed me," recounted Hobson, but passed on several miles south to Fisher's Hill, where Early too tried in vain to rally them. Some dispersed to the mountains, but most continued up the Valley Pike all night to New Market.[45]

The battle at Cedar Creek ended the threat from Early's army. More than a third of the six hundred men in Battle's brigade were listed as killed, wounded, or missing. About thirty Greensboro Guards had entered the battle under the command of a sergeant. At least three died from their wounds: James D. Webb Jr. (whose unofficial *Jr.* was added to distinguish him from his distant cousin and fellow Guard, J. D. Webb), who lost a leg above the knee; W. A. Lanier, shot in the chest; and Sergeant C. W. Hafner, shot in the hip. When he finally succumbed in December, Hafner was only nineteen and had been wounded at least three times previously. His obituary in the *Beacon,* which never spoke ill of the town's martyrs, described him as congenial, industrious, and courteous. At least a half dozen others were also wounded, and some of those were captured. By the end of the month, sixty-two of the eighty-one men listed on the Guards' muster roll could not report for duty.[46]

"When in the midst of danger," Hobson wrote to his fiancée following the battle, "the tender fingers of memory would gather together every word you said to me, . . . for what I did was in the discharge of my duty & not to gain any fame or to render myself conspicuous. I know if I but follow the path of duty, no matter into what danger it may lead me, you will look approvingly & forgivingly upon me."[47] But duty to whom? The self-made men of Greensboro's earliest years demonstrated little sense of duty beyond themselves and their families. But crisis had intensified these Greensborians' commitments to each other. The path of duty led to Greensboro.

★ ★ ★

"I think soldiers appreciate home more since this war than they ever did before," wrote Allen C. Jones' daughter, Julia, from Greensboro. The home folk reciprocated. "Our little town is quite gay at present," she continued; "there has been a large body of soldiers passing through for the last three days. . . . any excitement of that kind produces quite an effect upon the people."[48]

And who, then, were the people? During the spring offensive, "An Old Citizen" wrote a public letter to the *Beacon*. The occasion was an upcoming election for a judge to serve Alabama's seventh circuit, but the thrust of the letter was to distinguish the civilians from the soldiers fighting "the war of their choice" to secure independence for "their people." An Old Citizen gently advised military men to stick to military matters and let civilians fill political offices. The implications were clear enough, however, especially to the Guards fighting at the front. One of them, "Veteran," penned an immediate and indignant response. To begin with, he asserted, the war was not a choice made by the military men. "It was the choice of *the people*"—all the people, including both citizens and veterans. If An Old Citizen had opposed the war at its outset, then he certainly could not now that the Yankees had revealed their true character. All Southerners—both in the military and at home—must support their common cause by prosecuting the war to the bitter end. Civilian talk of ending the war was particularly discouraging to men in uniform. Entering service had been an act of conscience, "thinking and believing that the 'old citizens' left at home would guard and protect our interests and honor during our absence. With painful hearts we have seen many dispositions to betray this trust, till we have become somewhat jealous." If the veterans had anything to do with civilian matters—and they would—many like An Old Citizen would be thrown out when the peace had been won, "though it may be considered as yet dim in the future." The soldiers would return home and perhaps launch another revolution, this time against those who had betrayed them.[49]

This unique example of a split between the Guards and the town and the immediate response to the schism revealed just how close Greensborians remained even as the war turned against them. No Guard could continue to fight without reassurances that the people were behind him—indeed, that he embodied Greensboro's ideals. Those who dissented were betraying the cause. But evidence of weariness could not be ignored. The newspaper published virtually nothing but war news as civic life slowed and a formerly open society closed.

Distinctions were being voiced, certainly, but not so much between the soldiers and the people as between one people and another. Many of those with Northern roots, once easily accepted, now felt excluded. Henry Watson, the scion of a prominent Connecticut family, had long been the most conspicuous Yankee in Greensboro; he escaped much of the bitterness and intolerance by living in Europe during the war years. Others could not get away. Northern-born Cornelia Lockett wrote to her husband, a well-respected engineer in the Confederate army, as she prepared for an anticipated invasion by Union troops. For two weeks in early 1864, she had heard near-continuous cursing of every living Yankee. In the Selma hotel, several ladies with whom she had been sitting suddenly commenced a torrent of abuse toward Northerners. Their remarks cut close. Listening to such horrid words and expressions required Cornelia's perfect Christian forbearance and patience: "Is it my duty to forget the land of my birth, my own loved home, & the friends & associations of my childhood & adopt this as my country because it is yours? Is it my duty to forget habits contracted in my northern home & become in every way a Southerner! Tell me, how must I feel towards the *Yankees!*"[50] The war had created conflicts of allegiance in Greensboro that could not be decided merely by force of arms.

★ ★ ★

In late November, Sam Pickens arrived back in camp after a furlough home.[51] The division, now commanded by Brigadier General Bryan Grimes, was encamped near New Market. Pickens was surprised to find twenty-eight Guards in camp; he had expected seven or eight. By December 10, a heavy snowfall and wind resulted in two-foot snowdrifts up against the tents. Firewood was difficult to cut and gather, and food was exceptionally scarce. When the price of apples reached four or five dollars per dozen, Colonel Hobson cut the price to two, but then sellers withheld the good fruit.

Before daylight on December 14, Early's army marched up the Valley Pike. Snow was falling, and the route became sloppy under the men's feet. Pickens put a glove in the heel of his shoe to ease the pain. Many men competed to ride in ambulances. At night the soldiers scraped the snow off the ground and built hot hickory fires. Sleeping was difficult, with only oilcloths to put on the frozen ground. Some of the men said that the army was headed to Tennessee, where a couple of weeks earlier General John Bell Hood's Army of Tennessee had disastrously assaulted entrenched Federals at Franklin. Others thought that their ultimate destination was Georgia, where Sherman was laying siege to Savannah. Before noon on December 16, the Guards boarded a train at Staunton, sixty men to a boxcar, and about two hours before daybreak the next day they arrived in the capital. They knew now that their destination would be the trenches thinly stretched around Richmond and Petersburg, where Grant had finally trapped Lee.

The Guards had heard fearful accounts of the trenches, so they were relieved when they got off at Dunlop's Station, north of Petersburg along the Richmond and

Petersburg Railroad, and went into winter quarters at Swift Run, about three miles from Petersburg. In a piney woods, the officers laid out the ground in parallel lines a hundred yards apart. Pickens and his messmates soon were felling and notching small logs with their axes. The walls went up the next day on the sixteen-by-eighteen-foot hut. Young Idom managed to rive about 450 pine boards that John Carberry and Peter Hagins used as clapboards. J. C. McDiarmid and John H. Warren chinked the fireplace and walls. With bunks, a mantle, and floor planks, the men were snug. The entire company fit into only four huts. Food became particularly scarce that winter. Breakfast consisted of a biscuit and cup of coffee, and dinner was peas and corn bread. Hunger, "one of the few things cheap & easily obtained," served as sauce. The Guards celebrated Christmas dinner with a "hearty" meal of biscuits, beef, rice, and sweetened coffee. And after New Year's, the Alabamians took their positions in the trenches.

They were at the fork of the James and Appomattox Rivers. Before them were breastworks about twenty feet thick at the base and fifteen at the top, fronted by a ditch with pointed stakes to prevent the enemy from climbing over. Fifty yards beyond were the abatis of sharpened pine saplings. Behind the Guards, along the back edge of the trenches, small rude cabins had been placed where up to four men could sleep and keep warm. These were dug two or three feet below the surface, each with a door that opened directly into the trenches. Other cabins were crowded indiscriminately further back. Bombproof pits with beds of leaves were also part of the system. This formidable defense had precisely its intended effect. More than two miles away, the enemy held to its own frozen ground, Grant not wishing to repeat the mistakes of Cold Harbor. The Confederates walked their posts with a single man during the day and with two at night. But the pickets who kept the enemy out also kept the Confederates in. A standing order gave any man who shot an attempted deserter a thirty-day furlough.

The front could be quiet during the winter. The pickets stopped firing at each other (except when the Confederates saw black troops). Otherwise, the Yankees were peaceable enough and even traded coffee, tobacco, newspapers, and knives, despite strict orders forbidding such exchanges. A piece of Southern tobacco could get a jackknife, pipe, pocketbook, looking glass, or other small object. Confederate money was, of course, worthless, and besides, the Guards were not paid after November.

After a week in the trenches, the Guards happily marched back to camp, where life resumed its tedious routine of scrounging for food, sleeping, and fixing cabins before the next tour in the trenches. The weather was so cold at times that ink froze, and letter and diary writing came to a halt. The various rumors—of peace, reassignments, or moving the camp—had to be discussed and evaluated. Especially troubling was the accumulating evidence of the Confederacy's end. Fort Fisher fell on January 15, 1865, thus cutting off the Confederacy's last important port, Wilmington, North Carolina. "This is indeed a gloomy hour," wrote Pickens, adding his confident belief that "a merciful God will bless us with ultimate success." The Guards decided not to believe anything they heard. But then came news that General Hood had resigned his command of the devastated Army of Tennessee. In February the Guards learned that President Lincoln had spurned all Confederate efforts at a peace settlement. That same month, men in the brigade passed a series of resolutions declaring that they would never lay down their arms until independence was gained. But resolutions could not hold back the tide of bad news. Word had it that Columbia, South Carolina, had been evacuated and occupied by Sherman's troops. But by far the worst reports came from the Guards returning from their furloughs home to Greensboro. They told of frightful sentiments in Alabama, Georgia, and South Carolina. "Every body whipped & despairing of our cause:—wanting peace on any terms, reunion, submission—anything," lamented Pickens. "How shameful!" Desertions began to increase, even among Alabama regiments.[52]

Nineteen of the remaining twenty-seven Guards (the rest were sick, detailed, or otherwise engaged) marched out of camp on February 23. They moved toward Petersburg, turned west and crossed the Appomattox River on a pontoon bridge, then continued along the South Side Railroad to an oak woods with convenient water. There they again laid out their camp in neat lines and built log pens with leaves for floors and tents for roofs. This was comparatively pleasant duty, especially when rations included flour, meal, bacon, salt, sugar, coffee, smoking and chewing tobacco, and—surprisingly—whiskey. After a great many became too lively, Hobson ordered company commanders to watch each man drink his ration.

Whiskey, tobacco, and better rations could not prevent Lee's army from withering. In a single night, thirty-seven men deserted from the Forty-fifth North Carolina, and some Alabamians stole provisions from the North Carolinians' depot. "What shall I do!" their excited commander exclaimed, "my men are all deserting & the Alabamians are stealing every thing!"

The Guards again were told to strike tents. They zigzagged east on March 13, avoiding detection. By about ten that evening, broken down and suffering, they were back in the trenches at the Jerusalem plank road, just south of Petersburg near Fort Mahone. "The land is dug up in every direction as far as we can see: there is our line of work, the Yankee line, the two intermediate picket lines—fortified & then every hill top & elevated place is crowned with artillery." The opposing armies—only forty or fifty yards apart—no longer enjoyed the friendly terms of a couple of months earlier. At all times, a third of the men were ordered to be on guard, and firing continued all night. Whizzing minié balls made every imaginable sound—sometimes resembling a flying bird, at other times a howling dog or a squalling cat—until they hit their mark with a soft thud. One of the Livingston Rifles was shot through the head. The mortar batteries fired into the lines; during the day, the shots resembled india rubber balls, but at night their burning fuses gave them the look of meteors. "Shelling is an every day business here," wrote Pickens in his diary. By the end of March, the Guards were witnessing pyrotechnic displays unlike any they had previously seen. At one time fifteen or perhaps twenty shells would cross each other and explode like grand lightning bugs.

Petersburg's fate—and with it, Richmond's—was decided on April 1, when the Union sent the Confederates running at Five Forks. The next morning, while President Davis attended Sunday worship at St. Paul's, General Grant sent his Army of the Potomac at the entire Confederate line. Citizens were soon trying madly to get out of the capital. Flames consumed much of the town. Lee ordered his forces to abandon their positions between Richmond and Petersburg and to head west along various routes. He hoped to unite his disparate forces, feed them with supplies delivered along the South Side Railroad, and then march south into North Carolina.

Only one Guard made the march.

Sixteen Guards had been surprised in the Union's April 2 assault and were now captives in a massive prison camp at Point Lookout, Maryland, where they were searched and moved into a fenced enclosure with thousands of Confederates overseen by a Yankee corporal.[53] Food was the first problem. Pickens was fed only twice between his capture on Sunday morning and Wednesday. Without a fire, he had to eat a small mackerel raw. "Never so hungry in my life—almost desperate—felt like revolting." A cup of bean soup appeared, then bacon, crackers, and bread.

Rumors spread: that twenty thousand men had refused to follow General Lee out of Richmond, that Lynchburg had been burned, that the Army of Northern Virginia had suffered forty thousand casualties. And of course, the Yankees kept telling the prisoners that the war was as good as over. Then came a dreaded two hundred–gun salute in celebration of General Lee's surrender. Wrote Pickens, "Lord have mercy on us! How little we expected this!"

The Guards eventually learned that Lee's forces had headed west from their abandoned positions around Richmond and Petersburg with Grant's army, including infantry and cavalry, in vigorous pursuit. The two armies finally stopped near Appomattox Court House. Outnumbered by well over two to one, Lee finally yielded to his antagonist on the afternoon of April 9. Grant sent welcome food to those hungry and defeated men. Three days later, Major General John B. Gordon and his Second Corps led the Army of Northern Virginia in a formal surrender of its arms and banners. Only one member of the Greensboro Light Artillery Guards was there to witness the surrender: Ed Hutchinson.[54] "Oh! can it be possible that after all sacrifices made," wrote Pickens, the "immolation of so many noble heroes it is not to end in our favor—that we are to lose our independence & be in subjection to the Yankees! God forbid!"

Nearly two hundred men joined the Greensboro Guards during the war, plus twenty-one transfers from the Warrior Guards. At least thirty-three died—sixteen killed and the rest falling to disease. At least eighteen were discharged or put on detached service following battle wounds. About thirty others were discharged for illness or incompetence (all but six of them in 1861 or 1862). Seven were sent home for being too young or too old under the 1862 Conscription Act; two left after their first year's commitment because, as foreigners, they were not eligible for the draft. Only four deserted during the entire war, none of them from Greene County; these individuals lacked ties to that would have made their behavior the subject of retaliation back in Alabama. The company's low desertion rate may also reflect the heightened fear of a race war that initially drove Greensborians, who were so heavily tied to slavery, to support secession. And because some of the Guards transferred to other units while others stayed in only briefly (especially at the beginning of the war), the unit may appear larger—and casualty rates lower—than is warranted. Finally, many records are woefully incomplete, thus leaving open the possibility that more men deserted than can be tracked. By the war's end, fewer than thirty Guards, including those brought in from detached service, remained in uniform.[55]

The men passed the time in prison camp playing cards and gambling. Some used their liberties to learn how to swim in the Chesapeake. Entrepreneurs set up shops in camp selling everything from boots to horsehair vest chains. Books, especially trash novels and Bibles, were common among the twenty-six thousand prisoners, as was disease.

Paroles were granted in order of application. Those who had applied in writing to take the oath prior to the fall of Richmond left on May 15. The others waited. Finally, on June 16, 1865, Sam Pickens and Bob Price made their way to what Pickens dubbed the "machine where U.S. citizens are made out of rebel soldiers." After a long wait in the crowd, the two Guards were called into a house, where their particulars were recorded: name, rank, company, place and date of capture, and physical description. Thirty-two men then formed three sides of a hollow square. With hats removed, four men placed their right hands on a Bible and had the Oath of Allegiance to the United States read to them. Then they kissed the Bible and stood under an immense Stars and Stripes, twenty by thirty feet, stretched like a canopy above their heads. Each man was handed his oath and parole, which he signed and registered in two separate books. The men passed out the rear of the house and were marched to the parole camp to be released for home. But the machine that compelled a man's submission could not compel his loyalty.

PART IV

# Loyalty

# CHAPTER 10

# The Loyal Community

These afflictions will rather bind us more closely.

★ Eugene V. LeVert, 1865

"GLORIOUS NEWS," the *Alabama Beacon*'s headlines read, "Lincoln and Seward Assassinated! LEE DEFEATS GRANT." Greensborians were stung when they finally learned the truth, that it was Grant who had defeated Lee. But the end of the Confederacy did not deter editor John G. Harvey from warning Republicans against any insane attempts to abolish slavery, exact revenge on brave and chivalrous Southerners, or insist on dishonorable terms of settlement. Otherwise, he insisted, the conflict must go on.[1] But the conflict did not go on—if that meant flags waving, armies clashing, and cannon roaring.

At last the Guards began arriving home. Dick Adams told of spending twenty-one months in prison and attempting numerous escapes; at one point he nearly drowned after jumping from a ship.[2] Although Sam Pickens traveled most of the way by rail, he still did not reach Greensboro until well into July. The veterans found Southern University still standing, unlike the University of Alabama, which Union cavalry had burned to the ground. And many things seemed unchanged. Fences needed paint. On Sunday mornings, folks attended church. No one went out in the noonday sun without a hat. All in all, the town looked pretty much the same. Beneath Greensboro's veneer of normalcy, however, rancor raged.

First and foremost, slavery had ended, although some whites did not want to admit it. "Has the idea he is free," complained physician and planter John H. Parrish of a freedman who had settled his family without permission on the grounds of Henry Watson's home. White Greensborians could not accept such presumptuous behavior. A few minor accommodations perhaps, and postemancipation life might return to look a great deal like former days. Writers to the newspaper freely offered their opinions on how to get there. After praising the faithfulness of the black race during the war, "East Greene" suggested new municipal laws to check vagrancy and require employment. "A Planter" proposed that employment contracts run for a full year and that the courts declare as vagrants those who refused to sign such documents. The "vagrants" then could be arrested, apprenticed for a year, or put in

Main Street, Greensboro, 1873. (Courtesy Hale County Library, Greensboro, Alabama)

chain gangs: "The negro will soon learn that he cannot be either a vagabond or a criminal with impunity," for no man will labor voluntarily; he must be compelled. "An Old Citizen" urged the legislature to require all former slaves to be apprenticed for at least ten years. Alabama's legislators acted accordingly when they convened in January 1866 under a new state constitution. They quickly enacted a series of laws, known as Black Codes, circumscribing former slaves' labor and behavior. Conviction for vagrancy, for example, brought a prohibitively high fine of fifty dollars or a sentence to be hired out for six months. Leaving a job was forbidden, and black orphans were placed in the custody of their former masters. At a meeting in Dorman's Hall, Canebrake planters summed up their position: "*the labor,* upon which the planter has to rely, *must be subject to his control.*"[3]

Greensborians also assumed that the political order could, with just a little effort, revert more or less to prewar arrangements. Over the summer and fall of 1865, the state complied with President Andrew Johnson's directives for readmission into the Union. A constitutional convention renounced slavery, Alabama's Ordinance of Secession, and the state's war debt. In January 1866 the General Assembly sent former Unionist George S. Houston of north Alabama and military governor Lewis E. Parsons to the U.S. Senate. Reconstruction was now assumed to be virtually complete. The *Beacon*'s editor predicted that soon "the State will have been restored to all her former rights and privileges in the Union, the military withdrawn, the Freedmen's Bureau played out, and Alabama herself permitted to manage her own affairs in her own way, subject only to the Constitution of the United States."[4]

The assembly confidently went about creating new counties named after such Confederate heroes as Generals Robert E. Lee and Patrick R. Cleburne. Greene was changed as appeals from east of the Black Warrior persuaded the legislators to split the county along the river. After the townspeople pledged to supply a courthouse and jail, Greensboro became the seat of the new Hale County, named after Lieutenant Colonel Stephen F. Hale, a prominent Eutaw lawyer, legislator, Mexican War veteran, and Confederate martyr. Alfred H. Hutchinson, a veteran, son of the Reverend J. J. Hutchinson, and brother of Guard E. T. Hutchinson, won the race to serve as the new county's first probate judge; former Guards James E. Griggs and Edwin Nutting, whose brother had died carrying the flag at Gettysburg, ran successfully for sheriff and tax assessor. Colonel Edwin Lafayette Hobson was appointed to command a force of four county militia companies to replace the rough midwesterners in blue who patrolled Greensboro's dusty streets. Many Greensborians enlisted immediately to quell a rumored Christmas insurrection by the freedmen. At the meeting to elect officers, all the nominees except one were former Greensboro Guards (and the lone exception would join the company when it was briefly reincorporated in the mid-1870s). The veterans had promised to assume control when they returned home, and they had.[5]

It all seemed amazingly easy. But when Southern senators and representatives arrived in Washington, they discovered a Congress unwilling to seat them. Republicans charged that many of these individuals were traitors and lacking in contrition. Georgia, for example, sent to the U.S. Senate Alexander H. Stephens, the former vice president of the Confederacy. Local governments, such as those in Hale County and Greensboro, were clearly in the hands of former Confederates. And Congress labeled the Black Codes as merely Slave Codes under a new name. The Republicans demanded that the South be cleansed of these politicians; otherwise (in an echo of the Confederacy's argument) their sons in blue would have died in vain.

Greensborians had been mistaken, for life would not return to anything approaching earlier years. The newly freed people refused to acknowledge the authority of their former masters, and Congress was determined to effect a permanent change in Southern politics. White Greensborians had been profoundly altered by the war. Gone were too many fathers, husbands, sons, and brothers. Gone were fortunes. And gone were the premises of their society. Where autonomous young men had once rushed to make their fortunes, war-weary veterans now struggled back to the succor of their homes. These men were no longer proud individualists intent on advancing their personal self-interests, and the network of overlapping voluntary associations they had created in earlier decades no longer worked. "Our people are conquered, humiliated, ruined," declared Dr. Parrish immediately after the fighting stopped. Greensboro's whites felt alone, "cut off from the rest of the world."[6]

Exhausted residents endeavored to reestablish their civil society on the old footings, but the foundation would not hold. Following an initial burst of energetic activity after the war, membership in such associations as the Masons began a slow decline. Support for moral and educational reform also lapsed. This was not to say that Greensborians no longer solicited voluntary cooperation for particular projects. When a railroad promised to reach Greensboro in the late 1860s, townspeople again held rallies to drum up support. Harvey published a series of newspaper articles entitled "Railroads—What They Do for the Sections through Which They Pass," listing the usual material and cultural advantages: "Give us a railroad, and we should soon see new life and energy infused into the place. People would become hopeful as to the future." The road finally reached town in 1870 after Greensboro issued bonds for fifteen thousand dollars (with interest paid by a direct tax) and Hale County issued bonds for sixty thousand dollars.[7] Appeals to voluntary cooperation were still made, but not for holding disparate individualists together. For one thing, the people were no longer so disparate, having suffered together. And for another, the future was too precarious to trust to the caprice of individual choice.

Greensborians hardly saw the way clearly themselves, but casual expressions revealed an emerging consensus about what sort of community would replace voluntarism. When a Greensborian used the phrase *my people* before the war, it was a reference not to other Greensborians but to an individual's slaves. *My people* were my property, legally owned, with written documents as proof. During secession, Greensboro residents began to use the phrase *the people* to refer to Southerners as a group, using it as a weapon against dissenters and as a means of promoting unity. Finally, *the people* became *our people*, as in Dr. Parrish's offhand reference, a synonym for white Greensborians. Inclusion in the community was based on a shared experience, not on legal relationships or voluntary subscription. *Our people* supported the war and suffered through four critical years. *Our people* lost family. *Our people* were demoralized and ruined. *Our people* lived in Greensboro—not merely to make money and move on but because it was home.

This changed meaning of *our people* implied both a broader and a narrower understanding of community. The term included everyone who had supported the war, irrespective of economic, religious, or other differences. White Greensborians were finally united. Civil relationships seemed more natural among this select group. At the same time that *our people* included those who had supported the war, however, the term necessarily excluded those who had not: Yankees, freedmen, and a few apostates. *Our people* would broach no fence straddlers in this zero-sum equation.

Greensborians moved toward a community based not on prudent self-interest but on loyalty—an exclusive commitment to those who had shared their common struggle. Seemingly small statements again suggested larger transformations. In the summer of 1865, Provisional Governor Parsons penned an open letter, published in the *Beacon,* asking Alabamians to be loyal to the Union. "A Middle-Aged Citizen" took exception. The governor's brand of loyalty was "nothing more than a sincere and honest determination of mind to yield obedience to the laws and authority of the Government of the United States" in return for protection of liberty and property rights. The loyalty of Alabamians to their oppressors was a contract, in other words, although hardly a voluntary one (as Sam Pickens had learned when he took the oath of allegiance releasing him from prison camp). The correspondent had not a shadow of a doubt that the good people of his state would be loyal in this sense of the term. But no government, not even the victorious United States, had the power "to coerce the mind, the sentiments, the prejudices, the love, the attachment of the governed." This second sort of loyalty—"true loyalty," as he called it—involved much more. True loyalty moistened the eyes and quickened the heart when recalling the courage and endurance that Southern soldiers showed in a glorious endeavor, a struggle that commanded the world's respect and admiration. True loyalty twined a garland of glory around the immortal names of the illustrious dead. True loyalty loved and honored the state that these men represented. Northerners undoubtedly wished the conquered South to exhibit such an enthusiasm for the Union. But "if they ask us, if they expect us, to love and honor Connecticut as we love and honor Alabama—Beecher and Seward as we do Jas. D. Webb and Sydenham Moore, Lee and Longstreet—they must please excuse us."[8]

Greensborians had once asked how individualists could form a community. They had answered by building voluntary associations to further self-interest. The question they were now asking—To whom should we be loyal?—signaled that they were less individualistic, that they were seeing human relationships in different terms. The question had engaged the churches since the crisis began.

The Reverend W. M. Wightman, chancellor of Southern University, addressed the 1861 graduating class on July 3. With an unflinching tone he identified "corrupt ambition" and "base selfishness," particularly by politicians, as the direct source of the national conflict. He had in mind Yankees, of course, but his directives to the Southern University graduates clearly implied that they, too, could fall victim. "Better to be one of a poor people who maintain unsullied virtue," he pronounced, "than to have all seas whitened with the sails of our commerce, all nations tributary to our luxuries, and then to sink into the abyss of moral effeminacy, worship money, and hug the chains of despotism." The remedy lay in selfless duty and public service, in leaving behind the individualism that had brought Greensborians this far. The unity of the newly formed Confederate government suggested a fresh start, he suggested, because "the people, in blood, institutions, interests, manners, and customs, [are] one."[9]

When Richard Hooker Wilmer became Alabama's Episcopal bishop in 1862, he moved to the safety of Greensboro, from there directing Alabama's priests not to ask God for the health, prosperity, and long life of Abraham Lincoln. This "was not a question of loyalty," he insisted, but one of meaning. This particular prayer was for the safety of civil authority and not for the commander-in-chief of a foreign army. The Episcopalians held their annual council in Greensboro in early May 1865, only a few weeks after Lee's surrender, and Bishop Wilmer called for continuing the ban even after Lincoln's assassination. When military authorities stationed Federal soldiers at church doors and ordered Episcopal clergy to stop preaching or performing services until they agreed to return their allegiance to the United States, parishioners simply moved their services to private homes. The controversy was finally settled at a council meeting in Augusta that resolved to return to the old form of the prayer at the discretion of each bishop. Wilmer waited until the military lifted its ban before directing Alabamians to pray for the president of the United States.[10]

John M. P. Otts, the Presbyterian minister who had written the poem "To the Wounded of the Greensboro Guards," moved away from Greensboro in 1867. As someone who had so strongly urged the Guards to return to the fight, his departure suggests that he was turning his back on worldly problems. Indeed, that same year he published a small devotional book, *Nicodemus with Jesus,* about the prominent Pharisee who was told that salvation required a second birth. He picked as a subtitle, *Light and Life for the Dark and Dead World.* We owe our loyalty to Christ, he seemed to be saying, not to any mere worldly authority.

Alabama's long-serving Methodist bishop, James Osgood Andrew, wrote an open letter published in the *Beacon.* He asked Alabamians to invite the occupying soldiers to church, and he asked the ladies in particular to avoid expressing their bitter contempt for the Yankees. "God seems to have ordained that we should live together in civil compact with the North," he proclaimed, "and the sooner we can bring about a state of kind feeling between the two sections, the better for all concerned." Bishop Andrew called for greater spiritual piety across all differences in political allegiance.[11]

The Reverend Eugene LeVert, who for many years served Greensboro and various other Methodist churches around the Canebrake, saw more clearly than did others how the war had changed white Greensborians. The end of slavery, LeVert lamented, had prostrated the region because freedmen could not be induced to work either for pay or for the promise of improving their lives. On the contrary, "their conception of freedom consists in indulging in idleness & vag[a]bondism." Greensboro and Marion had escaped the reputed pillaging and burning by occupying troops, he noted, although rumors abounded of individuals being knocked on the head and robbed, houses plundered, and smallpox returning. He feared most for the poor, a group that now included those who had once been in comfortable circumstances. All of the reverend's sons had returned home from the war safely, and for that he was grateful. But they were in rags, unable to clothe themselves properly and without prospects. Their future, like that of many others, looked dark and cheerless. The recent disastrous war had impoverished them. Yet all these afflictions—the labor problems, lawlessness, and poverty—would not prove divisive but would "rather bind us more closely." Indeed, "we may still cultivate those feelings of affection which in some degree will enable us to bear the ills of life."[12]

Here was an idea that could work: loyalty. Young men on the make had once been too self-serving to consider melding their fates with each other, but things were now different. Loyalty to Greensboro meant charging Malvern Hill; loyalty to the Guards meant knitting socks; and loyalty to the Confederacy encompassed both. Individuals routinely juggle multiple allegiances. When loyalties conflict, the result is often tragic; when loyalties are combined to reinforce each other, however, the result can be powerful indeed. A single company could not defeat the perceived threat in Lincoln and the North, so Southerners turned to a new institution that held forth that possibility. Patriotic support for the Confederacy strengthened (perhaps even created) Greensborians' loyalty to each other and attachment to their hometown. By supporting the new nation, they were guarding Greensboro. Although the Confederacy was now gone (at least as an operating institution), the ties secured by soldiers and townspeople committing themselves to each other remained. Civil War experiences had established a new identity. This was not Greensborians' history so much as their heritage—a past they lived with, an inheritance that shaped them. "Let the past be our prophet for the future," a Greensborian proclaimed before one crucial political election.[13]

Being loyal did not mean that everyone would be treated in the same way—quite the opposite. Those who shared common bonds naturally warranted special treatment; like a family, a tribe, or even a Mason, each would have a niche—a specific role—in the community. Membership provided the reassurance that every soul was valued and part of something greater than the individual. People could rely on each other because they had been shaped and tested together. Thus, the identity of every white Greensborian became inextricably linked to the identity of every other. Loyal individuals were not autonomous individuals but together developed their own corporate personality—their own community—as they together faced unique challenges. And if some were included, others were not. A Middle-Aged Citizen knew that the loyalty he felt to Greensboro's sons forestalled loyalty to those who wore the blue.

The loyalists found little interest in appeals to rights. After all, many men had died trying to uphold the constitutionally guaranteed right to own slaves, and further, rights were the domain of self-interested liberalism. Instead, the loyal community stressed obligations, not merely between master and laborer but even more within the community. "Are we Doing our Duty?" asked Henry Tutwiler in an open letter printed in the *Beacon*. Widowed women and orphaned children, he claimed, were starving because their breadwinners had died in "our cause." Tutwiler called for public meetings, for a thousand dollars in contributions, and for concerned individuals to distribute supplies of corn to the suffering: "Shall we turn a deaf ear to their cry?" Several wealthier town fathers (including former Guards) made sizable contributions and encouraged others to follow their lead. Within a month the probate judge, Alfred Hutchinson, was distributing 264 bushels of corn to help feed the poor.[14] Greensborians had worked together before the war but had done so out of different motivations. Reform movements such as temperance, relief, and education sought to liberate individuals from the shackles of drink or ignorance that prevented them from achieving their own potential. But the war shifted their purposes from personal liberation to charity dispensed out of a shared sense of responsibility to "our people."

The freed people were no longer among "our people" to whom Greensboro's loyalties were obliged. True, many former slaves had remained faithful during the war. And they called themselves loyal, which led to some confusion. During Reconstruction, for example, freedmen overwhelmingly joined Greene County's Union League, an auxiliary of the Republican Party also known as the Loyal League. Republicans were proud that they had remained true to the Federal government. But this sort of loyalty was largely a synonym for patriotism. White Greensborians embraced loyalty of an entirely different sort, viewing former slaves who joined the Republicans as having renounced any illusions to being loyal members of their masters' households.

Loyalists hated betrayal as they hated no other sin. Voluntary communities, where relationships were based on contract and self-advancement, could not be betrayed. But friends, families, and this new type of community could be. Whatever bitterness loyalists felt toward the freed people paled beside their aversion to those few white Greensborians who joined the Republican Party. Scalawags did more than reject their community: they colluded with the enemy and deserved the sort of shunning practiced by the Amish or the banishment that the Puritans visited on Anne Hutchinson. Betrayal subverted the community because loyalty demanded a commitment that countenanced no others.

Postwar emigration might also have threatened Greensboro. Some former Confederates fled to avoid the long-anticipated race war; others simply left in search of better economic opportunities. Even as the Guards were returning home, a few white families were already on their way to Latin America. Such ventures would prove only marginally successful, if at all. Likelier destinations lay within the United States. Some touted Florida, others Tennessee (especially west Tennessee), and Texas (some Greensborians had moved to the Huntsville area before the war). But California seemed most to capture the imagination. During the fall of 1868, at least ten men traveled from Greensboro to the West Coast to look for promising sites to relocate their families. The list included such prominent names as Sledge, Tutwiler, Wright, and Borden. Some never returned, and a few left for a time and came back.[15] Unlike the emigration of earlier decades, however, this exodus drew closer together those white Greensborians who remained.

Greensboro's loyal community contrasted sharply with the expectations of the Republicans in general and the freed people in particular. Where the loyal community was local in its focus, the Republicans identified with the Union. Former slaves proudly flew the Stars and Stripes and celebrated the Fourth of July, Emancipation Day (January 1), and Lee's surrender (April 9). But for more than thirty years, loyal Greensborians refused to fly an American flag. Their most sacred day was Confederate Memorial Day (late in April), when they decorated the graves of their fallen sons and heard orators pay homage. Upon learning of Robert E. Lee's death in 1870, white citizens in nearby Uniontown stopped all activities to mourn.[16] As the Republicans looked forward to joining an expanding liberal America, loyal Greensborians turned back toward themselves.

The newly unshackled freed people were also trying to leave behind memories of their roots in slavery, renouncing identities given them by their historical roles. White Greensborians remembered what black Greensborians wanted to forget. Both groups were striving to create themselves but were headed in different directions. Caste and inherited obligations were the last things black Greensborians wanted to keep, so they stepped forward to champion the Constitution, Republican Party, and Federal government that promised to guarantee the universal personal rights denied to black Americans for generations.

The freed people's basic view of society thus contradicted at every turn the premises of loyalty.[17] Former slaves tied their future to a government that white Southerners had resisted for four years and would despise for much longer. Blacks boldly asked for equality, while loyalists believed that different people warranted different treatment; Black Codes, the elevation of veterans to leadership roles, and civic rituals such as Confederate Memorial Day all recalled and reinforced those special roles. Personal rights and independence implied contractual relationships predicated on equality—a notion acceptable to white Greensborians in the 1830s, but not now. Republican political rhetoric repeatedly tried to cross racial divides, inviting all to join together in moving the town and state forward, but loyal Greensborians rejected such overtures. Where they had once striven to keep their anomic town from flying apart, Greensborians were now proudly exclusive, using methods ranging from simple noncooperation or ostracism to overt murders and Klan intimidation. Seemingly minor episodes became symbolic community victories or defeats. Greensboro's loyal community was certainly not of one mind on all issues, but it was of one mind on the issues that mattered.

The failure of Reconstruction has been laid at the feet of virtually all participants: Republicans and Democrats, the Klan, Congress, Southerners and Northerners. The failure has not been examined, however, in the context of an underlying struggle over the meaning of—and membership in—the community. In villages and hamlets throughout the South, these problems had to be worked out on a daily, face-to-face basis. Without a consensus on what form that community would take, Reconstruction was doomed, and Southern towns such as Greensboro could hardly expect to reenter the American mainstream.

★ ★ ★

The loyalists did not wait long to strike the first blow.[18] During the summer of 1865, Greensboro was occupied by soldiers from Company H, Eleventh Missouri Infantry. Three of them entered Waller's store one afternoon on the last day of August, ate some fruit, and were turning to leave when the storekeeper asked for payment. The trio, who may have been drinking, refused to pay and continued their stroll up Main Street. Waller complained to their captain, who was standing in front of another building. The officer summoned his men, demanded that they pay for the fruit immediately, and threatened to hang them by their thumbs if they again tried to avoid paying for goods. The men paid Waller, who went back to tending his store.

In front of Waller's store sat some former Greensboro Guards. William S. ("Tood") Cowin had marched out of Greensboro in 1861 with his brother, Dr. John H. Cowin, and their father, Samuel. Another brother, Thomas, sat beside Tood. Tom had been too young to serve in the Guards but was wounded in the last days of the war while defending the approach to Selma, Alabama.[19] Robert Jeffries, whose leg had been amputated after the Guards attacked Malvern Hill, may have been there as well.

The three Union soldiers subsequently returned to Waller's store, and one of them, Joseph Adams, struck Tood Cowin in the face, presumably in some sort of retaliation. Both Cowin brothers immediately drew their pistols and fired at the Yankees. The first shots missed, so Adams ran to the other side of the street. As he reached the sidewalk in front of Stollenwerck's drugstore, Tood leveled his pistol across his left arm, slowly pulled the trigger, and with a curse sent a bullet through Adams' brain. Tom shot another Union soldier as he prepared to return the fire. The man fell in the gutter, dangerously but not fatally wounded in the side.

Greensborians ran into Main Street, and Union soldiers poured from their camp behind the Erwin place. Tood Cowin leaped onto one of John Hartwell Cocke's magnificent racing thoroughbreds and took off westward, with Union cavalrymen in hot pursuit. A half dozen miles west of town, Cowin left the main road and headed up a hill into a thicket. His pursuers passed by, but Cowin continued into Mississippi by another route.

Tom Cowin tried to escape by running into another store and out the back door, but the soldiers grabbed him. One of his captors placed a sword across Adams' dead body and swore an oath to hang Tom and burn Greensboro if his brother were not surrendered by sundown. Squads of soldiers moved from house to house, confiscating weapons. Others broke into Waller's store, threw his goods in the street, and helped themselves to his whiskey. Alarmed townspeople sent word to the regimental commander, then in Marion, that the soldiers were preparing to hang Tom in front of his father's hotel. They threw one end of the rope over a signboard and awaited the setting sun.

The sound of galloping horses finally came from the east. A lieutenant colonel rode up in his buggy and immediately stopped the lynching as a violation of military law, which demanded at least a court-martial. He ordered the troops to fall into ranks, under threat of being shot, and marched them back to camp. The rope was removed from Tom Cowin's neck, and he was taken first to the Greensboro camp. From there he was transferred under heavy guard to a Tuscaloosa prison.

Greensboro legend has it that the beautiful Irene Kohler set out to rescue her friend Tom Cowin. For many days she charmed the young lieutenant in charge of the prisoners, strolling about Tuscaloosa with her arm in his until he asked to marry her. She protested that she could never marry with Cowin behind bars, and shortly thereafter, the prisoner somehow escaped. She did not marry the Yankee officer (or Tom Cowin, for that matter). The Cowin brothers, never captured, returned to Greensboro a few years later. Rumors also spread that their father had contributed a twenty thousand dollar "loan" to secure their freedom.[20]

Over the years, Adams' shooting entered a twilight world of myth. By 1908, local historians had turned the "thrilling episode" into a blow by Greensboro's champions against dastardly and meddlesome outsiders. The Cowins had not only retaliated against an attacker but had once again stood up for Greensboro. The Guards were loyal and unafraid, purging the community of beasts.

Missing from this romantic account was one significant fact. The gunfight occurred on the same day that Alabamians were voting for delegates to a new state convention to end the Confederate experiment. The shooting of Adams was as much a political statement protesting the new government as retribution against rude bullies. Josiah Gorgas, former Confederate chief of ordnance, was in Eutaw on the election day. "This is the bitter end of four years of toil & sacrifices," he wrote in his diary. "What an end to our great hopes! Is it possible that we were wrong?"[21] Doubt, in time, would leave the South, as would the Yankee troops.

Not so the freedmen. They were not leaving and were instead demanding to enter into relationships that had heretofore been denied them. During the summer of 1865, former field hands refused to work, and some even filed legal claims against their former masters. Planters drew up legal contracts stipulating that they would furnish hands with food, clothing, a house, fuel, medical attendance, and a portion of the crop. In return, the workers agreed to do as the planters or their agents directed. For failing to work properly, former slaves could be discharged and forfeit all shares in the crop. They signed with their marks, and the masters with their signatures.[22]

From the planters' perspective, the contracts represented minimal concessions that would eventually lead to sharecropping and tenancy. Yet the contracts had other implications, for the explicit legal language tacitly recognized the rights of both parties. The freedmen had leveraged a rudimentary quid pro quo that traded their labor for recompense. Henry Watson could no longer buy and sell his house servants based on their ability to cook. The marketplace was forcing a grudging admission of the former slaves' humanity.

Neither party found the deal satisfactory. The failure to institute more sweeping changes created a divisive atmosphere that made radical politics compelling. The freedmen refused to work at their former pace, and the crop was reduced by half. By the middle of December 1865, when it was time to negotiate new contracts for the upcoming year, not a single contract had been signed, and many freedmen were simply not working. For their part, some planters blamed the first occupying garrison for spreading rumors that land soon would be redistributed and that the planters would brand and enslave those who signed new contracts. Other planters blamed black women for refusing to work outside of the home and expecting their husbands to care for them—like their white counterparts. Some planters persuaded workers to sign contracts by threatening to evict them. A few planters tried monthly wages of eight to ten dollars for a single male farmhand, seven dollars for women, and from thirteen to twenty-six dollars per family. Negotiations with such prominent men as Edward Bayol and Amassa Dorman failed completely, and their workers left for better conditions.[23]

Among planters, the consensus held that the unpredictability of free black labor was its undoing. Allowing laborers to contract with their former masters had made black workers feel "self-consequential" and perhaps even doomed them as a race on this continent. Most old planters, according to Allen C. Jones, were fed up with the situation and had decided to rent their lands to overseers and farmers in order to avoid personal involvement. New Union troops tried to work with the planters, threatening to tie up those freedmen who refused to work, but such attempts had only limited effect.[24] Frustrated planters placed their hopes in the Black Codes.

But Congress overturned those remedies when it rejected President Johnson's lenient plan of reconstruction and proceeded to impose its own "Radical" version. In early 1867 Alabama was again placed under military rule until another constitution was in place. Congress stipulated that this time black Americans must be allowed to vote, not only for convention delegates but also thereafter. Former Confederate leaders were denied both the vote and political office. Congress further required the state to ratify the Fourteenth Amendment, which extended federal citizenship to former slaves, forbade states from restricting individual rights, and mandated due process.

Some of Greensboro's white leaders asked for a town meeting to consider responses to these new measures. The group, which included such respected townspeople as Algernon Sidney Jeffries and Volney Boardman (both fathers of former Greensboro Guards), called on William T. Blackford, the physician who had served without commission as the Fifth Alabama's surgeon, to preside. Many who attended seemed to have been reluctant secessionists who were now considering the reconstruction of the state under the terms offered by congressional Republicans. These Greensborians decided to accept the measures imposed by Congress and to use their influence to secure white interests when Alabama's Republican Party convened for the first time.[25]

But the freed people were not to be denied. "I knew nothing more than to obey my master," admitted James K. Green of his days as personal servant to the exceptionally wealthy Gideon Nelson, onetime Greensboro Guard, "and there was thousands of us in the same attitude . . . but the tocsin of freedom sounded and knocked at the door and we walked out like free men and met the exigences as they grew up, and shouldered the responsibilities." Republicans began holding political rallies on Saturdays, calling on several white men who had attended the meeting in Greensboro to speak. All the invitees declined except for Dr. Blackford. Three thousand black men and women met in Newbern. The next week, some twenty-five hundred assembled at Mears' Grove in Greensboro, where, along with a few invited white friends, they organized a local chapter of the Union League and chose their delegates to the upcoming Republican convention. Again they unanimously called Dr. Blackford to the chair. He addressed the assembly, thanking the audience and then discussing black rights as determined by Congress. Various other speakers followed. The Reverend T. Y. Ramsey encouraged the freedmen to leave politics alone and to recall that white and black Southerners were the best of friends and dependent on each other. Major Charles W. Pierce of the Freedmen's Bureau subdistrict in Demopolis reminded the former slaves that for the past eighteen months he had been laboring on their behalf. And the local superintendent of freedmen's schools complimented the progress of the Greensboro schools. Local black leaders then spoke, acknowledging their political naïveté yet affirming their intention to exercise their political privileges and duties. Green, a rising star in Republican circles, honed his oratorical skills by interspersing humorous asides into zealous calls for reconstruction. In his deliberate way, Alex Webb told the gathering of the twenty-seven years of friendship he had shared with white Greensborians, a friendship that he wished to continue. The underlying assumption seemed to be that friendship might be the basis of cooperation and could overcome differences of race and former condition.[26]

The willingness of so many former slaves to attend the Mears' Grove meeting and the unprecedented outspokenness of their speakers surprised the white population. The assembly called for a convention to draft a new state constitution (as Congress had mandated), for a system of tax-supported common schools open to all, for governmental relief for the aged and infirm, and for harmony between the two races. No doubt these proposals were controversial to most white citizens, but the final two resolutions were wholly unacceptable. The interests of the landowner and the laborer, they declared, were identical and inseparable; when any one member of the community was injured, all were injured. And the freedmen avowed that the rights and privileges guaranteed in the Civil Rights Bill and elsewhere were unquestionably theirs—that is, "the equal rights of all men of every color before the law."[27]

The former slaves were asking to be included in a community of equals based solely on the individual rights of all persons. They asked for inclusion in a community with institutions to relieve and uplift all. And they asked that the community rise above its past. The freedmen failed to see that the loyal community of white Greensborians denied all these premises. Their community was not based on inalienable rights but on duties and obligations, not on equality but on differences, not on equal access to institutions but most emphatically on exclusion.[28]

The loyal community could hardly deny its heritage, could hardly forget that the freedmen were once slaves. Nor could the loyal community forget that Greensboro's sons had died in a war; to do so would render those lives meaningless. That freedmen appropriated organic phrases (when one was injured, all were injured) could only offend or amuse loyalists. Had the slaves grieved over the whites' loss of property through emancipation? Had they wept to learn of the Confederacy's defeat? No, they celebrated both events as holidays. An organic community might be possible if blacks were willing to accept a subordinate position, but that was not what the freedmen intended.

Hale County's delegates—Green, Dr. Blackford, and alternate Alex Webb—traveled to Montgomery for the first convention of Alabama's Republicans, held during the first week of June 1867. The party unanimously endorsed the Fourteenth Amendment and other congressional initiatives as well as many of the same resolutions that the Hale County assembly had endorsed, such as public education and racial harmony. The Republicans styled themselves "the party of hope—of strength, of security, of restoration," and pledged to "build up, restore, protect all—make us one people," an absurdity to Greensboro's loyal community.[29]

As a first step toward fulfilling the terms of Congressional Reconstruction, boards of one black and two white men began to register voters.[30] The black registrar for the Greene-Hale district was Alex Webb. On Thursday afternoon, a week after the Montgomery Republican convention, John C. Orrick, a former Greensboro Guard, walked down Main Street smoking his pipe. Orrick saw Webb and called to him, and the two began arguing. Orrick calmly drew out a pistol, aimed, and shot the unarmed Webb three times, killing him. Orrick soon rode out of town.

Greensboro's black residents immediately demanded revenge. Some threatened to set fire to the town and even to murder the white residents. One woman became so outraged, the *Beacon* reported, that she demanded the special privilege of tearing out the eyes of all the town's white children. Frightened Greensborians stayed awake for most of the night, many patrolling the streets.

The next morning, residents peeking out their windows saw crowds of black men armed with guns, pistols, knives, and bludgeons. Tensions remained high for the rest of the day. While some white men met with black leaders, someone sent word to Major Pierce of the Freedmen's Bureau. He at last arrived from Demopolis on Saturday night with news that a company of Federal troops was on its way from Selma. By Sunday morning, the excitement began to subside in Greensboro.

Events north of town, however, rekindled tensions. Armed black vigilantes fanned out in search of Orrick. They did not find him but instead surrounded and fired at Christopher Gewin, whom they mistook for Orrick.[31] The frightened young man fled into the woods in his nightclothes and wandered around until he was found sick and dazed by a second company of armed black men; they brought him back to Greensboro and marched him directly to Dr. Blackford's office. On hearing the facts, Blackford released Gewin, but a third company of black vigilantes soon tried to arrest the hapless innocent yet again.

Trying to forestall future problems, Dr. Blackford published an open letter in the *Beacon* denying that he had ever encouraged his black constituents to arm themselves or to burn the town. "I cherish the kindest feelings for this community," he concluded, "and hope I will not be condemned for entertaining different ideas of the weal or woe of a people."[32]

Editor Harvey took great pains to describe Webb's shooting as a private disagreement without political dimensions or even any relationship to Greensboro's white community, despite the claims of contemporary witnesses who heard Orrick vow never to be "registered by a nigger." Harvey insisted that the "community, then, is in no way responsible for the killing of Aleck Webb," adding that Webb's official position "had nothing whatever to do with the affair," including Orrick's escape. Orrick was never captured, despite a four hundred dollar reward posted by the governor.[33]

Prominent white townsmen testified that Orrick was indiscreet, high-handed, and rash. They conceded that he had deliberately walked out, shot Webb, and then coolly turned and walked right back to his office "as independently as if he had killed a pig." And they unanimously agreed that Webb was a well-meaning man, albeit meddlesome. They claimed that in this particular case, Webb had used his influence to prevent Orrick from trying to seduce a young mulatto girl who had some connection with Webb's family. Orrick discovered Webb's attempts to interfere and simply killed him. Several men even acknowledged that Webb had been trying to do the right thing.[34]

But whites could hardly concede that the murder was related to political activities, because such an admission risked destroying the town by fire and bullet. Nevertheless, Webb's visibility as a politically active black man gave the murder consequence. Even more than the killing of the Yankee soldier Adams a year and a half earlier—also coinciding with an election—the killing of the freedman Alex Webb was a statement about the limits of community. This murder signaled that a corner had been turned. Henceforth, no one could believe that Greensboro would become one people, as the Republicans intended. "And we doubt if these relations will ever again be as kind as they have heretofore been," opined Harvey. "Confidence, we are sorry to say, has been destroyed."

Despite Webb's murder, the registrars began their task of enrolling voters. Black men registered in overwhelming numbers, but white citizens were either ineligible or refused to register. In the Greensboro precinct, for example, 330 blacks and only 135 whites registered, a typical ratio for the state as a whole. (In all of Hale County, including the heavily black Canebrake, 3,363 blacks and only 823 whites had registered by early August.) Greensboro now prepared for a series of votes that would evict those who had spent four years trying to preserve slavery and establish the

Confederacy. The first elections would be held in early October for delegates to another constitutional convention, and then other elections would be called to ratify the new constitution and elect new county officers.[35]

On one dusty Saturday during the dog days of August, an estimated five or six thousand freedmen began walking to a Republican barbecue held near Caldwell Creek, a mile north of Greensboro, some coming from as far as fifteen miles away. The list of speakers represented the triumvirate of Southern Republicanism: the carpetbagger (a Pennsylvania Dutchman named Keffer), the freedman (Green), and the scalawag (Blackford), with Green and Blackford running as delegates to the constitutional convention. The doctor's rambling speech urged white Southerners to vote. The *Beacon* stated categorically that the speech was free from personal bitterness and lacked any attempt to excite animosity; nevertheless, alarmed white men wrote privately of "the most disgusting low down *incendiary* speeches, . . . calculated to make the most bitter feelings of hostility on the part of the negroes toward the white race." They complained that the region was filled with agents, "the meanest looking *Yankees* you ever saw," who socialized with blacks, taught them peculiar doctrines, and tried to establish Union Leagues devoted to the Republican Party. The war between the races, Greensboro's whites feared, was finally at hand. "Every thing tends to anarchy," complained a prominent Greensborian, Dr. Parrish.[36]

Ignoring all former political differences, Greensboro loyalists united against the Republicans. "I vote for the party in opposition to the radicals," stated Algernon Sidney Jeffries, the former Cooperationist who had once considered joining the Republicans. That meant the Conservative Union Party of Alabama, which he described as "conservative—old-line whigs and democrats acting together to put down the radicals." At both the state and the Hale County meetings, the Conservatives resolved to gain power by inviting the freedmen to cooperate; as a gesture, the party even named three former slaves to its Committee on Resolutions.[37]

The freedmen, however, remained unpersuaded. When Alabamians went to the polls in early October 1867—black men voting for the first time in the state's history—the election went resoundingly for the party of Lincoln: ninety-six of the one hundred delegates elected to the convention were Republicans, including sixteen blacks. The resulting state constitution (Alabama's fourth) was a moderate document, but former Confederates regarded it as tainted because such enemies as Blackford and Green had helped to write it. Blackford returned from Montgomery to urge his Republican constituency to secure its rights by using the ballot box to approve the new constitution. In local elections to be held on the same day, February 4, Dr. Blackford would be the Republican candidate for probate judge.[38]

Whether white Alabamians would accept the new constitution was another matter. At a state convention, they resolved to boycott the February referendum because the Reconstruction acts contained a clause stating that if a minimum number of registered voters did not cast ballots, the constitution could not be declared

The Hale County Courthouse, formerly Salem Baptist Church. (Special Collection, Samford University Library, Birmingham, Alabama)

binding, even if all the votes cast were in its favor. The proposal was endorsed at a meeting of prominent Hale County men that included several former Guards. For added insurance, a "special Committee" or "club" of young men was established to challenge the qualifications of every voter who might vote to approve the new constitution. White people would assert their rights, the men declared, "even in the face of the despotic bayonets with which our beloved country is so cruelly cursed."[39]

On election day, a half dozen "prudent and discreet men" came to watch the polls and challenge illegal voters. As the men entered the courthouse (the former Salem Baptist Church), Greensboro's Freedmen's Bureau agent, a German captain named Henry G. Claus, ushered them out. The special committee went outside and stood in front of the entrance to the building, but Claus moved them away from there as well. The purged challengers immediately called a public meeting to express the community's resentment of the occupying soldiers and specifically of Captain Claus. "In the judgment of the community," declared the committee, the captain's statements were "wantonly and wickedly false and slanderous in their character." The insolent Claus, a "miserable adventurer, of the basest order," had disturbed the community's equilibrium by procuring illegal voters even from the stench of the common jail. His actions merited "the scorn and execration of every man in whose breast there is a spark of honorable feelings." The crowd greeted the resolutions with prolonged and enthusiastic cheering. Two of the three who signed

the official complaint, William McDonald and Shelby Chadwick, had fought during the war as Greensboro Guards.[40]

The election results added to the furor. Nearly all the votes in favor of the new
constitution came from black voters. In Greensboro, 2,438 citizens voted, only 19 of
them white. (Only two other polling places existed in Hale County. In Havanna, 322
blacks and 5 whites voted; in Prairieville, the numbers were 632 and 1.) The *Beacon*
tried to learn and publish the names of the county's white voters in order to coerce
unanimity. Across the state, the minimum number of registered voters had not
gone to the polls, and thus the proposed new constitution failed on a technicality
and the white boycott succeeded. The uncertain status of the constitution also
put in doubt Dr. Blackford's election to the probate judgeship as well as all other
elections.[41]

While they waited during the first half of 1868 to see what Congress would do
about the vote, black and white Greensborians again came to blows. The violence
started when Captain Claus was struck in the head, apparently by Union soldiers
bribed with money and whiskey. Late on a Sunday night a few weeks later, someone
set fire to the livery stable. Circumstantial evidence pointed to black incendiaries.
The town's white men immediately formed a fire company, established and formally incorporated on the model of the Greensboro Guards. Within a month, on
March 20, an arsonist destroyed the Greene County Courthouse at Eutaw. The next
night, a similar attempt was made on the Hale County Courthouse at Greensboro.
The arsonists were never known, but white citizens suspected freedmen bent on revenge. A grocery keeper on the Newbern road was murdered, and two black men
were arrested for the crime; when lawmen attempted to take them to the stronger
jail in Marion, a band of armed and masked men kidnapped the two suspects and
presumably lynched them.[42]

The Wednesday morning after the attempted courthouse fire, Greensborians
awoke to find handbills posted along the streets:

> Headquarters Cyclops Circle, Spirit Cove, March 15, '68.
> Grand Cyclops, Hale County, Ala.:
>     Sprinkle ye the tombs with Blood! Brothers of the shroud take heed, and enforce ye
> these orders. Blood! Blood! Blood! Revenge! Revenge! Revenge! Let the
> guilty beware, the day of retribution is at hand—blood is our motto! Look wild
> Shrouds of Hale and enforce all these orders.
>     (A.M.U.) Grand Cyclops, K.K.K. Life Extinguishers

Harvey approved, writing in the *Beacon,* "Though harmless towards those who de-
port themselves as good citizens, *they prove a terror to evil doers. Incendiaries had
better beware!"*[43]

In his memoirs written many years later, John Hunnicutt claimed credit for
bringing the Ku Klux Klan to Greensboro. His self-serving account described how,
as a newly enrolled student at Southern University, he attended a local meeting to

address some farmers' concerns. They complained of a Connecticut man who was teaching school to freedpeople in the Canebrake and using his position to organize a local chapter of the Union League. Some suggested raising funds to bribe him to leave. Others wanted to appoint a committee to talk with him. One man asked to hear from Hunnicutt, who had already gained a reputation for knocking down freedmen who were not sufficiently deferential. He stood up and pledged that if the farmers would furnish five good saddle horses and a guide, the teacher would not be heard from again. William N. Knight, a former color-bearer in the Guards, offered the first horse. Another man from near Newbern said that he would show the way.[44]

Horses were waiting at a corner of the Southern University campus the next Saturday evening at eight o'clock. Hunnicutt and four other college mates he recruited mounted and rode off with their guide. They suspected the teacher of boarding with freedmen. Sharecropping had made the night riders' task easier, because black families were now living apart from each other rather than together in the quarters, where they could come to each other's defense. The students located the house where the teacher was staying, burst in with pistols blazing, threw him on the back of one of the horses, and galloped away to a big swamp above Newbern. There, the students cut switches about four feet long and as thick as a thumb. Hunnicutt asked the teacher if he realized how his sleeping in black people's homes and his organizing freedmen for unknown purposes had upset whites. Then Hunnicutt announced that he would not whip the teacher, as he would a slave, "but just wanted to show him how he stood in the community."

The next morning the teacher was the first to buy a ticket when the wicket opened at the Newbern train depot. Hunnicutt and his accomplices were hauled into court three weeks later, but the grand jury foreman turned out to be their friend William N. Knight. Nothing further came of the incident, Hunnicutt would boast years later in yet another instance of mythmaking.

The violence in Greensboro that surged in the spring of 1868 typified west Alabama. In nearby Marion, sixty or seventy young white men dispersed a parade of armed black men. White residents expressed their gratitude. In Eutaw, reported the *Beacon*, J. B. F. Hill, a Northern Methodist minister and Union Leaguer, had made himself abhorrent to the white residents by poisoning the minds of the freed people and laying the foundation for a race war. On the pretext that Hill had stolen wood, a dozen young men beat him. When they were taken before a military court, some were sentenced to two years of hard labor at Fort Jefferson in the Dry Tortugas. The indignant newspapers failed to mention that Hill taught in a black school and that the same night the local Freedmen's Bureau agent had been driven away. In Tuscaloosa, the vitriolic publisher of the *Independent Monitor* and leader of the local Klan, Ryland Randolph, stabbed a black man in a street brawl and later that summer drove out the newly appointed faculty of the rebuilt University of Alabama. Randolph had organized one of the first klaverns in late 1867 and called publicly for every community to have its own.[45]

The Southern University students followed Randolph's suggestion, especially because their first raid met with such success. Hunnicutt spent a week learning tactics from Klan leaders in Eutaw before returning to Greensboro to set up the organization there. The membership rolls of the Greensboro klavern never became public, but forty years after the events, a local history of Greensboro claimed unequivocally that most Klansmen had served in the Confederate army.[46] Given the number of Greensborians who had worn a uniform and given their public role in postwar resistance, it could hardly have been otherwise. This did not mean, however, that Greensboro's Klansmen operated in their own town. Many contemporaries insisted that they acted in adjacent counties in order to avoid detection.

The freedmen were determined to resist, and white Greensborians recoiled as the prospects of a race war seemed closer than at any time in the town's history. Harvey closely followed any rumors of armed freedmen congregating. He reported in the *Beacon* that on the first Saturday in September, a black man had spoken to a large crowd of freedmen armed with swords, pistols, guns, axes, hatchets, knives, bludgeons, and any other weapon they could find. The speaker claimed to be an envoy sent by General Ulysses S. Grant, the Republican candidate for president, to organize military companies. The speaker's message: this was their country and "they must *fight for it.*" The speaker organized a company with himself as captain, appointed his officers, and spent the rest of the day drilling and firing. In October, Harvey claimed that a freedman had been shot in the throat while resisting arrest. His friends, according to the editor, were determined that he not be taken and tried to hold off the law.[47] The real circumstances were never known.

White residents were scared and appalled. Harvey advised former slaves to attend to work instead of drilling in military companies and wasting time at political meetings. "The people," he said, again referring exclusively to Greensboro's white residents, "will not bear with any such proceedings much longer. Their patience is nearly exhausted." If the freedmen continued such practices, "the Jails and Penitentiaries of the country will be your homes."[48]

The Republican Congress in Washington finally made its decision on the election, and it was in no mood for legerdemain. Despite the boycott, Alabama's new constitution was pronounced ratified, and by July 1868, the state's delegation was seated in the U.S. House and Senate. Republican Charles W. Pierce, former head of the Freedmen's Bureau in the Demopolis subdistrict, represented the Fourth Congressional District, which included Greensboro. Soon Green and other black state legislators in Montgomery would also begin passing laws. In Greensboro, Dr. Blackford took his mandate to the courthouse, showed his commission, and demanded to be installed as probate judge. But the incumbent, Alfred H. Hutchinson, refused to leave until he had entered an official challenge in the court minutes. In his own hand, Hutchinson bitterly protested that he had been lawfully elected and qualified to serve as probate judge until March 1873. Yet "the claim of said W. T. Blackford is supported by a Military force which cannot be resisted. . . . And I now adjourn the Probate Court of Hale County until such time as law and justice again prevail in the State."[49]

"Politically our people are more discouraged than ever," concluded Dr. Parrish of his fellow white Greensborians. Congress had changed the rules. Black men were not only voting but also passing laws applicable to white men and women. Throughout Greensboro and the Canebrake, outraged loyalists issued warnings. Freedmen could vote as they wished, but their votes would be made known. And if they continued to elect Radicals such as Blackford, "the enemies of the Southern people, their old masters & employers & friends," then the blacks would have to find work elsewhere. "The white people are determined to make the laws & rule." Again, the loyalists were framing the issues in terms of a win-lose, us-versus-them contest. Former Guards had shot a Yankee soldier and a black Republican. The Klan had beaten or intimidated Freedmen's Bureau teachers and agents. Now white Greensborians prepared to remove a man they had once revered but now considered the Republicans' pied piper.[50]

★ ★ ★

Dr. Blackford described himself to U.S. senators investigating Klan activity as "thoroughly identified with" Greensboro before he entered politics. A native Virginian, he had arrived in the town in early 1857 to begin his medical practice, and that December he married into the Nutting family. But things soon unraveled. His wife died less than two years after their marriage (perhaps in childbirth), leaving the young widower with an infant daughter. During the secession crisis, Blackford expressed Unionist sentiments, at least until a vigilance committee threatened his life. To soothe feelings, he followed some friends' suggestions and gave up his large and lucrative practice to serve the Greensboro Guards (three of whom were his brothers-in-law) and the Fifth Alabama as an unpaid surgeon. His selfless act of bringing back the bodies of Sam Dorroh and William Willingham for reburial earned the public thanks of a grateful town. After the war, however, Blackford joined the Republican Party and became alienated from the white community, which blamed him for conferring "upon a lot of damned monkeys and baboons the right of suffrage." For that—for being "at war with the very decided and earnest sentiments of the community"—white Greensboro came to hate him.[51]

A few days after assuming his new office, Dr.—now Judge—Blackford addressed a crowd generally estimated at eight or ten thousand freed people who were celebrating Independence Day. The next morning he received the first of ten letters from the Klan, complete with a cartoon skull and crossbones captioned, "Behold what you will be in a few days" and signed with the standard bombast, "By order of the grand cyclops, in the caverns of death." Blackford's actions on the victorious Union's most sacred day had hit a vital nerve. The Klansmen warned that they intended to "avenge the death of the soldiers," thus raising again the matter of whether Greensboro's sons had died for no purpose. After eighteen mounted

Klansmen filed around Blackford's home on one moonlit night later that summer, he wrote to Governor William H. Smith, complaining that he had been threatened and ostracized by the "Slave oligarchy of middle ala" for doing all in his power to reconstruct the state and for the "*crime* of *loving the* Union of the States." Blackford also persuaded attorney James J. Garrett and other local leaders to write letters extolling his official conduct and readiness to serve.[52]

The November 1868 presidential elections both confirmed and deepened the breach between the loyal community and the Republicans led by Blackford. Greensboro had two polling places, one for each race. Of the 733 votes cast by the freedmen, 725 were for the Republican candidates, Ulysses S. Grant and Schuyler Colfax. Of the 209 white votes, 203 were for Democrats Horatio Seymour and Francis Preston Blair Jr. The *Beacon* cautioned the county's freedmen that they had aligned themselves with "the enemies of the South" and that white men would "look upon them and deal with them accordingly."[53]

With each new electoral contest—and there were many—tensions and violence increased. When in August 1869 a special election was held for a new congressman for Alabama's Fourth District, Blackford canvassed for the Republican, Charles Hays, a wealthy Greene County scalawag. As the doctor walked the streets of Greensboro, he overheard the residents remark, "There goes that damned radical," and "God damn him, we'll get him some of these days." On one occasion, Hunnicutt and his fellow students took Blackford's surrey and hung it from the belfry of Hamilton Hall, a university dormitory. And in the 1870 campaign, Democrats fired on a mass meeting of Republicans at the Greene County Courthouse in Eutaw, killing several and wounding dozens. The harassment worked, for Democratic gains in Greene, Sumter, and two other counties were crucial to putting a Democrat back in the Alabama governor's chair.[54]

The Democrats' success in the 1870 election campaign emboldened the Klan for a final attempt to get rid of Blackford.[55] On January 24, 1871, a Tuesday night, sixty or seventy armed and disguised men made their way into Greensboro. Perhaps by coincidence, perhaps by design, no Federal soldiers were in town at the time. The night riders reached the home of Maria Nutting, Blackford's mother-in-law and a resident of Greensboro since 1836. Blackford and his daughter lived there along with his brother-in-law, former Guard John S. Tucker, and his family. The Klansmen demanded to see Blackford but were told that he was not in. After thoroughly searching the house, they forced James E. Griggs, a former sheriff and Guard, to take them to the doctor's office. (That the Klansmen needed directions suggests that at least some were not from Greensboro.) But Blackford was not there either, so they grabbed his hat and some clothes, put them on a pole, and carried their prize into the street. "We have got his hat, and we will have him where we have got his hat."

Failing to find Judge Blackford, the Klansmen sprang a friend named McCrary from the calaboose. The prisoner, who may have been a former Guard, had been arrested for having stolen the horse of a Yankee living in Demopolis.[56] With their friend, the Klansmen moved back toward the Nutting house and started firing. One of the shots passed through the window of the room where Blackford's young daughter slept with her grandmother, missing the girl by inches. Someone blew a whistle, and the mob melted away.

The next morning, Blackford, who had managed to escape barefoot and in his nightclothes after a freedman ran to warn him, was outraged to discover the shots fired into his daughter's room. He confronted a couple of suspected Klansmen: "Any men that will go about in this manner, I look upon as cowards and villains, and therefore one of them would not fight, but maybe five of you will take up this fight." He then went to his office and armed himself. Several townspeople came up to him expressing their regret. For the next few nights, Blackford hid in the woods.

The freedmen took it on themselves to respond to the Klan's raid. The next night, just after eleven, another Greensboro livery stable was set ablaze. The fire company responded immediately, but the flames spread rapidly in the fodder and hay and consumed the stable, including two horses, a mule, three vehicles, and shop tools. The fire company was unable to stop the fire from reaching an adjacent wood and blacksmith shop, and a family of boarders suffered great material losses. Behind the livery stable was a well, but both buckets had been removed. A few days later, a black man named Phil Taylor was arrested on suspicion of trying to burn a gin house.[57]

White leaders called another public meeting "to guard the community against acts of *lawlessness*." They did not specify whether they meant the Klan's raid or the spate of fires—likely both. But the curious fact was their divided responses. Some discouraged any public demonstration, "as there would be a diversity of opinion as to what *ought to be done, we had best do nothing at all*." Such views, it is entirely possible, came from those who participated or condoned such Klan activity. But Harvey wrote for many who railed against such notions. Statements of common concern and purpose would instead produce "a greater unanimity as to what ought to be done. . . . we owe it to ourselves as a community, to declare our opposition to all sorts of lawlessness." Indeed, the Klan's raid on Greensboro threatened to divide the white community at a time when unanimity was especially needed. "There are questions involved which are of vital moment to the planting interest," the *Beacon*'s editor concluded. Many planters had initially supported Judge Blackford because they believed he would restrain the black workers and enforce labor contracts, but in time whites came to see him as a meddler who championed black rights for his own purposes. Planters who had previously supported Klan activities were now doubly disappointed. The 1871 Klan raid on Greensboro disrupted society and business just as Greensboro's long-hoped-for railroad was finally nearing completion. Even more alarming, night riding tended to stir up the freedmen, and planters depended on a stable labor force. The crisis needed to be handled quietly and with unanimity. Dissent or nonparticipation weakened the position and with it the community. Meanwhile, after an appeal by Blackford, the governor wrote to prominent Greensborians to organize a militia to put down the outrages. Allen C. Jones received one of the letters. The former captain of the Greensboro Guards responded that he dared not do any such thing because of his health. But the crux of the matter, according to Blackford, was that Jones had been a Confederate soldier and thus "could not and would not do anything in the way of raising a company" to protect freedmen and scalawags.[58]

After Blackford recounted his experience to a joint congressional subcommittee investigating Klan activity in Alabama, three respected Greensborians, representing the loyal community, testified against him. James J. Garrett described himself as an old-line Whig who had lived in Alabama since 1838. A lawyer and intendant of Greensboro, he claimed to have opposed secession although he later served in the Confederate army. Algernon Sidney Jeffries, father of a badly wounded Guard, came to the Canebrake in 1855 as a planter and merchant. He had run for a seat in the 1865 constitutional convention but now declared that he had always been a Unionist and opposed secession as irreconcilable with loyalty to the Union. And Charles L. Stickney lived three miles from Greensboro on an old family plantation where he farmed and manufactured shoes, harnesses, and other leather goods. The three took issue with the doctor on nearly every account.[59]

Far from being the selfless physician who had sacrificed his practice to care for wounded and ill Greensboro Guards, the witnesses portrayed Blackford as a lying, power-driven manipulator. Jeffries repeatedly accused the judge of being a notorious drinker who swore profanely. And Stickney regarded the doctor as a peculiar man of little consequence, "one among a thousand coming and going in our community," a man excluded from what Stickney termed "society." In this Stickney was right, for Blackford was certainly not part of Stickney's community. It may also be significant that Blackford was not a Mason, yet his most vocal or active opponents—Jeffries, Garrett, Alfred Hutchinson, Knight, and the Cowins—were.[60] Had Blackford been a Mason in good standing, he might have hesitated to align himself so publicly with the Republicans or his opponents might have confronted him privately.

Garrett, Jeffries, and Stickney also contradicted Blackford's account of the 1871 Klan raid. Garrett admitted that he had heard Blackford talk of shots that barely missed his daughter but stated, "I would doubt any declaration of Blackford himself where he was interested in producing a certain impression." The doctor was "constitutionally incapable of telling the truth." (In 1868, however, Garrett had written to the governor commending Blackford's official conduct.) Jeffries readily admitted that thirty or forty men had descended on Greensboro, released McCrary, and raided Blackford's office, bedroom, and home. Jeffries even admitted that the community had generally condemned the affair. He doubted, however, the existence of any Klan in Hale County. Stickney, too, admitted that the raid had occurred but thought the shots fired into the Nutting home were accidental shots discharged by decent young men who had been drinking. "As to these so-called Ku-Klux, or whatever you call these disguised men, I never have believed yet that they would commit an act of brutality, except under the influence of liquor." And then, in a masterful stroke of self-contradiction he added, "I do not believe in an organization," yet "I think that this so-called Ku-Klux organization, by the very name, has the effect as a terror to evil-doers." Over and again, the loyalists charged that Blackford had betrayed and thereby endangered the community. "He was constantly intermeddling," testified Jeffries. Garrett explained that Blackford's political sentiments and activities had made his presence "odious to the community."[61]

Greensborians chose to take care of their traitor in the same way that other loyal communities did: they banished him. On the Saturday after the raid—the same day that the gin house was nearly burned—a committee of "gentlemen" came to Blackford's office. Several were old personal friends, and one of them, Thomas Armstrong, had for years entrusted his family to the doctor's care. Armstrong took the doctor aside and spoke: "Sir, as your personal friend, I came to warn you to leave this town; you will certainly be assassinated, and those of us here would deprecate such a thing very much." After extensive negotiations, several townsmen agreed to buy Blackford's property for fifty-five hundred dollars—although the property had sold at public auction for sixty-seven hundred dollars only five years earlier. The committee suggested that Blackford conclude his business and personal matters in Greensboro as soon as possible since bitterness against him worsened with each passing day.[62]

One night in March 1871, less than two months after the Klan raid, Blackford stayed up late talking to his family as black volunteers stood guard. The next morning, a dozen armed freedpeople escorted Blackford to the railroad depot. The doctor boarded the train and was off to start a new life in Chattanooga. Despite the stipulation that he never return, Dr. Blackford occasionally slipped back to Greensboro on Friday or Saturday nights to visit his family. On Monday morning he would walk his daughter to the gate of the academy, carrying her books with her, and then depart. Blackford continued to deliver occasional speeches at Republican political meetings, and Greensborians continued to denounce his pernicious influence. "I detest the character of the man as much as any one," pronounced one loyalist.[63]

Dr. Blackford was driven out because he had betrayed the loyal community. Even more than the shootings of Adams and Webb, the presence of Blackford, an apostate white Southerner, undermined the unity and fidelity that this brand of loyalty demanded. And by actively colluding with former slaves and supporting the victorious Union, he had profaned Greensboro's dead sons.

With Blackford's departure in the spring of 1871, the Klan felt free to step up its activities in Hale County. During May, from twenty to forty Klansmen tried unsuccessfully to spring Peyton McDonald, who was being held in the Greensboro jail on charges of firing into the house of one black man and for trying to murder another on the same night. During the summer, hooded men burned the house of freedman Philip Greene, and two other freedmen were killed near Pinhook. A grand jury brought no charges. And on August 19, a few disguised men galloped up to a black prayer meeting in Hollow Square, west of Greensboro; when the order to disband was not obeyed, other disguised men rode up and shot indiscriminately into the crowd, wounding one man. The next night a gunfight broke out when armed black vigilantes surrounded the house of Mr. Monette, whom they believed to be one of the night riders. One black man was killed, the back of his head shot off. The jury of inquest called the death justifiable homicide, and the *Beacon* claimed that the man had been shot by one of his allies.[64] By the end of 1871, federal measures, such as the Ku Klux Klan Act, began to have an effect, and violence died down. At the same time, white townspeople grew increasingly confident that they would prevail.

★ ★ ★

The fourth Confederate Memorial Day, April 26, 1872, promised to be a special day for Greensborians had much to celebrate. For one thing, the detested Dr. Blackford was gone. Labor problems, too, had started to subside. Sharecropping and tenancy were well established, and those black families who could not adapt had begun to move off. Republican activist James K. Green tried to persuade his fellow laborers to follow him to Liberia. "We are delighted with the idea," opined the *Beacon*, "and would be glad to see the country purged of all insolent, lazy, and trifling men and women of that race." The real problem, Harvey continued, was that the majority of blacks were not satisfied with their station but demanded social equality. "They want to ride in the same public conveyances—eat at the same tables—sit side and side with whites, and no telling what not. This will *never* be the case in the South. The negro will *never* be the white man's equal in any respect." Harvey ended his diatribe with three simple words: "We say go." Many did go, although not to Liberia. A Montgomery convention of black laborers, including Green, adopted a report declaring that "the present condition of the colored people as a mass, is infinitely worse" than any other laborers in the known world. The most feasible scheme for salvation, the delegates decided, lay in emigration to Kansas. Within a couple of years, hundreds of black laborers from Hale and Greene Counties were at railroad depots preparing to make their way west, some to Louisiana, some to the newly opening Mississippi Delta, some to Kansas. Many planters now complained that they lacked hands, but others saw a hopeful change. With fewer laborers, planters would be forced to adopt more progressive farming techniques and to abandon the careless cultivation of too much land. Furthermore, fewer black laborers meant fewer Republican voters.[65]

Politics also seemed less confrontational. Later in 1872, the Republicans regained the governorship, but two years later, Alabama's political offices were "redeemed" for the Democrats for the next hundred years. Dr. Blackford had once charged that given the chance, the Democrats would not only repeal the Fifteenth Amendment (allowing black suffrage) but secede again "before daylight to-morrow morning."[66]

Leaving the Union was no longer an option, but the legislature quickly and deliberately eliminated Republican-initiated measures. Indeed, a new state constitution passed the next year, despite being voted down by a black majority in Hale County. The new document returned physical control of elections to white Democrats.

Politics, labor, and social relations were now rigidly reestablished beyond the power of any one individual to change. Gone were black hopes of an inclusive community that overcame differences in race and heritage. After years of struggle and doubts, loyal Greensborians had every reason to be confident when they celebrated their Memorial Day that Friday afternoon in 1872.

Businesses closed so that all townspeople could attend services. About four o'clock a procession formed at the Presbyterian church. Allen C. Jones, former captain of the Greensboro Guards and the day's marshal, directed the parade onto Main Street. The Greensboro Brass Band took the lead, followed by the fire company, the orator and committee for the occasion, and the Presbyterian, Methodist, and Episcopalian Sunday school children, with other residents on foot and in carriages at the procession's end. Every loyal Greensborian came—not merely those who had lost family members—because everyone shared the loss and because everyone was grateful.

After the procession reached the public cemetery, the Reverend Richard Hooker Cobbs of St. Paul's Episcopal Church climbed a stand and opened the occasion with a prayer. Jones then introduced the orator, local lawyer John T. Walker. His address—differing little from other Greensboro Memorial Day addresses for decades to come—paid tribute to the memories of such Confederate heroes as Robert E. Lee and Stonewall Jackson. When Walker praised the memories of such local heroes as J. D. Webb and Sydenham Moore, a sympathetic string vibrated in his listeners' hearts.[67]

The oration completed, Jones announced the decoration of the graves with beautiful bouquets provided by the ladies. A small marble obelisk stood in the town cemetery, having arrived a month before the Memorial Day unveiling and representing the culmination of at least a year of fund-raising efforts. On the obelisk were engraved the names of sixty-three local martyrs, twenty-seven of them members of the Guards. The keepers of the memory then placed wreaths of flowers and evergreens at the base of the obelisk.[68] The ritual ended, Greensborians went home to rock on the porch and retell heroic tales. The stories were theirs alone, not shared by those outside their community.

One last affront to the loyalists remained: the garrisons of occupying Federal troops. When these cavalrymen rode out of town, Southern University students celebrated by hauling out an old Confederate flag and flying it from Hamilton Hall. The Stars and Stripes did not fly again over Greensboro's public buildings until the United States declared war on Spain in 1898.[69]

Rumors began to circulate that the Guards were to be reactivated. In 1876 the legislature officially reincorporated the Guards, who then elected their officers ("gentlemen well versed in tactics—having graduated in the late unpleasantness between the States"), picked up their Springfield rifles, and had their uniforms sewn. The Greensboro Light Artillery Guards, as they were always officially known, held a formal military dress ball at Tom Cowin's home. The usual parades and musters would follow, but little else, for the company's exact role remained unclear. The Yankees were gone, the scalawag Blackford expelled, and the freedmen were back tilling the soil. The long-anticipated, much-dreaded war between the races had not erupted. Republicans were no longer a threat. Noah Gewin, another former Guard, even preached at a mock funeral for the defeated Radical Republican Party of Hale County. Former Guards occupied key local political posts, as promised. For example, Knight, the grand jury foreman who had helped the Klan, was now sheriff. The Guards had little left to do.[70]

The same could not have been said fifty years earlier. At that time, the Guards faced the two problems that seemed to threaten Greensboro's future: the lack of community and the threat of slave insurrections. Solving one required solving the other, as white citizens felt threatened by growing numbers of black slaves. But now those problems seemed less urgent. By allowing freedpeople to emigrate, emancipation had gradually diffused the fear of race war, and Greensborians who had once wondered how they could promote community feelings now stuck to each other like Canebrake mud.

After April 1878, the Guards made no noise for two years. They attempted to reorganize yet again in 1880 but apparently did not meet more than a time or two. Instead, a new military company, the Greensboro Rifles, organized in 1884 with the Guards' abandoned arms and accoutrements. The new company soon failed as well. The Greensboro Guards and their exploits would now continue only in the town's collective memory. Confederate veterans began to attend conventions in the mid-1880s and named their local camp after Allen C. Jones. "Tell them," urged one Memorial Day speaker, "that these and thousands of the bravest and best fought to save this land."[71] White Greensborians remained loyal—to each other and to a memory.

Late in his long life, *Beacon* editor Harvey composed an essay on loyalty. Loyalty was "dearer than life itself," giving meaning to integrity (loyalty to truth), valor (loyalty to courage), philanthropy (loyalty to humanity), and piety (loyalty to God). Loyalty had become the highest good, the key virtue by which all were judged. During the war, Dr. John H. Cowin had once ended a letter with the words "right is might and will prevail." But Harvey and other loyalists now knew better. Neither victory nor defeat mattered to the man whose character was built on commitment. "To such a man success or failure are mere incidents and do not effect his loyalty."[72] He was writing of the Guards and of his fellow Greensborians.

# CHAPTER 11

# The Stone Soldier

**To the memory of those heroes.**
★ William Edward Wadsworth Yerby, 1904

By April the dogwoods had long since dropped their creamy petals, and the temperature regularly reached the eighties. Memorial Day this year, 1904, lacked the usual fanfare, but not because of disinterest. This year, the main event was not Memorial Day but the annual state convention of the United Daughters of the Confederacy (UDC). They were meeting in Greensboro on May 12 to dedicate a new monument to the Confederate soldier.

The idea had originated with the Guards' former captain, J. W. Williams. His series of reminiscences published in the newspaper had, as he intended, reawakened the community's debt to its soldiers. Noting that the 1872 obelisk recognized only the dead (and only some of them), Williams pressed the idea of honoring all Confederate soldiers. At the same time, he suggested that Greensboro erect a monument to the faithful black servants who had accompanied their masters to the front.[1] Their loyalty, however, would never be so recognized.

At the appointed hour, veterans, UDC officials, and townspeople gathered in front of the courthouse. Before them stood a structure thirty feet high, hidden by drapes. A male quartet began the service with "Tenting on the Old Camp Ground." As one of the Daughters sang "The Bonnie Blue Flag," thirteen young women, representing the Confederate states (including Missouri and Maryland), formed a Southern Cross. William Yerby, editor of the local newspaper, delivered an appropriate address lauding the ladies' patriotism and devotion to the memory of the town's heroes. The singing of "Dixie" followed, and then former governor W. C. Oates delivered another speech. The benediction was pronounced by the Reverend Richard Hooker Cobbs, Greensboro's Episcopal priest, who had prayed at the dedication of the first monument three decades earlier. A bugler softly played "Taps." The moment had finally come. Miss Rebecca Erwin Jones pulled the cord, and the shroud fell. The unmoving marble man looked out over them all.[2]

And he stood for them all, particularly the five hundred locals whose names were inscribed on the pedestal. Their story—told around dinner tables, recounted

Dedication of Greensboro's Confederate Memorial, 1904. (*Confederate Veteran* 12 [1904]: 476)

by Captain Williams in the newspapers, passed from one generation to the next, ritualized every April, and now represented in stone—their story had established their community. By contributing to the story, by merging hundreds of episodes into one, by transforming experiences into a memories to be recalled again and again, a single individual extended his own life beyond the time God gave him.

For thousands of years, the Western world believed that individuals could not stand apart. Communities were elemental webs of social relations and institutions. All people inherited their lots in life. Some were born to rule, some to farm, some to nurse. All had a place. To withdraw from society, either psychically or physically, was to cease to be human, because communities arose naturally from humans' innate social spirit. "A man without a city is either a beast or a god," wrote Aristotle in book 1 of his *Politics.* To be fully human, one had to belong.

But nineteenth-century Americans saw it differently. Drunk with individualism, young men left home to pursue personal desires. For these self-made men, the frontier held a special place, not so much as a physical location but as a realm of opportunity to escape the stifling entanglements of their youth, a chance to build their own fortunes and families. But once on their own in the Canebrake, these men found no signposts to direct the way. In this world, all were created equal; the organic model of society had been discarded; loyalty was limited to spouse, parent, child. Even allegiance to one's country was more a matter of words than of blood. Self-interest permeated these men's lives, whether they were bargaining with peers or purchasing slaves.

Individualists had to find ways to create a civil society. Masons and evangelical Christians proposed elite communities distinguished by revelation or perhaps service. Town boosters tried to hold people together by building up material wealth and educational advantages. Social relations in such contexts were basically contracts—

extensions of the commercial world—among equals who collaborated in those limited projects that enhanced their own prospects. Thus, Greensboro's early years represented a striking example of the classical liberal society once described by John Locke. Such a society might be dismissed as merely an assemblage of people or, worse, a fiction. Yet that any sort of community could be created from such materials was indeed a remarkable achievement—a remarkably American achievement.

Although ostensibly just another voluntary association, the Greensboro Light Artillery Guards ultimately moved the town away from the American mainstream. The company cut across all differences of religion, economy, or nativity; the soldiers linked fraternity, voluntarism, and responsibility to the whole; and the Guards protected the populace from danger, particularly slave revolts. In this region where bound blacks vastly outnumbered free whites, Greensborians found their greatest fears nearly realized with Lincoln's election. The Guards were ready and marched off to protect their interests. They came back defeated four years later, but they brought with them a common story and standard of commitment by which to define their community.

Loyalty rests on an intuition that obligations among those with a common past and fate are not only desirable but morally superior. Instead of liberalism's unending search for equally applicable laws and moral codes, loyalty offers the calm assurance that comes from trusting those who are closest. Instead of championing equal rights, loyalty takes on duties and responsibilities. Unlike revocable contracts, loyalty is built of unbreakable social bonds. And loyalty denies the claim that solitary, unattached individuals lead fulfilling lives. ("The universe," observed Mr. Jarndyce at Bleak House, "makes an indifferent parent.") The Guards showed Greensborians the way back to an older, almost tribal form of community. From individualists came traditionalists, from gesellschaft emerged gemeinschaft, from an artificial society arose a natural one.[3]

Thus, the postwar years can be understood as a battle, not merely between the Republican Party and former Confederates but also over the meaning of community: the loyalists and their traditional community (ironically, only rather recently created) confronting liberal ideas of equality and rights that (excluding matters of race, of course) Greensborians had once embraced but now left behind. Although Reconstruction might have failed, the attempt to create a real community had at last triumphed.

But at what cost? The war had taken or crippled many of the town's hopes. The violence had not stopped at Appomattox, as Greensborians continued to attack garrisoned troops, scalawags, and especially former slaves well into the 1870s. Worse, the experience of the war had established relationships that precluded any possibility of a community that spanned racial, political, or historical differences. The mere existence of a community suggests a valuable set of obligations, but communities can also assume a willingness to enforce those obligations, sometimes with tragic results.

Confederate veterans on the steps of the second Hale County Courthouse, 1910. Top row, from left: John H. Turpin, H. T. Stringfellow, William G. Britton, T. J. Crawford, Cadwallader Jones, J. A. Ellerbe, J. C. Singley, J. Huggins, W. C. Christian, John G. Apsey. Front row, from left: T. J. Kinnaird, William N. Knight, Wiley C. Tunstall, R. B. Waller, H. T. Waller, Charles. E. Waller, George Nabors, N. B. Jones, Robert H. Jackson, A. J. Moore, Sam M. Hosmer. (Courtesy Alabama Historical Commission, Magnolia Grove Collection, Greensboro)

Greensboro might serve as a place to look for the distinctively Southern character. There have been many Souths, from Birmingham's industrial workers to black sharecroppers to plain folk. Greensboro undoubtedly differed from these other Souths by being unusually rich, Whiggish, and committed to a plantation economy. But just as certainly, I believe, Greensboro was typical—even archetypical—of the Confederate South, the South that would dominate the region. In the words of an 1869 participant in Greensboro's Memorial Day, "Let us show that we are becoming purer and truer by our trials, and that we intend to cling to this land rendered so dear by her 'ten thousand graves, vacant chairs and desolated homes.'"[4] Greensborians had once held no attachment to the land other than as a resource to be exploited. People had come and gone by the thousands. But the town had now been sanctified, the dross burned off.

With each passing Memorial Day, fewer veterans stood in front of the Hale County Courthouse for photographs. The hair on their chins longer than on the tops of their heads, each held one of the various Confederate flags. After the photographs were taken, the men would shuffle slowly toward the town cemetery. Children walking alongside heard them speak the names of distant yet personal places—Gaines' Mill, Malvern Hill, South Mountain, Spotsylvania Court House—

and of hardships that youngsters could not understand. The old men spoke in the present tense. At the town cemetery, the veterans sang old songs in ambiguous keys and laid wildflowers on friends' graves. The next year, a few more graves would need flowers. But the statue would remain to honor those who, while guarding Greensboro, were creating Greensboro.

# APPENDIXES

# APPENDIX A ★ POPULATION

Population of Greensboro, 1855–1900

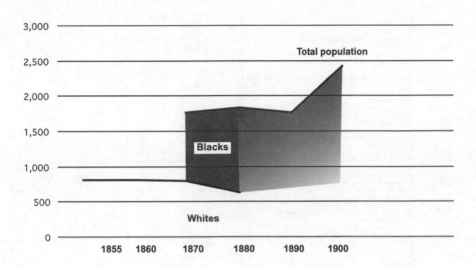

Population of Greene County, 1820–1867; Combined Population of Greene and Hale Counties, 1867–1900

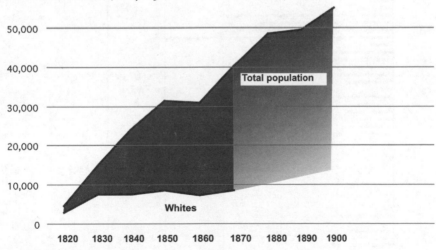

*Sources:* Manuscript and Compiled Census Reports, 1820–1900; *Greensboro Alabama Beacon,* June 8, 1855.

*Note:* The black-white ratios are estimated after 1880 in the town graph and after 1870 in the county graph.

Number Affiliating with the Masons, 1823–1899

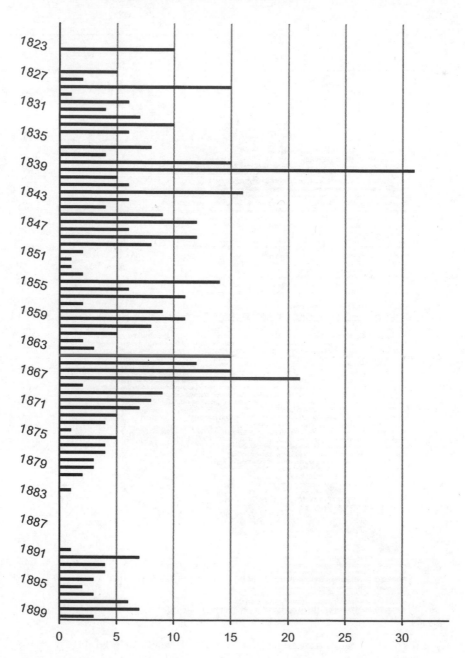

# Number of Master Masons, 1823–1899

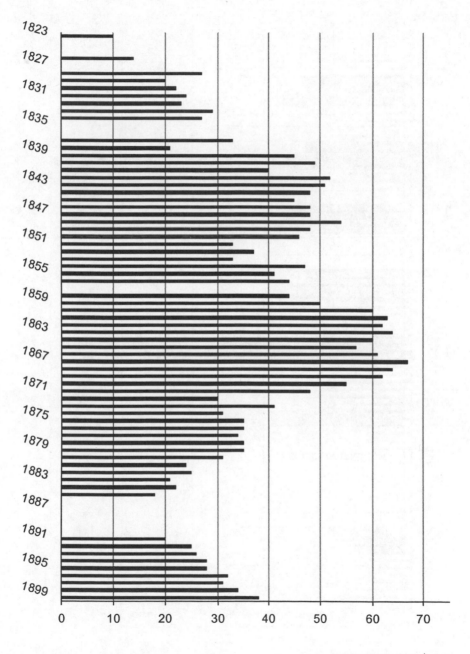

Persistence of Greensboro Masonic Lodge Members

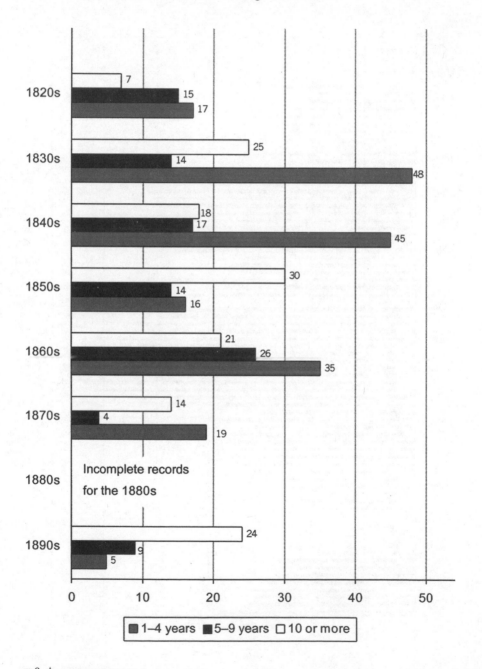

**1820s**
- 10 or more: 7
- 5–9 years: 15
- 1–4 years: 17

**1830s**
- 10 or more: 25
- 5–9 years: 14
- 1–4 years: 48

**1840s**
- 10 or more: 18
- 5–9 years: 17
- 1–4 years: 45

**1850s**
- 10 or more: 30
- 5–9 years: 14
- 1–4 years: 16

**1860s**
- 10 or more: 21
- 5–9 years: 26
- 1–4 years: 35

**1870s**
- 10 or more: 14
- 5–9 years: 4
- 1–4 years: 19

**1880s**
Incomplete records for the 1880s

**1890s**
- 10 or more: 24
- 5–9 years: 9
- 1–4 years: 5

Legend: ■ 1–4 years  ■ 5–9 years  □ 10 or more

*Source:* Membership rolls deposited in the Grand Lodge Free and Accepted Masons of Alabama, Montgomery.

*Note:* I entered every name appearing on the rolls of Greensboro's Lafayette Lodge No. 26 from 1823 through 1915, along with the first and last years that each name appeared. Those whose applications for membership were rejected were not included in this list. Using Masonic records to track persistence overcomes many of the problems inherent in using census records including the listing only of heads of households in the early enumerations; residents who were out of town when census takers came by, and the lack of records for those residents who came and went in between enumerations. My calculations confirm contemporary observations of a rootless population in the early years. Only 14 percent of those enrolled in the lodge in 1830, for example, remained members in 1840, but when those who joined between 1831 and 1839 are added, the persistence rate drops to 3 percent. The persistence rate climbed during the nineteenth century, reaching 50 percent in 1891, but this figure is somewhat misleading because the earliest Masons were far more likely to withdraw because they had moved away, while those in the latter half of the century left the rolls as a result of death or incapacity.

# APPENDIX C ★ WEALTH

Tax Assessments or Collections, Greene County, 1820–1872

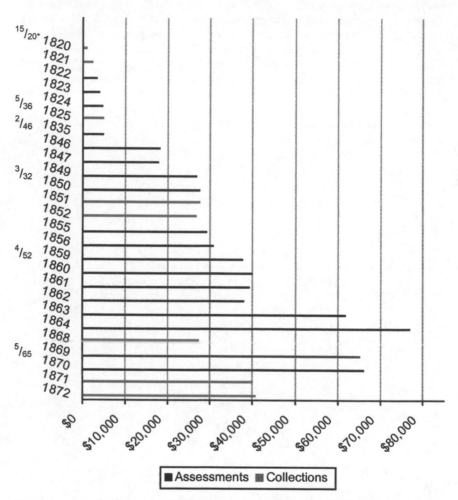

* Indicates rank of county among all Alabama counties. In 1820, for instance, Greene County ranked fifteenth among the state's twenty counties.

*Source:* Annual Reports of the Comptroller of Public Accounts of the State of Alabama to the General Assembly.

*Note:* I have used state taxes paid by the county as an index. These records are incomplete. After 1867, taxes paid by Greene and Hale Counties are combined. During Reconstruction, assessments vastly exceeded collections.

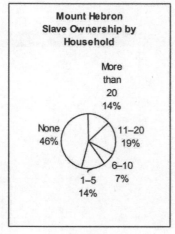

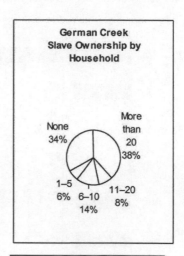

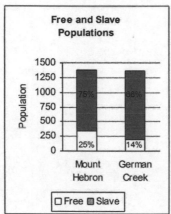

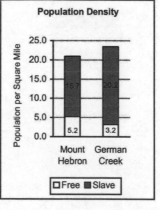

|  | Mount Hebron | | German Creek | |
|---|---|---|---|---|
|  | Mean | St. Dev. | Mean | St. Dev. |
| Cotton (in 400# bales) | 47 | 55 | 113 | 122 |
| Corn (in bushels) | 1,308 | 1,344 | 2,900 | 2,715 |
| Swine | 55 | 56 | 105 | 119 |
| Size of farm (in acres) | 553 | 665 | 957 | 1,315 |
| Value of farm | 7,941 | 10,849 | 27,335 | 50,993 |
| Improved Acreage | 46% | | 56% | |
| Portion of Precinct Surveyed | 75% | | 41% | |

*Sources:* 1860 Greene County Manuscript Census, Population, Slave, and Agricultural Schedules; Snedecor, *Directory;* Snedecor, 1858 Mount Hebron and German Creek Precinct maps, Alabama Department of Archives and History, Montgomery.

# APPENDIX E ★ THE GREENSBORO GUARDS

Greensboro Guards Enlistments, 1861–1864

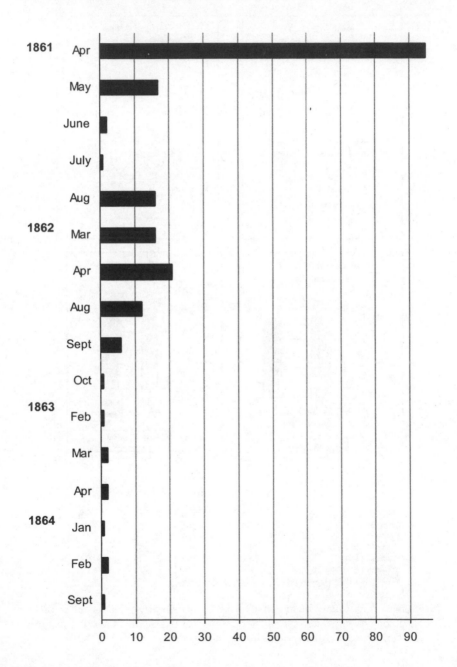

Greensboro Guards Effectives, 1861–1865

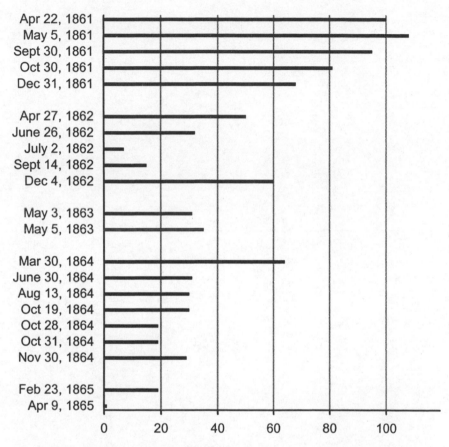

*Sources:* These data on Civil War enlistments and effectives are compiled from scores of different sources. The most important of these include muster rolls, governors' files, and militia records in the Alabama Department of Archives and History, Montgomery; compiled service records and the manuscript census from National Archives; and county records, newspaper articles, diaries, letters, Yerby's *History of Greensboro,* and J. W. Williams' reminiscences, published in the *Greensboro Watchman, Greensboro Record,* and *Montgomery Advertiser.*

*Notes:* The graph on enlistees includes the twenty-one Warrior Guards who transferred to the Greensboro Guards in April 1862; those months in which none enlisted are not included. The chart on effectives includes many gaps resulting from incomplete information. Only officers are known before the Creek War and after the Civil War because the muster rolls were apparently discarded.

# Rosters

The information included below has been culled from a host of incomplete and often contradictory records. I have used my best judgment but acknowledge that there must be errors, especially in the earliest names. This information should be seen as a general portrait of the company from 1823 to 1880.

## Greensboro Artillery Company Officers, 1823–1834

Names are culled from the Register of Officers, 1820–1832, Adjutant General's Papers, Administrative Files, Alabama Department of Archives and History (ADAH); and the Governors' Papers, Militia Election Returns, ADAH.

**Birdsong**, John.
**Black**, Archibald.
**Bostick**, Francis W. Commissioned lieutenant May 22, 1824; resigned October 13, 1826.
**Bullock**, Lawson. Ensign; resigned in October 1826.

**Carson**, Thomas K. *See* 1843–1846 entry.
**Carter**, William R. Commissioned lieutenant November 19, 1829.
**Cocke**, Jno. *See* **Cocke**, John, 1843–1846 entry.

**Dufphey**, William L. (died 1837). Mason 1823–1837; in 1830 reported forty slaves. Probably father of Guard William L. Dufphey.
**Dunn**, John C. Commissioned captain May 22, 1824; married in 1825; resigned October 13, 1826.

**Fife**, John. *See* 1843–1846 entry.

**Gage**, James B.

**Hatter**, Richard B. *See* 1843–1846 entry.
**Holdcroft**, Braxton.
**Hollinwork**, Alfred. Commissioned ensign November 19, 1829.

**Jones**, Claudius. *See* 1843–1846 entry.
**Jones**, William D. *See* 1843–1846 entry.

**Marrast**, William.
**McDunn**, Thomas.
**McFadin**, Andrew V.

**Norris**, Joseph E. Commissioned lieutenant October 25, 1826; Mason 1829–1833.

**Scott**, James B. (c. 1801–). Mason 1823–1834; married in 1827; in 1830 reported twenty slaves.
**Sizon**, John.

# Attention Guards !

You are hereby order-
ed to meet at the Court
House this (Friday) even-
ing, at 5 o'clock.

L. J. LAWSON,
Captain.

H. T. INGE,
1st. Sergeant.

(*Greensboro Alabama Beacon*, September 18, 1880)

**Sparks**, Thomas C. Commissioned ensign October 25, 1826; resigned January 26, 1828; married in 1828; in 1830 reported no slaves.

**Stephens**, William. Married in 1833.

**Stokes**, Peter (c. 1805–). Married in 1833; in 1840 reported four slaves; in 1850 a farmer with eleven children, reporting $5,000 in real estate and five slaves; in 1860 reported eleven slaves.

**Webb**, Henry. *See* Creek War of 1836 entry.

**Williams**, John. In 1840 reported three slaves.

## Greensborough Light Artillery Guards (Captain Webb's Company) in the Creek War of 1836

Names are from the Index to Compiled Service Records, Alabama Troops in the Creek War, National Archives.

**Alston**, Duncan D. In 1840, married with three slaves.

**Barnum**, Augustus. *See* 1843–1846 entry.

**Beck**, John E.

**Blair**, George W. Mason 1837–1838; in 1840 reported one slave.

**Briggs**, Duncan D. *See* 1843–1846 entry.

**Briggs**, Samuel G. *See* 1843–1846 entry.

**Brock**, John R.

**Chadwick**, Shelby W. (Sr.) *See* 1843–1846 entry.

**Cochran**, Hector.

Cocke, John. *See* 1843–1846 entry.
Cocke, William T. (c. 1813–).
Connor, William H.
Cowan, Samuel. *See* Cowin, Samuel C., 1861–1865 entry.

Eastham, Albert S. *See* 1843–1846 entry.

Fife, John. *See* 1843–1846 entry.
Franks, Britton J.

Goodwyn, William S.

Hardaway, William R. *See* 1843–1846 entry.
Harper, Henry (c. 1814, Georgia–). Married in 1852; moved to Arkansas.
Harrell, James (c. 1808, North Carolina–). In 1840 reported no slaves; in 1850 a farmer, married with three children; in 1860 a carpenter with five children, reporting $1,000 in real estate and $1,500 in personal estate.
Harrell, Wells (c. 1801, Virginia–). Mason 1836–1838; tailor.
Harrison, William S. *See* 1843–1846 entry.
Hart, John T. Fourth sergeant.
Hatter, Richard B. *See* 1843–1846 entry.
Heyle, William.

Jones, Claudius. *See* 1843–1846 entry.
Jones, William D. *See* 1843–1846 entry.

Locke, John. *See* 1843–1846 entry.
Locke, William A. Brother of Guard John Locke and father or uncle of Guard James W. Locke.

Parker, Thomas. Married in 1835.
Patterson, Douglas (c. 1805, Kentucky–). In 1850 a farmer.

Shackleford, Robert. *See* 1843–1846 entry.
Smith, Curtis S.
Smith, Henry H. *See* 1843–1846 entry.
Stainbeck, William M.
Stollenwerck, John A. Second lieutenant; Mason 1834–1838.

Vaughan, Algernon S. *See* 1843–1846 entry.

Webb, Henry (c. 1810, Maryland–). Captain; Mason 1832–1839; married in 1832; in 1860 a physician reporting $1,700 in personal estate. Probably brother-in-law of Guard Richard B. Hatter and father of Guard James Daniel Webb (Jr.).
Westbrooke, Thomas C. Married in 1823; in 1830 reported two slaves.
Williams, William D. Married in 1837.

## Greensboro' Light Artillery Guards, 1843–1846

Names are from the *Constitution and By-Laws of the Greensboro' Light Artillery Guards, adopted April 2, 1842,* 9–10; and the *Constitution and By-Laws of the Light Artillery Guards, at Greensboro', Alabama, adopted June 6th, 1846,* 13–14.

Albert, Kasper. Joined the Guards in 1838; Mason 1838–1846; in 1840 reported no slaves.
Allen, Thomas. Joined the Guards in 1842.

**Barnum**, Augustus (c. 1810, Pennsylvania–). Sergeant and assistant surgeon in Webb's Company; joined the Guards February 1, 1845; second lieutenant; Mason 1845–1852; officer in Sons of Temperance; in 1850 a physician, married with at least two sons, reporting $3,000 in real estate and six slaves; moved to Selma in 1852. Father of Guard David Barnum.

**Bayol**, Edward (c. 1808–April 29, 1880). Santo Domingan refugee; married in 1831; joined the Guards December 1, 1835; in 1850 reported eleven slaves; in 1860 a planter reporting $6,400 in real estate and $20,000 in personal estate, including eighteen slaves; in 1870 reported $3,000 in real estate and $200 in personal estate. Father of Guards Francis Edward Bayol and Jules Honoré Bayol.

**Bell**, William (c. 1818–). Joined the Guards July 4, 1842; ambiguous name in census records.

**Boast**, John. Joined the Guards June 1, 1844; Mason 1844–1850.

**Bragg**, Jno. H. (c. 1819, North Carolina–1850). Joined the Guards February 22, 1838; married in 1843; Mason 1846–1850; in 1850 a farmer reporting $4,500 in real estate and sixteen slaves.

**Briggs**, Duncan D. Joined March 1, 1834; married in 1839; in 1840 reported four slaves.

**Briggs**, Henry. In 1840 married with eight slaves; joined the Guards February 22, 1844; fourth corporal.

**Briggs**, Samuel G. (c. 1812, North Carolina–). Joined the Guards March 21, 1834; corporal; married in 1835; in 1840 reported eight slaves; in 1850 reported five slaves; in 1860 a bookkeeper with eight children, reporting $6,000 in real estate and $10,000 in personal estate, including seven slaves; in 1870 reported $2,500 in real estate and $1,000 in personal estate.

**Burrows**, Townsend. Joined the Guards January 8, 1841.

**Carson**, Thomas K. (c. 1813, North Carolina–>1880). Joined the Guards February 22, 1838; in 1840 reported eight slaves; in 1850 a merchant reporting $1,700 in real estate and four slaves; in 1860 reported $10,000 in real estate and $20,000 in personal estate, including eighteen slaves; married with eight children by 1870.

**Chadwick**, Jackson N. Joined the Guards December 11, 1840; in 1840 a merchant with two slaves; married in 1853.

**Chadwick**, Shelby W. (Sr.) (c. 1814, Kentucky–1854). Joined the Guards February 26, 1834; married in 1839; in 1850 a merchant with sixteen slaves. Father of Guard Shelby W. Chadwick (Jr.).

**Cherry**, Willis H. (c. 1820–). Joined the Guards November 2, 1842; married in 1843.

**Clements**, George M. Joined the Guards 1842; third corporal in 1846.

**Cocke**, James T. B. (c. 1825–). Joined the Guards February 22, 1845; fourth sergeant in 1846; married in 1851.

**Cocke**, John (c. 1805, Virginia–April 20, 1884). Mason 1826–1884; in 1830 reported thirty-eight slaves; joined the Guards February 22, 1834; lieutenant in Webb's Company; in 1850 a planter with sixty-six slaves, married with seven children; in 1860 reported $50,000 in real estate and $100,000 in personal estate, including eighty-two slaves. Not to be confused with John Hartwell Cocke.

**Connelly**, Randolph (c. 1808, Tennessee–). Joined the Guards December 11, 1840; Mason 1844–1850; mechanic; married with one daughter by 1850.

**Cottrell**, James L. Joined the Guards October 4, 1845; second corporal with duties of "collector with the powers of a constable" in 1846.

**Cowin**, Samuel. *See* 1861–1865 entry.

**Crawford**, Mathis. Joined the Guards July 4, 1846.

**Crawford**, William. Joined the Guards July 4, 1846.

**Croom**, Richard H. Joined the Guards May 1, 1846.

~~Croom, William J. Joined the Guards May 1, 1846.~~

**Crossland**, John V. Joined the Guards February 22, 1838; lieutenant in 1842; private in 1846; in 1840 reported three slaves.

**Davis**, Richard C. (c. 1807, Virginia–1877). Married in 1843; joined the Guards July 4, 1846; in 1850 a planter reporting $4,000 in real estate and sixteen slaves; Mason 1856–1877; in 1860 reported $8,000 in real estate and $22,000 in personal estate, including thirty-three slaves.

**Dew**, George A. Joined the Guards December 11, 1840; married in 1846.

**Dorman**, Amassa M. (c. 1816, Connecticut–1885). Married in 1839; joined the Guards February 23, 1841; first lieutenant in 1846; merchant, mayor, commissioner of free schools; in 1850 reported eleven slaves; in 1860 a merchant with nine children, reporting $20,000 in real estate and $17,000 in personal estate, including seventeen slaves; in 1870 reported $20,000 in real estate and $1,500 in personal estate; Mason 1872–1874.

**Eastham**, Albert S. Joined the Guards February 22, 1836; corporal in Webb's Company.

**Evans**, Williams P. Joined the Guards December 1, 1842.

**Fife**, John (c. 1809, Scotland–>1859). Mason 1830–1859; joined the Guards February 22, 1834; commissioned captain June 11, 1841; private in 1846; married in 1839; in 1840 reported no slaves; in 1850 the postmaster with one daughter and three slaves.

**Fowler**, William H. (June 15, 1826, North Carolina–murdered August 10, 1867, Marshall, Texas). Joined the Guards February 7, 1846; Mason 1850–1852; officer in Sons of Temperance; married with children; variously a teacher, journalist, editor, lawyer; secretary of 1861 secession convention; captain of the Warrior Guards, Fifth Alabama Infantry, in 1861; captain of Fowler's Battery in 1862; superintendent of army records for Alabama.

**Franklin**, Gray. Joined the Guards February 3, 1844.

**Gibson**, Jesse (c. 1810, Tennessee–). Mason 1838–1851; joined the Guards December 11, 1840; in 1840 reported twenty-nine slaves; in 1850 a brick mason, married with five children, reporting $200 in real estate and twelve slaves.

**Hanna**, William S. Joined the Guards April 3, 1841; Mason 1842–1847.

**Happell**, Phillip (c. 1816, France–). Joined the Guards February 22, 1838; Mason 1838–1869; married in 1844; in 1850 reported seven slaves; in 1860 reported five children and eleven slaves; in 1870 a retired merchant reporting $3,000 in real estate and $200 in personal estate.

**Hardaway**, William R. (c. 1820, North Carolina–). Joined the Guards June 3, 1836; married in 1838; in 1840 reported one daughter and three slaves; in 1850 a clerk; in 1860 a sheriff reporting $2,000 in real estate and $10,800 in personal estate, including four slaves.

**Harrison**, William S. (c. 1810, South Carolina–). Fourth corporal in Webb's Company; Mason 1831–1856; married in 1833; in 1860 a farmer reporting $10,000 in real estate.

**Harriss**, William T. Joined the Guards November 2, 1842; Mason 1842–1843; married in 1845; in 1850 reported seventeen slaves; Presbyterian.

**Hatter**, Richard B. Joined the Guards 1834; third sergeant, Webb's Company; in 1830 reported seventeen slaves; married in 1832; in 1840 reported eighteen slaves. Probably brother-in-law of Guard Henry Webb.

**Jackson**, John. Joined the Guards February 22, 1844. Probably John T. Jackson, in 1850 a farmer reporting $4,000 in real estate, but ambiguous name.

**Johnson**, Robert (c. 1817, North Carolina–). Joined the Guards July 4, 1846; by 1850 married with two children; Mason 1864–1874; in 1870 an illiterate gin maker reporting $2,000 in personal estate.

**Jones**, Claudius (c. 1809, Nova Scotia–June 17, 1864). Commissioned captain August 5, 1829; Mason 1830–1864; formally joined the Guards February 22, 1834; first sergeant, Webb's Company; captain in 1846; in 1840 reported seven slaves; in 1850 the town marshal, with four children; a master builder. Father of Guard Edwin Pompey Jones.

**Jones**, William D. Joined the Guards July 4, 1846. Ambiguous name.

**Kennedy**, Warren E. (c. 1814, North Carolina–). Joined the Guards July 4, 1842; in 1850 a planter, married with five children, reporting $7,672 in real estate and eighty-one slaves; in 1860 reported $3,000 in real estate and $25,000 in personal estate, including twenty-one slaves. Father of Guard William L. Kennedy.

**Kerr**, John P. (c. 1808, Scotland–). Mason 1830–1832; joined the Guards December 11, 1840; orderly sergeant c. 1857; married in 1834; in 1840 reported three slaves; in 1850 reported six children and six slaves.

**Livingston**, J. L. (c. 1814–). Joined the Guards February 22, 1838; in 1840 reported four slaves; in 1870 a tanner, married with two children, reporting $400 in real estate and $200 in personal estate.

**Locke**, John (died 1848?). Joined February 22, 1834. Brother of Guard William A. Locke and father or uncle of Guard James W. Locke.

**Marshall**, Jno. P. (c. 1821, Virginia–). Joined the Guards April 3, 1841; in 1850 an overseer.

**McDonald**, William J. *See* **McDonald**, William Jackson, 1861–1865 entry.

**Merridith**, Joseph C. (c. 1815, Kentucky–). Mason 1845–1851; joined the Guards July 4, 1846; in 1850 a clerk, married.

**Mitchell**, James M. (c. 1823, Georgia–). Joined the Guards May 1, 1844; in 1850 a farmer reporting $760 in real estate and seven slaves; in 1870 reported $1,500 in personal estate.

**Moore**, Jno. D. Joined the Guards December 11, 1840; married in 1843.

**Moore**, L. C. Joined the Guards December 1, 1841.

**Murray**, D. W. Joined the Guards October 1, 1838.

**Murray**, David S. (c. 1815, Virginia–). Joined the Guards February 22, 1838; Mason 1839–1866; in 1850 a merchant living in Cowin's hotel.

**Owen**, Stephen D. (c. 1817, North Carolina–). Joined the Guards December 11, 1840; married in 1849 or '50, with three slaves; in 1860 a broker and trader with four children, reporting $80,000 in real estate and $70,000 in personal estate, including forty-eight slaves.

**Palmer**, Beckham Dye. Joined the Guards June 6, 1840; officer in Sons of Temperance; a clerk, married in 1854; in 1860 a farmer with four children, reporting $10,000 in personal estate, including nine slaves.

**Pasteur**, Blovett. Joined the Guards February 22, 1838.

**Peteete**, Henderson (died 1843?). Joined the Guards December 11, 1840.

**Pittman**, William C. Joined the Guards December 11, 1840.

**Rice**, Robert G. Joined the Guards July 4, 1839; married in 1840; corporal in 1842; Mason 1845–1846.

**Rodgers**, Jonathan. Joined the Guards July 4, 1846.

**Seale**, Benjamin F. (c. 1803, Georgia–). Joined the Guards February 22, 1838; company secretary in 1846; in 1850 a farmer, married with eight children.

**Shackleford** or **Shackelford**, Robert (c. 1807, Georgia–>1877). Joined the Guards February

26, 1834; corporal in Webb's Company; Mason 1832–1855; in 1840 married with one son and four slaves; in 1850 a merchant reporting $3,000 in real estate and twelve slaves; in 1860 reported $10,000 in real estate and $13,000 in personal estate, including eleven slaves; in 1870 a retired merchant with nine children, reporting $500 in personal estate.

**Shaffer**, Rhodeham (c. 1815, South Carolina–). Joined the Guards February 5, 1842; married in 1844; living in Perry County by 1850.

**Sims**, George W. (c. 1819, Alabama–). Joined the Guards February 5, 1842; married in 1842; in 1840 reported fifteen slaves; in 1850 a farmer reporting $250 in real estate and fourteen slaves; in 1860 reported five children and $8,000 in real estate and $16,000 in personal estate.

**Sims**, Wilkins J. (c. 1802, Georgia–). Joined the Guards February 5, 1842, and July 4, 1846; married in 1827; in 1830 reported four slaves; in 1840 reported seventeen slaves; in 1850 reported twenty-three slaves; in 1860 reported thirty-six slaves.

**Smaw**, Isaiah B. (c. 1823–). Joined the Guards December 1, 1842; orderly sergeant in 1846; married in 1849; in 1860 a Boligee, Alabama, planter with two children, reporting $60,700 in real estate and $115,600 in personal estate; slaveholder.

**Smith**, Henry H. (c. 1802, Virginia–). Joined the Guards February 22, 1836; sportsman, unmarried.

**Stokes**, John F. Joined the Guards February 22, 1838; in 1840 reported two slaves; in 1850 reported six slaves.

**Thigpen**, Jason (c. 1825, North Carolina–). Joined the Guards July 4, 1846; in 1850 an overseer; in 1870 a farmer, married with three children, reporting $600 in real estate and $500 in personal estate.

**Tolson**, George W. (c. 1818, Alabama–). Joined the Guards December 11, 1840; Mason 1842–1849; third sergeant and treasurer in 1846; in 1850 reported $2,000 in real estate and nineteen slaves.

**Vaughan**, Algernon S. Mason 1831–1845; joined the Guards January 2, 1836; professor or engineer; in 1840 married with two children and four slaves.

**Vest**, Andrew J. Joined the Guards April 3, 1841.

**Webb**, James D. (Sr.). *See* **Webb**, James Daniel (J. D.), 1861–1865 entry.

**Webb**, Robert D. (died 1845). Joined the Guards February 22, 1834; Mason 1839–1845; in 1840 reported six slaves.

**Wells**, James C. Joined the Guards April 3, 1841.

**Wheeler**, Isaac C. (c. 1812, Kentucky–). Joined the Guards February 4, 1842; in 1840 married with one child and three slaves; in 1850 a farmer with five children, reporting $700 in real estate; in 1860 a planter and overseer, reporting $5,000 in personal estate, including three slaves. Father of Guard John E. Wheeler.

**Wilson**, Willis A. (c. 1815, South Carolina–) Joined the Guards April 3, 1841; Mason 1840–1852; married in 1845; in 1850 a farmer with two children, living with his father.

**Winters**, William. Joined the Guards April 3, 1841.

**Wright**, M. W. Joined the Guards February 22, 1838.

## Greensboro Guards at Fort Morgan, January 1861

Names are from the *Greensboro Alabama Beacon*, March 1, 1861.

**Atkins**, Joseph (c. 1829, Virginia–). Mason 1859–1875; in 1860 a druggist, married with no children, reporting $12,000 in personal estate, and a Democrat; in 1870 five children.

**Bauman**, Charles (c. 1833, Germany–). Tailor.

**Bayol**, Jules Honoré. *See* 1861–1865 entry.

**Benners**, Isaac Henricus (October 5, 1835, North Carolina–1884). Mason 1856–1870; married in 1857; in 1860 a farmer with two children, reporting $7,000 in real estate and $15,000 in personal estate, and sixteen slaves; candidate for the Alabama state legislature in 1861; moved to Texas and California after the Civil War.

**Black**, Jno. R. (c. 1832, South Carolina–). Married in 1857; in 1860 a farmer with one son, reporting $1,500 in real estate.

**Bounds**, William A. (c. 1830, Alabama–). Married in 1859; in 1870 a farmer with five children, reporting $500 in real estate.

**Breene**, Robert F. (c. 1831, Florida–). In 1860 a tinner reporting $1,000 in real estate and $12,000 in personal estate; in 1870 a dry goods merchant reporting $3,000 in real estate and $10,000 in personal estate.

**Britton**, William G. *See* 1861–1865 entry.

**Buchanan**, James S. (c. 1827, North Carolina–September 1898). Married in 1850; in 1860 a master carpenter reporting $2,300 in real estate and $4,000 in personal estate; in 1860 his father owned two slaves.

**Bulger**, W. F. *See* 1861–1865 entry.

**Burge**, Charles F. (c. 1817, Virginia–). Third corporal; in 1850 his mother owned thirteen slaves; in 1860 a farmer reporting $10,000 in real estate and $25,000 in personal estate; Mason 1866–1875; in 1870 a hotelier reporting $6,000 in real estate and $5,000 in personal estate.

**Burton**, James O. (c. 1838, Kentucky–). In 1860 a coach maker, married, and a Democrat.

**Carberry**, John. *See* 1861–1865 entry.

**Chadwick**, R. Y. Quartermaster.

**Childress**, Herbert C. (c. 1834, Alabama–). Married in 1850; Mason 1855–1885; second lieutenant in 1857; councilman in 1857; fifth sergeant at Fort Morgan; in 1860 owned one slave.

**Christian**, John F. *See* 1861–1865 entry.

**Coleman**, Thomas Wilkes (March 31, 1833, Alabama–>1907). Second corporal at Fort Morgan; captain of Company F, Fortieth Alabama; Mason; in 1860 a lawyer reporting $1,000 in real estate and $4,000 in personal estate, including five slaves; in 1860 a Democrat.

**Crowell**, J. W. *See* 1861–1865 entry.

**Davidson**, Robert J. (c. 1830, New York–). Fourth sergeant; in 1860 a painter, married with two sons, reporting $1,700 in real estate and $6,000 in personal estate, including four slaves.

**Davis**, William D. (c. 1832, Alabama–1868). In 1850 a laborer; married in 1854; in 1860 an overseer with one son; Mason 1860–1868.

**Dedman**, Marcus L. *See* 1861–1865 entry.

**DuBois**, Rufus U. (c. 1832, Alabama–1905). Third sergeant; in 1860 a dentist, married with two children, reporting $3,500 in real estate and $13,000 in personal estate, including eleven slaves; Mason 1862–1905.

**Dufphey**, London. *See* 1861–1865 entry.

**Erwin**, George W. (1835, Alabama–January 15, 1910). Second lieutenant; student at the University of Virginia in 1853–1854; married in 1857; in 1860 reported 35 slaves; in 1860, his father, attorney John Erwin, owned 169 slaves.

**Gewin**, Noah H. (November 24, 1839, Alabama–February 15, 1910). His family, with whom he lived until the mid-1860s, owned eleven slaves in 1830, forty-three slaves in 1850, and seventy-five slaves in 1860; in 1860 a farmer reporting $10,000 in personal estate, including seven slaves; joined the Guards January 7, 1861; in 1870 a farmer, married with two children, reporting $3,600 in real estate and $4,000 in personal estate; Mason 1874–1875.

**Hagy**, Andrew M. (c. 1816, Virginia–). In 1860 a blacksmith with one son.

**Hardaway**, Robert H. *See* 1861–1865 entry.

**Harris**, John Gideon (March 1, 1834, Alabama–July 7, 1908, Montgomery). Student at the Greene Springs School and Lebanon University; lawyer; Masonic grand master; his father owned fifteen slaves in 1850 and twenty-one slaves in 1860; during Civil War, captain, Company I, Twentieth Alabama.

**Harris**, Jno. F. (c. 1838, Alabama–). In 1860 a carpenter.

**Hill**, Richard (c. 1831, Alabama–). In 1850 a clerk; Mason 1859–1867; in 1860 a merchant, reporting $1,000 in real estate and $5,000 in personal estate, including two slaves; commissary at Fort Morgan; in 1870 a farmer, married with two children, reporting $8,000 in real estate and $1,000 in personal estate

**Hobson**, Edwin Lafayette. *See* 1861–1865 entry.

**Hooper**, William R. *See* 1861–1865 entry.

**Idom**, William Young. *See* 1861–1865 entry.

**Johnson**, Robert. *See* 1843–1846 entry.

**Jones**, Allen Cadwallader. *See* 1861–1865 entry.

**Jones**, Edwin Pompey. *See* 1861–1865 entry.

**Lavender**, Paul H. *See* 1861–1865 entry.

**McCall**, R. Scott. *See* **McCall**, Robert Scott, 1861–1865 entry.

**McCall**, William Alexander. *See* **McCall**, W. Alexander, 1861–1865 entry.

**McConnell**, Thomas H. Married in 1858; rejected as Mason in 1867.

**McDonald**, William Jackson. *See* 1861–1865 entry.

**McLemore**, Phillip B. (c. 1832, South Carolina–). First corporal; married in 1850; Democrat in 1860.

**Moore**, E. C.

**Moore**, Isaac D. (c. 1839, Alabama–). In 1860 a farmer.

**Moore**, Thomas G. *See* 1861–1865 entry.

**Nelson**, Algernon Sidney (1831, Alabama–December 17, 1871). Student at the University of Virginia in 1850–1853; Mason 1858–1872; married in 1859; in 1860 a planter with one child, reporting $72,000 in real estate and $135,000 in personal estate, including 120 slaves; in 1870 reported $48,150 in real estate and $5,000 in personal estate. Brother of Guard Gideon E. Nelson.

**Nelson**, Gideon E. *See* 1861–1865 entry.

**Nutting**, George. *See* 1861–1865 entry.

**Powers**, William Wesley (c. 1827, South Carolina–October 13, 1900). In 1860 a merchant reporting $4,000 in personal estate, and a Democrat; Mason 1865–1870; in 1870 a merchant and farmer reporting $12,000 in real estate and $24,000 in personal estate; no children.

**Rhodes**, Alva (c. 1837, Alabama–). In 1860 a gin maker, married with one child. Cousin of Guard Thomas Marshall Rhodes.

**Sanborn**, Henry A. (c. 1810, New Hampshire–). In 1850 a painter, married with four children; in 1860 a mechanic reporting $1,000 in real estate, and a Democrat; second sergeant at Fort Morgan; in 1870 reported $1,000 in real estate and $500 in personal estate.

**Steinhart**, Herman (c. 1820, Germany–). Married in 1849; in 1850 a merchant reporting $50 in real estate; in 1860 reported $4,000 in real estate and $8,000 in personal estate, including three slaves; Jewish.

**Stickney**, Richard Henry (c. 1838, Alabama–). In 1860 a clerk and merchant reporting $1,800 in real estate and two slaves; in 1880 a cotton factor, married with four children.

**Surles**, Marion (c. 1831, Georgia–). In 1860 a coach maker.

**Waddil**, Abner C. *See* **Waddell**, Abner C., 1861–1865 entry.

**Webb**, J. D. (Jr.). *See* **Webb**, James Daniel (Jr.), 1861–1865 entry.

**Williams**, Jonathan W. *See* 1861–1865 entry.

**Wilson**, George W. *See* 1861–1865 entry.

**Wright**, John J. *See* 1861–1865 entry.

**Wright**, Joseph L. *See* 1861–1865 entry.

**Wynne**, William A. (c. 1833, Alabama–1867 of yellow fever near Huntsville, Texas). In 1860 a lawyer living at home, and a Democrat. Brother of Guard John W. Wynne.

### Greensboro Guards, Fifth Alabama Infantry Regiment, April 1861–April 1865

Names and information are compiled from, among other sources, manuscript muster rolls, Fifth Alabama Infantry Regiment, June 30, August 31, September 1, October 31, December 31, 1861, February 8, 1862, March 30, June 30, August 31, October 31, 1864; the *Greensboro Alabama Beacon,* May 24, 1861, November 5, 1898; the *Greensboro Southern Watchman,* January 14, 1886; U.S. Government manuscript censuses 1860, 1870, 1880; Compiled Service Records, Fifth Alabama Infantry Regiment; William Edward Wadsworth Yerby, *History of Greensboro, Alabama, from its Earliest Settlement,* 42–45; J. W. Williams, "Company D, Fifth Alabama, C.S.A.: A Complete List of the Original Company"; and marriage and death records.

† Warrior Guards who transferred in April 1862

**Adams**, Benjamin Carter ("Buck") (1838–). Student at the University of Virginia in 1856; enlisted May 6, 1861, in Uniontown, Alabama; assistant regimental commissary with the rank of captain; brigade commissary in 1862; D. H. Hill's division commissary with the rank of major in 1863; cotton planter in 1878. Brother of Guards John M. Adams and Richard Henry Adams.

**Adams**, John M. Enlisted May 18, 1861 in Pensacola, Florida; discharged in September or October 1861 for a disability; later an assistant surgeon with the rank of captain. Brother of Guards Benjamin Carter Adams and Richard Henry Adams.

**Adams**, Richard Henry (Jr.) (April 21, 1841, Alabama–October 8, 1896). Enlisted May 6, 1861, in Uniontown, Alabama; wounded May 31, 1862; joined Partisan Rangers, Fifty-first Alabama Infantry; captured in Nashville and remained a prisoner for twenty-one months; civil engineer, postmaster. Brother of Guards Benjamin Carter Adams and John M. Adams.

**Allen**, W. Henry (c. 1844, Alabama–). In 1860 a student; son of a Havanna, Alabama, merchant reporting $1,000 in real estate and $5,800 in personal estate, including five slaves, in 1850; enlisted August 8 or 14, 1861, in Union Mills, Virginia; typhoid fever April 23–June 3, 1862; fourth corporal in March 1864; third corporal in August 1864; wounded in the thigh October 19, 1864, and sent home.

†**Arrington**, James Portis (died during war). From Forkland, Alabama; appointed aide-de-camp to Rodes with the rank of lieutenant in 1863.

**Avery**, Robert (c. 1844, Alabama–during war). In 1860 a student at the Greene Springs School; enlisted March 11, 1862, in Greensboro.

**Badenhausen**, Charles von (c. 1834, Germany–). Imperial cadet in the Austrian army 1852–1854, lieutenant 1854–1859; in 1860 a teacher at Faunsdale plantation, Marengo County, Alabama; enlisted May 6, 1861, in Uniontown, Alabama; chief musician; lost his left arm and a finger of his right hand July 1, 1862; discharged July 28, 1862.

**Bagley**, D. E. *See* **Bayley**, D. E.

**Bailey**, D. E. *See* **Bayley**, D. E.

**Barnum**, David (c. 1843, Alabama–). Enlisted August 23, 1861, in Union Mills, Virginia; captured September 14, 1862; appointed acting master, CS Navy at Charleston Harbor in August 1863. Son of Guard Augustus Barnum.

**Bayley** or **Bailey**, D. E. Enlisted August 25, 1862, in Pike County, Alabama; sick with: sciatica (February 1863), chronic rheumatism (January 1864), diabetes (June 1864); wounded May 5, 1864; in Lynchburg, Virginia, hospital (September and October 1864); in camp in February 1865; captured April 2, 1865.

**Bayol**, Francis Edward ("Ned") (c. 1835, Alabama–September 1900). Enlisted August 9, 1861, in Greensboro; wounded in the right leg September 14, 1862, in the right leg and hip May 3, 1863; detailed to the quartermaster department, Demopolis, Alabama; in 1880 a dancing instructor, married with five children. Son of Guard Edward Bayol and brother of Guard Jules Honoré Bayol.

**Bayol**, Jules Honoré (c. 1837, Alabama–July 1, 1862, at Malvern Hill). Enlisted August 9, 1861, in Greensboro; never married. Son of Guard Edward Bayol and brother of Guard Francis Edward Bayol.

**Beck**, Henry (c. 1839, Germany–). Arrived in Greensboro in 1857; in 1860 a merchant, married; enlisted April 18, 1861, in Greensboro but moved to the Jeff Davis Legion; exchanged with John S. Tucker to become brigade commissary clerk April 1, 1864; Mason 1870–1871; officer, Knights of Pythias; in 1870 a merchant with three children, reporting $30,000 in personal estate; moved to Birmingham in 1887; although he attended Christian services during the war, his son is described as Jewish in an 1892 issue of the *Greensboro Alabama Beacon*.

**Boardman**, James L. (c. 1841, Alabama–1876, Waco, Texas). His father was a silversmith and planter who owned twenty-two slaves in 1850 and more than forty-one slaves in 1860; enlisted April 13, 1861, in Greensboro; left in Montgomery with measles; third corporal in October 1861; clerk for Major Adams; division commissary clerk in 1864.

**Borden**, Frederick A. (c. 1839, Alabama–). In 1860 a student living in Newbern, Alabama, with his mother, who reported $80,000 in real estate and $9,000 in personal estate; enlisted April 18, 1861, in Greensboro; left in Knoxville with measles; transferred to the Jeff Davis Legion to be with his brothers in August 1862.

**Borden**, Joseph (January 27, 1828, North Carolina–1913, California). Married his stepsister, Frances S. "Fannie" Gray, in 1851; in 1860 reported thirty-two slaves; member of Greensboro Cavalry; enlisted in the Guards April 13, 1861, in Greensboro; third sergeant in April 1861; second sergeant in August 1861; second lieutenant April 27, 1862; wounded in July 1862; resigned December 12, 1863. Cousin of Guard James M. Jack.

**Borden**, William W. In 1860 a student; enlisted April 20, 1861, in Greensboro; typhoid fever in August 1861; discharged August 13, 1862, for being underage; in 1880 a farmer, married with four or five children.

**Bostick**, Lewis S. (died September 1862 while unloading a wagon of muskets). Enlisted March 10, 1862, in Greensboro; wagoner.

**Bridges**, D. J. Enlisted August 21, 1862, in Henry County, Virginia; wounded May 5, 1864; captured September 19, 1864, in Winchester, Virginia.

**Briggs**, Charles T. (c. 1842, Alabama–after 1906). In 1860 living at home; enlisted April 13, 1861, in Greensboro; discharged August 2, 1861, due to a disability; reenlisted November 20, 1862, in Middletown, Virginia; captured at Gettysburg; wounded May 8, 1864; typhoid fever in July 1864; sick in camp in February 1865; captured at Petersburg, April 2, 1865; in 1870 a dry goods clerk. Son of Guard Samuel G. Briggs.

**Britton**, William G. (c. 1843–after 1910). Enlisted April 13, 1861, in Greensboro; third corporal in August 1861; wounded in the shoulder May 3, 1863; first sergeant in 1864; wounded July 13, 1864; wounded and captured September 19, 1864, right arm amputated; in 1870 a farmer reporting $500 in personal estate; in 1880 a tax collector, married with five children.

**Brown**, Josiah McKendre (January 22, 1828, Greene County, Alabama–August 5, 1870). Enlisted April 16, 1861, in Greensboro; wounded in 1862; wounded and right leg amputated below the knee July 2, 1863; captured July 3, 1863; paroled September 25, 1863; married in 1868; farmer; Methodist.

**Bulger**, W. F. (died July 15, 1861, in Culpeper Court House, Virginia, of typhoid fever). Enlisted April 13, 1861, in Greensboro.

**Burton**, James (c. 1838, Kentucky–November 3, 1863, of smallpox in prison). Member of Greensboro Cavalry; in 1860 a coach maker, married, and a Democrat; enlisted March 6, 1862, in Greensboro; captured at South Mountain and at Gettysburg.

**Butler**, B. A. ("Bunk"). Enlisted March 8, 1862, in Greensboro; teamster in 1863; captured at Gettysburg; wounded and captured May 8, 1864.

**Carberry**, John. Enlisted April 13, 1861, in Greensboro; pioneer March–December 31, 1863; sick in camp in February 1865; captured April 2, 1865.

**Carroll**, D. L. (died May 14, 1863, following gunshot wound and an amputated arm after Chancellorsville). Enlisted before December 1862; wounded and captured May 3, 1863.

**Carter**, Benjamin A. (c. 1827, North Carolina–1870). Mason 1858–1870; in 1860 an overseer; enlisted April 13, 1861, in Greensboro; wounded May 3, 1863; surgical assistant.

**Chadwick**, Hanson M. Enlisted April 16, 1861, in Greensboro; captured November 21, 1863; released on oath of allegiance January 8, 1864.

**Chadwick**, Robert A. (c. 1845–). In 1860 a student; married Mary Willingham July 24, 1861; enlisted August 9, 1861, in Greensboro; discharged August 13, 1862, for being underage, but captured May 3, 1863, and on wounded furlough in 1864; moved to Austin, Texas, after the war.

**Chadwick**, Shelby W. (Jr.) (September 26, 1842, Alabama–1897). Enlisted in the Cahaba Rifles, Fifth Alabama Infantry, June 16, 1861; transferred to the Greensboro Guards August 1, 1861; wounded in the right hand in 1862; promoted from fourth sergeant to sergeant major in February 1864; taken prisoner April 2, 1865; Mason; clerk, merchant, surveyor, county treasurer; Methodist. Son of Guard Shelby W. Chadwick Sr.

**Chapman**, Alonzo B. (c. 1840–May 31, 1862, at Seven Pines). Enlisted April 13, 1861, in Greensboro after recent move from Dallas County, Alabama.

**Childress**, Henry R. (c. 1844, Alabama–). Enlisted March 6, 1862, in Greensboro; captured September 19, 1864, in Winchester, Virginia; exchanged October 30, 1864; captured April 2, 1865. Brother of Guard Jeff Childress.

**Childress**, Jeff. Left on thirty-day furlough March 11, 1864; in camp in February 1865. Brother of Guard Henry R. Childress.

**Chiles**, J. W. (c. 1840, Alabama–March 19, 1864). His father owned fifty-one slaves in 1860; enlisted August 26, 1862, in Pike County, Alabama; captured July 14, 1863. May have joined the federal service January 25, 1864. *Note:* Ambiguous records may refer to two individuals.

**Christian**, Henry (c. 1820, Virginia–). Enlisted August 9, 1861, in Greensboro; discharged July 22, 1862, due to inability to perform duty.

**Christian**, John F. (c. 1839, Alabama–). In 1860 a hotelier living with his widowed mother and six siblings, reporting $3,500 in personal estate, including five slaves; fourth corporal at Fort Morgan; enlisted April 13, 1861, in Greensboro; first sergeant May 13, 1861; brevet second lieutenant May 28, 1861; captured September 14, 1862, and May 3, 1863; elected third lieutenant March 30, 1863; wounded July 18, 1864; in camp February 23, 1865; captured April 2, 1865.

† **Clements**, J. W. (1835–). Student at the University of Virginia in 1854; from Eutaw, Alabama.

**Clifton**, William (c. 1819, South Carolina–). From Tuscaloosa, Alabama; enlisted February 16, 1863, in Grace Church, Virginia; detailed as a blacksmith in Carter's Battery in 1863; sick in camp in February 1865; captured April 2, 1865.

**Cobbs**, William Addison. Captured April 2, 1865.

**Coleman**, Alonzo G. ("Lonnie") (1837, Alabama–March 1899). Student at the University of Virginia in 1856; enlisted May 6, 1861, in Uniontown, Alabama; wounded May 31, 1862, and discharged; joined Partisan Rangers, Fifty-first Alabama Infantry; captured, escaped to Canada; cotton planter after the war.

**Cowin**, John Henry (1839, Alabama–May 3, 1863, at Chancellorsville). Attended the Greene Springs School; student at the University of Virginia in 1858; graduated from Jefferson Medical College in 1860; enlisted April 13, 1861, in Greensboro; corporal, orderly sergeant. Son of Guard Samuel C. Cowin and brother of Guard William S. Cowin.

**Cowin**, Samuel C. (c. 1813, Maryland–1886). In 1830 reported two slaves; married in 1836; enlisted in the Guards February 22, 1836; first corporal in 1846; in 1850 reported fifteen slaves; in 1860 a planter and hotelier with three sons, reporting $19,665 in real estate and $60,000 in personal estate, including fifty slaves; enlisted in the Guards April 13, 1861, in Greensboro; second lieutenant in October 1861; resigned in April 1862. Father of Guards John Henry Cowin and William S. Cowin.

**Cowin**, William S. ("Tood") (c. 1842, Alabama–). Student at the University of Alabama; enlisted April 13, 1861, in Greensboro; wounded in October 1862; brigade courier in May 1863; division commissary clerk in October 1864. Son of Guard Samuel C. Cowin and brother of Guard John H. Cowin.

† **Craddock**, J. N.

**Croom**, Wiley G. (c. 1844, Alabama–). In 1850 his parents in Newbern, Alabama, reported $10,000 in real estate and thirty-seven slaves; in 1860 reported $32,000 in real estate and $100,000 in personal estate, including fifty-nine slaves; enlisted April 22, 1861, in Greensboro.

**Crowell**, J. W. Enlisted April 13, 1861, in Greensboro; musician; wounded May 31, 1862; transferred to Thirtieth North Carolina Infantry April 7, 1863.

**Dedman**, Marcus L. (c. 1822, Virginia–c. 1867). In 1860 a marshal and mechanic, married with two children, reporting $1,000 in real estate, and a Democrat; enlisted April 13, 1861, in Greensboro; second lieutenant in April 1861; second lieutenant in May 1861; resigned in October 1861 to form his own company.

**Dorroh**, Samuel J. (c. 1840, Alabama–September 25, 1861, of typhoid). In 1860 living with his mother (Belinda) and father, who reported $12,500 in real estate and $50,000 in personal estate, including thirty-one slaves; enlisted April 20, 1861, in Greensboro. Cousin of Guards John J. Wright and Joseph L. Wright.

**Dufphey**, London. Slave who drummed in the Creek War, for the Greensboro Volunteers in Mexico, and for the Guards in the early part of the Civil War.

**Dufphey**, William L. (1832–). In 1860 his mother reported $30,000 in real estate and $45,000 in personal estate, including forty-eight slaves; member of the Greensboro Cavalry; enlisted April 18, 1861, in Greensboro; discharged December 19, 1861, due to a disability. Probably son of Guard William L. Dufphey.

**Elias**, Lewis. Enlisted July 18, 1861, in Montgomery; baker; wounded May 5, 1864; returned to his company under guard in December 1864; in camp in February 1865; deserted March 20, 1865.

† **Elliott**, Joseph Knox ("Old Elliott"). Discharged July 22, 1862, as unable to perform duty and detailed to quartermaster dept.

† **Elliott**, William. From Havanna, Alabama.

**Ellison**, William B. (c. 1838–June 27, 1862, at Gaines' Mill). Mason 1860–1862; enlisted August 9, 1861, in Greensboro; sutler.

**Farrier**, J. A. Enlisted August 23, 1862, in Washington County, Alabama; wounded in the arm and captured May 3, 1863; wounded May 5, 1864; in camp in February 1865; captured April 2, 1865.

† **Foster**, Ezra. Wounded May 31, 1862.

**Fowler**, Henry. Enlisted May 25, 1861, in Coffee County, Alabama; wounded in the arm May 3, 1863; discharged June 30, 1864.

† **Frierson**, Thomas McRea. Fourth corporal; captured September 14, 1862; transferred to cavalry in October 1862.

**Gawicki**, Stan (c. 1836, Poland or Germany–). In 1860 a tailor reporting $1,000 in personal estate; enlisted August 9, 1861, in Greensboro; musician; discharged October 27, 1862.

**Geddie**, H. Enlisted April 22, 1861, in Greensboro; wounded in August 1862; captured May 20, 1864; exchanged October 29, 1864; in camp in February 1865.

**Givens**, John J. (c. 1827, Alabama–November or December 1862 of pneumonia). Enlisted September 28, 1862, in Henry County, Alabama; farmer.

**Glover**, Walton N. (c. 1841, Alabama–). In 1860 living with his father, who reported $91,200 in real estate and $193,000 in personal estate, including 148 slaves; enlisted August 14, 1861, in Union Mills, Virginia; brigade commissary clerk; broke a leg in February 1863.

**Goslin**, A. J. Enlisted September 10, 1862, in Virginia.

**Grigg**, Joe A. Enlisted April 16, 1861, in Greensboro; wagon master and division courier for Rodes; captured September 14, 1862.

**Griggs**, James E. ("Squire") (c. 1813, Virginia–October 11, 1873). In 1860 a deputy sheriff; enlisted April 13, 1861, in Greensboro; fourth corporal in April 1861; wagon master in August 1861; discharged August 13, 1862, for being overage.

† **Haden**, W. B. Wounded May 31, 1862.

**Hafner**, Charles W. (1843–December 4, 1864, after Cedar Creek). In 1860 living with his father, a blacksmith who owned two slaves; enlisted March 16, 1862, in Greensboro; slightly wounded May 31, 1862; fifth sergeant; fourth sergeant in 1862; wounded September 14, 1862; fractured his left arm and captured May 3, 1863; fatally shot through the colon and rectum October 19, 1864. Brother of Guard William G. Hafner.

**Hafner**, William G. (December 17, 1842, South Carolina–). In 1861, a clerk living with mother and father, a Forkland, Alabama, blacksmith; enlisted August 9, 1861, in Greensboro; wounded May 1, 1864; in 1868 an officer in Greensboro Fire Company 1. Brother of Guard Charles W. Hafner.

**Hagins**, Peter (c. 1838–). In 1860 an overseer in Newbern, Alabama, living with his father, also an overseer, who reported $4,000 in personal estate, including five slaves; enlisted April 22, 1861, in Greensboro; captured May 3, 1863; acting regimental commissary sergeant in camp in February 1865.

**Hardaway**, Robert H. (c. 1827, Virginia–). In 1860 a deputy sheriff and clerk reporting $300 in personal estate; enlisted April 13, 1861, in Greensboro; discharged March 31, 1862.

† **Hargrove**, Andrew Coleman. Discharged for a disability, then raised his own company.

† **Hausman**, Christopher Jacob. Wounded May 2, 1863, and May 6, 1864.

**Herran**, J. C. N. (c. 1843, Alabama–December 16, 1861, in Richmond of disease). In 1860 living with his mother and father, a small farmer in Havanna, Alabama; enlisted April 25, 1861, in Greensboro.

**Hester**, J. A. No contemporary reference; possibly John H. Hester, overseer for Martin family.

**Hill**, Thomas Charles or Carter (c. 1847, Alabama–). In 1860 a Newbern, Alabama, physician and farmer who reported $20,000 in personal estate, including thirteen slaves; enlisted April 22, 1861, in Greensboro; first sergeant in August 1861; appointed assistant surgeon in the Fifth Alabama Infantry in 1863; later a surgeon; assigned to Lomax's cavalry division in 1864.

**Hobson**, Edwin Lafayette (1835, Alabama–November 2, 1901, Virginia). Attended the Greene Springs School; student at the University of Virginia in 1852; part of the Guards' 1857 reorganization; in 1860 a planter reporting $20,000 in real estate and $25,000 in personal estate, including twenty-seven slaves, with his mother reporting $20,000 in personal estate and other family members reporting ninety-five slaves; enlisted April 13, 1861, in Greensboro; elected captain May 13, 1861; elected major of the Fifth Alabama Infantry in April 1862; wounded in the left thigh May 2, 1863; wounded in the thigh May 8, 1864; colonel November 29, 1864; married daughter of J. R. Anderson of Tredegar Iron Works, where he worked after the war; ten children; Episcopalian.

**Holland**, H. T. (c. 1829–February 16 or 17, 1863, of disease). Enlisted September 21, 1862, in Henry County, Alabama; farmer.

**Holston**, G. W. (c. 1846, Alabama–). No contemporary reference; son of a Havanna, Alabama, farmer, reporting $1,000 in real estate in 1860.

**Hooper**, William R. (c. 1845, Alabama–). In 1860 a student; enlisted April 13, 1861, in Greensboro; wagoner; discharged August 13, 1862, for inability.

**Huggins**, Fred L. (c. 1844, Alabama–). In 1860 a student living in Newbern, Alabama, with his mother and father, who reported $2,500 in real estate and $10,000 in personal estate, including six slaves; enlisted April 22, 1861, in Greensboro; captured September 14, 1862; wounded September 3, 1864; captured September 25, 1864; wounded in the leg and captured October 19, 1864; in 1880 an unmarried store clerk.

**Huggins**, Noah F. Member of the Guards in 1864.

**Huggins**, Peter. *See* **Hagins**, Peter.

**Hutchinson**, Edward T. (January 20, 1844–December 3, 1927). Enlisted April 20, 1863, in Grace Court House, Virginia; captured May 3, 1863; wounded May 8, 1864, and October 19, 1864; sick in camp in February 1865; reputed the only Guard present at Appomattox; in 1870 a dry goods clerk and officer of Greensboro Fire Company 1; married in 1875. Son of the Reverend J. J. Hutchinson. *See also* 1876–1880 entry.

**Idom**, Edwin Young (c. 1843, Alabama–). In 1860 living with his mother and father, a well digger who reported $300 in real estate and $100 in personal estate; enlisted April 16,

1861, in Greensboro; brigade and division butcher; in 1870 a farmer, married with one son. Nephew of Guard William Young Idom.

**Idom**, William Young (c. 1825, Alabama–). Married in 1843; in 1860 a well digger with four children, reporting $1,300 in real estate and $1,600 in personal estate; enlisted April 13, 1861, in Greensboro; butcher, ambulance driver; discharged August 13, 1862, as overage but on duty again by May 1863; wounded in the thigh and back October 19, 1864; in camp in February 1865. Uncle of Guard Edwin Young Idom.

**Jack**, James M. (c. 1830, Alabama–). Attended the Greene Springs School; in 1860 attending the Havanna, Alabama, plantation of his father, who reported $23,000 in real estate and $100,000 in personal estate, including seventy slaves; enlisted April 20, 1861, in Greensboro; lost his left leg July 1, 1862; captain of home guards; married in 1867; in 1870 a Havanna farmer with one child, reporting $6,000 in real estate and $1,600 in personal estate; legislator in 1876; tax assessor in 1884. Cousin of Guard Joseph Borden.

**Jackson**, Andrew. Enlisted October 15, 1862, in Macon County, Alabama; prisoner of war in March 1864; captured October 19, 1864; exchanged January 17, 1865; illiterate. Brother of Guard Samuel B. Jackson.

**Jackson**, John F. (c. 1847–). Enlisted May 12, 1861, in Montgomery; ambulance driver; captured September 14, 1862.

**Jackson**, Norborne H. T. (c. 1843–). In 1860 a student at the Greene Springs School; enlisted April 17, 1861, in Greensboro; discharged October 5, 1861, for a disability; in 1870 a druggist, married with one child. Son of Guard John T. Jackson.

**Jackson**, Samuel B. From Linden, Marengo County, Alabama; enlisted May 12, 1861, in Montgomery; wounded May 2, 1863, and had three toes amputated. Brother of Guard Andrew Jackson.

**James**, Cunningham ("Cunny") (c. 1842, Virginia–). In 1850 his father owned twenty-two slaves; enlisted April 25, 1861, in Greensboro; discharged November 28, 1862, due to typhoid, pneumonia, and chronic diarrhea; joined the Jeff Davis Legion.

**James**, Gilliam (c. 1835, Virginia–). Enlisted April 25, 1861, in Greensboro; division courier cited by Rodes for great service at Chancellorsville; left company in December 1864 after an exchange with Private Wesson of the Jeff Davis Legion; in 1880 an unmarried farmer.

**Jeffries**, Robert H. (c. 1840–). In 1860 owned thirteen slaves and was attending the farm of his father, Algernon S. Jeffries, an 1861 Cooperationist candidate, who reported $51,900 in real estate and $57,000 in personal estate, including fifty slaves; enlisted April 13, 1861, in Greensboro; wounded July 1, 1862; foot and leg amputated.

**Johnson**, James M. Enlisted in April or May 1861; deserted June 30, 1861.

**Jones**, Allen Cadwallader (c. 1812, North Carolina–January 9, 1894). Commissioner of free schools in 1854, legislator, agriculturalist, member of the Joint Military Committee; in 1860 a planter, married with five children, reporting $30,000 in real estate and $78,000 in personal estate, including seventy-two slaves; reorganized the Guards and served as captain February 1857–April 1861; lieutenant colonel of the Fifth Alabama Infantry in May 1861; colonel in November 1861; resigned in April 1862; in 1870 reported $34,000 in real estate and $15,000 in personal estate. Brother-in-law of Guard George W. Erwin.

**Jones**, Edwin Pompey (c. 1841, Alabama–). Enlisted April 13, 1861, in Greensboro; corporal in June 1861; fourth sergeant in August 1861; orderly sergeant in April 1862; wounded in the right side and hand July 1, 1862; captured May 3, 1863; second lieutenant in May 1863; first lieutenant in 1864; captured July 18, 1864. Son of Guard Claudius Jones.

**Jones**, Matthew H. (July 15, 1845–). From Mobile; enlisted April 20, 1863, in Santee, Virginia; wounded in the hand and foot May 2, 1863; appointed CSA cadet September 18, 1863.

**Jones**, Napoleon B. (c. 1831, Alabama–after 1910). In 1860 living as a planter with or near his father, a planter and physician, who reported $121,357 in real estate and $250,000 in personal estate; enlisted April 25, 1861, in Greensboro; appointed first corporal of a company of mounted infantry in May 1863.

**Jones**, William J. (c. 1842, Alabama–). Enlisted April 20, 1861, in Greensboro; second corporal in 1863.

**Kennedy**, William L. ("Tink") (c. 1842, Alabama–). In 1860 a student; enlisted April 13, 1861, in Greensboro; color corporal in August 1861; color sergeant May 31, 1862; wounded in September 1862; wounded September 19, 1864; exchanged October 30, 1864; captured at Amelia Court House April 5, 1865. Son of Guard Warren E. Kennedy.

**Knight**, Sam. Enlisted September 22, 1862, in Washington County, Alabama; declared deserted in August 1863 after a furlough for typhoid fever.

**Knight**, William N. (c. 1840, Alabama–after 1910). Enlisted May 8, 1861, in Pensacola, Florida; discharged for a disability in October 1861; reenlisted and made captain of another company; Mason 1867–1903; in 1870 a farmer, married with two sons, reporting $33,000 in real estate and $7,000 in personal estate.

**Knowlen, Knowles**, or **Noland**, John T. (c. 1824, Washington, D.C.–). In 1850 a painter, married, with one slave; enlisted May 13, 1861, in Pensacola, Florida; wounded May 31, 1861; captured July 2, 1863.

**Lanier**, Robert B. (c. 1840, North Carolina–). In 1860 living with his mother and father, a farmer reporting $10,735 in real estate and $25,000 in personal estate; enlisted April 22, 1861, in Greensboro; discharged for a constricted urethra January 11, 1862. Brother of Guard William A. Lanier.

**Lanier**, William A. (c. 1841, North Carolina–November 17, 1864, from chest wound at Cedar Creek). In 1860 a student living with his parents; enlisted April 22, 1861, in Greensboro; wounded May 31, 1862; wounded in the head and captured July 2, 1863; exchanged April 27, 1864; shot in the lung and captured October 19, 1864. Brother of Guard Robert B. Lanier.

**Lavender**, Paul H. (c. 1833, Alabama–May 27, 1883). In 1860 a merchant clerk reporting $2,500 in personal estate, including one slave; enlisted April 13, 1861, in Greensboro; wounded in the thigh July 1, 1863; detailed as a clerk in Richmond in June 1864; represented a New York firm in Mobile by 1879.

**Lawrence**, Elijah (died during the war). In the hospital with scurvy in May 1863.

**Layne**, G. W. (c. 1838, Tennessee–). In 1860 owner of a livery stable, reporting $1,600 in real estate and $5,000 in personal estate; enlisted March 6, 1862, in Greensboro.

**Lee**, James H. Enlisted in June 1861 in Linden, Alabama; musician; fractured his right leg in July 1863.

**Lester**, James A. (c. 1843, Virginia–). In 1860 a clerk in Newbern, Alabama; enlisted April 13, 1861, in Greensboro; discharged in July 1861 for a disability.

**Lewis**, Elias. *See* **Elias**, Lewis.

**Little**, W. J. A. In company in January 1863.

**Locke**, James W. (c. 1842, Alabama–). Enlisted April 13, 1861, in Greensboro; discharged August 9, 1862, due to a disability; second corporal of a company of mounted infantry in 1863; in 1870 a farmer reporting $4,000 in real estate and $500 in personal estate; in 1880 a tax collector, married with two children. Son of Anne Locke Kerr. Probably nephew or son of Guards John Locke and William A. Locke.

**Logan**, Dudley (c. 1846, Alabama–). No contemporary references; in 1860 an apprentice wagon maker in Havanna, Alabama.

**Long**, W. W. ("Old Man") (c. 1820, South Carolina–1865). In 1860 a planter, married with two children, reporting $7,200 in real estate and $50,000 in personal estate, including forty-six slaves; enlisted February 8, 1864, in Eutaw, Alabama; in camp in February 1865.

**Lyles**, William (c. 1841, Alabama–). In 1860 a farmer, married with six children, reporting $1,000 in real estate; entered the Guards from the Forty-third Alabama in February 1865, after an exchange with J. Sterling Speed; captured April 2, 1865; illiterate.

**Madison**, John W. (c. 1825, Alabama–). Enlisted April 22, 1861, in Greensboro; discharged in September or October 1861 for a disability; in 1870 a farmer in Havanna, Alabama, married with three children, reporting $800 in real estate and $2,000 in personal estate.

**Madison**, William J. (c. 1830, Alabama–). His Nova Scotia–born illiterate father owned twenty-eight slaves in 1850 and thirty-two in 1860; enlisted March 2, 1863, in Greensboro; by 1863 detailed to provost guard in Selma, Alabama; in 1870 a farmer, married, reporting $195 in real estate and $150 in personal estate.

**Markstein**, Max (c. 1842, Germany–). Clerk; enlisted April 22, 1861, in Greensboro; discharged August 14, 1862; in 1880 a merchant, married with three children.

**Martin**, Edward Thomas (c. 1829, Alabama–). In 1860 a farmer, married with five children, reporting $2,000 in real estate and $3,000 in personal estate; enlisted April 20, 1861, in Greensboro; regimental butcher in 1863; wounded and captured May 5, 1864.

† **Martin**, John M. Sergeant major; later raised his own company.

**McCall**, Robert Scott (c. 1845, Alabama–). In 1860 living with his mother and father, a trader with four children, reporting $2,200 in real estate; enlisted April 13, 1861, in Greensboro; wounded May 31, 1862; discharged August 13, 1862, for being underage. Brother of Guard W. Alexander McCall.

**McCall**, W. Alexander (c. 1843–). Enlisted April 13, 1861, in Greensboro; second sergeant in 1864; in command of the Guards October 19, 1864. Brother of Guard Robert Scott McCall.

**McCrary**, Budd (c. 1840, Alabama–). In 1860 a farmer in Havanna, Alabama, married; enlisted March 11, 1862, in Greensboro; discharged for a disability April 1, 1864. Brother of Guard William H. McCrary.

**McCrary**, William H. (c. 1843, Alabama–). In 1860 living with his mother and father, a farmer in Havanna, Alabama, who reported $2,000 in real estate; enlisted March 13, 1862, in Greensboro; wounded in the arm in July 1864; guarding baggage in February 1865. Brother of Guard Budd McCrary.

**McDiarmid**, **McDiermaid**, or **McDiermid**, Joel Calvin (October 30, 1836, North Carolina–October 25, 1900, Goodwater, Alabama). In 1838 his family moved to Talladega County, Alabama; in 1860 a clerk in Havanna, Alabama; enlisted April 13, 1861, in Greensboro; court-martialed for leaving the battlefield at Fredericksburg; wounded October 19, 1864; on work detail February 23, 1865; captured April 2, 1865. Married in 1880.

**McDonald**, William Jackson (c. 1825, Alabama–). Joined the Guards June 6, 1846; in 1850 a clerk, married with two children; in 1860 an architect, married with six children, reporting $20,000 in real estate and $12,000 in personal estate; enlisted April 13, 1861, in Greensboro; third sergeant; discharged August 2, 1861; in 1870 a merchant reporting $5,000 in real estate and $140 in personal estate, his wife reporting $2,500 in real estate and $1,500 in personal estate.

† **McGee** or **McGehee**, James C. Captured September 14, 1862.

**McNeil**, Q. C. No contemporary references.

**McNeil**, W. W. (died January 7 or 8, 1863, in Richmond of pneumonia).

**Miller**, William D. (c. 1838, Alabama–). Enlisted April 13, 1861, in Greensboro; discharged for a disability August 2, 1861.

**Moore**, Augustus H. ("Gus") (c. 1836, Alabama–May 31, 1862, at Seven Pines). Attended the Greene Springs School; in 1860 a physician living with his mother and father, a planter reporting $36,000 in real estate and $55,000 in personal estate; enlisted April 13, 1861, in Greensboro; color corporal. Brother of Guards James Pickens Moore and Thomas G. Moore.

**Moore**, James Pickens ("Pick") (c. 1839, Alabama–). Student at the University of Virginia in 1858; in 1860 a merchant living with his parents; enlisted April 13, 1861, in Greensboro; corporal in January 1863; division courier for Rodes in 1864; in 1878 a cotton planter. Brother of Guards Augustus H. Moore and Thomas G. Moore.

**Moore**, Rick. *See* **Moore**, James Pickens.

**Moore**, Thomas G. (c. 1842, Alabama–July 2, 1907). Attended the Greene Springs School; in 1860 a student living with his parents; enlisted April 13, 1861, in Greensboro; brigade courier in April 1863. Brother of Guards Augustus H. Moore and James Pickens Moore.

**Moorman**, W. B. (died September 14, 1862, at South Mountain). Enlisted May 6, 1861, in Uniontown, Alabama; captured in Williamsburg, Virginia.

**Morris**, A. R. On the Guards' muster roll in January 1863.

**Morris**, J. C. No contemporary references.

**Nelson**, Gideon E. (c. 1824, Alabama–June 1867). In 1850 a planter reporting $9,700 in real estate and 46 slaves; Mason 1855–1867; in 1860 a planter, married with six children, reporting $10,000 in real estate and $165,000 in personal estate, including 145 slaves; commissioned first lieutenant April 27, 1857; enlisted April 13, 1861, in Greensboro; resigned May 28, 1861, due to a disability. Brother of Guard Algernon Sidney Nelson.

**Noland**, John T. *See* **Knowlen**, John T.

**Nutting**, Edwin (c. 1841, Alabama–). In 1860 living with his mother and father, a master carpenter reporting $2,000 in real estate and $7,000 in personal estate, including seven slaves; enlisted March 6, 1862, in Greensboro; wounded May 31, 1862; discharged December 5, 1862. Brother of Guard George Nutting; brother-in-law of Guard John S. Tucker.

**Nutting**, George ("Tean") (c. 1843, Alabama–July 1, 1863, at Gettysburg). In 1860 living with parents; enlisted April 13, 1861, in Greensboro; color corporal; wounded May 31, 1862; captured May 3, 1863. Brother of Guard Edwin Nutting; brother-in-law of Guard John S. Tucker.

**Orrick**, John C. (1844, Alabama–1923, Texas). In 1860 living with his mother and father, a dentist reporting $1,000 in real estate; enlisted April 13, 1861, in Greensboro; discharged for being underage; joined Mosby's guerrillas as a scout; in 1867 killed freedman Alex Webb and escaped to Central America and Mexico; changed his name to Arrington and served as a captain in the Rangers and later as sheriff of Wheeler, Texas, and attached counties; retired as a rancher near Canadian, Texas.

† **Owens**, F. E.

**Parker**, J. W. Enlisted in April or May 1861.

† **Parrish**, R. C.

**Pasteur**, Edward T. (c. 1836, Alabama–September 1, 1904). In 1860 living with his mother, a planter reporting $25,000 in real estate and $40,000 in personal estate, including thirty-three slaves; enlisted April 13, 1861, in Greensboro; corporal in January 1863; wounded and captured May 3, 1863; declared unfit for battle and detailed to the quartermaster department in Greensboro in 1864; in 1870 a farmer, married with two children, reporting $3,000 in real estate and $2,000 in personal estate; Episcopalian.

**Paulding**, Robert. Enlisted May 6, 1861, in Uniontown, Alabama; captured July 12, 1861.

† **Pearson**, Tom.

**Perrin** or **Perren**, Robert. Unsuccessful candidate for the Alabama state house of representatives in 1861.

**Pickens**, James ("Jamie") (July 30, 1842, Alabama–). Attended the Greene Springs School; student at the University of Virginia in 1859; in 1860 living in Sawyerville, Alabama, with his mother, who reported $209,600 in real estate and $250,000 in personal estate, including 201 slaves; enlisted January 22, 1864, in Eutaw, Alabama; in 1870 married with one child. Brother of Guard Samuel Pickens.

**Pickens**, Samuel (June 9, 1841, Alabama–September 9, 1890). Student at the University of Virginia in 1859; in 1860 living with his mother; enlisted September 3, 1862, in Gainesville, Alabama; captured May 3, 1863; first corporal in April 1864; wounded September 19, 1864; captured April 2, 1865. Brother of Guard James Pickens.

**Pickering**, Robert (died during war). Enlisted in March 1862 in Greensboro.

**Pope**, William M. (c. 1829–June 20, 1863, of typhoid). In 1850 an overseer; division blacksmith in 1863.

**Price**, George T. (1838, North Carolina–June 27, 1862, at Gaines' Mill). Enlisted April 18, 1861, in Greensboro; sergeant; unmarried.

**Price**, Robert Belton (died 1865). Enlisted April 18, 1861, in Greensboro; captured September 14, 1862; wounded in the leg and hip May 2, 1863; detailed to South Carolina Conscript Bureau in 1864; returned to the Guards February 2, 1865; captured April 2, 1865.

† **Quarles**, W. R.

**Ramsey**, Matthew S. (died June 27, 1862, at Gaines' Mill). Physician just settled in Greensboro when he enlisted there April 16, 1861; third lieutenant in 1861; second lieutenant in October 1861; first lieutenant in April 1862.

**Ray**, John C. Enlisted August 17, 1862, in Tallapoosa County, Alabama; captured July 2, 1863; exchanged February 18, 1865.

**Rencke**, Jacob (died December 11, 1864, of pneumonia). Enlisted March 27, 1863, in Grace Church, Virginia; captured July 12, 1864.

**Rhodes**, Thomas Marshall (died September 11, 1863). Shot May 3, 1863, in the groin. Cousin of Guard Alva Rhodes.

**Roberts**, J. C. Enlisted August 17, 1862, in Choctaw County, Alabama; reported deserted in August 1863 while on furlough for typhoid fever.

**Rowland**, T. B. (died September 16, 1863, of fever in prison). Enlisted April 18, 1861, in Greensboro; wagon and forage master; captured in July 1863.

**Sadler**, Benjamin F. (c. 1838, Ireland–). In 1860 a clerk; enlisted April 18, 1861, in Greensboro; ward master, Charlottesville, Virginia, hospital in 1864; chronic eye problems.

**Sample**, Joseph (c. 1825, Alabama–). In 1850 a student and farmer living with his father, who reported $6,500 in real estate and thirty-two slaves; enlisted April 18, 1861, in Greensboro; discharged in October 1861 for a disability.

† **Sanders**, J. W. Badly wounded May 31 or June 1, 1862.

**Selden**, William M. (February 20, 1844, Virginia–). Student of medicine; enlisted May 6, 1861, in Uniontown, Alabama; discharged in September 1861 for a disability.

**Sellers**, James D. Enlisted August 23, 1862, in Pike County, Alabama; wounded in June 1864; sick in camp in February 1865.

**Semple**, John P. (c. 1830, Virginia–). Druggist; enlisted May 6, 1861, in Selma, Alabama; on detached service in December 1861; transferred to CS Navy April 4, 1864.

**Shelden**, Charles A. (c. 1847, Alabama–). In 1860 a student living with his mother and father, a merchant in Havanna, Alabama, who reported $5,000 in real estate and $10,000 in personal estate; enlisted March 11, 1862, in Greensboro; discharged due to underage and delicate constitution; Mason 1879–1903. Brother of Guards Christopher C. Shelden and William H. H. Shelden.

**Shelden**, Christopher C. (c. 1844, Alabama–). In 1860 a student living with his parents; enlisted April 18, 1861, in Greensboro; wounded in 1862 and 1863; transferred to the Jeff Davis Legion in 1863; candidate for sheriff in 1867; in 1880 a farmer, married, reporting $500 in personal estate. Brother of Guards Charles A. Shelden and William H. H. Shelden.

**Shelden**, William H. H. (c. 1841, North Carolina–). In 1860 a student living with his parents; enlisted April 18, 1861, in Greensboro; in camp in February 1865; in 1870 no occupation listed, married with two children. Brother of Guards Charles A. Shelden and Christopher C. Shelden.

**Sherron**, Patrick H. (c. 1821, New York–). In 1860 a gin maker, married with four children; enlisted August 9, 1861, in Greensboro; detailed to make artillery wagons; discharged in August 1862 for being overage.

**Simonds**, Richard H. (c. 1843, Alabama–). In 1860 a student living with his father, a physician who reported $2,000 in real estate and $28,000 in personal estate, including twenty-six slaves; enlisted March 6, 1862, in Greensboro; severely wounded May 3, 1863; applied for a cadet appointment in February 1864; discharged in March 1864 due to a gunshot wound.

**Sims**, William A. (c. 1839, Alabama–). In 1860 living with his father, a farmer reporting $12,260 in real estate and $30,000 in personal estate; enlisted April 13, 1861, in Greensboro; wounded in May or June 1862; captured May 3, 1863; division courier for Rodes, teamster, and forage master; hospitalized in 1864 with syphilis; married Ann Briggs in 1864; in camp in February 1865; captured April 2, 1865; illiterate; in 1870 reported one child and $2,200 in real estate and $800 in personal estate.

**Sledge**, Alexander A. (1787, North Carolina–August 12, 1861). Physician who graduated from the University of Pennsylvania; married in 1817; moved to Alabama in 1822; moved to Marengo County in 1827; Methodist; enlisted in the Guards April or May 1861 and went to Pensacola, Florida; and Virginia. Ambiguous name.

**Southworth**, Larrison D. (c. 1839, Alabama–). In 1860 living with his father, an illiterate farmer who reported $400 in personal estate; enlisted in April 1861.

**Speed**, J. Sterling (c. 1824, North Carolina–). In 1850 an unmarried farmer; Mason 1861–1874; enlisted September 2, 1864, in Greensboro; exchanged with William Lyles; in 1870 a farmer, married with five children, reporting $280 in real estate and $1,000 in personal estate.

**Stephenson**, H. C. Enlisted September 6, 1862, in Pike County, Alabama; wounded May 12, 1864.

**Stokes**, William W. (c. 1840, Alabama–August 27 or 28, 1863, of measles). In 1860 an overseer, reporting $300 in real estate; wounded in the leg and captured July 1 or 2, 1863; married with four children in 1863.

**Thomas**, Wade R. Transferred to the Greensboro Guards in August 1863 from the Livingston Rifles, Fifth Alabama Infantry.

**Tinker**, William (1838–). Student at the University of Virginia in 1856–1857; in 1860 living with his mother, who reported $100,000 in real estate and $125,000 in personal estate, including 232 slaves; enlisted April 13, 1861, in Greensboro; Mason 1864–1870; in 1870 a farmer reporting $12,500 in real estate and $2,000 in personal estate.

**Trawick**, R. J. Enlisted August 28, 1862, in Dale or Pike County, Alabama; admitted to a hospital in May 1863; severely wounded October 19, 1864.

**Tucker**, John S. (died June 18, 1880). Mason 1858–1880; in 1860 a clerk, married to Annie Nutting; enlisted March 6, 1862, in Greensboro; regimental and division commissary clerk; entered the Jeff Davis Legion after an exchange with Henry Beck April 1, 1864; in 1870 a dry goods merchant with two children living with his in-laws, reported $2,000 in real estate and $150 in personal estate; murdered in a Newbern, Alabama, robbery. Brother-in-law of Guards George Nutting and Edwin Nutting.

**Tunstall**, Wiley C. (c. 1840, Alabama–1916). In 1860 living with his mother, who reported $40,000 in real estate and $90,000 in personal estate, including eighty-six slaves; enlisted April 25, 1861, in Greensboro; third lieutenant in April 1862; resigned in October 1862, citing chronic diarrhea; in 1880 married with five children.

† **Ullman**, L. Captured September 14, 1862.

**Waddell**, Abner C. (c. 1833, Virginia–). In 1860 a saddler, married; enlisted August 9, 1861, in Greensboro; ambulance driver and teamster; brigade quartermaster department; in camp in February 1865; in 1870 reported $1,500 in real estate and $250 in personal estate.

**Walker**, William T. (1832, Alabama–). Druggist; enlisted May 18, 1861, in Pensacola, Florida; discharged June 15, 1862, due to a bladder stone.

**Wall**, L. P. Enlisted May 6, 1861, in Uniontown, Alabama; discharged August 2, 1861, for a disability.

**Walthall**, Thomas. No contemporary references.

**Ward**, Alfred G. (c. 1841–November 1908). In 1860 a clerk living with an upholsterer; Knight of Pythias; enlisted August 9, 1861, in Greensboro; sergeant major; wounded May 31, 1862; head fractured by a minié ball at Chancellorsville, where he was captured and cited for gallantry.

**Ward**, Thomas R., Sr. (1826, North Carolina–November 14, 1897). Student at Charleston Medical College and Cincinnati Medical College; Mason 1854–1897; married in 1858; in 1860 a physician with one child, reporting $3,800 in real estate; enlisted March 6, 1862, in Greensboro; wounded and captured May 3, 1863; third corporal in August 1863; wounded and captured May 5, 1864; in camp in February 1865; in 1870 reported $6,000 in real estate and $2,500 in personal estate. *See also* 1876–1880 entry.

**Warren**, John H. (c. 1839, North Carolina–). In 1860 a clerk living with a shoemaker; enlisted April 13, 1861, in Greensboro; wounded May 31, 1862; in camp in February 1865; in 1870 a merchant, married with one child.

**Webb**, James Daniel (Jr., to distinguish from older Guard and distant relative with the same name) (c. 1839–February 26, 1865, following Cedar Creek). In 1860 a clerk living with his father and reporting $2,000 in real estate; enlisted April 13, 1861, in Greensboro; captured September 14, 1862; corporal; wounded and captured October 19, 1864; a leg amputated above the knee October 20, 1864. Probably son of Guard Henry Webb.

**Webb**, James Daniel (J. D.) (February 26, 1818, North Carolina–July 19, 1863). Mason 1839–1854; married in 1853; in 1860 a lawyer with five children, reporting $7,000 in real estate and $20,400 in personal estate, including nineteen slaves; enlisted in the Guards December 7, 1844; ensign in 1846; enlisted April 1861 in Greensboro; quartermaster of the Fifth Alabama Infantry with the rank of captain; with J. T. Morgan, established Partisan Rangers, Fifty-first Alabama Infantry.

**Webb**, James Ed. (c. 1841, Alabama–). Student at the University of Alabama in 1859; in 1860 a law student living in Eutaw, Alabama, with his father, who reported $5,000 in real estate and $26,600 in personal estate; enlisted April 18, 1861, in Greensboro; promoted to lieutenant and division ordnance officer in 1863; assigned to W. H. F. Lee's cavalry division; after the war became a Birmingham lawyer.

**Webb**, Sydney V. (c. 1832, Alabama–). In 1860 a physician reporting $5,000 in personal estate; enlisted April 20, 1861, in Greensboro.

**Webster**, Daniel T. (c. 1838, Alabama–). In 1860 a clerk living with his father, who reported $18,360 in real estate and $48,570 in personal estate, including forty-five slaves; enlisted April 18, 1861, in Greensboro; brigade commissary with the rank of major; married Bettie Wynne in 1865; cotton factor in 1866.

**Wells**, John. No contemporary references.

**Wesson**, ———. Transferred into the Guards December 29, 1864, from the Jeff Davis Legion after an exchange with Gilliam James.

**Westcott**, Gideon G. (c. 1834, Rhode Island–). In 1860 living with Guard Charles Shelden; enlisted April 13, 1861, in Greensboro; corporal in August 1861; brigade commissary clerk; Mason 1867–1870; in 1870 a dry goods clerk, married with two children, reporting $500 in real estate and $300 in personal estate.

**Wheeler**, John E. (c. 1843, Alabama–). Enlisted April 13, 1861, in Greensboro; discharged in July 1861 due to a disability. Son of Guard Isaac C. Wheeler.

**Whelan**, Lee T. (c. 1840, Alabama–). In 1860 living with his mother and father, a grocery merchant reporting $1,700 in personal estate; enlisted August 9, 1861, in Greensboro; discharged June 8, 1862, for a disability brought on by disease; in 1870 a druggist.

**Wilder**, Lott M. (died after 1907). Enlisted August 14, 1862, in Montgomery; repeatedly in the hospital; in camp in February 1865.

**Williams**, Charles L. (c. 1837, Alabama–). Mason 1859–1867; in 1860 married and attending a farm; enlisted February 1, 1864, in Eutaw, Alabama; discharged June 1864 for a disability. Brother of Guard Jonathan W. Williams.

**Williams**, Davis G. (c. 1842, Alabama–). Student at the Greene Springs School; in 1860 living with his mother and father, a farmer reporting $6,000 in real estate and $8,000 in personal estate; enlisted April 13, 1861, in Greensboro; wounded May 31, 1862; courier and division commissary department; wounded October 19, 1864.

**Williams**, Jonathan W. (c. 1840, Alabama–April 24, 1908). In 1860 living with his brother, Charles; Mason 1861–1885; enlisted April 13, 1861, in Greensboro; corporal in April 1861; second lieutenant in June 1861; first lieutenant in October 1861; captain in April 1862; captured September 14, 1862; wounded in the shoulder and captured May 3, 1863; wounded May 10, 1864; married Carrie Avery in 1864; resigned February 8, 1865, because of chronic diarrhea; in 1880 attending to his father's Havanna, Alabama, farm with seven children; ran the county poor farm. Brother of Guard Charles L. Williams.

**Willingham**, Samuel M. (c. 1838, South Carolina–). In 1860 living with his mother and father, a planter reporting $5,000 in real estate and $20,000 in personal estate, including twenty-one slaves; enlisted April 13, 1861, in Greensboro; captured September 14, 1862; skull fractured in 1864; in 1880 a farmer, married with three children.

**Willingham**, William H. (c. 1841, Alabama–October 3, 1861, of typhoid pneumonia). In 1860 living with his mother and father, an overseer reporting $2,000 in personal estate; enlisted April 29, 1861, in Greensboro.

**Wilson**, George W. (c. 1841, Alabama–). Enlisted April 13, 1861, in Greensboro; in 1860 farming with his father, who reported $3,000 in real estate and $12,000 in personal estate; in 1860 reported twelve slaves.

**Wilson**, James Ezra (c. 1835, South Carolina–June 1884). In 1860 a farmer reporting $11,000 in real estate and $50,000 in personal estate; enlisted August 14, 1861, in Union Mills,

Virginia; suffered broken thigh in July 1862; Knight of Pythias; in 1880 a dry goods clerk; died without family.

† **Witherspoon**, William Dick. Assistant surgeon with the rank of captain; captured September 14, 1862; wounded in the shoulder May 3, 1863; transferred to the Eleventh Alabama in 1864 as assistant surgeon.

† **Woodruff**, Daniel W. Clerk for R. E. Rodes.

**Wright**, John J. (c. 1839, Alabama–January 3, 1862, of pneumonia). In 1860 a printer/tinner living with his father, also a tinner; enlisted April 13, 1861, in Greensboro. Brother of Guard Joseph L. Wright and cousin of Guard Samuel J. Dorroh.

**Wright**, Joseph L. (c. 1841, Alabama–September 16, 1863, of congestion). In 1860 living with his father; tavern keeper; enlisted April 13, 1861, in Greensboro; fourth corporal in October 1861; regimental drummer; captured May 3, 1863; wounded in the shoulder July 2, 1863; promoted to fourth corporal in August 1863. Brother of Guard John J. Wright and cousin of Guard Samuel J. Dorroh.

**Wright**, Sam (c. 1846, Alabama–). Enlisted March 11, 1862, in Greensboro; discharged June 23, 1862, due to disability caused by chronic diarrhea.

**Wynne**, John W. (c. 1838, South Carolina–). In 1860 owned eight slaves and farmed with his father, a planter who reported $15,000 in real estate and $100,000 in personal estate, including eighty-five slaves; enlisted April 13, 1861, in Greensboro; wounded in June 1864; sergeant commanding a company in February 1865. Brother of Guard William A. Wynne.

**Youngblood**, Jacob B. Enlisted August 23, 1862, in Pike County, Alabama; wounded May 3, 1863, and May 12, 1864; in camp in February 1865; captured April 2, 1865.

**Youngblood**, John L. ("Jack"). Enlisted August 23, 1862, in Pike County, Alabama; wounded and captured May 5, 1864; in camp in February 1865; captured April 2, 1865.

## Greensboro Guards Officers, 1876–1880

Names are from the *Greensboro Alabama Beacon*, February 12, June 3, 1876, April 7, 1877; and the *Greensboro Southern Watchman*, November 7, April 25, 1877, August 2, 1880. Although the Guards during these years were required to keep muster lists in the mayor's office and with the state adjutant general, none seem to have survived.

**Bayol**, J. F. First corporal in 1877.

**Bell**, J. F. Third corporal in 1880.

**Bondurant**, E. D. Third sergeant in 1880.

**Briggs**, W. G. Fourth corporal in 1880.

**Coleman**, A. A. (Jr.) (c. 1862–). First corporal and a student in 1880; his father was a lawyer.

**Cowin**, Thomas E. First lieutenant in 1880; Mason 1871–1885.

**DuBois**, John E. (c. 1841, Alabama–). In 1870 a merchant reporting $10,000 in real estate and $3,000 in personal estate; Mason 1871–1872; second lieutenant in 1876.

**Ernst**, Joseph. Orderly sergeant in 1876; Mason 1876–1879.

**Findlay**, John. Second sergeant in 1880.

**Gayle**, Edward. Second sergeant in 1876.

**Hamilton**, Jesse D. (c. 1845, Alabama–). In 1870 the town marshal, living with his father, a boot maker reporting $1,000 in real estate and $300 in personal estate; third sergeant in 1876; second lieutenant in April 1877; resigned in November 1877.

**Hutchinson**, Edward T. Orderly sergeant in 1877; second lieutenant in 1880. *See also* 1861–1865 entry.

**Inge**, H. T. First sergeant in 1877; orderly sergeant in 1880.

**Lane**, Charles. Fifth sergeant in 1876.
**Latimer**, J. T. Third sergeant in 1877.
**Lawrence**, B. R. Fourth corporal in 1877.
**Lawson**, Lewis J. (c. 1856, Alabama–). Mason 1870–1910; first lieutenant in 1876; captain in 1877; first lieutenant in 1877; captain in 1880; in 1880 a merchant living with his father, also a merchant.

**Marx**, S. M. Second corporal in 1880.
**McFaddin**, Thomas J. (c. 1851–). Fourth sergeant in 1876.

**Powers**, A. J. Third corporal in 1877.

**Stockton**, John T. (c. 1852, Alabama–). In 1870 a dry goods clerk living with his mother; fourth sergeant in 1877.

**Tutwiler**, Pascal A. (c. 1850, Alabama–). Second corporal; in 1880 a lawyer, married with one child. Son of Henry Tutwiler.

**Ward**, Thomas R., Sr. Fourth sergeant. *See also* 1861–1865 entry.
**Wiley**, J. B. Second sergeant in 1877.

**Young**, William B. Captain in 1876, 1877.

# Notes

## Preface

1. Typical of the many attempts to portray the Confederate South as torn by rigid class distinctions is David Williams' 1998 study, *Rich Man's War*. Williams, whose subject is Alabama's eastern Black Belt, argues that class conflict was "the crucial factor" in deciding the outcome of the Civil War. He finds the South so riven, in fact, that "the Confederacy as a nation never really existed at all" (184).

Anyone taking such an extreme position certainly finds it difficult to account for the Confederacy's lasting four years (despite an appalling toll in dead and wounded) and for those of all economic and social strata who remained committed to the Confederacy and the Lost Cause. (I find it amusing that among the photographs in Williams' volume is William Andrews, who, as an old man, still proudly wore his Confederate veteran badges.) The ties that held Southerners together clearly were stronger than the forces that pulled them apart.

William Blair makes these and a great many more points in *Virginia's Private War*, published the same year as *Rich Man's War*. Like my work, Blair's study of three Virginia counties suggests a much more complex society in which planters, civic leaders, and an independent-minded electorate all engaged in a rowdy democracy. He argues that rather than resulting in flagging support for the war and increased class divisions, the conflict created a new Confederate identity that merged well with local loyalties. Blair continued his investigation of Confederate identity in "Maryland, Our Maryland."

Another study of the Civil War that meshes easily with mine is Margaret deMontcourt Storey's "Southern Ishmaelites," which argues that the alleged poverty and isolation of Alabama Unionists have been vastly exaggerated. Instead, particular factors (she focuses on personality, experience, ideology, the influence of kin and family, and neighborhoods that cut across class lines) drove individuals to support the Union rather than the Confederacy; these individuals subsequently formed political and social alliances. The end of hostilities found Alabama Unionists, like my Greensborians, with a new sense of community.

## Chapter 1. The Stone Soldier

1. In "The South's Hidden Heritage," historian Eric Foner observes that Confederate memorials are vastly more common than memorials to other Southerners.

## Chapter 2. A Land of Strangers

1. Yerby, *History*, 3; Platt and Brantley, "Canebrakes," 8–21; Lyell, *Second Visit*, 68; H. Cobbs, "Geography," 89.

2. Letter from Dr. J. W. Heustis, *Cahawba Press*, June 2, 1821, reprinted in Abernethy,

Formative Period, 22; Withers, "Geological Notices," 188; Henry Watson Jr. to Julius Reed, February 28, 1831; Henry Watson Jr. to Theodore Watson, March 23, 1834, Henry Watson Jr. Papers, Rare Book, Manuscript, and Special Collections Library, Duke University, Durham, North Carolina; McGuire, "On the Prairies," 93–98. Edmund Ruffin's description in Notes is less credible because of its late date (1860), the small amount of the Canebrake that he actually saw, and the drastic changes the Canebrake encountered under intensive farming.

3. See for example, John Hartwell Cocke diary, January 20, March 24, 1838, John Hartwell Cocke Papers, Special Collections, University of Virginia Library, Charlottesville.

4. See, for example, Henry Watson Jr. diary, December 29, 1830, Watson Papers; Ruffin, Notes, 5, 4; William B. Beverley to his father, January 21, 1831, Beverley Family Papers, Virginia Historical Society, Richmond.

5. Israel Pickens to William B. Lenoir, January 1, 1815, December 8, 1816, Chilab S. Howe Papers, Southern Historical Collection, University of North Carolina, Chapel Hill (hereafter cited as SHC).

6. Israel Pickens to William B. Lenoir, June 5, 1819, January 29, 1820; Israel Pickens to Thomas Lenoir, December 30, 1819; Doster, "Land Titles," 108–124. The price of land dropped during the Panic of 1837.

7. Israel Pickens to William B. Lenoir, November 25, 1823, Howe Papers. Pickens seems to exemplify Oakes' portrayal in The Ruling Race of slaveholders as eager participants in the market economy.

8. Israel Pickens to William B. Lenoir, March 22, 1822, November 25, 1823, Lenoir Family Papers.

9. "Account of Sundries Sold . . . October 1827 . . . estate of Israel Pickens deceased," Pickens Family Papers, Alabama Department of Archives and History, Montgomery (hereafter cited as ADAH).

10. Greensboro Alabama Beacon, August 23, 1845, March 8, 1853; Yerby, History, 3. See also "Reminiscences of Eliza Picton," Eliza Gould Picton Collection, ADAH.

11. Greensboro Alabama Beacon, May 20, 1881. Greensboro was typical; see Tolbert, Constructing Townscapes.

12. Juliet Bestor Coleman to mother and sister, January 5, 1834, in Coleman, Connecticut Yankee, 30.

13. Henry Watson Jr. to Henry Watson Sr., January 26, February 10, 1834, Watson Papers; Greensboro Watchman, March 18, 29, April 19, 1888. See also Mansell, Hale County.

14. Henry Watson Jr. to Henry Watson Sr., December 14, 1834, Watson Papers.

15. Henry Watson Jr. to Henry Watson Sr. January 26, February 10, 1834; Henry Watson Jr. to Henry Barnard, July 2, 1835, Watson Papers; William B. Beverley to father, June 9, 1831, Beverley Papers. See also appendix A.

16. Cocke diary, February 14, 1840; Willie Withers to uncle, May 24, 1855, LeVert Family Papers, SHC; N. Cobbs, "Alabama's 'Wonder,'" 163–180.

17. See appendixes A and D; U.S. Bureau of the Census, Ninth U.S. Census (1870), Compendium, vol. 1, Population, 24; Watson diary, January 10, 1831.

18. Henry Watson Jr. to Theodore Watson, March 23, 1834; Henry Watson Jr. to Alfred Watson, March 14, 1834, Watson Papers; U.S. Census Bureau, Sixth Census (1840), Compendium, vol. 2, Mines, Agriculture, Commerce, and Manufactures, 260.

19. Martha Hatch to grandmother, December 26, 1832, [January 4, 1833], Cullen B. Hatch Collection, North Carolina State Archives, Raleigh; John S. Haywood to George W. Haywood, April 4, 1835, Ernest Haywood Papers, SHC; William B. Beverley to father, April 1, 1831, December 22, 1833, Beverley Papers; Henry Watson Jr. to William Watson, April 30, 1834,

Watson Papers. Sarah Gayle's journal presents the views of another woman in Greensboro at this time; see Gorgas Family Papers, W. S. Hoole Special Collections Library, University of Alabama, Tuscaloosa.

20. U.S. Bureau of the Census, *Seventh U.S. Census* (1850), *Compendium,* vol. 1, *Population,* 429; U.S. Bureau of the Census, *Eighth U.S. Census* (1860), *Compendium,* vol. 2, *Agriculture,* 2. See also appendix C.

21. Thomas Johnston to George M. Johnston, December 15, 1832, July 5, August 10, 1833, George M. Johnston Papers, Rare Book, Manuscript, and Special Collections Library, Duke University, Durham.

22. Benjamin King to Alfred Williams, May 15, 1832, North Carolina State Archives, Raleigh; C. C. Scott to John, August 29, 1832, Scruggs Collection, Birmingham Public Library, Alabama.

23. William B. Beverley to father, January 21, 1831, Beverley Papers.

24. Henry Watson Jr. to mother, May 18, 1834, Watson Papers.

25. Juliet Bestor to mother and sister, January 5, 1834, in Coleman, *Connecticut Yankee,* 29; Henry Watson Jr. to mother, April 24, 1836, Watson Papers. Some historians argue that the Southwest endured boom and bust cycles before emerging in more stable form during the 1840s, thus implying that voluntary communities emerged as a response to changed economic conditions. See Dupre, *Transforming the Cotton Frontier;* Morris, *Becoming Southern.*

26. Watson diary, April 30, 1831; N. Cobbs, "Alabama's 'Wonder,'" 170–174 (modern dams have reduced the height of the bluff); Robert W. Withers Papers, vol. 2, folder 3, SHC. Like Israel Pickens, Withers conforms to Oakes' portrait of Southern slaveholders who solidified their wealth with a series of professional and mercantile activities; see *Ruling Race.*

27. Watson diary, April 30, 1831; *Greensboro Watchman,* March 15, 1888; Tayloe quoted in Cashin, *Family Venture,* 62.

28. Tocqueville, *Democracy,* 2:148. On American character, see esp. Pessen, *Jacksonian America,* chap. 2, "The Jacksonian Character: A Contemporary Portrait of American Personality, Traits, and Values," 4–32; Kohl, *Politics.*

29. Israel Pickens, "Oration Delivered at St. Stephens Alabama, on the Fourth of July, 1820," Pickens Family Papers; Baldwin, *Flush Times,* 238; Horace B. Barbour to Henry Watson Jr., December 28, 1833, Watson Papers. Hunt examines the last passage in "Organizing a New South," 110–111. For an analogous treatment of mobility, kinship networks, and frontier expansion, see Faragher, *Women and Men.*

30. Cashin's study of immigration to the Southwest, *Family Venture,* has been widely criticized as too extreme in its portrayal of male autonomy. Baptist, for example, states flatly that the "need and desire of these men of the planter class to emigrate along with relatives overwhelmed any inclination for isolated, manly independence" ("Migration," 553). Faragher, too, argues for kinship immigration and identifies "families in association" with the Sugar Creek community of Illinois (*Sugar Creek,* 56). Boucher's study of Alabama families, particularly those living in Forkland, reveals a divergence between image and reality concerning family roles. She also notes contemporary admissions that during the antebellum years, some men gained status from membership in influential families and after the Civil War they found considerable security; see "Wealthy Planter Families," 77–78, 174, 181. In "South by Southwest," James David Miller acknowledges the effort at manly independence but argues that it was overcome by the desire for order.

31. *Greensboro Watchman,* June 27, 1898.

32. Thomas Johnston to George M. Johnston, December 21, 1833, Johnston Papers; *Greensboro Watchman,* April 19, 1888; Yerby, *History,* 26–28.

33. Yerby, *History,* 30–35. Wyatt-Brown considers some of the issues raised by this incident in *Southern Honor,* 339–350.

34. Baldwin, *Flush Times,* 47, 84, 238. According to Johanna Nicol Shields (introduction to Hooper, *Adventures,* vii–lxix), Baldwin exaggerated the contrast between the rowdy disorder he found in Alabama and the stultifying society of his native Virginia in an attempt to raise his reputation. He claimed, for example, to have come to the frontier alone, when he actually rode with a relative by marriage and his two brothers joined him a year or two later. In contrast to William Gilmore Simms, Baldwin was enthusiastic about the frontier, eventually moving to California during its Flush Times.

35. *Erie Greene County Gazette,* September 26, 1830; Baldwin, *Flush Times,* 89.

36. Hooper, *Adventures,* 35, 50.

37. Simms, *Richard Hurdis;* Hoole, "Alabama and W. Gilmore Simms," 85–107, 185–199.

38. Simms, *Richard Hurdis,* 274, 275.

39. Baldwin, *Flush Times,* 229–230, 88–89, 85, 84. Tocqueville observed the same absence of society in the new states in the West (*Democracy,* 1:51).

40. Simms, *Richard Hurdis,* 51. Simms developed a theme of brotherly rivalry on the frontier that Tuscaloosan Alexander B. Meek criticized in his review of *Richard Hurdis.*

41. Henry Watson Jr. to Henry Watson Sr., February 6, 1836; Henry Watson Jr. to mother, September 27, 1836, Watson Papers.

42. *Greensborough Green[e] County Sentinel,* August 9, 1834; William B. Beverley to father, April 1, August 1, 1831, Beverley Papers; Henry Watson Jr. to William Watson, April 30, 1834, Watson Papers. Kasson, *Rudeness and Civility,* 103–111, examines this problem of appearance and confidence men in individualized America; although he deals with northeastern cities, the problem of distinguishing the genuine from the counterfeit was everywhere.

43. Watson diary, April 21, 1831; Henry Watson Jr. to mother, July 15, 1834, Watson Papers; William B. Beverley to father, April 1, 1831, Beverley Papers. These separate social spheres for men and women in early Greensboro accord very well with eighteenth-century Chesapeake society as outlined in Kulikoff, *Tobacco and Slaves,* 217–231, which argues that the informal pursuits of the men—muster, courthouses, hunting, cockfights, horse races, taverns, and stores—furthered their individuality and competition, while the social circles favored by women fostered cooperation and charity.

44. Henry Watson Jr. to William Watson, April 30, 1834, Watson Papers; see appendixes A and B. Such figures are consistent with the 80 to 90 percent of Black Belt slaveholders Oakes estimates did not stay put for more than two decades (*Ruling Race,* 78). In his study of Dallas County (in the Black Belt southeast of Greene County) during the 1850s, Barney computes a persistence rate of 32 percent for all white males over the age of nine ("Towards the Civil War," 148). Faragher (*Sugar Creek,* 249 n.14) finds a persistence rate of about 30 percent from 1820 to 1840 and a little over 20 percent from 1840 to 1860 in a rural region of southern Illinois. Wiener calculates a high persistence rate among 236 large slaveholders of 43 percent during the 1860s (*Social Origins,* 9–22). Formwalt, "Antebellum Planter Persistence," questions Wiener's figures.

45. Henry Watson Jr. to mother, September 27, 1836, Watson Papers.

46. Henry Watson Jr. to Henry Watson Sr., February 6, 1836, Watson Papers; Sam Pickens to W. A. Lenoir, October 3, 1837, Lenoir Family Papers.

47. Castellano, "Railroad Development."

48. William Beverley to father, January 20, 1837, Beverley Papers; William Lenoir to Thomas Lenoir, April 11, 1839, Lenoir Family Papers.

49. Henry Watson Jr. to Henry Watson Sr., February 6, 1836, Watson Papers; bankruptcy probated January 16, 1838, in Greene County Deed Record Book H, 477–489, Greene County

Courthouse, Eutaw, Alabama. Bankruptcies were ordinarily filed with the circuit court, whose records were destroyed in an 1868 courthouse fire. This particular bankruptcy was registered as a sale, however, and was recorded in the probate office, whose deed books survive.

50. Baldwin, *Flush Times*, 240; Henry Watson Jr. to mother, March 28, 1839, Watson Papers.

## Chapter 3. Voluntary Communities

1. Eugene V. LeVert to Francis J. LeVert, September 13, 1838, LeVert Papers; although LeVert lived for many years in Greensboro, he wrote this letter from Arcadia, near Linden, Marengo County. This interpretation agrees with much in Cashin's *Family Venture*. Although her argument about male independence and emigration has been criticized as overstated and contradicted by kinship networks, I believe that the strength of her argument lies in the realm of perception. Young men clearly had compelling psychological reasons to exaggerate their independence. Greene County's settlement seems to follow the same pattern outlined by Morris in *Becoming Southern*. He argues that kinship groups formed in rural areas (such as the Canebrake), while people living in towns (such as Greensboro) formed communities based on voluntary associations.

2. My comparison of reform groups indicates not only overlapping membership but also overlapping leadership. These individuals were often but not always prosperous. Although participation in such endeavors is characteristically Whiggish and Greene County tended to vote Whig, political affiliation was no predictor of participation. The two organizations that included the most leaders were the Masons and the local militia company (see chap. 4). Leadership was hardly limited to these individuals, however.

3. The phrase *voluntary community* comes from Doyle, *Social Order*, 156–193. The experiences of community-formation in Greensboro and Jacksonville, Illinois, paralleled each other in striking ways. Of course, in *Democracy in America*, Tocqueville explored Americans' willingness to join voluntary associations.

4. A similar pattern emerged elsewhere. Charleston, South Carolina, in particular, justified a railroad as a civic project and appealed to public spirit for support; see Pease and Pease, *Web*, 56–62. See also Dupre, *Transforming the Cotton Frontier*, esp. 107–133.

5. William B. Beverley to father, December 26, 1833, Beverley Papers; Henry Watson Jr. to Henry Watson Sr., February 10, 1834, Watson Papers. See also J. Miller, *South by Southwest*, 277–278. Studies of the changing antebellum landscape include Cronon, *Nature's Metropolis*; Stilgoe, *Common Landscape*.

6. *Greensboro Alabama Beacon*, August 12, 1848; N. Cobbs, "Alabama's 'Wonder,'" 165–171.

7. Robert W. Withers, undated notes found in vol. 2, no. 3235, p. 274, Withers Papers; *Erie Greene County Gazette*, February 28, 1831.

8. Castellano, "Railroad Development"; *Greensboro Alabama Beacon*, January 23, 1847, November 10, 1849, January 2, 1852,

9. Samuel Pickens to William Lenoir, July 5, 1854, Lenoir Family Papers; Castellano, "Railroad Development."

10. *Greensboro Alabama Beacon*, May 5, 1849, February 15, 1851, October 29, November 5, 19, 26, December 3, 1852.

11. Ibid., October 29, November 5, 12, 26, December 3, 10, 1858, September 2, 23, 1859. Greensboro was not served by a rail link until 1870, and only after 1882 was the track continued westward. An unpublished study of shareholders in Alabama's Northeast and Southwest

Railroad during the 1850s made by Robert J. Norrell of the Department of History at the University of Tennessee, Knoxville, determined that proximity to the line overwhelmed all other factors in attracting subscribers.

12. *Greensboro Alabama Beacon,* November 25, December 2, 1848, March 17, August 26, 1849, February 2, 1850, March 26, April 12, 1851, July 13, 1855. Other locales engaged in similar attempts to build canals and cotton factories to use technology to promote wealth and community-building. See Pease and Pease, *Web,* chap. 4, "Charleston's Dream of Prosperity," 40–52; Dupre, *Transforming the Cotton Frontier,* 123.

13. Robert Withers journal, vol. 2, folder 3, p. 160, Withers Papers; Watson diary, April 30, 1831; Withers, "Geological Notices"; Isaac Croom, "Address Delivered before the Greensboro' Agricultural Society, on the 2d of May, 1850," W. S. Hoole Special Collections Library, University of Alabama, Tuscaloosa; *Greensboro Alabama Beacon,* November 10, 1849, August 24, 1850, May 14, 1852; Norrell, *Promising Field,* 21–22. Some of these ideas are also explored in J. Miller, "South by Southwest," 107–117.

14. *Greensboro Alabama Beacon,* February 25, 1853.

15. This overview of Freemasonry is based on Bullock, "Pure and Sublime System"; Bullock, "Revolutionary Transformation"; and on Bullock's more comprehensive work, *Revolutionary Brotherhood.* See also Doyle, *Social Order,* 184–187; Carnes, *Secret Ritual.*

16. *Greensboro Halcyon,* December 20, 1823. I thank the Grand Lodge Free and Accepted Masons of Alabama, Montgomery, for generously permitting me to examine the membership rolls of Greensboro's lodge. Membership in the Masons jumped again in the 1860s (see appendix B).

17. See appendix B.

18. Richard G. Earle, "Address Delivered before Hiram Lodge No. 42 on the 24 of June 1848," James Crow Papers, ADAH.

19. Ibid.

20. Ibid.

21. Kutolowski, "Freemasonry and Community," 550–551, argues that Episcopalians dominated local lodges.

22. Holcombe, *History,* 66; *Erie Greene County Gazette,* November 1, 1830, March 17, November 17, 1831; Yerby, *History,* 3–4. Faragher, *Sugar Creek,* 156–170, stresses the role of churches in bringing kinship groups together into a single communion.

23. Henry Watson Jr. to Rosanna Reed, April 9, 1834, Watson Papers; Julia to Emma Lewis, August 20, 1836, John F. Speight Papers, SHC (written from Tuscaloosa).

24. Yerby, *History,* 175.

25. William Scarborough to Daniel Scarborough, December 1, 1839, North Carolina State Archives, Raleigh; 129; John Witherspoon to daughter, July 9, 1846, Witherspoon-McDowall Papers, SHC. Scarborough's complaints exemplify Hatch's interpretation of religion on the frontier in *Democratization.* See also Loveland, *Southern Evangelicals,* chap. 4, "The Church and the World," 91–129.

26. E. V. LeVert to brother, December 19, 1855, LeVert Papers (written from Marion).

27. West, *History,* 679–680. See, for example, *Greensboro Alabama Beacon,* May 8, 1859.

28. The historiography of yeomen begins with Owsley, *Plain Folk.* Owsley tried to distinguish a yeoman society in Greene County by using the maps of Tax Assessor V. G. Snedecor (whose personal records have unfortunately not survived). I found, however, that the evidence pointed away from a distinct society. During the Civil War all would fight together, and small farmers would rise in the ranks to command wealthy planters.

29. The boredom is evident in the diary of one of the quilt signers, Daniel W. W. Smith,

a lawyer whose American flag block is the most unusual on the quilt. Smith's days during the late 1850s were consumed with visiting friends, traveling to Tuscaloosa, or just wandering about aimlessly in search of something new. Smith apparently went on to have an undistinguished career in the Thirty-eighth Alabama Infantry. The desire to escape such routine surely helped to motivate Smith and others to go off to fight Yankees, but to what extent this was a factor will probably never be known. Smith's diaries are in the ADAH. This analysis of the Lanford quilt is based on Cargo and Hubbs, "Stitches in Time." The quilt has been presented to the Birmingham Museum of Art.

30. Quilts of this general design are known as Baltimore album quilts because this design became popular in that city in the 1840s and '50s. The quilts were often sewn as presentation pieces for a bride or especially a Methodist minister. Methodists in America trace their formal organization to Baltimore in 1784, and it is likely that Methodists brought the idea of an album quilt with them to the western states (Cargo and Hubbs, "Stitches in Time").

31. Statistics gleaned from the 1860 Greene County Manuscript Census, Population, Slave, and Agricultural Schedules; from Snedecor, *Directory*; and from Snedecor's 1858 Mount Hebron Precinct map, ADAH.

32. See appendix D.

33. *Greensboro Alabama Beacon*, January 23, February 27, April 3, 1847. My working definition of *reformer* comes from Quist, *Restless Visionaries*.

34. *Erie Greene County Gazette* July 5, December 22, 1831, January 5, 12, March 29, 1832. See Quist, *Restless Visionaries*, especially chap. 3, "Toward the Sober Slaveholder: Temperance in Tuscaloosa County," 155–234. Quist found that slaveholders "saw no contradiction between their cause and the peculiar institution" (234)

35. See appendix A; *Greensboro Alabama Beacon*, March 1, September 13, 1845.

36. *Greensboro Alabama Beacon*, August 19, 1848; Quist, *Restless Visionaries*, 191–192; Cocke diary, January 17, 1849; Henry Watson Jr. to brother and sister, August 14, 1849, Watson Papers.

37. *Greensboro Alabama Beacon*, January 23, 1850.

38. Serano Watson, "Address to the Greensboro Temperance Association," August 22, 1857, Watson Papers.

39. Henry Watson Jr. to Mary Ann McFaddin, September 20, 1858, Watson Papers.

40. Israel Pickens to William B. Lenoir, March 3, 1822, Lenoir Family Papers; diary of Mrs. John Gayle, quoted in A. Tutwiler, "White Education," 5; Watson diary, December 22, 1830; Henry Watson Jr. to Julius Reed, January 8, February 28, 1831, quoted in Dale, "Connecticut Yankee," 60.

41. Henry Watson Jr. to mother, July 15, 1834, Watson Papers; *Greensboro Alabama Beacon*, February 15, 1845.

42. A. Tutwiler, "White Education," 18.

43. F. Peck to Sophia Peck, November 4, 1834, Watson Papers; A. Tutwiler, "White Education," 10–11; minutes of the Greensboro Female Academy, December 17, 1853, Yerby-Lawson Papers, Auburn University Special Collections and Archives, Auburn, Ala.; *Catalogue*, 17; *Greensboro Alabama Beacon*, March 27, 1847.

44. Lamb, "James G. Birney," 111.

45. Henry Tutwiler to James G. Birney, April 11, 1832, in Birney, *Letters*, 1:18n; H. Tutwiler, *Sketch;* Willie Withers to uncle, October 11, 1856, LeVert Papers.

46. This interpretation is based on Hunt's "Organizing a New South." See also Hunt, "Home, Domesticity, and School Reform." Alabama reformers' views on separate male and female education were consistent with the most progressive expressions from New England, where the most influential proponent of education for domesticity was Catharine Beecher.

It is impossible to trace influence, but some Greensborians sent their children to New England for their education. See Sklar, *Catharine Beecher*.

47. *Greensboro Alabama Beacon*, April 28, July 14, 1854, July 24, 1857; Yerby, *History*, 80–82.

48. Holcombe, *History*, 72–75. Greensboro's efforts again mirrored those in towns throughout the West; see Doyle, *Social Order*, 62–91.

49. I have based this account of the origins of Southern University on Parks and Weaver, *Birmingham-Southern College*, 5–38. Christenberry, *Semi-Centennial History*, is marred by errors.

50. *Greensboro Alabama Beacon*, February 9, 16, 1855.

51. Ibid., February 23, 1855.

52. Ibid., June 15, 1855.

53. Ibid., June 8, 1855.

54. Ibid., December 7, 1855.

55. Augustus Benners diary, July 6, 1855, transcript of original in possession of Glenn Linden. Across the state, Auburnites pursued the same path. Undeterred by the Methodists' decision to build Southern University in Greensboro, they turned to the legislature. A week after Southern University's 1856 charter, the same legislators created East Alabama Male College over a gubernatorial veto.

56. *Charter and Ordinances*, 15.

57. Cocke diary, March 1, 1857; *Greensboro Alabama Beacon*, March 6, 1857.

58. *Greensboro Alabama Beacon*, June 19, 1857. The efforts of Greensboro's voluntary communities to promote reform are consistent with Quist's demonstration (*Restless Visionaries*, 462–470) that Tuscaloosa's reformers were in the American mainstream (except, of course, for the antislavery movement).

59. *Greensboro Alabama Beacon*, November 11, 18, 1859.

60. Snedecor, *Directory*, 60–63. Southern University was demolished in 1873 following extensive tornado damage; according to Ed Lowery, editor of the *Greensboro Watchman*, the contents of the cornerstone had been ruined by water.

61. Testimony of Charles L. Stickney, October 28, 1871, U.S. Congress, Joint Select Committee, *Report*, 1518. See, for example, *Greensboro Alabama Beacon*, February 15, 1851. Among the many personal letters describing moves or planned moves by successful Canebrakers or Greensborians are Julia Pickens Howe to Louisa L. Lenoir, July 15, 1844, Lenoir Family Papers; Thomas A. Sharpe to Lucy Melissa Young, August 6, 1845, William D. Simpson Papers, SHC. See also *Greensboro Alabama Beacon*, April 24, 1857, August 26, 1859. Mansell, *Hale County*, catalogs Greensboro's structures.

## Chapter 4. Guards and Slaves

1. The standard work on the antebellum militia is Cunliffe, *Soldiers and Civilians*. Alabama's state militia is analyzed in Pitcavage, "Equitable Burden." Other writings on the Alabama militia include Rodgers, "Alabama's Volunteer Militia"; Napier, "Martial Montgomery." See also Flynn, *Militia*; Laver, "Rethinking the Social Role."

2. The relationship between slavery and the military is discussed in a long controversy over whether the antebellum South had a distinctive martial character. See Higginbotham, "Martial Spirit"; May, "Dixie's Martial Image." A study of an Old Northwest town and its militia company, corresponding to this study of Greensboro and its Guards, would go far in answering the question of Southern military distinctiveness. Faragher, *Sugar Creek*, 35, notes

a "continuing glorification of and fascination with things military" in Illinois' Sugar Creek region, a phenomenon he attributes to a legacy of the pioneer period.

3. Alabama, *Digest*, 609–622.

4. Patrick May to Governor John Murphy, January 13, 1828, W. Tindels to Governor John Murphy, November 22, 1828, Governors' Papers, Militia Correspondence, ADAH.

5. Longstreet, *Georgia Scenes*, 145–151.

6. Meek, *Supplement*, 140–145.

7. A. McAlpine to James J. Pleasants, May 30, 1823, Governors' Papers, Militia Election Returns, ADAH; R. D. Huckabee to Governor R. H. Chapman, December 26, 1848, Governors' Papers, Militia Files, ADAH; Patrick May to Governor John Murphy, January 13, 1828, Governors' Papers, Militia Correspondence. The Greensboro Cavalry, about which very little is known, met off and on as late as 1861, but for reasons that remain unclear never enjoyed the same success as the Guards and did not enter Confederate service as a unit.

8. *Erie Greene County Gazette*, June 14, July 12, 1830.

9. Ibid., March 1, 8, 1832.

10. Alabama, *Acts Passed*, 148–149 (the act was passed January 17, 1834); John C. Pickens to John F. Thompson, June 6, 1839, Benson-Thompson Family Papers, Rare Book, Manuscript, and Special Collections Library, Duke University, Durham, North Carolina. The Greensboro Guards' uniforms are described in minute detail in their constitutions of 1842 and 1846; see *Constitution and By-Laws of the Greensboro' Light Artillery Guards, adopted April 2, 1842*, and *Constitution and By-Laws of the Light Artillery Guards, at Greensboro', Alabama, adopted June 6, 1846*, both in John Cocke Papers, W. S. Hoole Special Collections Library, University of Alabama, Tuscaloosa. The design was basically a single-breasted dark blue broadcloth dress coat and pants; white pants were substituted for summer. White straps crossed the chest. The seven-and-a-half-inch-tall black leather cap was trimmed with a ten-inch white plume tipped with red.

11. *Constitution and By-Laws, 1842*, 9. See also John C. Pickens to John Thompson, July 25, 1837, Benson-Thompson Family Papers.

12. See Rosters.

13. The general outlines of the war are taken from Valliere, "Creek War"; Ellisor, "Second Creek War."

14. Clement C. Clay, "Annual Message for 1836," in Alabama, Senate, *Journal*, 6, 8, 9; James C. Adams to E. D. King, March 7, 1836, Governors Papers, Administrative Files—Creek War, ADAH.

15. William D. Jeffreys to Robert N. Jeffreys, February 9, 1836, William A. Jeffreys Papers, North Carolina State Archives, Raleigh; roster of "Captain Smith's Company of Mounted Volunteers, Green[e] County, Alabama," Alabamians at War File, ADAH. My analysis of the members of Captain Smith's company is based on a detailed examination of the manuscript census and county records.

16. William D. Jeffreys to Robert N. Jeffreys, February 9, 1836, Jeffreys Papers.

17. Henry Watson Jr. to Henry Watson Sr., March 20, 1836, Watson Papers.

18. P. S. Wyatt to Governor Clement C. Clay, March 9, 1836, Governors Papers, Administrative Files—Creek War; William Beverley to father, March 13, 1837, Beverley Papers; Henry Watson Jr. to Henry Watson Sr., March 20, 1836, Watson Papers.

19. Yerby, *History*, 97; Henry Watson Jr. to mother, June 8, 1836, Watson Papers. The rumors of Bestor's murder were false; he returned to supervise the Greensboro Female Academy and to serve in the legislature.

20. Henry Webb to Governor Clement C. Clay, February 12, 17, 1836; "A Member of the

Greensborough Light Artillery Guards" to Governor Clement C. Clay, May 25, 1836, Governors Papers, Administrative Files—Creek War.

21. Governor Clement C. Clay to Henry Webb, May 30, 1836, Governor Clement C. Clay to Major General Benjamin Patterson, June 1, 1836; Governor Clement C. Clay to Major J. B. Brant, July 4, 1836; Henry Webb to Governor Clement C. Clay, February 12, 1836, Governors Papers, Administrative Files—Creek War; Compiled Service Records, Alabama Troops in the Creek War, index, National Archives; untitled list, June 3, 1836, John Cocke Papers; *Greensboro Alabama Sentinel,* quoted in *Greensboro Watchman,* September 18, 1913.

22. Eufaula quoted in Clinton, *Matt Clinton's Scrapbook,* 52; Clay, "Annual Message," 15.

23. Henry Watson Jr. to Henry Watson Sr., August 30, 1836, Watson Papers.

24. Hooper, *Adventures,* 117. Suggs' military campaign is related in chaps. 7–10.

25. William D. Jeffreys to Robert N. Jeffreys, July 15, 1836, Jeffreys Papers.

26. Reeves, *Napoleonic Exiles,* 551/29; Tharin, *Directory,* 57. Unless otherwise noted, this account is taken from Smith, *Days of Exile,* which collects and summarizes much of what has been written on the exiles in Alabama.

27. Stollenwerck and Orum, *Stollenwerck, Chaudron, and Billon Families,* 54–55.

28. Eaton, *Growth,* 128; Fredrickson, *Black Image,* 8–9, 69; Freehling, *Prelude,* 58–60, 112. A conference entitled "The Impact of the Haitian Revolution on the Atlantic World" was held on October 15–17, 1998, at the College of Charleston at Charleston, South Carolina.

29. Smith, *Days of Exile,* 70–71. A portrait of Adele Fournier hangs in the ADAH.

30. Ibid., 77.

31. Memoir of Mrs. Sylvanie Bayol, in Will T. Sheehan, "French Exiles in Alabama," *Montgomery Advertiser,* October 10, 1905, reprinted in Smith, *Days of Exile,* 74–75; Mrs. J. C. Webb, untitled and undated memoir, Walsh (Aimee Shands) and Family Papers, Mississippi Department of Archives and History. For the account of Marc Antoine Frenage's escape, see Griffin, "History," 375–376.

32. *Erie Greene County Gazette,* October 4, 25, 1830, September 8, 1831; Henry Watson Jr. to Rosanna Reed, April 9, 1834, Watson Papers; H. Cobbs, "Geography," 96.

33. Henry Watson Jr. to Rosanna Reed, April 9, 1834, Watson Papers.

34. *Erie Greene County Gazette,* September 20, 1830.

35. Turner quoted in Gray, *Confessions,* 3–23, 225–245.

36. J. J. Cribbs to Henry Watson Jr., November 16, 1831, Watson Papers; *Erie Greene County Gazette,* October 6, 27, 1831.

37. J. J. Cribbs to Henry Watson Jr., November 16, 1831, Watson Papers.

38. *Charter and Ordinances,* 8. Other Southern states and towns reacted similarly; see, for example, Pease and Pease, *Web,* 162–166.

39. William B. Beverley to father, December 26, 1833, Beverley Papers. In *Transforming the Cotton Frontier,* Dupre does not report an 1833 slave insurrection in Madison County.

40. Henry Watson Jr. to Henry Watson Sr., August 23, 1835; Henry Watson Jr. to Julius Reed, August 23, 1835, Watson Papers. Morris, "Event," 93–111, argues that such scares helped frontiersmen establish community organization and interpersonal networks. For the Clinton insurrection's effect in Madison County, Alabama, see Dupre, *Transforming the Cotton Frontier,* 225–236.

41. *Erie Greene County Gazette,* September 9, 1835.

42. John D. Phelan to brigadier general, December 14, 1840, Governors' Papers, Correspondence and Files, ADAH; *The Liberator,* January 22, 1841.

43. C. Jones et al. to Governor Joshua L. Martin, January 8, 1846; Governor Joshua L. Martin to "Gentlemen," April 21, 1846; R. D. Huckebee to R. H. Chapman, December 26,

1846, Governors' Papers, Militia Files ; George W. Crabb to John Ford Thompson, November 8, 1838, in Benson-Thompson Family Papers; *Constitution and By-Laws, 1842; Constitution and By-Laws, 1846.* For the militia's roll in slave patrols, see Pitcavage, "Equitable Burden," 432–444.

44. *Greensborough Greene County Patriot,* August 31, 1825.

45. T. Nixon Van Dyke to James G. Birney, November 25, 1832, in Birney, *Letters,* 42–43; *Erie Greene County Gazette,* March 1, 1832.

46. Henry Tutwiler to James Gillespie Birney, August 20, 1832, in Birney, *Letters,* 42–43; Lamb, "James G. Birney"; 1860 manuscript U.S. census, slave schedule, Havanna Precinct, p. 333. Former slaves remembered Tutwiler as an uncommonly kind master; see "Some Recollections of Legrand Tutwiler, Former Slave of Dr. Henry Tutwiler of Greene Springs, Alabama," Henry Tutwiler Papers, W. S. Hoole Special Collections Library, University of Alabama, Tuscaloosa.

47. Except where noted, this account of Cocke is taken from R. Miller, *Dear Master,* introduction; Eaton, *Mind,* chap. 2, 23–43.

48. Cocke diary, January 20, 1838.

49. Ibid., February 26, 1841.

50. Ibid., January 28, 1848.

51. Lucy Skipwith to John Hartwell Cocke, May 19, 1855, in R. Miller, *Dear Master,* 198.

52. Cocke diary, January 3, February 1, 1850.

53. J. Williams, *Narrative.* The greater severity of slavery in the Southwest (with examples from Greene County) is discussed in Cashin, *Family Venture,* 112–118.

54. J. Williams, *Narrative.*

55. Cocke diary, February 3, 1850; Israel Pickens to William B. Lenoir, March 3, 1822, Lenoir Family Papers; John Bell to John Springs, October 24, 1847, Springs Family Papers, SHC (from Perry County). See also Dr. J. N. Carrigan to Henry Watson Jr., November 6, 1852, Watson Papers; Thomas Caufield to "Henry," November 9, 1851, Caufield Family Papers, Texas Collection, Baylor University, Waco.

56. See Rosters; Watson diary, January 10, 1831; Henry Watson Sr. to Henry Watson Jr., February 6, 1831; Henry Watson Jr. to Henry Watson Sr., August 23, 1835, Watson Papers. Watson's slaveholdings are examined in Gutman, *Black Family,* 159–167.

57. Henry Watson Jr. to mother, November 7, 1847, Watson Papers.

58. Henry Watson Jr. to Sophia Watson, November 27, 1851, Watson Papers, quoted in Oakes, *Ruling Race,* 219.

59. Henry Watson Jr. to Sarah A. Carrington, January 28, 1861, Watson Papers. Genovese, *Roll, Jordan, Roll,* treats at great length the contradictions between the slaveholders' demand for their slaves' loyalty on the one hand and the way in which they treated their slaves as property on the other. He suggests that the sort of paternalism that Watson exhibited was self-serving, fulfilling a master's need for his slaves' affection even as he tried to accommodate the cruelty that slavery necessarily involved.

60. Sophia Watson to Henry Watson Jr., July 31, 1848, Watson Papers.

61. John Witherspoon to Susan K. McDowall, July 9, 1846, Witherspoon-McDowall Papers. See Cashin, *Family Venture.* Rable, *Civil Wars,* 114–118, explores the shift from paternalism during the Civil War. Historians of the West have also concluded that women and men experienced emigration to the frontier differently; see Faragher, *Women and Men,* chaps. 3–5, 66–143.

62. John W. Womack to J. L. Womack, August 30, 1835, Marcus Joseph Wright Papers, SHC.

63. Estes, *Defence;* Matthew Estes to Bates, Hooper, and Company, October 9, November 18, 1846, January 16, 1847, Thomas Hill Watts Papers, ADAH; *Greensboro Alabama Beacon,* January 2, March 13, 1847.

64. Estes, *Defence,* 227, 244. In all the vast literature on proslavery writings, I have never found Estes' book considered.

65. Ibid., 38–40, 43–44.

66. Ibid., 127, 185, 233.

67. *Greensboro Alabama Beacon,* September 20, 1845. Houston approached Greensboro from Marion, his wife's hometown.

68. William Kerr and John E. Lipscomb to Governor Joshua L. Martin, May 13, 1846, Governors' Papers, Militia Files; *Greensboro Alabama Beacon,* June 6, 1846.

69. *Fort Worth Star-Telegram,* July 10 or 11, 1916, in Alabamians at War File; Nat Murphy and John L. Croom to Governor Joshua L. Martin, May 26, 1846; Richard H. Croom and John L. Croom to Governor Joshua L. Martin, n.d.; A. L. Pickens to Governor Joshua L. Martin, May 30, 1846, Governors' Papers, Militia Files; Nunnelee, "Alabama," 417; *Greensboro Alabama Beacon,* June 6, 1846; Sydenham Moore, "Diary of the Mexican War," June 4, 5, 15, 1846, Sydenham Moore Papers, ADAH.

70. This account is taken from Moore, "Diary."

71. *Greensboro Alabama Beacon,* October 24, 1846.

72. Of the 145 names that appear in the volunteers' muster rolls (less than 100 men departed from Mobile), 89 do not appear in the manuscript census or marriage records, thus suggesting that they were transients or at least did not remain in Greensboro after the war with Mexico. Of the 145, only 2 (both Greensboro Guards) were known to be members of the Sons of Temperance, and 2 were Masons (including 1 of the Guards). By 1850, 18 volunteers were listed as married, although at least 5 of these marriages occurred after the men returned from Mexico. Seventeen of the 145 (surely a low figure) either held slaves or were associated with families that did so. The Greensboro Guards, conversely, were far more prominent and settled than those Greensborians who went to Mexico. The Guards in 1846 numbered 55, of whom only 12 are unknown (and 2 of those have ambiguous names). Of the 55, 9 were members of the Sons of Temperance (in 1851, more than half the local officers were Guards), and 20 were Masons. Twenty-seven of the Guards were married, and 29 were members of slaveholding families. The names of the members of Captain Pickens' Greensboro Volunteers, Company A, First Alabama Volunteer Regiment, have been compiled from *Greensboro Alabama Beacon* June 6, 1846, July 12, 1851; A. L. Pickens to Governor Joshua L. Martin, May 30, 1846, "Members of the Greensboro Independent Volunteers" (undated handwritten copy), Governors' Papers, Militia Files; typescript muster rolls, April 30, June 2, 1847, Mexican War Muster Rolls Collection, ADAH; Yerby, *History,* 49–50; *Fort Worth Star Telegram,* July 10 or 11, 1916. See also Rosters.

73. John Witherspoon to Susan K. McDowall, July 9, 1846, Witherspoon-McDowall Papers; Henry D. Caufield to William E. Young, August 23, 1847; Lizzie to sister, November 24, 1852, Caufield Family Papers.

74. Andrew Pickens Calhoun to John C. Calhoun, February 4, 1847, in C. N. Wilson and Cook, *Papers,* 104; *Greensboro Alabama Beacon,* January 30, 1847, July 1, 15, 1848.

75. *Greensboro Alabama Beacon,* November 11, 25, 1848, February 17, 3, 1849.

76. Ibid., April 14, 1849, April 20, 1850, September 14, 1850.

77. *Greensboro Alabama Beacon,* October 12, 1850.

78. Samuel Pickens to William A. Lenoir, June 8, 1851, Lenoir Family Papers.

79. *Greensboro Alabama Beacon,* September 27, October 4, 11, 18, 19, 1851, February 27, March 5, 19, 26, April 2, 9, 30, May 7, 14, 1852.

80. *Charter and Ordinances,* 14; William [Hays?] to Cornelia [Hays?], November 19, 1852, Mary Hays Papers, ADAH.

81. *Greensboro Alabama Beacon,* September 4, 11, October 2, 9, 1857; Henry Watson Jr. to mother, June 19 [22], 1858, Watson Papers.

82. *Greensboro Alabama Beacon,* February 20, 1857.

83. Ibid., February 27, April 10, 1857.

84. Ibid., April 10, 1857.


## Chapter 5. One Voice

1. According to philosopher David Carr, "Narrative and the Real World," 128, 127, "A community in this sense exists by virtue of a story which is articulated and accepted." "It is not my experience but *ours,* not *I* who act but *we* who act in concert." For a fuller treatment, see Carr, *Time, Narrative, and History.* My portrait of the Guards' merging their experiences is not inconsistent with that drawn by Piston and Hatcher in *Wilson's Creek.* Piston and Hatcher argue that going to war was a collective experience whereby soldiers and their hometowns collaborated to uphold their reputations and honor.

2. *Greensboro Alabama Beacon,* May 15, June 20, July 10, 17, 1857. Rable, *Civil Wars,* 40–42, and others note how unusual it was for women to make public speeches.

3. *Greensboro Alabama Beacon,* July 17, 1857.

4. Ibid., July 10, November 10, 1857, February 26, July 9, November 16, 1858, January 14, 21, May 8, 1895; John Gideon Harris journal, July 7, 1858, Tanglewood/Bishop Collection, W. S. Hoole Special Collections Library, University of Alabama, Tuscaloosa.

5. *Greensboro Alabama Beacon,* April 9, October 8, 1858, July 1, 1859; Harris journal, October 5, 1858, May 18, June 28, 1859.

6. *Greensboro Alabama Beacon,* December 2, 1859.

7. Ibid., January 27, March 2, 1860; Alabama, General Assembly, *Acts, 1859,* 36–41; Hubbs, "Lone Star Flags"; Bailey, "Regulation Uniform." The governor and his aides almost surely failed to adopt a flag, which would have been Alabama's first.

8. *Greensboro Alabama Beacon,* January 13, April 13, 1860.

9. See, for example, Benners diary, July 20–23, 1853.

10. My understanding of Democratic and Whig ideology has been influenced by Berlin, "Two Concepts"; Kohl, *Politics;* Thornton, *Politics.* A succinct version of these views may be found in Thornton, "Jacksonian Democracy."

11. Thornton, *Politics,* 238.

12. *Greensboro Alabama Beacon,* November 5, 1848.

13. Thornton, *Politics,* 32, 437, 443.

14. Benners diary, November 3, 1856.

15. *Greensboro Alabama Beacon,* January 27, 1860.

16. Ibid., July 6, July 13, 1860.

17. Thornton, *Politics,* 401–403.

18. Philip Henry Pitts diary, June 1860, Philip Henry Pitts Papers, SHC; Serano Watson to Henry Watson Jr., September 4, 1860, Watson Papers; Benners diary, August 14, 1860. Greensborians' reasons for embracing secession seem consistent with Channing's description of South Carolinians (*Crisis of Fear,* 286–293): they feared that the Republican Party would end slavery and precipitate a race war. Channing admits that other causes of secession may have been at work, but the fear of emancipation was so overwhelming that it consumed all other issues. References to rights—constitutional, state, and property—and other apologies merely masked true fears.

19. *Greensboro Alabama Beacon,* November 16, 1860; Duckworth, "Role," 93–102, analyzes voting patterns.

20. *Greensboro Alabama Beacon,* November 9, 16, 1860.

21. Serano Watson to Henry Watson, November 17, 1860, Watson Papers. In January 1861, Moore stepped down as a member of the U.S. Congress and returned to Alabama.

22. *Greensboro Alabama Beacon,* November 30, 1860.

23. Ibid.

24. Ibid.

25. Serano Watson to Henry Watson, November 17, 1860; Henry Watson Jr. to Thayer and Peck, December 14, 1860; Henry Watson Jr. to Henry Barnard, December 23, 1860, Watson Papers; Benners diary, December 29, 1860; U.S. Congress, Joint Select Committee, *Report,* 8:1272. Statistical studies confirm the reported change in sentiment following Lincoln's election; see Duckworth, "Role," 93–102.

26. Thornton, *Politics,* 347, 343. Barney's study of secession in Alabama, *Secessionist Impulse,* attempts to correlate voting with wealth, place of residence, and nativity (67, 250–257). He comes close to equating Unionists and Cooperationists, an interpretation that may apply to the mountainous regions of the state but does not apply to Greene County.

27. "Delegates," 420–421, 396–397; 1860 manuscript census, slave schedules, pp. 383, 379–381, 261, 398, National Archives. J. D. Webb, then nearly forty-three years old, was born in North Carolina, graduated from the University of Alabama in 1836, and after studying law began a practice in Greensboro in 1838. He served sporadically in the legislature and in 1860 owned at least 25 slaves. He had supported Bell in the 1860 election but now ran as an Immediatist. In April he joined the Greensboro Guards. His running mate, Herndon, was born in Erie in 1828 and received degrees from the University of Alabama as well as a law degree from Harvard in 1848. He practiced law in Eutaw even as he edited the *Eutaw Democrat* and oversaw his family's substantial Erie plantation, which had more than 159 slaves. William P. Webb owned 10 slaves. His running mate, Jeffries, was a wealthy Greensboro planter who kept 50 slaves on his Canebrake plantation six miles west of Greensboro; Jeffries' son, Robert, enlisted in the Guards in April 1861.

28. West, *History,* 731–732; Parks and Weaver, *Birmingham-Southern College,* 23; J. J. Hutchinson File, Alabama–West Florida Conference Archives, United Methodist Church, Huntingdon College, Montgomery, Alabama; J. J. Hutchinson, "Address," December [5], 1860, Rare Book, Manuscript, and Special Collections Library, Duke University, Durham, North Carolina.

29. *Greensboro Alabama Beacon,* December 7, 1860.

30. *Tuscaloosa Monitor,* February 11, 1860; *Greensboro Alabama Beacon,* December 21, 1860.

31. Duckworth, "Role," 97–98; J. D. Webb to Justina Webb, January 12, 1861, Walton Family Papers, sнc. The county's 8 percent higher vote for immediate secession may reflect the increased sense of vulnerability that isolated white Canebrakers felt while living among vast numbers of slaves.

32. Serano Watson to Julia Watson, January 12, 1861, Watson Papers.

33. Benners diary, January 16, 1861; *Greensboro Alabama Beacon,* January 25, 1861, June 18, 1870; *Greensboro Watchman,* May 2, 1907.

34. At least twenty-six Guards were members of slaveholding families, although only thirteen can be directly linked to farming or planting. The ranks included eight merchants or clerks, seven artisans or mechanics, four in the building trades, two lawyers, and two in the healing arts. The backgrounds of only three are unknown. Seventeen were clearly living with their parents; the rest were presumably independent, with at least twenty-four married.

See Rosters. Studies of Civil War soldiers are rich and extensive, among them Wiley, *Life;* McPherson, *For Cause and Comrades;* Mitchell, *Civil War Soldiers;* Robertson, *Soldiers.*

35. Henry Watson Jr. to mother, January 15, 1861, Watson Papers; *Greensboro Alabama Beacon,* January 18, 25, 1861; Jules Honoré Bayol to mother, January 31, 1861, Bayol Family Papers, Virginia Historical Society, Richmond.

36. George Erwin to wife, January 18, 1861, George Erwin Papers, ADAH; Samuel Henry Lockett to wife, February 18, 1861, Samuel Henry Lockett Papers, SHC.

37. *Greensboro Alabama Beacon,* March 1, 1861; Fanny Erwin to Cadwallader Jones, February 23, 1861, Cadwallader Jones Papers, SHC.

38. Henry Watson Jr. to mother, February 27, 1861; Henry Watson Jr. to Julia Watson, March 8, 1861, Watson Papers; Benners diary, March 7, 1861; *Greensboro Alabama Beacon,* March 8, 1861; Jessie Webb to Mrs. J. L. Walton, February 27, 1861, Walton Family Papers.

39. John S. Haywood to George M. Haywood, January 8, 1861, Ernest Haywood Papers, SHC; *Greensboro Alabama Beacon,* March 1, 8, 1861.

## Chapter 6. Greene County's Still

1. Benners diary, March 7, 1861; J. D. Webb to Justina Webb, March 5, 1861, Walton Family Papers; Pitts diary, March 4, 1861; Henry Watson Jr. to mother, March 17, 1861; Henry Watson Jr. to M. L. Filley, March 17, 1861, Watson Papers.

2. Henry Watson Jr. to unknown, April 11, 1861, Watson Papers; *Greensboro Alabama Beacon,* January 25, April 12, 19, 1861. Over the next few years, Fowler would serve in a number of administrative positions, collecting service claims and records. See Owen, *History,* 3:607–609.

3. Story, "Pocket Diary," April 13, 1861, 86; John H. Cowin diary, April 22, 1861, W. S. Hoole Special Collections Library, University of Alabama, Tuscaloosa, published in its entirety in Hubbs, *Voices; Greensboro Alabama Beacon,* May 3, 1861. Much of my analysis of the Guards and their relationship to Greensboro during the Civil War is consistent with Mitchell's depiction in *The Vacant Chair.*

4. *Greensboro Alabama Beacon,* April 26, May 10, 1861. My rather extensive analysis of the company members is summarized in appendix E, a compilation drawn from contemporary sources that includes many who stayed in the company only briefly; rosters drawn after the war tend to list only soldiers whose length of service seemed to merit recognition. These data, based largely on the 1860 manuscript census, are consistent with those derived for two other volunteer military companies from nearby Dallas County. See Barney, "Towards the Civil War."

5. Cowin diary, preface.

6. Ibid. Cowin was probably typical of the students examined by Kilbride in "Southern Medical Students."

7. Cowin diary, April 22, 1861; J. D. Webb to Justina Webb, May 21, May 19, July 29, 1861, Walton Family Papers.

8. Cowin diary, May 5, 1861; Joseph Borden to Fannie Borden, May 5, 1861, in Borden and Borden, *Legacy,* 14; *Greensboro Alabama Beacon,* May 10, 17, 1861. Although the county was a mere three or four decades old, by the 1850s the phrase "Old Greene" had already started to crop up; see *Greensboro Alabama Beacon,* March 27, April 13, 1850, December 7, 1860, May 10, 1861, April 15, 1864; Ruffin Gray to Fannie Borden, November 29, 1862, in Borden and Borden, *Legacy,* 123

9. List courtesy of Alan Pitts, Birmingham, who has compiled and corrected the records on the Fifth Alabama and other state regiments from manuscript sources in the ADAH. See also Terry, "Record," 304.

10. Cowin diary, May 5, 9, 1861; *Greensboro Alabama Beacon,* May 17, 10, 1861; Joseph Borden to Fannie Borden, May 17, 1861, in Borden and Borden, *Legacy,* 16; J. D. Webb to Justina Webb, May 12, 1861, Walton Family Papers.

11. J. D. Webb to Justina Webb, May 14, 1861, Walton Family Papers; Cowin diary, May 13, 1861.

12. Joseph Borden to Fannie Borden, May 19, 25, 1861, in Borden and Borden, *Legacy,* 16, 18; Cowin diary, May 12, 1861; J. D. Webb to Justina Webb, May 16, 21, 1861, Walton Family Papers.

13. Cowin diary, May 1861; *Greensboro Alabama Beacon,* May 31, 1861.

14. Joseph Borden to Fannie Borden, May 30, June 11, 2, 10, 1861, in Borden and Borden, *Legacy,* 19, 22–23, 21–22; *Greensboro Alabama Beacon,* July 12, June 28, 1861; Cowin diary, June 1861.

15. Cowin diary, June 1861.

16. Ibid., June, July 7, 1861; *Greensboro Alabama Beacon,* July 26, 1861.

17. Cowin diary, June, July 1, 3, 9, 13, 1861; Joseph Borden to Fannie Borden, June 15, July 25–26, 1861, in Borden and Borden, *Legacy,* 23–24; *Greensboro Alabama Beacon,* July 26, 1861.

18. Cowin diary, July 3, 4, 15, 1861.

19. *Greensboro Alabama Beacon,* August 9, 16, 1861; Cowin diary, July 17, 1861. On courage, see Linderman, *Embattled Courage.*

20. Joseph Borden to Fannie Borden, July 19, 31, 1861, in Borden and Borden, *Legacy,* 28–29, 34; Cowin diary, July 20, 1861.

21. Cowin diary, July 21, 1861; *Greensboro Alabama Beacon,* August 9, 1861; Joseph Borden to Fannie Borden, July 24, 31, 1861, in Borden and Borden, *Legacy,* 30.

22. Cowin diary, July 22, 23, 1861; *Greensboro Alabama Beacon,* August 9, 1861.

23. Joseph Borden to Fannie Borden, July 26, 1861, in Borden and Borden, *Legacy,* 31; J. D. Webb to Justina Webb, [July 1861], Walton Family Papers; Sydenham Moore to wife, July 23, 1861, Moore Papers.

24. Cowin diary, July 22, 1861; J. D. Webb to Justina Webb, 1861 [after July 21], Walton Family Papers; Joseph Borden to Fannie Borden, July 26, 1861, in Borden and Borden, *Legacy,* 31.

25. Joseph Borden to Fannie Borden, July 26, 9, 1861, in Borden and Borden, *Legacy,* 31, 27.

26. Winn, *Great Victory;* J. A. Wemyss to Henry Watson Jr., July 22, 1861, Watson Papers; *Greensboro Alabama Beacon,* April 26, May 3, 1861.

27. *Greensboro Alabama Beacon,* July 26, August 16, 1861; James Pickens to Sam Pickens, July 7, 1863, Mrs. Pickens to Sam Pickens, September 9, 1863, McCall Family Papers, Selma, Alabama; Justina Webb to J. D. Webb, September 10, 1861, Walton Family Papers; *Greensboro Alabama Beacon,* July 26, August 2, 16, 1861; Cowin diary, August 2, 1861.

28. *Greensboro Alabama Beacon,* August 2, 1861; Benners diary, June 24, 27, July 8, 20, 1861; *Greensboro Alabama Beacon,* August 2, 1861; Cowin diary, October 9–15, 1861.

29. Sterkx, *Partners,* 106, 94; *Greensboro Alabama Beacon,* September 13, August 9, 1861, February 14, September 19, 1862; Justina Webb to J. D. Webb, September 29, June 3, [June?] 18, 1861, Walton Family Papers.

30. John Gideon Harris, "Fellow Officers in the Confederate Army from the State of Alabama," April 1862, John Gideon Harris Papers, ADAH (another copy is in Bishop/Tanglewood Collection). The story of the ladies' gunboats and the gunboat quilts appears in Henley, "Gunboat Quilts"; see also *Greensboro Alabama Beacon,* March 14, 1862. The child's quilt was eventually presented to the Reverend Hutchinson, and his children displayed it from time to time; see *Greensboro Watchman,* November 23, 1893, December 14, 1899.

31. A. McAlpine to Jas. J. Thornton, May 28, 1825, Governors' Papers, Militia Election Returns; William Kerr to Joe Riggs, March 21, 1861, Governors' Papers, Military Correspondence.

32. *Greensboro Alabama Beacon,* April 26, May 3, 31, June 14, July 19, 26, September 13, 1861; Story, "Pocket Diary," April 19, 26, October 11, 1861, 88, 89, 114; Dr. John H. Parrish to Henry Watson, June 29, 1861, Watson Papers. The muster roll of the Young Rebels reveals that many had fathers who served in the Guards and that many served in the Greensboro Guards during the next four years (*Greensboro Alabama Beacon,* June 28, 1861).

33. Cowin diary, August 2, 1861; *Greensboro Alabama Beacon,* August 2, 1861. Captain Harris' company was accepted as Company I, Twentieth Alabama Infantry Regiment, and immediately ordered to the defense of Mobile. The company later fought in some decisive battles of the western theater, including Port Gibson, Missionary Ridge, and Nashville and the retreat through Georgia. After the war, Harris edited the *Alabama Baptist,* served as grand master of the Grand Lodge of Alabama, and was appointed state superintendent of education; see Tanglewood/Bishop Collection.

34. Greene County Marriages, book C-44; 1850 Greene County manuscript census, p. 253; U.S. Government, 1860 Greene County manuscript census, p. 844; *Greensboro Alabama Beacon,* May 31, July 12, September 13, 1861; Joseph Borden to Fannie Borden, May 25, 1861, in Borden and Borden, *Legacy,* 18; J. D. Webb to Justina Webb, May 21, 23, 1861, Walton Family Papers; "Sister" [Fanny Erwin?] to Cadwallader Jones, May 30, 1861, Jones Papers.

35. *Greensboro Alabama Beacon,* June 28, 1861; Snedecor, *Directory,* 63; Cowin diary, July 5, 11, August 3, 14, 19, 20, 30, September 12–14, 16–24, 25, 1861.

36. Cowin diary, September 26, 27, October 3, 4, 1861. Captain Fowler's Warrior Guards joined the Greensboro Guards at the graves.

37. Cowin diary, November 4, 1861; *Greensboro Alabama Beacon,* November 8, 15, 1861; U.S. Congress, Joint Select Committee, *Report,* 8:1272. Blackford later served in the Thirty-first Alabama, as needed, until the end of the war.

38. F. E. and J. H. Bayol to father, August 27, 1861, Bayol Family Papers; James L. Boardman to father, August 16, 1861, James L. Boardman to sister, August 17, 1861, James L. Boardman Papers, Rare Book, Manuscript, and Special Collections Library, Duke University, Durham, North Carolina.

39. Cowin diary, October 26, 27, 1861; J. D. Webb to Justina Webb, November 3, 1861; James E. Webb to aunt, Walton Family Papers; *Greensboro Alabama Beacon,* June 23, 1849; Eugene Blackford to Mary B. Blackford, February 20, 1861, Gordon-Blackford Collection, Maryland Historical Society, Baltimore. See also J. H. Bayol to parents, November 21, 1861, Bayol Family Papers.

40. F. E. and J. H. Bayol to father, August 27, 1861, Bayol Family Papers.

41. Cowin diary, October 7, 19, 30, November 11, 1861; F. E. and J. H. Bayol to father, August 27, 1861; F. E. Bayol to sister, November 10, 1861; J. H. Bayol to parents, November 21, 1861, Bayol Family Papers.

42. Joseph Borden to Fannie Borden, November 9, December 7, 10, 25, 1861, January 1, 1862, in Borden and Borden, *Legacy,* 46, 47, 48, 64; J. D. Webb to Justina Webb, December 9, 1861, Walton Family Papers; J. H. Bayol to father, November 27, 1861, Bayol Family Papers.

43. F. E. Bayol to brother, October 20, 1861, Bayol Family Papers; *Greensboro Alabama Beacon,* June 18, 1870; Cowin diary, July 3, 1861; *Greensboro Watchman,* May 2, 1907.

44. Cowin diary, September 18, November 8, 1861; J. H. Bayol to sister, December 1861, Bayol Family Papers.

45. Cowin diary, July 24, August 25, 26, 31, September 7, October 14, 21, 31, 1861. Red flannel seems to have been a common choice among Alabama companies. In addition to the

Greensboro Guards, both the Young Rebels and the Canebrake Guards wore red flannel shirts. See Bridges, "Juliet Opie Hopkins," 86.

46. This line of thought is developed by several scholars, particularly by Mitchell in *The Vacant Chair*, esp. chap. 2, "The Northern Soldier and His Community," 19–37 (also in Vinovskis, *Toward a Social History*). See also Linderman, *Embattled Courage;* McPherson, *For Cause and Comrades*, chap. 4, "If I Flinched I Was Ruined," 46–61.

47. *Greensboro Alabama Beacon*, July 12, 1861.

## Chapter 7. Beyond a Simple Calculus

1. Justina Webb to J. D. Webb, May 25, 1861, Walton Family Papers.

2. *Greensboro Alabama Beacon*, August 9, 1861; John Haywood to George W. Haywood, November 1, 1861, Haywood Papers; Joseph Borden to Fannie Borden, January 4, 14, 1862, in Borden and Borden, *Legacy*, 64, 66; Justina Webb to J. D. Webb, January 30, 1862, Walton Family Papers.

3. James L. Boardman to sister, August 17, 1861, Boardman Papers; John F. Christian [?] to Annie, October 22, 1861, John Beverley Christian Papers, Rare Book, Manuscript, and Special Collections Library, Duke University, Durham, North Carolina; J. H. and F. E. Bayol to father, February 2, 1862, Bayol Family Papers; Joseph Borden to Fannie Borden, February 8, 1862, in Borden and Borden, *Legacy*, 68; *Greensboro Alabama Beacon*, March 7, 1862.

4. Joseph Borden to Fannie Borden, January 23, February 25, 1862, in Borden and Borden, *Legacy*, 67, 69; Eugene Blackford to William M. Blackford, February 9, 1862, Gordon-Blackford Collection; *Greensboro Alabama Beacon*, February 7, 1862. The remnants of the Warrior Guards joined the Greensboro Guards in April 1862.

5. *Greensboro Alabama Beacon*, March 7, 28, May 2, 1862.

6. *Greensboro Alabama Beacon*, April 4, 1862; Justina Webb to J. D. Webb, March 31, 1862, Walton Family Papers.

7. A. Moore, *Conscription and Conflict*, 14. Webb was mortally wounded in an 1863 skirmish near Elk River, Tennessee.

8. Richard H. Adams diary, April 27, 1862, Richard H. Adams Papers, Virginia Military Institute, Lexington, and reprinted in Hubbs, *Voices;* John S. Tucker diary, April 27, 1862, ADAH (portions of the Tucker diary are also published in Hubbs, *Voices*); Joseph Borden to Fannie Borden, April 28, 1862, in Borden and Borden, *Legacy*, 75.

9. List courtesy of Alan Pitts, Birmingham. Along with the Fifth Alabama, Rodes' brigade at this point included the Sixth and Twelfth Alabama, the Twelfth Mississippi, and Carter's Artillery Battery.

10. J. D. Webb to Justina Webb, April 7 [9], 1862, Walton Family Papers; Tucker diary, April 8, 12, 1862; Adams diary, April 7, 8, 9, May 1, 1862; Joseph Borden to Fannie Borden, April 11, 13, 1862, in Borden and Borden, *Legacy*, 71–72; Eugene Blackford to parents, April 22, 1862, Gordon-Blackford Collection.

11. Tucker diary, April 13, 20, 1862; Eugene Blackford to parents, April 22, 1861, Gordon-Blackford Collection; Adams diary, April 14, 30, 1862; Joseph Borden to Fannie Borden, April 22, 27, 1862, in Borden and Borden, *Legacy*, 73.

12. Joseph Borden to Fannie Borden, April 19, 1862, in Borden and Borden, *Legacy*, 72; Eugene Blackford to parents, April 22, 1862, Gordon-Blackford Collection; Adams diary, May 2, 3, 1862.

13. Tucker diary, May 3, 4, 1862; Eugene Blackford to Mary B. Blackford, May 11, 1862, Gordon-Blackford Collection.

14. Tucker diary, May 4, 1862.

15. Eugene Blackford to Mary B. Blackford, May 11, 1862, Gordon-Blackford Collection; Adams diary, May 5, 1862.

16. Adams diary, May 5, 1862; Eugene Blackford to Mary B. Blackford, May 11, 1862, Gordon-Blackford Collection. Casualty figures are taken from Livermore, *Numbers and Losses*, 80–81.

17. Tucker diary, May 6–18, 1862; Eugene Blackford to parents, May 20, 1862; Eugene Blackford to Mary B. Blackford, May 11, 1862, Gordon-Blackford Collection; Adams diary, May 6–18, 1862; Joseph Borden to Fannie Borden, May 30, 24, 1862, in Borden and Borden, *Legacy*, 78, 77.

18. Joseph Borden to Fannie Borden, May 29, 1862, in Borden and Borden, *Legacy*, 78; Tucker diary, May 25, 26, 1862; Eugene Blackford to parents, May 20, 1862, Gordon-Blackford Collection; Adams diary, May 28, 29, 1862.

19. Adams diary, May 31, 1862; Tucker diary, May 31, 1862; *War of the Rebellion* (hereafter cited as OR), ser. 1, vol. 11, pt. 1, p. 971.

20. OR, ser. 1, vol. 11, pt. 1, pp. 972, 978; Park, *Sketch*, 29; Adams diary, May 31, 1862; Eugene Blackford to William M. Blackford, June 6, 1862, Gordon-Blackford Collection.

21. *Greensboro Watchman*, March 29, 1900.

22. OR, ser. 1, vol. 11, pt. 1, pp. 978, 973; Tucker diary, May 31, 1862.

23. Adams diary, May 31, 1862.

24. OR, ser. 1, vol. 11, pt. 1, pp. 975, 978; Tucker diary, June 1, 1862; *Greensboro Alabama Beacon*, June 13, 1862.

25. Eugene Blackford to William M. Blackford, June 6, 1862, Gordon-Blackford Collection; Adams diary, May 31, 1862; F. E. Bayol to parents, June 21, 1862, Bayol Family Papers; OR, ser. 1, vol. 11, pt. 1, p. 976; Livermore, *Numbers and Losses*, 81.

26. *Greensboro Alabama Beacon*, June 13, July 25, 1862, September 25, 1869; Julius [Jules] Honoré Bayol, "Map of Seven Pines Battlefield," ADAH.

27. James L. Boardman to father, June 17, 1862, Boardman Papers.

28. OR, ser. 1, vol. 11, pt. 2, p. 630; *Greensboro Alabama Beacon*, October 17, 1862; E. L. Hobson to H. A. Whiting, July 19, 1862, Hobson Family Papers, Virginia Historical Society, Richmond; Livermore, *Numbers and Losses*, 82.

29. Tucker diary, July 16, 1862; *Greensboro Alabama Beacon*, October 17, 1862; OR, ser. 1, vol. 11, pt. 2, p. 632; E. L. Hobson to H. A. Whiting, July 19, 1862, Hobson Family Papers.

30. OR, ser. 1, vol. 11, pt. 2, pp. 625–626; *Greensboro Alabama Beacon*, October 17, 1862; Veteran of Company D, "More War Records" [extracts from a diary], *Greensboro Alabama Beacon*, March 11, 1899.

31. J. H. Bayol to parents, June 28, 1862, Bayol Family Papers; Livermore, *Numbers and Losses*, 82–83; E. L. Hobson to H. A. Whiting, July 19, 1862, Hobson Family Papers; OR, ser. 1, vol. 11, pt. 2, pp. 632, 633.

32. *Greensboro Alabama Beacon*, October 17, 1862.

33. As cited in Freeman, *Lee's Lieutenants*, 1:589; McPherson, *For Cause and Comrades*, 469.

34. OR, ser. 1, vol. 11, pt. 2, pp. 627–628, 634.

35. Ibid., 628; Forsyth, *History*, 36, quoted in McPherson, *Battle Cry*, 470; *Greensboro Alabama Beacon*, July 18, 1862.

36. J. W. Williams, "The Faithful Body Servant," *Greensboro Record*, October 22, 1903.

37. Joseph Borden to Fannie Borden, August 11, 1862, in Borden and Borden, *Legacy*, 117.

38. *Greensboro Alabama Beacon*, October 17, 1862; Tucker diary, August 19, 20, 1862.

39. Unless otherwise noted, this account of the Guards' adventures during and after the Maryland campaign is from J. W. Williams' reminiscences in the *Greensboro Record*: "From

Richmond to Stone Mountain: Company D's Part in That Memorable Campaign in Maryland," December 3, 1903; "Memorable March into Maryland: A Interesting Account of Company D, the Greensboro Guards' Part in This Campaign," December 17, 1903; "Company D Captured at the Battle of South Mountain: Thrilling Narrative of a Fight against Overpowering Numbers: The Greensboro Guards Captured and Sent Prisoners to Fort Delaware," December 24, 1903; "A Search for a Sword: Captain J. W. Williams Tries to Find His Captured Weapon; A Few of the Replies Received from Wearers of Blue, Who Witnessed Its Surrender," September 3, 1903; and "Company D Leave Fort Delaware, Being Returned as Prisoners They Make Sensational Escape through the Lines," January 14, 1904. This newspaper series was written forty years after the war and must be read in the context of a man of unfaltering pride in his adventures with the Guards. Nevertheless, I have found his memory reliable, with only trivial discrepancies from contemporary accounts.

40. Tucker diary, September 2, 1862.

41. Ibid., September 3, 1862.

42. *Greensboro Alabama Beacon*, October 17; 1862, OR, ser. 1, vol. 19, pt. 1, p. 1019.

43. Tucker diary, September 6, 11, 1862; F. E. Bayol to parents, September 9, 1862, Bayol Family Papers.

44. F. E. Bayol to parents, September 9, 1862, Bayol Family Papers.

45. Samuel Pickens diary, October 3, 1862, McCall Family Papers, Selma, Alabama. The complete diary is also reproduced in Hubbs, *Voices*.

46. Ibid.

47. Priest, *Before Antietam*, 324.

48. *Greensboro Alabama Beacon*, October 3, 1862.

49. Ibid.

50. Samuel Pickens diary, October 3, 1862; *Greensboro Alabama Beacon*, October 3, 1862. The Combined Service Records list only nine Guards taken prisoner; Williams recalled twelve or thirteen. The sword was engraved with the name of Gideon E. Nelson, a prosperous planter and former Guard who presented the weapon to Williams. At the turn of the century, Williams tried to locate his sword, apparently without success.

51. Livermore, *Numbers and Losses*, 92–93; *Greensboro Alabama Beacon*, October 17, 1862. For an excellent account of Rodes' brigade at Sharpsburg, see Krick, "Mutual Extermination."

52. Fannie Borden to Joseph Borden, July 4, 1862, in Borden and Borden, *Legacy*, 90. Rable, "Hearth, Home, and Family," analyzes the complex relationship of soldier to home and family.

53. Livermore, *Numbers and Losses*, 86; OR, ser. 1, vol. 11, pt. 2, pp. 633, 635; Eugene Blackford to mother, July 18, 1862, Gordon-Blackford Collection.

54. Fannie Borden to Joseph Borden, July 19, 1862; Joseph Borden to Fannie Borden, July 9, 11, 15, 28, 1862, in Borden and Borden, *Legacy*, 99, 92, 95, 97, 107; *Greensboro Alabama Beacon*, August 1, July 18, 1862; Compiled Service Records, Fifth Alabama Infantry Regiment, reel 136, National Archives.

55. This account appears in J. W. Williams, "Faithful Body Servant."

56. *Greensboro Alabama Beacon*, June 13, July 11, February 23, 1862.

57. Ibid., July 25, 1862.

58. Ibid., July 4, 1862; Joseph Borden to Fannie Borden, June 28, 1862, in Borden and Borden, *Legacy*, 89.

59. *Greensboro Alabama Beacon*, July 11, 1862; J. H. Bayol to parents, November 21, 1861, June 28, 1862, Bayol Family Papers; Smith, *Days of Exile*, 71–75, 135.

60. Joseph Borden to Fannie Borden, June 28, 1862, in Borden and Borden, *Legacy*, 89.

61. Fannie Borden to Joseph Borden, July 10, 1862, in ibid., 93–94.

62. Fannie Borden to Joseph Borden, July 14, 19, 1862, in ibid., 96–97, 99, 101.

63. Fannie Borden to Joseph Borden, July 24, 29, August 10, 1862; Joseph Borden to Fannie Borden, July 24, 17, 1862, in ibid., 104–105, 108, 114, 104, 99.

64. Joseph Borden to Fannie Borden, December 24, 1862; Benjamin Borden to Joseph Borden, December 25, 1862, in ibid., 132–133, 134.

65. Fannie Borden to Joseph Borden, December 25, 1862, in ibid., 134–136.

66. Fannie Borden to Joseph Borden, January 7, 1, 1863, in ibid., 143, 139.

67. Fannie Borden to Joseph Borden, January 7, March 18, 1863, in ibid., 143, 155–156; Joseph Borden to General S. Cooper, November 25, 1863, Compiled Service Records, Fifth Alabama Infantry Regiment, reel 137. The Bordens moved to California in the late 1860s; see Borden and Borden, *Legacy*, iv, 170.

68. Fannie Borden to Joseph Borden, July 10, 1862, in Borden and Borden, *Legacy*, 93–94. Rable, *Civil Wars*, chap. 3, "The War as Family Crisis," 50–72, also casts these incidents as undermining a war effort that people still supported. Faust, *Mothers of Invention*, 238–244, argues that pleas to come home such as those made by Fannie Borden were examples of an independence and self-interested individualism that was replacing earlier political forms based on virtue and community. The experiences of Greensborians suggest that women who assumed greater responsibilities at home were not becoming more individualistic but, if anything, were deepening their exclusive commitments to others.

69. *Greensboro Alabama Beacon*, May 15, 1863; Harris, "Fellow Officers." Although the most recent study of Civil War soldiers' motives, McPherson's *For Cause and Comrades*, is consistent with the statements of Greensboro troops, I would stress an evolution in their beliefs as they sought to reconcile their experiences with their motivations. From an initial desire to preserve slavery, Greensborians began broadening their apologies with appeals to rights and other tactics. Greensborians ultimately came to fight largely out of a sense of duty and out of the fear that to quit would render their comrades' deaths meaningless. See Hubbs, "What They Fought For." Hess, *Union Soldier*, 101, stresses the changes that combat experience brought to soldiers and argues that "ideology was the most potent explanation for self-sacrifice in the war."

70. Thanks to David D. Nelson of Tuscaloosa, Alabama, for sharing this poem with me. These sentiments exemplify the role of civilians in encouraging courageous endeavors on the battlefield; see Linderman, *Embattled Courage*, 83.

## Chapter 8. Confidence and Despair

1. Joseph Borden to Fannie Borden, December 4, 11, 1862, in Borden and Borden, *Legacy*, 124, 126; Samuel Pickens diary, November 21–29, December 3, 1862.

2. Samuel Pickens diary, December 12, 1862; OR, ser. 1, vol. 21, p. 643.

3. Samuel Pickens diary, December 13, 1862.

4. *Greensboro Alabama Beacon*, March 27, 1863.

5. Eugene Blackford to father, March 24, 1863, Gordon-Blackford Collection; Samuel Pickens diary, March 5, 26, 27, 30, April 14, 1863.

6. OR, ser. 1, vol. 25, pt. 1, p. 950. Unless otherwise noted, this account of the Guards at the battle of Chancellorsville is taken from Samuel Pickens' diary, April 29–May 3, 1863; J. W. Williams, "Recollections of the Battle of Chancellorsville," *Greensboro Watchman*, April 3, 10, 1902; J. W. Williams, "The Flag of the Fifth Alabama Regiment," *Montgomery Advertiser*, April 11, 1905. Not surprisingly, their accounts occasionally differ from modern ones, such as Furgurson's *Chancellorsville* and Sutherland's *Fredericksburg and Chancellorsville*.

7. *Greensboro Alabama Beacon,* June 5, 1863; OR, ser. 1, vol. 25, pt. 1, p. 947.

8. Veteran of Company D, "More War Records," portions of which are published in Hubbs, *Voices.*

9. *Greensboro Alabama Beacon,* June 5, 1863.

10. OR, ser. 1, vol. 25, pt. 1, p. 954; *Greensboro Alabama Beacon,* June 5, 1863.

11. *Greensboro Alabama Beacon,* June 5, 1863.

12. Ibid.

13. Ibid.; OR, ser. 1, vol. 25, pt. 1, pp. 954–955; J. W. Williams, "Company 'D,' Fifth Alabama," *Greensboro Watchman,* February 4, 1897. The flag is now in the ADAH.

14. Livermore, *Numbers and Losses,* 98–99; Sutherland, *Fredericksburg and Chancellorsville,* 180.

15. Joseph Borden to Fannie Borden, May 11, 1863, in Borden and Borden, *Legacy,* 162; *Greensboro Alabama Beacon,* June 5, 1863; OR, ser. 1, vol. 25, pt. 1, p. 1052. The Confederate Congress established the Roll of Honor in November 1862.

16. Samuel Pickens diary, May 6–7, 1863.

17. Ibid., May 8, 1863.

18. Ibid., May 11–13, 1863.

19. Ibid., May 14, 1863.

20. F. E. Bayol to his parents, May 21, 1863, Bayol Family Papers; Joseph Borden to Fannie Borden, May 17, 1864, in Borden and Borden, *Legacy,* 163; Samuel Pickens diary, May 15–20, 1863.

21. Samuel Pickens diary, May 21, 1863; J. W. Williams, "Company 'D,' Fifth Alabama."

22. Samuel Pickens diary, May 29, 1863.

23. Unless otherwise noted, this account of the Pennsylvania campaign is based on Samuel Pickens diary, June 4–July 14, 1863.

24. OR, ser. 1, vol. 27, pt. 2, p. 596.

25. *Greensboro Watchman,* January 19, 1911; Tucker diary, July 1, 1863.

26. Veteran of Company D, "More War Records."

27. Livermore, *Numbers and Losses,* 102–103; *Greensboro Alabama Beacon,* July 24, September 4, 1863; *Greensboro Watchman,* January 19, 1911. This outline of the despair that Greensborians felt after the July 1863 losses should not be an endorsement of the claim that a lack of will caused the Confederacy's defeat. The more important point is that the Union refused to quit despite an astonishing two-year record of defeats. Despair had more impact on Southern identity. See McPherson, "American Victory, American Defeat."

28. *Greensboro Alabama Beacon,* September 25, October 23, 1863.

29. Ibid., August 14, September 4, 1863; Benners diary, July 17, 1863. Gallagher, "'Lee's Army,'" disputes the claim that all Southerners recognized Gettysburg as a disastrous defeat.

30. *Greensboro Alabama Beacon,* September 4, 1863. For a Confederate context, see Faust, *Creation,* chap. 3, "'Sliding into the World': The Sin of Extortion and the Dynamic of Confederate Identity," 41–57. Harvey of course had almost been thrown out of town during the secession crisis as a result of his Unionist views.

31. *Greensboro Alabama Beacon,* September 4, 1863. The standard work on the Confederate decision to arm slaves is Durden, *The Gray and the Black,* which does not report the Eutaw Resolutions. For a contrast with other Southern towns (although a year later), see Dillard, "Confederate Debate." The idea of arming slaves to fight for the Confederacy had been advanced as a boast before the bombing of Fort Sumter; see *Greensboro Alabama Beacon,* March 8, 1861. One correspondent from Arkansas submitted the proposal to the war department in mid-1861; see OR, ser. 4, vol. 1, pp. 482, 529.

32. *Montgomery Mail,* September 9, 1863, reprinted in Durden, *The Gray and the Black,* 30–32.

33. *Greensboro Alabama Beacon,* September 4, 1863, November 4, 1864; Cowin diary, October 9, 1861; Eugene Blackford to Mary B. Blackford, November 3, 1864, Gordon-Blackford Collection; James L. Boardman to father, August 16, 1861, Boardman Papers; Jonathan W. Williams, "Faithful Body Servant." Litwack, *Been in the Storm,* 39–45, examines the faithful servant and the decision to arm slaves.

34. *Gainesville Independent,* November 26, 1864; *Greensboro Alabama Beacon,* January 20, 27, February 3, March 10, 1865; Langdon, *Question.*

35. *Greensboro Alabama Beacon,* November 11, 1864, January 20, March 10, 1865; Samuel Pickens diary, February 17, 1865. Durden covers some of the debate among the army commanders in *The Gray and the Black,* 204–224. After the Confederate government finally decided to arm slaves, Augustus Benners wrote from Greensboro that "the institution of Slavery it seems has rec'd a severe blow by Nigger bill" (Benners diary, March 17, 1865).

36. See, for example, Thomas, *Confederate Nation,* chap. 12. Rable, *Confederate Republic,* 287–296, interprets the proposal for arming slaves as an act of desperation. Faust, *Creation,* also stresses the conflicts between the ideology and the reality of wartime slavery.

37. J. A. Wemyss to Henry Watson, July 22, 1861, January 28, 1862, Watson Papers; John Haywood to George W. Haywood, November 1, 1862, Haywood Papers.

38. John Haywood to George W. Haywood, November 1, 1862, March 11, June 6, July 6, 1863, January 27, February 24, June 27, 1864, Haywood Papers; Washington Pickens Nance to Louisa Lawler Nance, August 5, 1864, in Nance, "Washington Pickens Nance Letters," 48.

39. Justina Webb to J. D. Webb, April 19, 1863, Walton Family Papers; Fannie Borden to Joseph Borden, July 24, 1862, in Borden and Borden, *Legacy,* 105; *Journal of the Thirty-second Annual Council,* 68.

40. *Greensboro Alabama Beacon,* October 9, 1863.

41. Ibid., September 25, 1863. Mitchell, *The Vacant Chair,* explores these aspects of the relationship between home and soldier.

## Chapter 9. Defying the Machine

1. James Pickens to Samuel Pickens, April 27, May 12, 1862, McCall Family Papers; Benners diary, January 14, 1862.

2. Samuel Pickens to mother, January 15, 1864, McCall Family Papers.

3. Linderman, *Embattled Courage,* 216–229, finds a growing estrangement between soldier and civilian as the war continued, but I found no evidence for such a split in Greensboro.

4. Samuel Pickens diary, July 15–August 4, 1863.

5. *Greensboro Alabama Beacon,* October 2, 1863.

6. Tucker diary, August 16, 1863, quoted in Freeman, *Lee's Lieutenants,* 3:217; Samuel Pickens diary, August 10, 1863.

7. Samuel Pickens diary, August 14, 16, 1863; Freeman, *Lee's Lieutenants,* 3:218–219; J. W. Williams, "Promotions in Company 'D,'" *Greensboro Record,* September 17, 1903.

8. *Greensboro Alabama Beacon,* February 5, 1865; James Pickens diary, April 28, 1864, McCall Family Papers. The complete diary is also published in Hubbs, *Voices.*

9. Eugene Blackford to William M. Blackford, September 19, 1863, Gordon-Blackford Collection; Samuel Pickens diary, September 19–20, 1863.

10. This account is based on J. W. Williams, "Hard Lines for Company 'D,'" *Greensboro Record,* October 1, 1903; J. W. Williams, "Promotions in Company 'D'"; Eugene Blackford to William M. Blackford, October 20, 1863, Gordon-Blackford Collection; Park, *Sketch,* 58–61.

11. Livermore, *Numbers and Losses*, 108; Park, *Sketch*, 64.

12. *Greensboro Alabama Beacon*, February 5, 1864.

13. Ibid., April 8, 1864.

14. Ibid.; Samuel Pickens diary, January 25, 1864. See also service record for J. W. Williams, Compiled Service Records, Fifth Alabama Infantry Regiment, reel 140.

15. *Greensboro Alabama Beacon*, April 22, 1864; "Military Volunteer Family Assistance Reports," Governors' Papers, Files, ADAH; Benners diary, May 4, 1864. Greene County had relatively few indigent families and, because of its wealth, best supported its families; see Martin, *Desertion*, 54–57, 173–174.

16. J. W. Williams, "Company D at the Battle of the Wilderness," *Greensboro Record*, July 2, 16, 1903; Moore, *Conscription and Conflict*, 308.

17. James Pickens diary, March 17, 1864.

18. Ibid., March 31, April 24, 29, May 13, 1864.

19. Ibid., May 4, 1864.

20. Ibid.

21. Unless otherwise noted, the following account of the Battle of the Wilderness comes from Jonathan W. Williams, "Company D at the Battle of the Wilderness"; J. W. Williams, "Battles around 'The Bloody Angle,'" *Greensboro Record*, July 30, 1903; J. W. Williams, "The Bloody Angle," *Greensboro Record*, August 6, 1903.

22. James Pickens diary, May 5, 1864.

23. Robert Key, "Battle of Wilderness, Fifth Day of May, 1864," Sanguinetti Collection, United Confederate Veterans Scrapbook, ADAH.

24. Veteran of Company D, "More War Records"; James Pickens diary, May 5, 1864.

25. Samuel Pickens to mother, May 7, 1864, McCall Family Papers.

26. Ibid.; Livermore, *Numbers and Losses*, 110–111; Rhea, *Battle of the Wilderness*, 440, 435.

27. James Pickens diary, May 8, 1864; Veteran of Company D, "More War Records."

28. James Pickens diary, May 9, 1864.

29. Briggs contracted typhoid fever shortly thereafter, lost forty pounds, and made his way back to Greensboro with great difficulty (*Greensboro Alabama Beacon*, July 29, 1864).

30. James Pickens diary, May 11, 1864; James Pickens to mother, May 16, 1864, McCall Family Papers.

31. Livermore, *Numbers and Losses*, 112–113; Park, *Sketch*, 104–105; James Pickens diary, May 12, 1864; *Mobile Advertiser and Register*, June 1, 1864; Rhea, *Battles for Spotsylvania Court House*, 311–312. J. W. Williams, "Bloody Angle," states that the Fifth Alabama did not participate in the action of May 12; however, he had been wounded on May 10 and evacuated to a Richmond hospital and was thus unaware of the Guards' participation in the counterattack.

32. This account from Spotsylvania to Cold Harbor is taken from J. W. Williams, "Fighting on the Old Battle Fields about Richmond in 1864," *Greensboro Record*, August 20, 1903. A modern account can be found in Trudeau, *Bloody Roads*.

33. In conversation with the author, Robert Krick, historian at the Fredericksburg and Spotsylvania National Military Park, claims that careful modern scholarship has determined that the usual figure of seven thousand Union men lost in half an hour is inaccurate (Catton repeats this number in *Stillness*, 163). See also Furgurson, *Not War but Murder*, 277–280.

34. *Greensboro Watchman*, December 10, 1891. Typesetting errors have been silently amended, as have paragraph breaks. Hutchinson's story is confirmed by Henry Beck in his diary, May 14, June 3, 4, 12, 1864, Birmingham Public Library, Alabama (also published in Hubbs, *Voices*). See also J. W. Williams, "Faithful Body Servant"; *Greensboro Alabama Beacon*, September 25, 1869; Hutchinson File.

35. J. W. Williams, "Fighting on the Old Battle Fields."

36. Beck diary, June 25, 1864; Joel Calvin McDiarmid diary, June 25, 1864, Malcolm Macmillan Papers, Auburn University Special Collections and Archives, Auburn, Alabama (also published in Hubbs, *Voices*); Park, *Sketch*, 71; Veteran of Company D, "More War Records" Freeman, *Lee's Lieutenants*, 3:557. Modern treatments of the 1864 Valley campaign include Wert, *From Winchester to Cedar Creek;* Gallagher, *Struggle.*

37. Samuel Pickens to mother, June 28, 1864, McCall Family Papers; Freeman, *Lee's Lieutenants*, 3:558, 524.

38. Samuel Pickens to mother, July 18, 1864, McCall Family Papers; McDiarmid diary, June 28–July 3, 1864; Park, *Sketch*, 72–73.

39. Samuel Pickens to mother, July 18, 1864, McCall Family Papers; McDiarmid diary, June 28–July 12, 1864; Park, *Sketch*, 74–76; Veteran of Company D, "More War Records"; *Greensboro Alabama Beacon*, August 26, 1864.

40. Samuel Pickens to mother, July 18, 1864, McCall Family Papers; Park, *Sketch*, 77.

41. Samuel Pickens to mother, July 23, 27, August 20, 30, September 7, 1864, McCall Family Papers; McDiarmid diary, July 13–August 25, 1864; *Greensboro Alabama Beacon*, August 26, 1864; Park, *Sketch*, 82–88.

42. Samuel Pickens to mother, September 26, 1864, McCall Family Papers; Park, *Sketch*, 93–94; Beck diary, September 19, 1864. Modern estimates of killed and wounded put Early's losses between 1,900 and 2,000, of which Rodes' division alone numbered 686, while Union casualties totaled more than 5,000 (Wert, *From Winchester to Cedar Creek*, 103).

43. Samuel Pickens to mother, September 26, 1864, McCall Family Papers; Park, *Sketch*, 91–94; Beck diary, October 19, 1864; *Greensboro Alabama Beacon*, November 11, 1864; Freeman, *Lee's Lieutenants*, 3:600.

44. McDiarmid diary, October 19, 1864; *Greensboro Alabama Beacon*, November 11, 1864; Edwin Lafayette Hobson to Fannie, October 23, 1864, and typescript of report, Hobson Family Papers; *Greensboro Alabama Beacon*, November 11, 1864. The battery, named as the Sixth Maine's, was probably Lamb's.

45. Edwin Lafayette Hobson to Fannie, October 23, 1864, and typescript of report, Hobson Family Papers; Beck diary, October 19, 1864.

46. *Greensboro Alabama Beacon*, October 28, 1864, February 10, 1865; Company D, Fifth Alabama Infantry Regiment roster, October 31, 1864, Confederate Muster Rolls Collection, ADAH (copy of original from National Archives). Union casualties at Cedar Creek officially numbered more than fifty-six hundred, and inaccurate Confederate casualties were more than twenty-nine hundred (Wert, *From Winchester to Cedar Creek*, 246).

47. Edwin Lafayette Hobson to Fannie, October 23, 1864, Hobson Family Papers.

48. Julia Erwin Jones to Cadwallader Jones, May 3, 1864, Jones Papers.

49. *Greensboro Alabama Beacon*, April 15, May 20, 1864. As noted earlier, Linderman, *Embattled Courage*, 234, argues that as individual experience yielded to comradeship and the collective work of fighting a war, soldiers became alienated from their communities. The Guards, however, appear to have become more rather than less attached to Greensboro.

50. J. A. Wemyss to Henry Watson, August 8, 1861; L. D. Hatch to Henry Watson, December 14, 1861, Watson Papers; Cornelia Lockett to Samuel Lockett, February 20, 1864, Lockett Papers.

51. James Pickens to mother, November 13, 1864, McCall Family Papers. Unless otherwise noted, this account of the Guards from November 1864 until June 1865 is taken from the Samuel Pickens diary and occasionally from McDiarmid diary.

52. *Greensboro Alabama Beacon*, March 3, 1865; Samuel Pickens diary, February 9, 1865.

53. The number of Guards captured on April 2 is computed from the Compiled Service Records, Fifth Alabama Infantry Regiment.

54. J. W. Williams, "Company D, Fifth Alabama, C.S.A.: A Complete List of the Original Company," *Greensboro Record,* June 4, 1903.

55. These casualty figures are compiled from the same records used in the Rosters. The four deserters were James M. Johnson in June 1861, Sam Knight and J. C. Roberts in August 1863, and Lewis Elias in March 1865. Johnson enlisted on April 13, 1861, but nothing else is known of him. Knight joined on September 22, 1862, in Washington County, Alabama, and suffered from typhoid fever during the summer of 1863. Roberts, too, did not return from a furlough for typhoid fever. Elias had joined for the duration of the war in Montgomery on July 18, 1861, served briefly as a baker, and was wounded on May 5, 1864. The low number of Guards who deserted is consistent with the findings of Martin, *Desertion,* 42–48, that deserters were far more prominent in Alabama's mountain counties than in the Black Belt and Tennessee Valley.

## Chapter 10. The Loyal Community

1. *Greensboro Alabama Beacon,* March 17, 31, April 21, May 5, 12, 1865. An alternative reaction to Appomattox was voiced in Cornelia Lockett to Samuel Henry Lockett, May 4, 1865, Lockett Papers.

2. Adams diary.

3. *Greensboro Alabama Beacon,* August 25, September 15, 1865, January 19, 1866, November 23, December 7, 1867; "Planters Convention," for the *Messenger,* November 20, 1867, John Witherspoon DuBose Papers, ADAH. At an 1873 meeting, the planters decided to create the Greensboro Grange of the Order of Patrons of Husbandry. The Grangers, who included large planters and many former Guards, called for collective action for those in agriculture against those they identified as conspiring against them (*Greensboro Alabama Beacon,* September 27, October 4, 11, 1873). Wiener's controversial class-based interpretation of these events appears in *Social Origins.*

4. *Greensboro Alabama Beacon,* September 15, 1865.

5. Ibid., November 3, December 1, 1865, July 14, September 29, 1866, January 12, 26, February 9, 1867; Yerby, *History,* 133, 134; C. S. Gayle to Henry Watson, October 28, 1865, Watson Papers; Lewis E. Parsons to E. L. Hobson, September 28, 1865, Hobson Family Papers. The four militia companies were to be located at Greensboro, Newbern, Eutaw, and Burton's Hill; unfortunately, their muster lists were not kept.

6. John H. Parrish to Henry Watson, June 25, 1865, Watson Papers. The more pertinent studies of postwar reactions to emancipation include Litwack, *Been in the Storm;* Gilmour, "Other Emancipation"; Carter, *When the War Was Over.* The cautious and conservative leaders who emerged in Greene County following the war seem consistent with Carter's portrayal.

7. See appendix B; *Greensboro Watchman,* June 4, 1885; James E. Webb to Zemma[?], August 21, 1870, James E. Webb Papers, ADAH; Liestman, "Chinese Laborers"; Yerby, *History,* 69–72; *Greensboro Alabama Beacon,* May 15, 22, 29, June 5, 12, 26, July 17, 1869; Jay, "General N. B. Forrest." The railroad was not extended to connect with the Alabama Great Southern line at Akron until 1882.

8. *Greensboro Alabama Beacon,* August 25, 1865.

9. "Baccalaureate Address."

10. *Journal of the Proceedings of an Adjourned Meeting,* 14; Wilmer, *Recent Past,* 143–144; Gorgas, *Journals,* July 2, 1865, 179; *Journal of the Proceedings of the Thirty-second Annual Council,* 14. This episode is succinctly summarized in J. Moore, "Praying."

11. *Greensboro Alabama Beacon,* June 23, 1865; "First Quarterly Conference for Greene

Circuit Convened at Selma Church on Saturday January 27th 1866," Alabama Church Records, Greene Circuit—Methodist, ADAH. Bishop Andrew had precipitated the 1844 split of the Methodist Episcopal Church when he inherited two slaves; see Norwood, *Story,* 197–199.

12. Eugene V. LeVert to his brother, August 4, November 18, 1865, Eugene V. LeVert to "Mr. LeVert," August 11, 1865, LeVert Family Papers.

13. *Greensboro Southern Watchman,* October 12, 1882. Examinations of the problem of nationalism, especially Confederate nationalism, begins with Potter, "Historian's Use of Nationalism." Subsequent treatments include Faust, *Creation;* Blair, *Virginia's Private War,* esp. chap. 6, "The Problem of Confederate Identity," 134–152.

My understanding of loyalty was especially stimulated by Fletcher, *Loyalty,* esp. chap. 1, "The Historical Self," 3–32. I was also struck by Hoffer's lines in *The True Believer:* "forms of dedication, devotion, loyalty and self-surrender are in essence a desperate clinging to something which might give worth and meaning to our futile, spoiled lives" (15). Other relevant works include Held, "Mothering versus Contract"; Bender, *Community and Social Change.*

14. *Greensboro Alabama Beacon,* March 23, April 13, 20, May 18, 1867.

15. John H. Parrish to Henry Watson, June 19, 1865, September 3, 1868, Watson Papers; *Greensboro Alabama Beacon,* February 16, December 1, 1866, November 16, 1867, February 22, 1868, January 16, 1869, July 30, October 29, December 31, 1870; M. G. Borden to Fannie Borden, April 4, 1872; Fannie Borden to Joseph Borden, November 23, December 20, 1868, May 30, August 26, 1869, May 29, 1871, in Borden and Borden, *Legacy,* 188, 171, 172, 174–176, 179, 184.

16. L. J. Lawson, quoted by Lester, "Greensboro, Alabama," 88; Pitts diary, October 13, 1870. C. R. Wilson, *Baptized,* esp. chap. 1, "Sacred Southern Ceremonies: Ritual of the Lost Cause," 18–36, carefully examines the role of ritual in the postwar Southern mind. Greensborians were typical in observing such ceremonies as special days, funerals of veterans, and dedication of monuments.

17. Historians have generally identified the black community—both slave and free— with family life, extended kinship, and churches. Although tempting to label Greensboro's postbellum black community as artificial and as structured like that of white Greensborians before the war, little is known about Greensboro's black community. Greensboro's freedpeople did begin to form voluntary associations, generally fraternal and benevolent, that they registered at the Hale County Courthouse. Studies of the black community in general include Blassingame, *Slave Community;* Gutman, *Black Family;* Burton, *In My Father's House,* a community study that attempts to meld black and white families into a social portrait.

18. This account is taken from *Greensboro Alabama Beacon,* September 8, 1865; Gorgas, *Journals,* September 6, 1865, 186–187; Benners diary, September 7, 1865. The melodramatic account supplied by Yerby, *History,* 51–59, must be taken with skepticism; written forty years later, it differs in some details from contemporary reports.

19. *Greensboro Alabama Beacon,* April 5, 1865.

20. Mabel Yerby Lawson named Irene Kohler in the 1963 edition of Yerby, *History,* 204.

21. Gorgas, *Journals,* August 31, 1865, 186.

22. John H. Parrish to Henry Watson Jr., June 25, 1865, "Contract between Henry Watson and the negroes named herein," June 26, 1865, Watson Papers; see also "Labor Regulations, Demopolis Alabama, June 1st, 1865," Haywood Papers.

23. John H. Parrish to Henry Watson Jr., June 25, 1865; Henry Watson Jr. to Serano Watson, December 10, 1865; Henry Watson Jr. to Julia Watson, December 16, 1865; Henry Watson Jr. to James Dixon, December 20[?], 1867; Henry Watson Jr. to unknown, January 26, 1866, Watson Papers; "Contract of Thos. M. Johnston Adm. of Estate of R. H. McFadden and

Freedmen on Canebrake place 1866," Johnston-McFadden Papers, SHC; "Contract with laborers for 1866," Haywood Papers. Fitzgerald explores the relationship between planters and the freedpeople's attraction to Radicalism; see his *Union League,* chap. 5, "Land, Labor, and the Loyal League," 136–176, which deals specifically with Hale County.

24. Henry Watson Jr. to unknown, January 26, 1866; Henry Watson Jr. to Serano Watson, December 10, 1865, Watson Papers; *Greensboro Alabama Beacon,* November 30, 1867; Allen C. Jones to Cadwallader Jones Jr., July 29, 1866, Jones Papers.

25. U.S. Congress, Joint Select Committee, *Report,* 1296, 1289; *Greensboro Alabama Beacon,* November 15, 1861. Blackford later served in the Thirty-first Alabama, as needed, until the end of the war. For more on Boardman, see Adams, *Made in Alabama,* 293.

26. U.S. Congress, Senate, Committee on Education and Labor, *Report,* 451; U.S. Congress, Joint Select Committee, *Report,* 1297; John S. Haywood to G. W. Haywood, May 21, 1867, Haywood Papers; *Greensboro Alabama Beacon,* May 25, 1867. The political struggles of former slaves in Hale County are consistent with Litwack's *Been in the Storm.* The standard work on the Union League, Fitzgerald, *Union League,* deals largely with Alabama and Hale County; see esp. 141–149. See also Bureau of Refugees, Freedmen, and Abandoned Lands, Reports of the Operations from the Subdistricts. Because the regional office was in Greensboro, these records of the Freedmen's Bureau were generally cursory and unfortunately much less helpful than I anticipated.

27. *Greensboro Alabama Beacon,* May 25, 1867.

28. A simple example of this exclusion occurred not long after the railroad to Greensboro was finished. A black schoolteacher named La Mott walked into the ladies' car and took his seat. The conductor, Captain Jack English, came up to the teacher and informed him that he was in the wrong car and that he would find accommodations in the front car. La Mott replied that he was an American citizen and was unwilling to move. But when he learned that he would be put off the train if he did not move promptly, he moved to the car assigned to black people. "Captain English is not the man for an experiment of that sort to be tried with," observed the *Beacon* on June 18, 1870. Rabinowitz, *First New South,* 135–139, suggests that black demands for separate but equal accommodations were attempts to gain access that was denied them by exclusion.

29. *Greensboro Alabama Beacon,* June 1, 1867.

30. This clearly biased account of the Webb murder comes from ibid., June 22, 1867.

31. Gewin's older brother, Noah, had gone to Fort Morgan as a Guard.

32. *Greensboro Alabama Beacon,* June 22, 1867.

33. Ibid. Harvey had confused Alex Webb with Aleck Webb, another freedman active in politics; see *Eutaw Whig and Observer,* December 3, 1874. Greensboro tradition claims that Orrick was hidden by a black janitor first at Southern University and then in a cemetery vault. Orrick's descendants confirmed in a letter to Birmingham-Southern College that Orrick changed his name to Arrington and wandered through Central America and the United States before becoming a Texas Ranger, a sheriff, and a cattle rancher near Canadian, Texas (*Greensboro Watchman,* August 29, 1963).

34. U.S. Congress, Joint Select Committee, *Report,* 1479, 1492, 1521; Fitzgerald, *Union League,* 142.

35. W. W. Rogers et al., *Alabama,* 243–244; *Greensboro Alabama Beacon,* July 6, August 3, 1867.

36. *Greensboro Alabama Beacon,* August 17, 1867; John H. Parrish to Henry Watson Jr., August 13, 6, 1867, Watson Papers.

37. U.S. Congress, Joint Select Committee, *Report,* 1498–1499; *Greensboro Alabama Beacon,* August 31, 1867.

38. *Greensboro Alabama Beacon,* November 16, 1867, December 21, 28, 1867.

39. Ibid., December 28, 1867, January 18, 25, 1868.

40. Yerby, *History,* 134; *Greensboro Alabama Beacon,* February 8, 15, 22, 1868.

41. *Greensboro Alabama Beacon,* February 15, 1868.

42. U.S. Congress, Joint Select Committee, *Report,* 1286; *Greensboro Alabama Beacon,* March 7, 21, 28, April 4, 11, 1868; Yerby, *History,* 130–131.

43. Yerby, *History,* 63; *Greensboro Alabama Beacon,* March 28, 1868. The date on the handbills indicated that they had been printed before the courthouse burning.

44. Hunnicutt's account of the Klan in Greensboro appears in *Reconstruction in West Alabama,* 48–58. Hunnicutt's dating of the events does not correspond exactly with contemporary sources. The schoolteacher may have been the same man Blackford described in his testimony; see U.S. Congress, Joint Select Committee, *Report,* 1287. After serving in the Guards, Knight became captain of the Planters' Guards (Company I, Twentieth Alabama Infantry Regiment).

45. *Greensboro Alabama Beacon,* March 21, May 16, 1868; Trelease, *White Terror,* 84; Hubbs, *Tuscaloosa,* 48–51. A story of mission schools in Greensboro and Marion appears in Paterson, "To Teach."

46. Yerby, *History,* 61.

47. *Greensboro Alabama Beacon,* September 12, October 3, 1868.

48. Ibid., October 3, 1868.

49. Hale County Probate Minutes, book A, July 28, 1868, 172–173, Hale County Courthouse, Greensboro, Alabama.

50. John H. Parrish to Henry Watson Jr., April 16, 1868, Watson Papers; U.S. Congress, Joint Select Committee, *Report,* 1272, 1476; A. Y. Sharpe to Lucy M. Young, August 31, 1868, Simpson Papers (this letter is from Demopolis).

51. U.S. Congress, Joint Select Committee, *Report,* 1486; J. H. Bayol to Emma [Charles], December 17, 1857, in possession of E. P. Whatley Jr., Moundville, Alabama. Blackford's testimony appears in U.S. Congress, Joint Select Committee, *Report,* 1271–1302. Blackford's three brothers-in-law in the Guards were John S. Tucker, George Nutting, and Edwin Nutting. Blackford also served as a surgeon with the Thirty-first Alabama. The portrait of scalawags developed by Wiggins, *Scalawag,* seems consistent with Blackford.

52. William T. Blackford to William H. Smith, September 12, 1868; James J. Garrett to William H. Smith, October 19, 1868; J. E. Love to William H. Smith, December 19, 1868; B. L. Whelan to William H. Smith, December 19, 1868; Governors' Papers, General Correspondence, ADAH.

53. *Greensboro Alabama Beacon,* November 7, 1868. Blair was also one of the three Senate subcommittee members who subsequently took Blackford's testimony; Confederates (possibly including some Guards) had burned the Maryland home of his brother, Montgomery Blair, in 1864.

54. W. W. Rogers Jr., *Black Belt Scalawag,* 44; Hunnicutt, *Reconstruction in West Alabama,* 65–66; Hennessey, "Political Terrorism."

55. U.S. Congress, Joint Select Committee, *Report,* 1272–1274; *Greensboro Alabama Beacon,* January 28, February 4, 1871. Blackford originally gave the date as January 19 but corrected this mistake.

56. U.S. Congress, Joint Select Committee, *Report,* 1484.

57. *Greensboro Alabama Beacon,* February 4, 1871.

58. Ibid., February 11, 1871; U.S. Congress, Joint Select Committee, *Report,* 1486, 1275. Wiener's assertion that the Klan "was an instrument of the planter class" (*Social Origins,* 61) is simplistic and disproved by Fitzgerald "Ku Klux Klan."

59. *Greensboro Alabama Beacon,* August 25, 1865. The testimony of Garrett, Jeffries, and Stickney appears in U.S. Congress, Joint Select Committee, *Report,* 1475–1491, 1491–1504, 1518–1537.

60. U.S. Congress, Joint Select Committee, *Report,* 1492, 1493, 1501, 1518; Membership rolls of Greensboro Lafayette Lodge No. 26, Grand Lodge Free and Accepted Masons of Alabama, Montgomery. See also appendix B.

61. U.S. Congress, Joint Select Committee, *Report,* 1484, 1530, 1532, 1495, 1486.

62. Blackford discussed his departure in ibid., 1275–1289.

63. Ibid., 1277–1278; *Greensboro Alabama Beacon,* August 17, 1872.

64. *Greensboro Alabama Beacon,* August 26, 1871.

65. John H. Parrish to Henry Watson Jr., September 3, 1868, Watson Papers; *Greensboro Alabama Beacon,* August 29, 1868, January 21, July 22, 1871; U.S. Congress, Senate, Committee on Education and Labor, *Report,* 450; *Greensboro Southern Watchman,* February 8, 1883; M. G. Borden to Fannie Borden, April 4, 1872, in Borden and Borden, *Legacy,* 187; *Greensboro Alabama Beacon,* January 25, March 1, May 31, 1873. Green settled in Montgomery as a carpenter and continued agitating for black laborers.

66. U.S. Congress, Joint Select Committee, *Report,* 1287–1289.

67. *Greensboro Alabama Beacon,* May 4, 1872.

68. Ibid. The present base on which the obelisk rests was the result of a program by one of the women of the Greensboro Memorial Association, who solicited nickels and dimes from children to provide a block of granite. The plan was to keep alive the stories of the marches, the companies, and the battles by learning the stories from fathers, brothers, and friends, those "Heroes of Our Homes" (*Greensboro Watchman,* February 1, 1900).

69. According to tradition and to a 1956 interview with Greensborian L. J. Lawson, the last garrisons rode out in 1872 (Lester, "Greensboro, Alabama," 88), but post returns were filed from Greensboro as late as December 1874; see U.S. Adjutant General's Office, Post Returns, National Archives.

70. *Greensboro Alabama Beacon,* January 22, April 1, June 3, 17, October 21, 1876, February 17, April 7, 1877; *Greensboro Southern Watchman,* May 30, August 15, 29, 1877.

71. *Greensboro Alabama Beacon,* August 7, 1876, August 14, 21, 1880, June 12, 1883, December 25, 1884, May 28, December 24, 1885; *Greensboro Southern Watchman,* August 19, 26, 1880, October 12, May 11, 1882, May 17, 1883.

72. *Greensboro Alabama Beacon,* May 31, 1892, March 27, 1863.

## Chapter 11. The Stone Soldier

1. J. W. Williams, "Faithful Body Servant."

2. Yerby, *History,* 67–68; "Monument in Greensboro, Alabama"; *Greensboro Alabama Beacon,* April 27, 1904; *Greensboro Watchman,* April 24, 1904.

3. My analysis does not merely refute the conventional declension theory but turns it on its head. Building on Tonnies, *Community and Society* (1887), declension and its related modernization theorists argue that modern urban societies inevitably destroy traditional communities. But such notions have come under withering attack in the past few decades from empirical studies of ethnic immigrant neighborhoods and from such theoretical studies as Bender, *Community and Social Change* (1978). What set white Greensborians apart (and Southerners, too, I suspect) is that their defeat in the Civil War moved them away from the American mainstream; instead of building their communities on modern forms of voluntary association, they turned to traditional notions of loyalty.

4. *Greensboro Alabama Beacon,* May 15, 1869.

# Bibliography

## Manuscript Collections

ALABAMA

Alabama Department of Archives and History, Montgomery
  Richard H. Adams Papers (portion covering the Greensboro Guards included in Hubbs,
    *Voices*)
  Adjutant General's Papers
    Administrative Files
    Register of Officers, 1820–1832
  Alabama Church Records
  Alabamians at War File
  Julius [Jules] Honoré Bayol, "Map of Seven Pines"
  Comptroller of Public Accounts of the State of Alabama, *Annual Reports to the General
    Assembly*
  Confederate Muster Rolls Collection
  James Crow Papers
  John Witherspoon DuBose Papers
  George Erwin Papers
  Governors' Papers
    Administrative Files—Creek War
    General Correspondence and Files
    Military and Militia Correspondence, Election Returns, 1820–1861, and Files
  John Gideon Harris Papers
  Mary Hays Papers
  Mexican War Muster Rolls Collection
  Sydenham Moore Papers
  Pickens Family Papers
  Eliza Gould Picton Collection
  Sanguinetti Collection
  Daniel W. W. Smith Diaries
  V. Gayle Snedecor, map of Greene County, 1856 (also available at the W. S. Hoole Special
    Collections Library, University of Alabama) and map of Greene County precincts,
    1858
  John S. Tucker Diary, photocopy and transcript of original diary (also published as "The
    Diary of John S. Tucker: Confederate Soldier from Alabama," ed. Gary Wilson, *Ala-
    bama Historical Quarterly* 43 [1981]: 5–33; portions included in Hubbs, *Voices*)
  War with Mexico File

Thomas Hill Watts Papers

James E. Webb Papers

Alabama–West Florida Conference Archives, United Methodist Church, Huntingdon College, Montgomery

Joseph Johnston Hutchinson file

Auburn University Special Collections and Archives, Auburn

Joel Calvin McDiarmid Diary, in Malcolm Macmillan Papers, transcript of original, present location unknown (included in Hubbs, *Voices*)

Yerby-Lawson Papers

Birmingham Public Library

Henry Beck Diary, transcript of original, present location unknown (included in Hubbs, *Voices*)

Scruggs Collection

Grand Lodge Free and Accepted Masons of Alabama, Montgomery

Membership rolls, Lafayette Lodge No. 26

Greene County Courthouse, Eutaw

Greene County Deed Record Book H

Greene County Marriages, book C-44

Hale County Courthouse, Greensboro

Hale County Probate Minutes, book A

W. S. Hoole Special Collections Library, University of Alabama, Tuscaloosa

John Cocke Papers

*Constitution and By-Laws of the Greensboro' Light Artillery Guards, adopted April 2, 1842*

*Constitution and By-Laws of the Light Artillery Guards, at Greensboro', Alabama, adopted June 6th, 1846*

John H. Cowin Diary, photocopy of original owned by Ron Cartee of Martinsburg, West Virginia (included in Hubbs, *Voices*)

Gorgas Family Papers

Isaac Croom, "Address Delivered before the Greensboro' Agricultural Society, on the 2d of May, 1850"

Tanglewood/Bishop Collection

Henry Tutwiler Papers

MARYLAND

Maryland Historical Society, Baltimore

Gordon-Blackford Collection

MISSISSIPPI

Mississippi Department of Archives and History, Jackson

Walsh (Aimee Shands) and Family Papers

NORTH CAROLINA

Rare Book, Manuscript, and Special Collections Library, Duke University, Durham

Benson-Thompson Family Papers

James L. Boardman Papers

John Beverley Christian Papers

Sarah A. G. Crawford Papers

J. J. Hutchinson, "Address," December 3 [5], 1860
George M. Johnston Papers
Henry Watson Jr. Papers (also available in *Records of Ante-Bellum Southern Plantations from the Revolution through the Civil War,* ser. F, pt. 1, reels 10–18)
North Carolina State Archives, Raleigh
Cullen B. Hatch Collection
William A. Jeffreys Papers
Miscellaneous letters
Benjamin King to Alfred Williams, May 15, 1832 (PC1048.1)
William Scarborough to Daniel Scarborough, December 1, 1839 (PC906.1)
Southern Historical Collection, University of North Carolina, Chapel Hill
Ernest Haywood Papers (also available in *Records of Ante-Bellum Southern Plantations from the Revolution through the Civil War,* ser. J, pt. 7)
Chilab S. Howe Papers
Johnston-McFadden Papers (also available in *Records of Ante-Bellum Southern Plantations from the Revolution through the Civil War,* ser. J, pt. 7)
Cadwallader Jones Papers
Lenoir Family Papers
LeVert Family Papers
Samuel Henry Lockett Papers
Philip Henry Pitts Papers
William D. Simpson Papers
John F. Speight Papers
Springs Family Papers
Walton Family Papers
Robert W. Withers Papers
Witherspoon-McDowall Papers
Marcus Joseph Wright Papers

TEXAS

Texas Collection, Baylor University, Waco
Caufield Family Papers

VIRGINIA

Virginia Historical Society, Richmond
Bayol Family Papers
Beverley Family Papers
Hobson Family Papers
Special Collections, University of Virginia Library, Charlottesville
John Hartwell Cocke Papers
Henry Tutwiler Papers
Virginia Military Institute, Lexington
Richard H. Adams Papers (portion covering the Greensboro Guards included in Hubbs, *Voices*)

WASHINGTON, D.C.

National Archives

Bureau of Refugees, Freedmen, and Abandoned Lands, Reports of the Operations from the Subdistricts, Records of the Assistant Commissioner for the State of Alabama, microfilm no. 809, reel 18

Compiled Service Records, Alabama Troops in the Creek War, Index, microfilm no. 244

Compiled Service Records, Fifth Alabama Infantry Regiment, microfilm no. 311, reels 136–149

Manuscript Muster Rolls, Fifth Alabama Infantry Regiment

U.S. Adjutant General's Office, Post Returns, microfilm no. 617, reel 1512

U.S. Government, Manuscript Census for 1830 through 1880, Greene and Hale Counties, microfilm no. F150–F156; *compendia* to each census were also consulted, especially in the preparation of certain appendixes

PRIVATE COLLECTIONS

Nicholas Cobbs, Greensboro, Alabama
  V. Gale Snedecor, map of Hale County, 1870
Glenn Linden, Southern Methodist University, Dallas
  Augustus Benners Diary, transcription of original
McCall Family Papers, Selma, Alabama
  James Pickens Diary and Letters (transcripts of the diary can be found in the W. S. Hoole Special Collections Library, University of Alabama, and in the Alabama Department of Archives and History; also included in Hubbs, *Voices*)
  Samuel Pickens Diary and Letters (transcripts of the diary can be found in the W. S. Hoole Special Collections Library, University of Alabama, and in the Alabama Department of Archives and History; also included in Hubbs, *Voices*)
David D. Nelson, Tuscaloosa
  John M. P. Otts, "To the Wounded of Greensboro Guards"
E. P. Whatley Jr., Moundville, Alabama
  J. H. Bayol to Miss Emma [Charles], December 17, 1857

Newspapers

*The Liberator* (Boston)
*Erie Greene County Gazette* (copies in Greene County Courthouse, Eutaw, Alabama)
*Eutaw Whig and Observer*
*Gainesville Independent*
*Greensboro Alabama Beacon*
*Greensboro Alabama Sentinel*
*Greensboro Record*
*Greensboro Southern Watchman*
*Greensboro Watchman*
*Greensborough Green[e] County Sentinel*
*Greensborough Greene County Patriot* (copies in Rare Book, Manuscript, and Special Collections Library, Duke University, Durham, North Carolina)
*Mobile Advertiser and Register*
*Montgomery Advertiser*
*Montgomery Mail*

## Published Sources, Conference Papers, Dissertations, and Theses

Abernethy, Thomas Perkins. *The Formative Period in Alabama, 1815–1828*. Montgomery: Brown, 1922.

Adams, E. Bryding. *Made in Alabama: A State Legacy*. Birmingham: Birmingham Museum of Art, 1995.

Alabama. *A Digest of the Laws of the State of Alabama: Containing the Statutes and Resolutions in Force at the End of the General Assembly in January, 1823*. Compiled by Harry Toulmin. Cahawba, Ala.: Ginn and Curtis, 1823.

Alabama. General Assembly. *Acts of the Seventh Biennial Session of the General Assembly of Alabama, Held in the City of Montgomery, Commencing on the Second Monday in November, 1859*. Montgomery: Shorter and Reid, 1860.

———. *Acts Passed at the Annual Session of the General Assembly of the State of Alabama, Begun . . . 1833*. Tuscaloosa: May and Ferguson, 1834.

Alabama. Senate. *Journal of the Senate of the State of Alabama, Begun and Held in the Town of Tuscaloosa on the First Monday in November, 1836*. Tuscaloosa: David Ferguson, 1837.

"Baccalaureate Address of W. M. Wightman, D.D., LL.D." *Quarterly Review of the Methodist Episcopal Church, South* 15 (October 1861): 525–531.

Bailey, Michael. "The Regulation Uniform for Alabama Volunteer Troops." *Camp Chase Gazette*, May 1985, 22–25.

Baldwin, Joseph Glover. *The Flush Times of Alabama and Mississippi: A Series of Sketches*. 1853; reprint, with an introduction and notes by James H. Justus, Baton Rouge: Louisiana State University Press, 1987.

Baptist, Edward E. "The Migration of Planters to Antebellum Florida: Kinship and Power." *Journal of Southern History* 62 (1996): 527–554.

Barney, William L. *The Secessionist Impulse: Alabama and Mississippi in 1860*. Princeton: Princeton University Press, 1974.

———. "Towards the Civil War: The Dynamics of Change in a Black Belt County." In *Class, Conflict, and Consensus: Antebellum Southern Community Studies*, edited by Orville Vernon Burton and Robert C. McMath Jr., 146–172. Westport, Conn.: Greenwood, 1982.

Bender, Thomas. *Community and Social Change in America*. Baltimore: Johns Hopkins University Press, 1982.

Berlin, Isaiah. "Two Concepts of Liberty." In *Four Essays on Liberty*, 118–172. New York: Oxford University Press, 1970.

Birney, James Gillespie. *Letters of James Gillespie Birney, 1831–1857*. Edited by Dwight L. Dumond. New York: D. Appleton-Century, 1938.

Blair, William A. "Maryland, Our Maryland: Or How Lincoln and His Army Helped to Define the Confederacy." In *The Antietam Campaign*, edited by Gary W. Gallagher, 74–100. Chapel Hill: University of North Carolina Press, 1999

———. *Virginia's Private War: Feeding Body and Soul in the Confederacy, 1861–1865*. New York: Oxford University Press, 1998.

Blassingame, John W. *The Slave Community: Plantation Life in the Antebellum South*. Rev. ed. New York: Oxford University Press, 1979.

Borden, Fannie, and Joseph Borden. *The Legacy of Fannie and Joseph*. Compiled by Winifred Borden. Montgomery, Ala.: privately printed, 1992.

Boritt, Gabor S., ed. *Why the Confederacy Lost*. New York: Oxford University Press, 1992.

Boucher, Ann Williams. "Wealthy Planter Families in Nineteenth-Century Alabama." Ph.D. diss., University of Connecticut, 1978.

Bridges, Edwin C. "Juliet Opie Hopkins and Alabama's Civil War Hospitals in Richmond, Virginia." *Alabama Review* 53 (2000): 83–111.

Bullock, Steven C. "A Pure and Sublime System: The Appeal of Post-Revolutionary Freemasonry." *Journal of the Early Republic* 9 (1989): 359–373.

————. *Revolutionary Brotherhood: Freemasonry and the Transformation of the American Social Order, 1730–1840.* Chapel Hill: University of North Carolina Press, 1996.

————. "The Revolutionary Transformation of American Freemasonry, 1752–1792." *William and Mary Quarterly,* 3d ser., 47 (1990): 347–369.

Burton, Orville Vernon. *In My Father's House Are Many Mansions.* Chapel Hill: University of North Carolina Press, 1985.

Cargo, Robert, and G. Ward Hubbs. "Stitches in Time: The Lanford Album Quilt." *Alabama Heritage* 1 (summer 1986): 2–11.

Carnes, Mark C. *Secret Ritual and Manhood in Victorian America.* New Haven: Yale University Press, 1989.

Carr, David. "Narrative and the Real World: An Argument for Continuity." *History and Theory* 25 (1986): 117–131.

————. *Time, Narrative, and History.* Bloomington: Indiana University Press, 1986.

Carter, Dan. *When the War Was Over: The Failure of Self-Reconstruction in the South, 1865–1867.* Baton Rouge: Louisiana State University Press, 1985.

Cashin, Joan E. *A Family Venture: Men and Women on the Southern Frontier.* Baltimore: Johns Hopkins University Press, 1994.

Castellano, Donna M. "Railroad Development in Antebellum Alabama." Paper presented at the Alabama Historical Association meeting, Birmingham, April 19, 1997.

*Catalogue of the Trustees, Teachers, and Pupils of the Greensboro Female Academy.* N.p., 1844.

Catton, Bruce. *A Stillness at Appomattox.* Garden City, N.Y.: Doubleday, 1953.

Channing, Steven A. *Crisis of Fear: Secession in South Carolina.* New York: Norton, 1974.

*Charter and Ordinances of the Town of Greensborough, Alabama, March 1860.* Mobile: J. Y. Thompson, 1860.

Christenberry, Daniel P. *The Semi-Centennial History of the Southern University, 1856–1906.* Greensboro, Ala.: D. P. Christenberry, 1908.

Clinton, Matt. *Matt Clinton's Scrapbook: 150 Years in the Life of Tuscaloosa and Northport.* [Tuscaloosa]: Portals, 1979.

Cobbs, Hamner. "Geography of the Vine and Olive Colony." *Alabama Review* 14 (1961): 83–98.

Cobbs, Nicholas H., Jr. "Alabama's 'Wonder of the Earth.'" *Alabama Review* 49 (1996): 163–180.

Coleman, Juliet Bestor. *Connecticut Yankee in Early Alabama: Juliet Bestor Coleman, 1833–1850.* Edited by Mary Morgan Ward Glass. N.p.: National Society of Colonial Dames of America in the State of Alabama, 1980.

Cronon, William. *Nature's Metropolis: Chicago and the Great West.* New York: Norton, 1991.

Cunliffe, Marcus. *Soldiers and Civilians: The Martial Spirit in America, 1775–1865.* Boston: Little, Brown, 1968.

Dale, William Pratt. "A Connecticut Yankee in Ante-Bellum Alabama." *Alabama Review* 6 (1953): 59–70.

"Delegates to the Alabama Secession Convention." *Alabama Historical Quarterly* 3 (1941): 368–426.

Dillard, Philip D. "The Confederate Debate over Arming Slaves: Views from Macon and Augusta Newspapers." *Georgia Historical Quarterly* 79 (1995): 117–146.

Doster, James F. "Land Titles and Public Land Sales in Early Alabama." *Alabama Review* 16 (1963): 108–124.

Doyle, Don Harrison. *The Social Order of a Frontier Community: Jacksonville, Illinois, 1825–1870.* Urbana: University of Illinois Press, 1983.

Duckworth, Peggy Jane. "The Role of Alabama Black Belt Whigs in the Election of Delegates to the Secession Convention." Master's thesis, University of Alabama, 1961.

Dupre, Daniel S. *Transforming the Cotton Frontier: Madison County, Alabama, 1800–1840.* Baton Rouge: Louisiana State University Press, 1997.

Durden, Robert F. *The Gray and the Black: The Confederate Debate on Emancipation.* Baton Rouge: Louisiana State University Press, 1972.

Eaton, Clement. *The Growth of Southern Civilization, 1790–1860.* New York: Harper, 1963.

———. *The Mind of the Old South.* Rev. ed. Baton Rouge: Louisiana State University Press, 1967.

Ellisor, John. "The Second Creek War: The Unexplored Conflict." Ph.D. diss., University of Tennessee, 1996.

Estes, Matthew. *A Defence of Negro Slavery, as It Exists in the United States.* Montgomery: Alabama Journal, 1846.

Faragher, John Mack. *Sugar Creek: Life on the Illinois Prairie.* New Haven: Yale University Press, 1986.

———. *Women and Men on the Overland Trail.* New Haven: Yale University Press, 1979.

Faust, Drew Gilpin. *The Creation of Confederate Nationalism: Ideology and Identity in the Civil War South.* Baton Rouge: Louisiana State University Press, 1988.

———. *Mothers of Invention: Women of the Slaveholding South in the American Civil War.* Chapel Hill: University of North Carolina Press, 1996.

Fitzgerald, Michael W. "The Ku Klux Klan: Property Crime and the Plantation System in Reconstruction Alabama." *Agricultural History* 71 (1997): 186–206.

———. *The Union League Movement in the Deep South: Politics and Agricultural Change during Reconstruction.* Baton Rouge: Louisiana State University Press, 1989.

Fleming, Walter L. *Civil War and Reconstruction in Alabama.* 1905; reprint, Spartanburg, S.C.: Reprint Company, 1978.

Fletcher, George P. *Loyalty: An Essay on the Morality of Relationships.* New York: Oxford University Press, 1993.

Flynn, Jean Martin. *The Militia in Antebellum South Carolina Society.* Spartanburg, S.C.: Reprint Company, 1991.

Foner, Eric. "The South's Hidden Heritage." *New York Times,* February 22, 1997.

Formwalt, Lee W. "Antebellum Planter Persistence: Southwest Georgia—A Case Study." *Plantation Society* 1 (1981): 410–429.

Forsyth, Charles. *History of the Third Alabama Regiment, CSA.* 1866; reprint, University, Ala.: Confederate Publishing, n.d.

Fredrickson, George M. *The Black Image in the White Mind: The Debate on Afro-American Character and Destiny, 1817–1914.* 1971; Middletown, Conn.: Wesleyan University Press, 1987.

Freehling, William W. *Prelude to Civil War: The Nullification Controversy in South Carolina, 1816–1836.* 1966; New York: Oxford University Press, 1992.

Freeman, Douglas Southall. *Lee's Lieutenants: A Study in Command.* 3 vols. New York: Scribner's, 1944.

Furgurson, Ernest B. *Chancellorsville, 1863: The Souls of the Brave.* New York: Knopf, 1992.

———. *Not War but Murder: Cold Harbor 1864.* New York: Knopf, 2000.

Gallagher, Gary W. "'Lee's Army Has Not Lost Any of Its Prestige': The Impact of Gettysburg on the Army of Northern Virginia and the Confederate Home Front." In *The Third Day at Gettysburg and Beyond,* ed. Gallagher, 1–30. Chapel Hill: University of North Carolina Press, 1995.

———. *Struggle for the Shenandoah: Essays on the 1864 Valley Campaign.* Kent, Ohio: Kent State University Press, 1991.

Genovese, Eugene D. *Roll, Jordan, Roll: The World the Slaves Made.* New York: Random House, 1972.

Gilmour, Robert Arthur. "The Other Emancipation: Studies in the Society and Economy of Alabama Whites during Reconstruction." Ph.D. diss., University of Michigan, 1972.

Gorgas, Josiah. *The Journals of Josiah Gorgas, 1857–1878.* Edited by Sarah Woolfolk Wiggins. Tuscaloosa: University of Alabama Press, 1995.

Gray, Thomas R. *The Confessions of Nat Turner.* 1831. Photo reproduction in *Slavery, Race, and the American Legal System, 1700–1872,* edited by Paul Finkelman, ser. 4, vol. 1, *Slave Rebels, Abolitionists, and Southern Courts: The Pamphlet Literature.* New York: Garland, 1988.

Griffin, Martin I. J. "History of the Church of Saint John the Evangelist, Philadelphia." *Records of the American Catholic Historical Society of Philadelphia* 20 (1907): 350–405.

Gutman, Herbert G. *The Black Family in Slavery and Freedom, 1750–1925.* New York: Pantheon, 1976.

Hatch, Nathan O. *The Democratization of American Christianity.* New Haven: Yale University Press, 1989.

Held, Virginia. "Mothering versus Contract." In *Beyond Self-Interest,* edited by Jane J. Mansbridge, 287–304. Chicago: University of Chicago Press, 1990.

Henley, Bryding Adams. "Gunboat Quilts." *Alabama Heritage* 8 (spring 1988): 14–25.

Hennessey, Melinda Meek. "Political Terrorism in the Black Belt: The Eutaw Riot." *Alabama Review* 33 (1980): 35–48.

Hess, Earl J. *The Union Soldier in Battle: Enduring the Ordeal of Combat.* Lawrence: University Press of Kansas, 1997.

Higginbotham, R. Don. "The Martial Spirit in the Antebellum South: Some Further Speculations in a National Context." *Journal of Southern History* 58 (1992): 3–26.

Hoffer, Eric. *The True Believer.* New York: Harper, 1951.

Holcombe, Hosea. *A History of the Rise and Progress of the Baptists in Alabama.* Philadelphia: King and Baird, 1840.

Hoole, William Stanley. "Alabama and W. Gilmore Simms." *Alabama Review* 16 (1963): 85–107, 185–199.

Hooper, Johnson Jones. *Adventures of Captain Simon Suggs, Late of the Tallapoosa Volunteers; Together with "Taking the Census" and Other Alabama Sketches.* 1858; reprint, with an introduction by Johanna Nicol Shields, Tuscaloosa: University of Alabama Press, 1993.

Hubbs, G. Ward. "Lone Star Flags and Nameless Rags." *Alabama Review* 39 (1986): 271–301.

———. *Tuscaloosa: Portrait of an Alabama County.* Northridge, Calif.: Windsor, 1987.

———, ed. *Voices from Company D: Diaries by the Greensboro Guards, Fifth Alabama Infantry Regiment, Army of Northern Virginia.* Athens: University of Georgia Press, 2003.

———. "What They Fought for . . . in Greensboro, Alabama." *Southern Historian* 19 (1998): 5–13.

Hunnicutt, John L. *Reconstruction in West Alabama: The Memoirs of John L. Hunnicutt,* edited by William Stanley Hoole, with an introduction by Allen J. Going. Tuscaloosa: Confederate Publishing, 1959.

Hunt, Robert Eno. "Home, Domesticity, and School Reform in Antebellum Alabama." *Alabama Review* 46 (1996): 253–275.

———. "Organizing a New South: Education Reformers in Antebellum Alabama, 1840–1860." Ph.D. diss., University of Missouri, 1988.

Jay, John C. "General N. B. Forrest as a Railroad Builder." *Alabama Historical Quarterly* 24 (1962): 15–31.

*Journal of the Proceedings of an Adjourned Meeting of the Thirtieth Annual Convention of the Protestant Episcopal Church in the Diocese of Alabama, Held in St. Paul's Church, Selma, on Thursday, November 21, 1861 [1862].* Montgomery: Montgomery Advertiser, 1863.

*Journal of the Proceedings of the Thirty-second Annual Council of the Protestant Episcopal Church in the Diocese of Alabama, Held in St. Paul's Church, Greensboro', on May 7, 8, and 9, 1863.* Montgomery: Montgomery Advertiser, 1863.

*Journal of the Proceedings of the Thirty-fourth Annual Council of the Protestant Episcopal Church in the Diocese of Alabama, Held in St. Paul's Church, Greensboro', on Wednesday, May 3, 1865.* Montgomery: Montgomery Advertiser, 1866.

Kasson, John F. *Rudeness and Civility: Manners in Nineteenth-Century Urban America.* New York: Hill and Wang, 1990.

Kilbride, Daniel. "Southern Medical Students in Philadelphia, 1800–1861: Science and Sociability in the 'Republic of Medicine.'" *Journal of Southern History* 65 (1999): 697–732.

Kohl, Lawrence Frederick. *The Politics of Individualism: Parties and the American Character in the Jacksonian Era.* New York: Oxford University Press, 1989.

Krick, Robert K. "It Appeared as Though Mutual Extermination Would Put a Stop to the Awful Carnage: Confederates in Sharpsburg's Bloody Lane." In *The Antietam Campaign,* edited by Gary W. Gallagher, 223–258. Chapel Hill: University of North Carolina Press, 1999.

Kulikoff, Allan. *Tobacco and Slaves: The Development of Southern Cultures in the Chesapeake, 1680–1800.* Chapel Hill: University of North Carolina Press, 1968.

Kutolowski, Kathleen Smith. "Freemasonry and Community in the Early Republic: The Case for Antimasonic Anxieties." *American Quarterly* 34 (1982): 542–561.

Lamb, Robert Paul. "James G. Birney and the Road to Abolitionism." *Alabama Review* 47 (1994): 83–134.

Langdon, Charles Carter. *The Question of Employing the Negro as a Soldier! The Impolicy and Impracticability of the Proposed Measure Discussed.* [Mobile]: Advertiser and Register Steam Job Press, 1864.

Laver, Harry S. "Rethinking the Social Role of the Militia: Community-Building in Antebellum Kentucky." *Journal of Southern History* 68, no. 4 (2002): 777–816.

Lester, Richard Irwin. "Greensboro, Alabama—1861–1874." Master's thesis, Alabama Polytechnic Institute, 1956.

Liestman, Daniel. "Chinese Laborers in Reconstruction Alabama." *Alabama Heritage* 8 (spring 1988): 2–14.

Linderman, Gerald F. *Embattled Courage: The Experience of Combat in the American Civil War.* New York: Free Press, 1987.

Litwack, Leon F. *Been in the Storm So Long: The Aftermath of Slavery.* New York: Vintage, 1979.

Livermore, Thomas L. *Numbers and Losses in the Civil War in America, 1861–1865.* 1900; reprint, Bloomington: Indiana University Press, 1957.

Long, E. B., with Barbara Long. *The Civil War Day by Day: An Almanac, 1861–1865.* 1971; reprint, New York: Da Capo, n.d.

Longstreet, Augustus Baldwin. *Georgia Scenes, Characters, Incidents &c., in the First Half Century of the Republic by a Native Georgian.* 2d ed. New York: Harper, 1852.

Loveland, Anne C. *Southern Evangelicals and the Social Order, 1800–1860.* Baton Rouge: Louisiana State University Press, 1980.

Lyell, Sir Charles. *A Second Visit to the United States of North America.* Vol. 2. New York: Harper, 1849.

Mansell, Jeff. *Hale County, Alabama: An Inventory of Significant and Historic Resources.* Brierfield, Ala.: Cahaba Trace Commission, 1992.

Martin, Bessie. *Desertion of Alabama Troops from the Confederate Army: A Study in Sectionalism.* New York: Columbia University Press, 1932.

May, Robert E. "Dixie's Martial Image: A Continuing Historiographical Enigma." *Historian* 40 (1978): 213–234.

McGuire, W. W. "On the Prairies of Alabama." *American Journal of Science and Arts* 26 (1834): 93–98.

McPherson, James M. "American Victory, American Defeat." In *Why the Confederacy Lost,* edited by Gabor S. Boritt, 15–42. New York: Oxford University Press, 1992.

———. *Battle Cry of Freedom: The Civil War Era.* New York: Oxford University Press, 1988.

———. *For Cause and Comrades: Why Men Fought in the Civil War.* New York: Oxford University Press, 1997.

[Meek, Alexander B.] Review of *Richard Hurdis. Southron* 1 (1839): 52–62.

———. *A Supplement to Aikin's Digest of the Laws of the State of Alabama.* Tuscaloosa: White and Snow, 1841.

Miller, James David. "South by Southwest: Planter Emigration and Elite Ideology in the Deep South, 1815–1861." Ph.D. diss., Emory University, 1996.

Miller, Randall M., ed. *Dear Master: Letters of a Slave Family.* 1978; reprint, Athens: University of Georgia Press, 1990.

Mitchell, Reid. *Civil War Soldiers: Their Expectations and Their Experiences.* New York: Viking, 1988.

———. "The Northern Soldier and His Community." In *Toward a Social History of the American Civil War: Exploratory Essays,* edited by Maris A. Vinovskis, 78–92. Cambridge: Cambridge University Press, 1990.

———. *The Vacant Chair: The Northern Soldier Leaves Home.* New York: Oxford University Press, 1993.

"Monument in Greensboro, Alabama." *Confederate Veteran* 12 (1904): 476–477.

Moore, Albert Burton. *Conscription and Conflict in the Confederacy.* New York: Macmillan, 1924.

Moore, Janie M. "Praying for the President." *Alabama Heritage* 24 (spring 1992): 32–39.

Morris, Christopher. *Becoming Southern: The Evolution of a Way of Life, Warren County and Vicksburg, Mississippi, 1770–1860.* New York: Oxford University Press, 1995.

———. "An Event in Community Organization: The Mississippi Slave Insurrection Scare of 1835." *Journal of Social History* 22 (1988): 93–111.

Nance, Washington Pickens. "The Washington Pickens Nance Letters, March–December 1864." Edited by R. B. Rosenburg and William C. Duckworth Jr. *Alabama Review* 54 (2001): 54–62.

Napier, John Hawkins, III. "Martial Montgomery: Ante Bellum Military Activity." *Alabama Historical Quarterly* 29 (1967): 107–132.

Norrell, Robert J. *A Promising Field: Engineering at Alabama, 1837–1987.* Tuscaloosa: University of Alabama Press, 1990.

Norwood, Frederick A. *The Story of American Methodism.* Nashville: Abingdon, 1974.

Nunnelee, S. F. "Alabama in Mexico War: Letter to Dr. W. S. Wyman from S. F. Nunnelee (Written June 14, 1906)." *Alabama Historical Quarterly* 19 (1957): 415–433.

Oakes, James. *The Ruling Race: A History of American Slaveholders.* New York: Vintage, 1983.

Otts, John Martin Philip. *Nicodemus with Jesus; or, Light and Life for the Dark and Dead World.* Philadelphia: Claxton, 1867.

Owen, Thomas McAdory. *History of Alabama and Dictionary of Alabama Biography.* 4 vols. Chicago: S. J. Clarke, 1921.

Owsley, Frank Lawrence. *Plain Folk of the Old South.* Baton Rouge: Louisiana State University Press, 1949.

Park, Robert Emory. *Sketch of the Twelfth Alabama Infantry of Battle's Brigade, Rodes' Division, Early's Corps, of the Army of Northern Virginia.* Richmond, Va.: Jones, 1906.

Parks, Joseph H., and Oliver C. Weaver Jr. *Birmingham-Southern College, 1856–1956.* Nashville: Parthenon Press, 1957.

Paterson, Judith Hillman. "To Teach the Negro." *Alabama Heritage* 40 (spring 1996): 6–17.

Pease, William H., and Jane H. Pease. *The Web of Progress: Private Values and Public Styles in Boston and Charleston, 1828–1843.* New York: Oxford, 1985.

Pessen, Edward. *Jacksonian America: Society, Personality, and Politics.* Rev. ed. Homewood, Ill.: Dorsey Press, 1978.

Pierrepont, Alice Vaughan Duncan. *Reuben Vaughan Kidd, Soldier of the Confederacy.* Petersburg, Va.: n.p., 1947.

Piston, William Garrett, and Richard W. Hatcher III. *Wilson's Creek: The Second Battle of the Civil War and the Men Who Fought It.* Chapel Hill: University of North Carolina Press, 2000.

Pitcavage, Mark. "An Equitable Burden: The Decline of the State Militias, 1783–1858." Ph.D. diss., Ohio State University, 1995.

Platt, Steven G., and Christopher G. Brantley. "Canebrakes: An Ecological and Historical Perspective." *Castanea* 62 (March 1997): 8–21.

Potter, David M. "The Historian's Use of Nationalism and Vice Versa." In *The South and the Sectional Conflict,* 34–83. Baton Rouge: Louisiana State University Press, 1968.

Power, J. Tracy. *Lee's Miserables: Life in the Army of Northern Virginia from the Wilderness to Appomattox.* Chapel Hill: University of North Carolina Press, 1998.

Priest, John Michael. *Before Antietam: The Battle for South Mountain.* Shippensburg, Pa.: White Mane, 1992.

Quist, John W. *Restless Visionaries: The Social Roots of Antebellum Reform in Alabama and Michigan.* Baton Rouge: Louisiana State University Press, 1998.

Rabinowitz, Howard N. *The First New South, 1865–1920.* Arlington Heights, Ill.: Harlan Davidson, 1992.

Rable, George C. *Civil Wars: Women and the Crisis of Southern Nationalism.* Urbana: University of Illinois Press, 1991.

———. *The Confederate Republic: A Revolution against Politics.* Chapel Hill: University of North Carolina Press, 1994.

———. "Hearth, Home, and Family in the Fredericksburg Campaign." In *The War Was You and Me: Civilians in the American Civil War,* ed. Joan E. Cashin, 85–111. Princeton: Princeton University Press, 2002.

Reeves, Jesse S. *The Napoleonic Exiles in America: A Study in American Diplomatic History, 1815–1819.* Baltimore: Johns Hopkins Press, 1905.

Rhea, Gordon C. *The Battle of the Wilderness, May 5–6, 1864.* Baton Rouge: Louisiana State University Press, 1994.

———. *The Battles for Spotsylvania Court House and the Road to Yellow Tavern, May 7–12, 1864.* Baton Rouge: Louisiana State University Press, 1997.

Robertson, James I., Jr. *Soldiers Blue and Gray.* Columbia: University of South Carolina Press, 1988.

Rodgers, Thomas G. "Alabama's Volunteer Militia, 1850–1861." *Military Collector and Historian* 42 (summer 1990): 56–62.

Rogers, William Warren, Robert David Ward, Leah Rawls Atkins, and Wayne Flynt. *Alabama: The History of a Deep South State.* Tuscaloosa: University of Alabama Press, 1994.

Rogers, William Warren, Jr. *Black Belt Scalawag: Charles Hays and the Southern Republicans in the Era of Reconstruction.* Athens: University of Georgia Press, 1993.

Ruffin, Edmund. *Notes on the Cane-Brake Lands, of the Cretaceous Region of Alabama.* Richmond: n.p., 1860.

Simms, W. Gilmore. *Richard Hurdis: A Tale of Alabama.* 1855; reprint, ed. John Caldwell Guilds, Fayetteville: University of Arkansas Press, 1995.

Sklar, Kathryn Kish. *Catharine Beecher: A Study in American Domesticity.* New Haven: Yale University Press, 1973.

Smith, Winston. *Days of Exile: The Story of the Vine and Olive Colony in Alabama.* [Tuscaloosa, Ala.: W. B. Drake,] 1967.

Snedecor, V. Gayle. *A Directory of Greene County for 1855–1856.* Mobile: Strickland, 1856.

Sterkx, H. E. *Partners in Rebellion: Alabama Women in the Civil War.* Rutherford, N.J.: Fairleigh Dickinson University Press, 1970.

Stilgoe, John R. *Common Landscape of America, 1580–1845.* New Haven: Yale University Press, 1982.

Stollenwerck, Frank, and Dixie Orum. *The Stollenwerck, Chaudron, and Billon Families in America.* N.p., 1948.

Storey, Margaret deMontcourt. "Southern Ishmaelites: Wartime Unionism and Its Consequences in Alabama, 1860–1874." Ph.D. diss., Emory University, 1999.

Story, James Osgood Andrew. "Pocket Diary for 1861." Edited by Llerena Friend. *Alabama Historical Quarterly* 28 (1966): 51–120.

Sutherland, Daniel E. *Fredericksburg and Chancellorsville: The Dare Mark Campaign.* Lincoln: University of Nebraska Press, 1998.

Terry, James G., comp. "Record of the Alabama State Artillery." *Alabama Historical Quarterly* 20 (1958): 141–447.

Tharin, W. C. *A Directory of Marengo County, for 1860–61.* Mobile: Farrow and Dennett, 1861.

Thomas, Emory. *The Confederate Nation, 1861–1865.* New York: Harper and Row, 1979.

Thornton, J. Mills, III. "Jacksonian Democracy." In *Encyclopedia of Southern Culture,* edited by Charles Reagan Wilson and William Ferris, 629–631. Chapel Hill: University of North Carolina Press, 1989.

———. *Politics and Power in a Slave Society: Alabama, 1800–1860.* Baton Rouge: Louisiana State University Press, 1978.

Tocqueville, Alexis de. *Democracy in America.* 2 vols. Translated by Phillips Bradley. 1835, 1840; New York: Vintage, 1990.

Tolbert, Lisa C. *Constructing Townscapes: Space and Society in Antebellum Tennessee.* Chapel Hill: University of North Carolina Press, 1999.

Tonnies, Ferdinand. *Community and Society (Gemeinschaft und Gesellschaft).* Translated by Charles P. Loomis. 1887; reprint, New York: Harper and Row, 1963.

Trelease, Allen W. *White Terror: The Ku Klux Klan Conspiracy and Southern Reconstruction.* New York: Harper and Row, 1971.

Trudeau, Noah Andre. *Bloody Roads South: The Wilderness to Cold Harbor, May–June 1864.* Boston: Little, Brown, 1989.

Tutwiler, Agnes. "The Story of Private White Education in Greensboro, Alabama, prior to 1900." Master's thesis, University of Alabama, 1938.

Tutwiler, H. *Sketch of Greene Springs School for Thirty Years*. Greensboro, Ala.: Williams, 1877.

U.S. Congress. Joint Select Committee on Condition of Affairs in the Late Insurrectionary States. *Report of the Joint Select Committee to Inquire into the Condition of Affairs in the Late Insurrectionary States*. 42d Cong., 2d sess., House Report 22, vol. 8, Alabama. Washington D.C.: Government Printing Office, 1872.

U.S. Congress. Senate. Committee on Education and Labor. *Report of the Committee of the Senate upon the Relations between Labor and Capital, and Testimony Taken by the Committee*. 48th Cong., vol. 4, Testimony. Washington, D.C.: Government Printing Office, 1885.

Valliere, Kenneth L. "The Creek War of 1836, a Military History." *Chronicles of Oklahoma* 57 (1980): 463–485.

Veteran of Company D. "More War Records." *Greensboro Alabama Beacon*, February 4, 11, 18, March 4, 11, 18, 25, 1899. Portions of this diary are reprinted in Hubbs, *Voices*.

*The War of the Rebellion: A Compilation of the Official Records of the Union and Confederate Armies*. 128 vols. Washington, D.C.: Government Printing Office, 1880–1901.

Wert, Jeffry D. *From Winchester to Cedar Creek: The Shenandoah Campaign of 1864*. New York: Simon and Schuster, 1989.

West, Anson. *A History of Methodism in Alabama*. Nashville: Publishing House of the Methodist Episcopal Church, South, 1893.

Wiener, Jonathan M. *Social Origins of the New South: Alabama, 1860–1885*. Baton Rouge: Louisiana State University Press, 1978.

Wiggins, Sarah Woolfolk. *The Scalawag in Alabama Politics, 1865–1881*. University: University of Alabama Press, 1977.

Wiley, Bell Irvin. *The Life of Johnny Reb: The Common Soldier of the Confederacy*. Baton Rouge: Louisiana State University Press, 1943.

Williams, David. *Rich Man's War: Class, Caste, and Confederate Defeat in the Lower Chattahoochee Valley*. Athens: University of Georgia Press, 1998.

Williams, J. W. "Company 'D,' Fifth Alabama," *Greensboro Watchman*, February 4, 1897; "Recollections of the Battle of Chancellorsville," *Greensboro Watchman*, April 3, 10, 1902; "Company D, Fifth Alabama, C.S.A.: A Complete List of the Original Company," *Greensboro Record*, June 4, 1903; "Company D at the Battle of the Wilderness," *Greensboro Record*, July 2, 16, 1903; "Battles around 'The Bloody Angle,'" *Greensboro Record*, July 30, 1903; "The Bloody Angle," *Greensboro Record*, August 6, 1903; "Fighting on the Old Battle Fields about Richmond in 1864," *Greensboro Record*, August 20, 1903; "A Search for a Sword: Captain J. W. Williams Tries to Find His Captured Weapon; A Few of the Replies Received from Wearers of Blue, Who Witnessed Its Surrender," *Greensboro Record*, September 3, 1903; "Promotions in Company 'D,'" *Greensboro Record*, September 17, 1903; "Hard Lines for Company 'D,'" *Greensboro Record*, October 1, 1903; "The Faithful Body Servant," *Greensboro Record*, October 22, 1903; "From Richmond to Stone Mountain: Company D's Part in That Memorable Campaign in Maryland," *Greensboro Record*, December 3, 1903; "Memorable March into Maryland: A Interesting Account of Company D, the Greensboro Guards' Part in this Campaign," *Greensboro Record*, December 17, 1903; "Company D Captured at the Battle of South Mountain: Thrilling Narrative of a Fight against Overpowering Numbers: The Greensboro Guards Captured and Sent Prisoners to Fort Delaware," *Greensboro Record*, December 24, 1903; "Company D Leave Fort Delaware, Being Returned as Prisoners They Make Sensational Escape through the Lines," *Greensboro Record*, January 14, 1904; and "The Flag of the Fifth Alabama Regiment," *Montgomery Advertiser*, April 11, 1905.

Williams, James. *Narrative of James Williams, an American Slave, Who Was for Several Years a Driver on a Cotton Plantation in Alabama.* New York: American Anti-Slavery Society; Boston: Isaac Knapp, 1838.

Wilmer, Richard H. *The Recent Past from a Southern Standpoint: Reminiscences of a Grandfather.* New York: Thomas Whittaker, 1887.

Wilson, Charles Reagan. *Baptized in Blood: The Religion of the Lost Cause, 1865–1920.* Athens: University of Georgia Press, 1980.

Wilson, Clyde Norman, and Shirley Bright Cook, eds. *The Papers of John C. Calhoun.* Columbia: University of South Carolina Press, 1998.

Winn, T. S. *The Great Victory at Manassas Junction. God the Arbiter of Battles. A Thanksgiving Sermon, Preached in the Presbyterian Church, at Concord, Greene County, Alabama, on the 28th day of July, 1861.* Tuscaloosa: Warren, 1861.

Withers, Robert W. "Geological Notices Respecting a Part of Greene County, Alabama." *American Journal of Science* 24 (1833): 187–189.

Wyatt-Brown, Bertram. *Southern Honor: Ethics and Behavior in the Old South.* New York: Oxford University Press, 1982.

Yerby, William Edward Wadsworth. *History of Greensboro, Alabama, from its Earliest Settlement.* 1908; reprint, Northport, Ala.: Colonial Press, 1963.

# Index

Italicized page numbers refer to illustrations.

Blair, Francis Preston, Jr., 220
Blair, Montgomery, 188
Blount, Robert P., 104
Boardman, James L., 115, 120, 131, 165
Boardman, Volney, 210
Boatright, James M., 34
Boligee, Ala., 74
Borden, Fannie, 105, 108, 141, 143–145, 150, 168
Borden, Joseph, 105, 106, *107*, 108–109; reasons of, to fight, 109; disgust of, with malingerers, 122; during Peninsula campaign, 125, 141; and wife, Fannie, 143–145
Brandy Station, Va., 159
Breckinridge, John C., 91
Bridges, D. J., 180
Briggs, Charlie, 181, 182, 183
Britton, William G., 105, 157, *230*
Brown (merchant), 17
Brown, Joseph, 160
Bull Run, 108, 114
Bunker Hill, Va., 189
Burnside, Ambrose, 148
Butler, B. A. ("Bunk"), 181
Butler, Benjamin, 177

Cahaba River, 7
Caldwell Creek, 214
Calhoun, Andrew Pickens, 75
Camargo, Mexico, 73
Camp life, 117–118
Camps: Jeff. Davis, 104; Masked Battery, 115; Winder, 140
Canebrake, the, *8;* description and early settlement of, 7–13; problems with water in, 9, 11, 12; development of, 27, 29, 30; French in, 57–60; and slavery, 63, 65–68
Carberry, John, 193
Carlisle, Pa., 160
Carson, Thomas K., 110
Cass, Lewis, 75
Casualties: during the Peninsula campaign, 126–127, 129, 132, 141; at Sharpsburg and South Mountain, 139; at Chancellorsville, 156, 157; at Gettysburg, 161; during the Overland campaign 180, 181, 183, 185; at Cedar Creek, 190

Centreville, Pa., 160
Chadwick, Shelby, 141, 155, 156, 170, 172, 175, 189, 216
Chambersburg, Pa., 159, 189
Chancellorsville, Va., 152–156 passim
Chapman, Alonzo B. ("Lonnie"), 129, *130*, 142–143, 146
Charlestown, W.Va., 188, 189
Charlottesville, Va., 187
Chesapeake and Ohio Canal, 136
Chickahominy River, 127, 131, 132
Childress, Henry, 179
Christian, John F., 122
Christian, W. C., *230*
Christianity, 33–35
Churches: Concord Presbyterian, 109; Greensboro Methodist, 39; Greensboro Presbyterian, 52, 225; Salem Baptist, 33, 215; Sardis Methodist, 35; St. Paul's Episcopal, 5, 34; St. Paul's Episcopal (Richmond), 158, 195; Wesley Chapel, 170
City Point, Va., 157
Civic virtue, 31, 118
Civil War, 81–196
Clarksburg, Md., 188
Claus, Henry G., 215–216
Clay, C. C., 54, 55, 140
Cleburne, Patrick, 164, 201
Clinton, Ala., 62
Cobbs, Richard Hooker, 225, 227
Cocke, John (a Guard), 65
Cocke, John Hartwell, 49, 64–66, 79, 144
Cold Harbor, Va., 131, 184–185, 187
Coleman, Alonzo G. ("Lonnie"), 129
Colfax, Schuyler, 220
Commitment, 84, 226; during the war, 118–120, 124, 145, 171, 177, 191. *See also* Duty; Loyalty
Community: and anomie, 16–22, 25; building of, 25–48 passim, 49, 52; and civil society, 26, 201, 228; exclusive or inclusive, 202, 205–207, 211; and familial society, 25; loyalty to, 84, 120, 124, 199–231; meaning of, 228–229; and nature of society, 32, 71–72; rural, 35–37; and slavery, 71–72; and state of nature versus social contract, 19, 28, 45–46, 77; voluntary, 25–48, 201–203

Locke, James W., 113
Lockett, Cornelia, 192
Longstreet, Augustus Baldwin, 50–51, *51*
Longstreet, James, 158, 161, 178, 180, 203
L'Ouverture, Toussaint, 58
Loyalty: as basis of community, 84, 111, 197–231; to Confederacy, 145, 196; meaning of, 202–207, 226; and slavery, 69–70. *See also* Commitment
Lyell, Charles, 27
Lyles, William, 4
Lynchburg, Va., 187

Madison's Mills, Ala., 111
Magruder, John Bankhead, 124
Malvern Hill, Va., 132–133
Manassas, Va., 113, 115, 117, 134, 135
Manassas Gap, 172
Marching, 134–136, 187–188
Marion, Ala., 86–87, 112, 217
Martin, Edward Thomas, 180
Martin, Joshua L., 63
Masons. *See* Freemasonry
Matamoros, Mexico, 73
May, Helen, 84
May, John L., 74
McCall, Alex, 136, 138
McClellan, George B., 124, 127, 131, 132, 137
McCrary, Mr., *48*
McCrary, William H., 188, 221, 222
McDiarmid, J. C., 193
McDonald, Peyton, 223
McDonald, William, 216
McLean, Wilmer, 108
Meade, George, 177–178
Mears' Grove, 211
Mechanicsville, Va., 131
Melton, Jesse J., 73
Methodism, 42–48 passim
Mexican War, 72–74
Migration, 9–22, 40, 74, 206, 226
Military Units
    Brigades in which Fifth Alabama (i.e., the Guards) fought: Ewell's, 108; Rodes, 115, 124, 127–129, 131–133, 135, 141, 150; O'Neal's, 151, 152, 155, 160–161; Battle's, 174, 176, 178, 182, 189–190
    Companies (other than Greensboro Guards): Barbour Greys, 106, 123, 126; Cahaba Rifles, 104, 124; Captain Smith's company for the Creek War, 54–55; Dixie Guards, 112; Eutaw Rangers, 73–74, 112; Greensboro Cavalry, 52, 74, 85, 99, 112, 113; Greensboro Confederates, 122; Greensboro Home Guards, 112; Greensboro Rifles, 226; Greensborough Independent Volunteers (for Mexico), 73–74; Grove Hill Guards, 104, 124; Haymouth Guards, 123–124, 137–139; Livingston Rifles, 103–104, 124; Marion Rifles, 99; Mobile Continental State Artillery, 104, 105; Monroe Guards, 104, 123, 136; Pickensville Blues, 104, 118, 124, 136–139, 182; Planters' Guards, 112–113, 122; Selma Blues, 103, *103*; Sumter Rifle Guard, 104, 124, 136; Talladega Artillery, 104, 123; Tuscaloosa Warrior Guards, 100, 103–104, 123; Young Rebels, 112
    Fifth Alabama Infantry Regiment: organization of, 104; at Manassas and Fairfax County, 106–109; reorganization of, 123–124; during Peninsula campaign, 127, 141; in spring 1863, 151; at Chancellorsville, 152–156; at Gettysburg, 160–161; at the Wilderness, 179; at the Mule Shoe and Bloody Angle, 182–183; at Bethesda Church, 184
    Miscellaneous: Canebrake Legion, 122
    Regiments (excluding Fifth Alabama): Alabama, Third, 131, 179; —, Fourth, 108; —, Sixth, 128, 129, 139, 152, 179, 184; —, Eleventh, 112; —, Twelfth, 172; —, Twenty-sixth, 131–132, 176; —, Fifty-first, 123; —, Sixty-first, 176, 178, 179; Louisiana, Fifth, 125; Massachusetts Colored, Fifty-fourth, 164; Mississippi, Twelfth, 128, 131; Missouri, Eleventh, 207; North Carolina, Forty-fifth, 194; Pennsylvania Reserves, Fifth, 138; Pennsylvania Volunteers, 111th, 156; Virginia, Twenty-fourth, 125
Militia, 50–57, 85–86, 201, 222
"Militia Company Drill, The" (Longstreet), 50–51, *51*
Millwood, Va., 159
Mine Run, 174

*Also by G. W. Hubbs*

# Voices from Company D

*Diaries by the Greensboro Guards, Fifth Alabama Infantry Regiment,*
*Army of Northern Virginia*

Now available from The University of Georgia Press